LOGISTICS AND SUPPLY CHAIN MANAGEMENT
BUS 1055

School of Business
George Brown College

MCGRAW-HILL RYERSON LIMITED

Toronto   Montréal   Boston   Burr Ridge, IL   Dubuque, IA   Madison, WI   New York   San Francisco
St. Louis   Bangkok   Bogotá   Caracas   Kuala Lumpur   Lisbon   London   Madrid   Mexico City   Milan
New Delhi   Santiago   Seoul   Singapore   Sydney   Taipei

Table of Contents

CHAPTER

1 The Role of Logistics in the Economy and Organization

Chapter Outline

Chapter Objectives

- To identify how logistics affects the economy and the profitability of corporations.
- To briefly explore how logistics has developed over time.
- To understand how logistics contributes to value creation.
- To understand the concept of the systems approach as it relates to logistics and marketing, the total cost concept, and profitability.

Introduction

Logistics Has Many Implications for Consumers

Logistics is a broad, far-reaching function which has a major impact on a society's standard of living. In a modern society, we have come to expect excellent logistics services, and tend to notice logistics only when there is a problem. To understand some of the implications to consumers of logistics activity, consider:

- The difficulty in shopping for food, clothing, and other items if logistical systems do not conveniently bring all of those items together in one place, such as a single store or a shopping mall.
- The challenge in locating the proper size or style of an item if logistical systems do not provide for a wide mix of products, colors, sizes, and styles through the assortment process. This was a continual problem in the former Soviet Union.
- The frustration of going to a store to purchase an advertised item, only to find out the store's shipment is late in arriving.

These are only a few of the issues often taken for granted which illustrate how logistics touches many facets of our daily lives. Because of the magnitude of the impact of logistics on society and individuals, a macro approach is taken in this initial chapter.

This chapter focuses on how logistics has developed over time, explains the systems approach as it applies to logistics, explores the role of logistics in the economy and the firm, and examines the key interfaces of logistics with other marketing activities. This chapter also shows the relationship between the systems concept and the total cost of ownership perspective. The discussion closes with a summary of key trends and current issues in logistics management.

Definition of Logistics Management

Because logistics is the topic of this textbook, it is important to establish the meaning of the term. Logistics has been called by many names, including the following:

- Business logistics
- Channel management
- Distribution
- Industrial logistics
- Logistical management
- Materials management
- Physical distribution
- Quick-response systems
- Supply chain management
- Supply management

What these terms have in common is that they deal with the management of the flow of goods or materials from point of origin to point of consumption, and in some cases

The logistics of supplying products to highly populated cities such as Hong Kong is difficult and complex. Highly efficient and effective logistics systems provide consumers with goods and services that improve their standard of living.

even to the point of disposal. The Council of Logistics Management (CLM), one of the leading professional organizations for logistics personnel, uses the term *logistics management* to describe:

Logistics Management Defined

the process of planning, implementing and controlling the efficient, effective flow and storage of goods, services, and related information from point of origin to point of consumption for the purpose of conforming to customer requirements.[1]

Throughout this text, the CLM definition is used. This definition includes the flow of materials and services in both the manufacturing and service sectors. The service sector includes entities such as the government, hospitals, banks, retailers and wholesalers.[2] In addition, the ultimate disposal, recycling, and reuse of the products need to be considered because logistics is becoming increasingly responsible for issues such as removing packaging materials once a product is delivered and removing old equipment.

Logistics Is Relevant to All Types of Organizations

Logistics is not confined to manufacturing operations alone. It is relevant to all enterprises, including government, institutions such as hospitals and schools, and service orga-

---

[1] Council of Supply Chain Management Professionals (CSCMP)

Moving materials and personnel to space stations orbiting the Earth can be a daunting task. Overcoming the enormous distances challenges the logistics capabilities of NASA, but offers significant opportunities for furthering future space exploration.

nizations such as retailers, banks, and financial service organizations. Examples from these sectors will be used throughout the book to illustrate the relevance of logistics principles to a variety of operations.

Some of the many activities encompassed under the logistics umbrella are given in Figure 1–1, which illustrates that logistics is dependent upon natural, human, financial, and information resources for inputs. Suppliers provide raw materials which logistics manages in the form of raw materials, in-process inventory, and finished goods. Management actions provide the framework for logistics activities through the process of planning, implementation, and control. The outputs of the logistics system are competitive advantage, time and place utility, efficient movement to the customer, and providing a logistics service mix such that logistics becomes a proprietary asset of the organization. These outputs are made possible by the effective and efficient performance of the logistics activities shown at the bottom of Figure 1–1. Each of these activities will be explained in varying depth in this chapter and throughout the book.

FIGURE 1–1

Components of logistics management

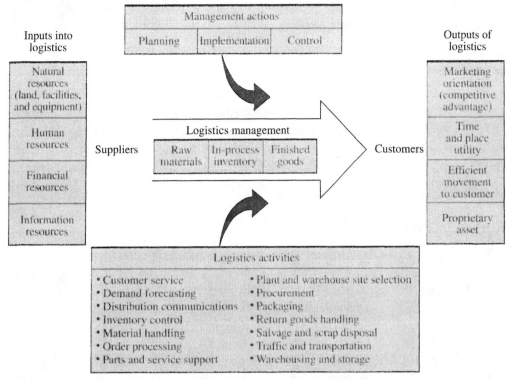

Development of Logistics

Logistics activity is literally thousands of years old, dating back to the earliest forms of organized trade. As an area of study however, it first began to gain attention in the early 1900s in the distribution of farm products,[3] as a way to support the organization's business strategy,[4] and as a way of providing time and place utility.[5]

Military Logistics

Following the clear importance of the contribution of logistics toward the Allied victory in World War II, logistics began to receive increased recognition and emphasis. Just as in the Persian Gulf War in 1990–1991, the ability to efficiently and effectively distribute and store supplies and personnel were key factors in the success of the U.S. Armed Forces.[6]

---

[3]John F. Crowell, *Report of the Industrial Commission on the Distribution of Farm Products,* vol. 6 (Washington, DC: U.S. Government Printing Office, 1901).

[4]Arch W. Shaw, *An Approach to Business Problems* (Cambridge: Harvard University Press, 1916).

[5]L. D. H. Weld, *The Marketing of Farm Products* (New York: Macmillan, 1916).

[6]William G. Pagonis, *Moving Mountains: Lessons in Leadership and Logistics from the Gulf War* (Boston: Harvard Business School Press, 1992).

The first dedicated logistics texts began to appear in the early 1960s,[7] which also is the time that Peter Drucker, a noted business expert, author, and consultant, stated that logistics was one of the last real frontiers of opportunity for organizations wishing to improve their corporate efficiency.[8] These factors combined to increase the interest in logistics.

Deregulation

Shippers Have More Options

To further fuel the focus on logistics, deregulation of the transportation industry in the late 1970s and early 1980s gave organizations many more options and increased the competition within and between transportation modes. As a result, carriers became more creative, flexible, customer-oriented, and competitive in order to succeed. Shippers are now faced with many more transportation options. They can focus on negotiation of rates, terms, and services, with their overall attention directed toward getting the best transportation buy.

Competitive Pressures

Global Logistics

With rising interest rates and increasing energy costs during the 1970s, logistics received more attention as a major cost driver. In addition, logistics costs became a more critical issue for many organizations because of the globalization of industry. This has affected logistics in two primary ways.

First, the growth of world class competitors from other nations has caused organizations to look for new ways to differentiate their organizations and product offerings. Logistics is a logical place to look because domestic organizations should be able to provide much more reliable, responsive service to nearby markets than overseas competitors.

Second, as organizations increasingly buy and sell offshore, the supply chain between the organization and those it does business with becomes longer, more costly, and more complex. Excellent logistics management is needed to fully leverage global opportunities.

Cost Control

Another factor strongly contributing to the increased emphasis and importance of logistics is a continued and growing emphasis on cost control. A survey of chief executive officers of Fortune 500 manufacturing firms and Fortune 500 service firms indicated that they believed that the most important way to improve company profitability was through cost cutting and cost control.[9] Thus, despite all the talk and emphasis on other issues, such as quality and customer service which CEOs rated as second and third in importance, cost cutting is still seen as the most important factor.

Information Technology

At about this same time, information technology really began to explode. This gave organizations the ability to better monitor transaction intensive activities such as the ordering, movement, and storage of goods and materials. Combined with the availability of comput-

---

[7]See, for example, Edward W. Smykay, Donald J. Bowersox, and Frank H. Mossman, *Physical Distribution Management* (New York: Macmillan, 1961).

[8]Peter F. Drucker, "The Economy's Dark Continent," *Fortune* (Apr. 1962), pp. 103, 265–70.

[9]"CEO's Still Don't Walk the Talk," *Fortune* (Apr. 18, 1994), pp. 14–15.

erized quantitative models, this information increased the ability to manage flows and to optimize inventory levels and movements. Systems such as materials requirements planning (MRP, MRP II), distribution resource planning (DRP, DRP II), and just-in-time (JIT) allow organizations to link many materials management activities, from order processing to inventory management, ordering from the supplier, forecasting and production scheduling.

Other factors contributing to the growing interest in logistics include advances in information systems technology, an increased emphasis on customer service, growing recognition of the systems approach and total cost concept, the profit leverage from logistics, and the realization that logistics can be used as a strategic weapon in competing in the marketplace. These, and other factors, will be discussed throughout this book.

Channel Power

Shifting of Channel Power from Manufacturers to Retailers

The shifting of channel power from manufacturers to retailers, wholesalers, and distributors has also had a profound impact on logistics. When competition rises in major consumer goods industries, there is a shakeout of many suppliers and manufacturers, so that a few leading competitors remain. Those remaining are intensely competitive and offer very high-quality products. In many cases, the consumer sees all of the leading brands as substitutes for each other. Lower brand-name loyalty decreases a manufacturer's power. This increases the retailer's power because sales are determined by what is in stock, not by what particular brands are offered.

Profit Leverage

The profit leverage effect of logistics illustrates that $1.00 saved in logistics costs has a much greater impact on the organization's profitability than a $1.00 increase in sales. In most organizations, sales revenue increases are more difficult to achieve than logistics cost reductions. This is particularly true in mature markets, where price cuts are often met by the competition, and revenue in the whole industry thus declines. The impact of the profit leverage effect is illustrated in Table 1–1.

The Profit Impact of Logistics Cost Savings

There are many costs associated with a sale, such as the cost of goods sold and logistics-related costs. Thus, a $1.00 increase in sales does not result in a $1.00 increase in profit. If, for example, an organization's net profit margin (sales revenue less costs) is 2 percent, the firm only receives a before tax profit of $0.02, from each sales dollar. Yet, any dollar saved in logistics does not require sales or other costs to generate the savings. Therefore, a dollar saved in logistics costs is a dollar increase in profit! As a result, logistics cost savings have much more leverage, dollar for dollar, than an increase in sales. Thus, the term, the "profit leverage effect of logistics," is relevant.

Systems Approach/Integration

The systems approach is a critical concept in logistics. Logistics is, in itself, a system; it is a network of related activities with the purpose of managing the orderly flow of material and personnel within the logistics channel. This is illustrated in Figure 1–2. It shows a

TABLE 1–1   Profit Leverage Provided by Logistics Cost Reduction

If Net Profit on the Sales Dollar is 2.0 Percent, Then. . .

A Saving of	Is Equivalent to a Sales Increase of
$ 0.02	$ 1.00
2.00	100.00
200.00	10,000.00
2,000.00	100,000.00
20,000.00	1,000,000.00

Source: Bernard J. LaLonde, John R. Grabner, and James F. Robeson, "Integrated Distribution Systems: A Management Perspective," *International Journal of Physical Distribution Management,* October 1970, p. 46.

FIGURE 1–2

Distribution channel: Logistics manages to flow through the channel

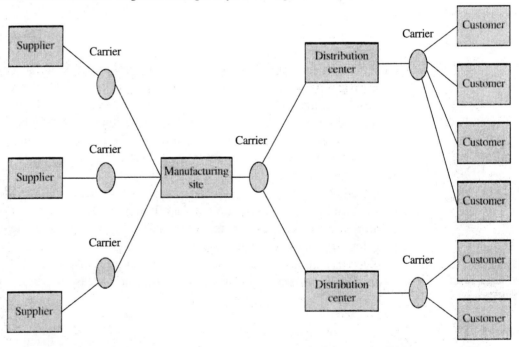

While the flow is primarily left to right, logistics is also responsible for returns, or movements from right to left, hence the term *reverse logistics* has developed.

Global

Hewlett-Packard's Systems Approach to Inventory Management

Hewlett-Packard (HP) is a leading global supplier of computer printers, particularly the ink-jet and laser-jet variety. It has over $3 billion invested in inventory worldwide. HP has a division located in Vancouver, Washington, which manufactures and distributes the DeskJet Plus printer worldwide. It has three distribution centers, one each in North America, Europe, and Asia.

HP faced a situation where high inventories of printers, approximately seven weeks' worth, were required to meet their 98 percent service goal in Europe. High inventories were required in part because each country has unique power cord and transformer requirements, and needs the proper language manual. Initially, the "differentiation" of the printers to meet the needs of the local market was done at the Vancouver facility. HP apparently faced the prospect of high inventory costs or reduced customer service levels, neither of which was an acceptable option.

The management at the Vancouver site considered many options for reducing inventory while maintaining customer service. They first worked on improving the logistics system by reducing delivery variability. They considered faster shipping modes, such as air, to reduce transit inventory, and inventory held to cover lead times. That alternative proved too costly.

However, by looking at the entire system as a whole, HP was able to develop a better solution. It could delay the differentiation of printer power sources and manuals until firm orders were received. This allowed HP to reduce inventory to five weeks while maintaining 98 percent service levels. This saved over $30 million annually. In addition, transportation dropped by several million dollars because generic printers can be shipped in larger volumes than printers specific to a particular country. Because HP viewed the system as a whole and understood the interactions, they were able to develop this innovative logistical solution.

Source: Adapted from Tom Davis, "Effective Supply Chain Management," *Sloan Management Review*, 34, no. 4 (Summer 1993), pp. 35–46; and Corey Billington, "Strategic Supply Chain Management," *OR/MS Today* 21, no. 2 (Mar.–Apr. 1994), pp. 20–27.

simplified example of the network of relationships that logistics has to manage in a channel of distribution.

The Systems Approach Defined

The systems approach is a simplistic yet powerful paradigm for understanding interrelationships. The **systems approach** simply states that all functions or activities need to be understood in terms of how they affect, and are affected by, other elements and activities with which they interact. The idea is that if one looks at actions in isolation, he or she will not understand the big picture or how such actions affect, or are affected by, other activities. In essence, the sum, or outcome of a series of activities, is greater than its individual parts.[10]

---

[10]For a more thorough discussion of the systems approach, see C. W. Churchman, *The Systems Approach and Its Enemies* (New York: Basic Books, 1979); R. L. Ackoff, "Science in the Systems Age: Beyond IE, OR and MS," *Operations Research* 21, no. 3 (1973), pp. 661–71; Heiner Müller Merback, "A System of Systems Approaches," *Interfaces* 24, no. 4 (July–Aug. 1994), pp. 16–25; and Peter Senge, *The Fifth Discipline* (New York: Doubleday/Currency, 1990).

While it might be desirable to have high inventory levels in order to improve customer order fulfillment, high inventory levels increase storage costs as well as the risk of obsolescence. Those unfavorable factors must be "traded off" with the favorable aspects of a decision before arriving at a decision on inventory levels. Without considering the impact of decisions on the larger system, such as the firm or the distribution channel, suboptimization often occurs. That means while the individual activities in that system appear to be operating well, the net result on the total system is relatively poor performance. To understand the opportunities for improvement, and the implication of those opportunities, the system must be viewed as a whole.

Systems Must Be Viewed as a Whole

Without understanding the channelwide implications of logistics decisions to improve service levels, excess inventory will begin to build up at the links along the supply chain. This excess inventory will tend to increase costs throughout the channel, but it serves as a buffer to protect against the uncertainty of how other channel members will behave. Thus, the system as a whole is less efficient than it could otherwise be. To get around that issue, organizations like Hewlett-Packard's DeskJet Division have taken a systems approach to managing channel inventories.

The systems approach is at the core of the next several topics discussed. The systems approach is key to understanding the role of logistics in the economy, its role in the organization, including its interface with marketing, the total cost concept, and logistics strategy.

The Role of Logistics in the Economy

Logistics Is an Important Component of GDP

Logistics plays a key role in the economy in two significant ways. First, logistics is one of the major expenditures for businesses, thereby affecting and being affected by other economic activities. In the United States, for example, logistics contributed approximately 10.5 percent of GDP in 1996. U.S. industry spent approximately $451 billion on transportation of freight and about $311 billion on warehousing, storage, and carrying inventory. These and other logistics expenses added up to about $797 billion.[11]

In 1980, logistics expenditures accounted for around 17.2 percent of GDP. If logistics expenditures were still that high by 1996, an additional $510 billion would have been spent on logistics costs in the United States. This would translate into higher prices for consumers, lower profits for businesses, or both. The result could be a lower overall standard of living and/or a smaller tax base. Thus, by improving the efficiency of logistics operations, logistics makes an important contribution to the economy as a whole.

Second, logistics supports the movement and flow of many economic transactions; it is an important activity in facilitating the sale of virtually all goods and services. To understand this role from a systems perspective, consider that if goods do not arrive on time, customers cannot buy them. If goods do not arrive in the proper place, or in the proper condition, no sale can be made. Thus, all economic activity throughout the supply chain will suffer.

---

[11]Robert V. Delaney, "CLI's 8th Annual 'State of Logistics' Report," remarks to the National Press Club, Washington, DC (June 2, 1997), pp. 3–6.

Logistics Adds Value by Creating Time and Place Utility

One of the fundamental ways that logistics adds value is by creating utility. From an economic standpoint, utility represents the value or usefulness that an item or service has in fulfilling a want or need. There are four types of utility: form, possession, time, and place. The later two, time and place utility, are intimately supported by logistics.

Form utility is the process of creating the good or service, or putting it in the proper form for the customer to use. When Honda of America Manufacturing transforms parts and raw materials into a car, form utility is created. This is generally part of the production or operations process.

Possession utility is the value added to a product or service because the customer is able to take actual possession. This is made possible by credit arrangements, loans, and so on. For example, when General Motors Acceptance Corporation extends a loan to a prospective auto purchaser, possession utility becomes possible.

The Five Rights of Logistics

While form and possession utility are not specifically related to logistics, neither would be possible without getting the right items needed for consumption or production to the right place at the right time and in the right condition at the right cost.[12] These "five rights of logistics," credited to E. Grosvenor Plowman, are the essence of the two utilities provided by logistics: time and place utility.

Time utility is the value added by having an item when it is needed. This could occur within the organization, as in having all the materials and parts that are needed for manufacturing, so that the production line does not have to shut down. This occurs when the logistics function at Pillsbury delivers flour from one of its mills to a production facility so that cake mix may be produced on schedule. Or it could occur in the marketplace, as in having an item available for a customer when the customer wants it. The item does the customer no good if it is not available when it is needed.

This is closely related to **place utility,** which means having the item or service available where it is needed. If a product desired by consumers is in transit, in a warehouse, or in another store, it does not create any place utility for them. Without both time and place utility, which logistics directly supports, a customer could not be satisfied.

The Role of Logistics in the Organization

In recent years, effective logistics management has been recognized as a key opportunity to improve both the profitability and competitive performance of firms. By the late 1980s and early 1990s, customer service took center stage in many organizations. Even organizations that had previously adhered to the "marketing concept" were reexamining what it meant to be customer-driven. The trend toward strong customer focus continues today.

Logistics Supports Marketing

The Marketing Concept

The **marketing concept,** as mentioned above, is a "marketing management philosophy which holds that achieving organizational goals depends on determining the needs and

---

[12]George A. Gecowets, "Physical Distribution Management," *Defense Transportation Journal* 35, no. 4 (Aug. 1979), p. 5.

FIGURE 1–3

Marketing/logistics management concept

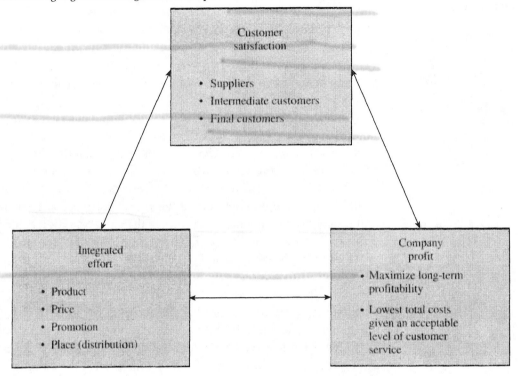

wants of target markets and delivering the desired satisfactions more effectively and efficiently than competitors."[13] Thus, the marketing concept is a "customer-driven" perspective which holds that a business exists to meet customer needs. The relationships between logistics and the three critical elements of the marketing concept (customer satisfaction, integrated effort/systems approach, and adequate corporate profit), are shown in Figure 1–3. Logistics plays a key role in each of these elements in several ways.

The "Four P's" of the Marketing Mix

The "four P's" of the marketing mix require that for a firm to be successful, any marketing effort must integrate the ideas of having the right product, at the right price, publicized with the proper promotion, and available in the right place. Logistics plays a critical role particularly in support of getting the product to the right place. As discussed previously in conjunction with utility, a product or service provides customer satisfaction only if it is available to the customer when and where it is needed. Figure 1–4 summarizes the trade-offs required between and among the major elements of the marketing mix and logistics.

Thus, the organization needs to use the "systems approach" in linking the needs foreseen by marketing with production as well as logistics. Achieving customer satisfaction requires an integrated effort both internally and with suppliers and ultimate customers.

---

[13]Phillip Kotler and Gary Armstrong, *Principles of Marketing,* 5th ed. (Englewood Cliffs, NJ: Prentice Hall, 1993), p. 22.

FIGURE 1–4

Cost trade-offs required in marketing and logistics

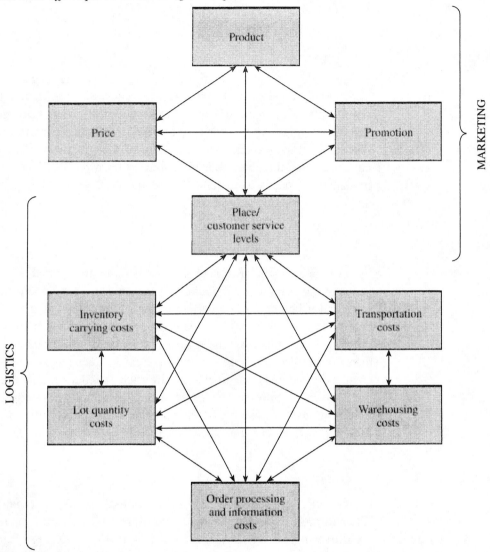

Marketing objective: Allocate resources to the marketing mix to maximize the long-run profitability of the firm.
Logistics objective: Minimize total costs given the customer service objective where Total costs = Transportation costs + Warehousing costs + Order processing and information costs + Lot quantity costs + Inventory carrying costs.

Source: Adapted from Douglas M. Lambert, *The Development of an Inventory Costing Methodology: A Study of the Costs Associated with Holding Inventory* (Chicago: National Council of Physical Distribution Management, 1976), p. 7.

Making Trade-Offs in Logistics Is Important

Also, it is important to understand that a central goal of an organization is to maximize long-term profitability or effective use of assets in the public or nonprofit sectors. One of the key ways to accomplish that, as shown in Figure 1–4 and presented later, is through examining trade-offs among alternatives, thereby reducing the overall total cost of activities within a system.

To better understand Figure 1–4, the sections below explore the manner in which each of the major elements of the marketing mix interact and are affected by logistics operations.

Product

Product refers to the set of utilities/characteristics that a customer receives as a result of a purchase. In an effort to lower price, management may decide to reduce product quality, eliminate product features, reduce the breadth of product offerings, reduce customer service or warranty support, or increase the time between model changes. However, any of these actions may reduce the attraction of the product for consumers, creating a loss of customers and thereby a reduction in long-term profits. To avoid making poor decisions, management needs to understand the trade-off and interrelationships between logistics and other marketing activities.

Price

Price is the amount of money that a customer pays for the product or service offering. Some of the items that should be factored into price include discounts for buying in quantities or for belonging to a certain class of customers, discounts for prompt payment, rebates, whether inventory is offered on consignment, and who pays delivery costs. A supplier may attempt to increase sales by reducing the price of its product, changing the terms or service offering. Unless the item in question is very price sensitive (i.e., sales change dramatically due to changes in price), such a strategy may create higher unit sales, but not enough to offset the lower price, yielding lower profit. This is particularly true in mature industries where customer demand is relatively fixed and the competition may follow the price decrease. The sales and the profitability of the entire industry suffer.

Promotion

Selling Value-Added to Customers

Promotion of a product or service encompasses both personal selling and advertising. Whereas increasing advertising expenditures or the size of the direct sales force can have a positive impact on sales, there is a point of diminishing returns. A point exists where the extra money being spent does not yield sufficiently high increases in sales or profits to justify the added expense. It is important for organizations to understand when they reach that point, so that they can avoid misallocating funds. A more prudent idea may be to try to use those funds more effectively, perhaps training the sales force to provide more value-added services to the customer, or make the customer more aware of the value added it currently provides through superior logistics service.

Place

Place is the key element of the marketing mix with which logistics interfaces directly. Place expenditures support the levels of customer service provided by the organization. This includes on-time delivery, high order fill rates, consistent transit times, and similar issues.

Customer Service Is an Output of the Logistics System

Customer service is an output of the logistics system. On the other hand, when the organization performs well on all the elements of the marketing mix, customer satisfaction occurs.

For many organizations, customer service may be a key way to gain competitive advantage.[14] By adjusting customer service levels to meet what the customer desires and is willing to pay, the organization may simultaneously improve service levels and reduce cost. All of the logistics trade-offs illustrated in the bottom of Figure 1–5 must be considered in terms of their impact on customer service levels. To accomplish this analysis, the total cost concept must be used.

Total Cost Concept

The **total cost concept** is the key to effectively managing logistics processes. The goal of the organization should be to reduce the *total* cost of logistics activities, rather than focusing on each activity in isolation.[15] Reducing costs in one area, such as transportation, may drive up inventory carrying costs as more inventory is required to cover longer transit times, or to balance against greater uncertainty in transit times.[16] National Semiconductor was actually able to reduce costs while improving logistics performance (see the Creative Solutions box at the end of this chapter) by taking a total cost approach.

There Are Six Major Logistics Cost Categories

Management should be concerned with the implications of decision making on all of the costs shown in Figure 1–5. These six major cost categories cover the 14 key logistics activities that will be discussed in this text. Figure 1–5 illustrates how the logistics activities drive the six major logistics cost categories. To provide a better understanding of the total cost concept, each of these activities will be briefly described.

Key Logistics Activities

Outlined below are the key activities required to facilitate the flow of a product from point of origin to point of consumption. All of these activities, listed alphabetically below, may be considered part of the overall logistics process.

Major Logistics Activities

- Customer service
- Demand forecasting/planning
- Inventory management
- Logistics communications
- Material handling

---

[14]Joseph B. Fuller, James O'Conor, and Richard Rawlinson, "Tailored Logistics: The Next Advantage," *Harvard Business Review* 71, no. 3 (May–June 1993), pp. 87–98.

[15]This section draws heavily on work by Douglas M. Lambert, *The Development of an Inventory Costing Methodology: A Study of the Costs Associated with Holding Inventory* (Chicago: National Council of Physical Distribution Management, 1976), pp. 5–15, 59–67.

[16]Joseph Cavinato, "A Total Cost/Value Model for Supply Chain Competitiveness," *Journal of Business Logistics* 13, no. 2 (1992), pp. 285–301.

f

Figure 1–5

How logistics activities drive total logistics costs

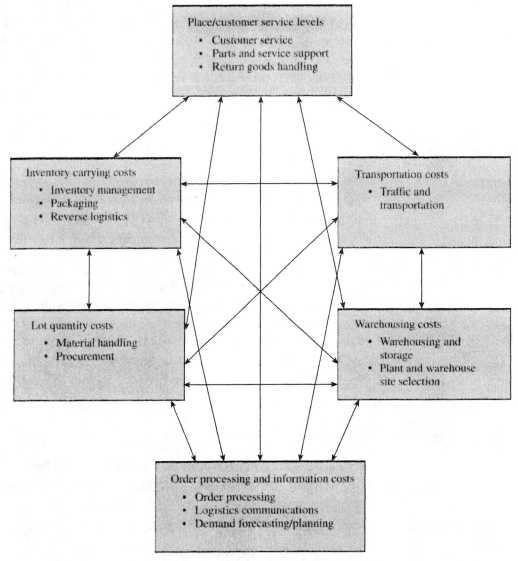

Source: Adapted from Douglas M. Lambert, *The Development of an Inventory Costing Methodology: A Study of the Costs Associated with Holding Inventory* (Chicago: National Council of Physical Distribution Management, 1976), p. 7.

- Order processing
- Packaging
- Parts and service support
- Plant and warehouse site selection
- Procurement
- Return goods handling
- Reverse logistics

- Traffic and transportation
- Warehousing and storage

While all organizations may not explicitly consider these activities to be part of logistics activities, each activity affects the logistics process, as shown in Figure 1–1.

Customer Service

Good Customer Service Supports Customer Satisfaction

Customer service has been defined as "a customer-oriented philosophy which integrates and manages all elements of the customer interface within a predetermined optimum cost-service mix."[17] Customer service is the output of the logistics system. It involves getting the right product to the right customer at the right place, in the right condition and at the right time, at the lowest total cost possible. Good customer service supports customer satisfaction, which is the output of the entire marketing process. Customer service is the topic of the next chapter.

Demand Forecasting/Planning

There Are Many Types of Demand Forecasts

There are many types of demand forecasts. Marketing forecasts customer demand based on promotions, pricing, competition, and so on. Manufacturing forecasts production requirements based on marketing's sales demand forecasts and current inventory levels. Logistics usually becomes involved in forecasting in terms of how much should be ordered from its suppliers (through purchasing), and how much of finished product should be transported or held in each market that the organization serves. In some organizations, logistics may even plan production. Thus, logistics needs to be linked to both marketing and manufacturing forecasting and planning.

Forecasting is a complex issue, with many interactions among functions and forecast variables. This topic will be explored in greater depth in Chapters 5 and 13.

Inventory Management

The Financial Impacts of Inventories

Inventory management involves trading off the level of inventory held to achieve high customer service levels with the cost of holding inventory, including capital tied up in inventory, variable storage costs, and obsolescence. These costs can range from 14 to over 50 percent of the value of inventory on an annual basis![18] With high costs for items such as high-tech merchandise, automobiles, and seasonal items that rapidly become obsolete, many organizations, including Hewlett-Packard, Xerox, and Sears, are giving inventory management much more attention.[19] These issues will be explored in Chapters 4 and 5.

---

[17]Bernard J. La Londe and Paul H. Zinszer, *Customer Service: Meaning and Measurement* (Chicago: National Council of Physical Distribution Management, 1976), p. iv.

[18]Lambert, *The Development of an Inventory Costing Methodology,* pp. 104–24.

[19]Tom Davis, "Effective Supply Chain Management," *Sloan Management Review* 34, no. 4 (Summer 1993), pp. 35–46.

Logistics Communications

Communications are becoming increasingly automated, complex, and rapid. Logistics interfaces with a wide array of functions and organizations in its communication processes. Communication must occur between:

1. The organization and its suppliers and customers.
2. The major functions within the organization, such as logistics, engineering, accounting, marketing, and production.
3. The various logistics activities listed previously.
4. The various aspects of each logistics activity, such as coordinating warehousing of material, work in process, and finished goods.
5. Various members of the supply chain, such as intermediaries and secondary customers or suppliers who may not be directly linked to the firm.

Communication Is Vital

Communication is key to the efficient functioning of any system, whether it be the distribution system of an organization or the wider supply chain. Excellent communications within a system can be a key source of competitive advantage. Part of Wal-Mart's success can be attributed to computerized advance communications systems which link their suppliers to their actual customer sales on a regular basis, so that the suppliers can plan based on up-to-date demand information, and provide timely and adequate replenishment to Wal-Mart stores. This is presented in more depth in Chapter 3, which describes information systems.

Materials Handling

Materials handling is a broad area that encompasses virtually all aspects of all movements of raw materials, work in process, or finished goods within a plant or warehouse. Because an organization incurs costs without adding value each time an item moves or is handled, a primary objective of materials management is to eliminate handling wherever possible. That includes minimizing travel distance, bottlenecks, inventory levels, and loss due to waste, mishandling, pilferage, and damage. Thus, by carefully analyzing material flows, materials management can save the organization significant amounts of money, as illustrated in Chapter 9.

Order Processing

Order processing entails the systems that an organization has for getting orders from customers, checking on the status of orders and communicating to customers about them, and actually filling the order and making it available to the customer. Part of the order processing includes checking inventory status, customer credit, invoicing, and accounts receivable. Thus, order processing is a broad, highly automated area. Because the order processing cycle is a key area of customer interface with the organization, it can have a big impact on a customer's perception of service and, therefore, satisfaction.[20] In-

---

[20]Benson P. Shapiro, V. K. Rangan, and J. J. Sviokla, "Staple Yourself to an Order," *Harvard Business Review* 70, no. 4 (July–Aug. 1992), pp. 113–22.

creasingly, organizations today are turning to advanced order-processing methods such as electronic data interchange (EDI) and electronic funds transfer (EFT) to speed the process and improve accuracy and efficiency. This will be described in greater depth in Chapter 3.

Packaging

Packaging Promotes and Protects

As Chapter 9 will explain, packaging is valuable both as a form of advertising/marketing, and for protection and storage from a logistical perspective. Packaging can convey important information to inform the consumer. Aesthetically pleasing packaging also can attract the consumer's attention. Logistically, packaging provides protection during storage and transport. This is especially important for long distances over multiple transportation modes such as international shipping.

Packaging can ease movement and storage by being properly designed for the warehouse configuration and materials handling equipment.

Parts and Service Support

In addition to supporting production through the movement of materials, work in process, and finished goods, logistics also is responsible for providing after-sale service support. This may include delivery of repair parts to dealers, stocking adequate spares, picking up defective or malfunctioning products from customers, and responding quickly to demands for repairs. Downtime can be extremely costly to industrial customers who may have to stop or delay production while awaiting repairs! This is discussed in conjunction with materials handling in Chapter 9.

Plant and Warehouse Site Selection

Determining the location of the company's plant(s) and warehouse(s) is a strategic decision that affects not only the costs of transporting raw materials inbound and finished goods outbound, but also customer service levels and speed of response. This topic is overviewed in Chapter 8. Issues to consider include the location of customers, suppliers, transportation services, availability and wage rates of qualified employees, governmental cooperation, and so on.

Intel Corporation Locates a Semiconductor Facility

In recent times, there has been a great deal of competition for new manufacturing facilities. An example of this is Intel Corporation's decision regarding where to locate a semiconductor facility. It received bids from a number of major cities, including Portland, Oregon; Austin, Texas; and Chandler, Arizona, a suburb of Phoenix. Ultimately, Intel chose Chandler because it already had a facility there, the Phoenix area was growing and had an attractive labor force, and the company had a good relationship with and was provided attractive incentives by the local government.[21]

---

[21]"Intel Building $1.5 Billion Plant," *Rocky Mountain Construction* 74, no. 24 (Dec. 20, 1993), p. 15; and William Carlisle, "States Are Closing Firms' 'Candy Store,'" *Arizona Republic* (July 24, 1994), pp. 1E–2E.

Procurement

Procurement Defined

With the increase in outsourcing of goods and services, the procurement function plays a more important role in the organization. Most U.S. industries spend from 40 to 60 percent of their revenues on materials and services from sources outside of the organization.[22] **Procurement** is the purchase of materials and services from outside organizations to support the firm's operations from production to marketing, sales, and logistics. Procurement, also referred to as purchasing, supply management, and by a number of other names, includes activities such as supplier selection, negotiation of price, terms and quantities, and supplier quality assessment. As organizations form longer-term relationships with fewer key suppliers, procurement continues to grow in importance and contribution to the organization. This is examined in greater depth in Chapter 10.

Return Goods Handling

Return Goods Handling Is Complex and Costly

Returns may take place because of a problem with the performance of the item or simply because the customer changed his or her mind. Return goods handling is complex because it involves moving small quantities of goods back from the customer rather than to the customer as the firm is accustomed. Many logistics systems have a difficult time handling this type of movement. Costs tend to be very high. The cost of moving a product backward through the channel from the consumer to the producer may be as much as nine times as high as moving the same product forward from the producer to the customer.[23] Thus, this significant cost and service area is beginning to receive more attention. The topic is discussed in Chapter 9.

Reverse Logistics

Logistics is also involved in removal and disposal of waste materials left over from the production, distribution, or packaging processes. There could be temporary storage followed by transportation to the disposal, reuse, reprocessing, or recycling location. As the concern for recycling and reusable packaging grows, this issue will increase in importance. This is of particular concern in Europe, which has very strict regulations regarding removal of packaging materials and even obsolete product due in part to limited landfill space.

Traffic and Transportation

A key logistics activity is to actually provide for the movement of materials and goods from point of origin to point of consumption, and perhaps to its ultimate point of disposal as well. Transportation involves selection of the mode (e.g., air, rail, water, truck, or

---

[22]Michiel Leenders and Harold E. Fearon, *Purchasing and Materials Management,* 10th ed. (Burr Ridge, IL: Richard D. Irwin, 1993).

[23]Douglas M. Lambert and James R. Stock, *Strategic Logistics Management,* 3rd ed. (Burr Ridge, IL: Richard D. Irwin, 1993), p. 18.

Growing concerns about the quality of the environment have made materials recycling an important aspect of logistics.

pipeline), the routing of the shipment, assuring of compliance with regulations in the region of the country where shipment is occurring, and selection of the carrier. It is frequently the largest single cost among logistics activities. Transportation issues are covered in Chapter 7.

Warehousing and Storage

Warehousing supports time and place utility by allowing an item to be produced and held for later consumption. It can be held near the location where it will be needed, or transported later. Warehousing and storage activities relate to warehouse layout, design, ownership, automation, training of employees, and related issues. These issues are presented in Chapter 8.

The Relationship of Logistics Activities to Logistics Costs

Logistics costs are driven or created by the activities that support the logistics process. Each of the major cost categories—customer service, transportation, warehousing, order processing and information, lot quantity and inventory carrying—are discussed below.

Customer Service Levels

The key cost trade-off associated with varying levels of customer service is the cost of lost sales. Monies that are spent to support customer service include the costs associated with order fulfillment, parts, and service support. They also include the costs of return goods handling, which has a major impact on a customer's perception of the organization's service as well as the ultimate level of customer satisfaction.

Cost of a Lost Sale

The cost of lost sales includes not only the lost contribution of the current sale, but also potential future sales from the customer and from other customers due to word-of-mouth negative publicity from former customers. A recent estimate indicated that every disgruntled customer tells an average of nine others about his or her dissatisfaction with the product or service.[24] It is no wonder that it is extremely difficult to measure the true cost of customer service!

The Objective Is to Minimize Total Costs Given the Customer Service Objectives

Thus, the best approach is to determine desired levels of customer service based on customer needs, and how those needs are affected by expenditures on other areas of the marketing mix. The idea is to minimize the total cost, given the customer service objectives. Because each of the other five major logistics cost elements work together to support customer service, good data are needed regarding expenditures in each category.

Transportation Costs

The activity of transporting goods drives transportation costs. Expenditures that support transportation can be viewed in many different ways, depending on the unit of analysis. Costs can be categorized by customer, product line, type of channel such as inbound versus outbound, and so on. Costs vary considerably with volume of shipment (cube), weight of shipment, distance, and point of origin and destination. Costs and service also vary considerably with the mode of transportation chosen. These costs will be described in more depth in Chapter 7.

Warehousing Costs

Warehousing costs are created by warehousing and storage activities, and by the plant and warehouse site selection process. Included are all of the costs that vary due to a change in the number or location of warehouses. Warehousing costs are explored in Chapter 8.

Order Processing/Information Systems Costs

This category includes costs related to activities such as order processing, distribution communications, and forecasting demand. Order processing and information costs are an

---

[24]George R. Walther, *Upside-Down Marketing* (New York: McGraw-Hill, 1994), summarized by Audio-Tech Books, no. 2 (Mar. 1994), p. 8.

**Examples of Order
Processing Costs**

extremely important investment to support good customer service levels and control costs. Order processing costs include such costs as order transmittal, order entry, processing the order, and related internal and external costs such as notifying carriers and customers of shipping information and product availability. Shippers and carriers have invested a great deal in improving their information systems, to include technology such as electronic data interchange (EDI), satellite data transmission, and bar coding and scanning shipments and sales. There also has been a growth in more sophisticated information technology, such as decision support systems, artificial intelligence (AI), and expert systems. These are the topics of Chapter 3.

Lot Quantity Costs

The major logistics lot quantity costs are due to procurement and production quantities. **Lot quantity costs** are purchasing- or production-related costs that vary with changes in order size or frequency and include:

**The Components of
Lot Quantity Costs**

1. *Setup costs.*
   a. Time required to set up a line or locate a supplier and place an order.
   b. Scrap due to setting up the production line.
   c. Operating inefficiency as the line begins to run, or as a new supplier is brought on board.
2. *Capacity lost* due to downtime during changeover of line or changeover to a new supplier.
3. *Materials handling,* scheduling, and expediting.
4. *Price differentials* due to buying in different quantities.
5. *Order costs* associated with order placement and handling.

These costs must not be viewed in isolation because they also may affect many other costs. For example, a consumer goods manufacturer that produces large production runs may get good prices from suppliers and have long efficient production runs, but requires more storage space to handle large runs. Customer service levels may suffer as order fulfillment declines because products are produced infrequently, in large batches, and with inventory going to zero and creating stockout situations in between runs. This may increase information and order processing costs, as customers frequently call to check on availability of back-ordered products, and cancel back orders.

Transportation costs also may rise as customers are sent partial or split shipments. Inventory carrying costs will rise as large quantities of inventory are held until depleted, due to large batch sizes. The implication of one cost upon another must be explicitly considered. Transportation issues are further detailed in Chapter 7.

Inventory Carrying Costs

The logistics activities that make up inventory carrying costs include inventory control, packaging, and salvage and scrap disposal. Inventory carrying costs are made up of many elements. For decision-making purposes, the only relevant inventory costs to consider are

The Relevant Inventory Costs Are Those That Vary with the Amount of Inventory

those that vary with the amount of inventory stored. These costs will be explored in detail in Chapter 4. The four major categories of inventory cost are:

1. **Capital cost,** or **opportunity cost,** which is the return that the company could make on the money that it has tied up in inventory.

2. **Inventory service cost,** which includes insurance and taxes on inventory.

3. **Storage space cost,** which includes those warehousing space-related costs which change with the level of inventory.

4. **Inventory risk cost,** including obsolescence, pilferage, relocation within the inventory system, and damage.

Developing Logistics Strategy

Understanding the organization's overall strategy and the key trade-offs in that organization are important to developing logistics strategy. The primary goal of logistics in any organization is to support the organization's customer service goals in an effective and efficient manner. To do that, the logistics function and the organization's management need to know:

Primary Goal of Logistics Is to Provide Customer Service

1. What do customers desire in terms of customer service levels and capabilities?

2. How is the competition performing in terms of customer service?

3. How is the organization performing today compared with the competition and, particularly, on those areas that the customer perceives as important?

Logistics costs also are an important aspect of analyzing alternative logistics service offerings. The next section provides an overview of some of the key issues in developing logistics strategy.

External and Internal Audits Provide Information for Decision Making

Answering questions one and two above can be accomplished through a marketing and logistics audit of the external environment. This is outlined briefly in Chapter 15. Answering the third question can be accomplished by conducting an internal audit in conjunction with customer service, as described in Chapter 2, and in Chapter 15, in conjunction with strategy.

Based on this analysis, an organization can identify its own strengths and weaknesses, and what may be potential opportunities and hazards in the marketplace. Objectives or goals for the logistics function are thus formulated. Based on the objectives, alternative strategies or plans of action need to be developed in support of those objectives. The analysis should include the implications of each alternative on other functions and performance parameters, as well as an analysis of the total cost of each alternative. Thus, a systems approach is required.

Once a decision has been made concerning logistics strategy, the organization must ensure that its current logistics structure is adequate to achieve that strategy, or adjust the channel structure accordingly. Proper channel design is an important concern for logistics professionals. The next section addresses some additional future challenges facing logistics professionals, and highlights some key areas for logistics performance improvement.

Future Challenges and Areas for Logistics Performance Improvement

This section presents some of the key challenges and issues that logistics faces today and will continue to face in the future. These themes will be integrated throughout this text to provide continuity and an understanding of how these issues affect the performance and perceived importance of various logistics activities.

As the role of logistics grows and takes on greater importance in achieving the overall goals of the organization, logistics needs to meet the challenge and improve its performance to support those goals. Some areas of opportunity include:

- Greater participation in setting organizational strategy and the strategic planning process.
- Total quality management (TQM).
- Identification of opportunities for using logistics as a competitive weapon/marketing strength.
- Just-in-time (JIT) logistics.
- The use of quick response (QR) and efficient consumer response (ECR) techniques.
- Improved understanding of and accounting for logistics costs.
- Better understanding of global logistics issues and improved logistics information systems.
- Greater participation of logistics professionals on work teams.
- Appropriate understanding and use of outsourcing, partnerships, and strategic alliances.
- Greater understanding and appropriate application of technology.
- Green marketing.

Each of these issues is explored below.

Strategic Planning and Participation

Strategic Planning at Bergen Brunswig

Table 1–2 shows the increasing participation of the logistics function in competitive strategy. Activities such as logistics budgeting and control, inventory planning and positioning, and customer service have become important parts of the organization's strategic planning process. A study supported by the Council of Logistics Management illustrates that strategic planning is performed by the majority of logistics organizations studied.[25] Bergen Brunswig, a multibillion dollar drug wholesaler, reports that logistics participation in strategic planning is critical, with the vice president of Logistics attending corporate strategy meetings and serving on the task force which thinks strategically about the future.[26]

---

[25]Martha C. Cooper, Daniel E. Innis, and Peter R. Dickson, *Strategic Planning for Logistics* (Oak Brook, IL: Council of Logistics Management, 1992), p. 10.

[26]Ibid., p. 105.

TABLE 1–2   Strategic Planning by Departments

	Planning Level				
	Corporate	*Marketing*	*Manufacturing*	*Logistics (Staff)*	*Logistics (Function)*
Is strategic planning done at this level?	97%	93%	86%	82%	70%
Is there a formal written plan at this level?	90%	85%	75%	65%	55%
How many years has this formal system existed?	8	8	5	4	3
How many people are involved?	11	10	10	5	5

Note: Percentage of survey respondents indicating a "Yes" response.

Source: Based on the mail survey; Martha C. Cooper, Daniel E. Innis, and Peter R. Dickson, *Strategic Planning for Logistics* (Oak Brook, IL: Council of Logistics Management, 1992), p. 10.

Total Quality Management

Total quality management (TQM) is a philosophy that should be embedded in all aspects of logistics operations. Going beyond simple "quality control," which monitors for problems in actual performance after the fact, TQM is a philosophy that is integrated in designing logistics systems to achieve desired results, performing logistics activities, and monitoring results. Total quality management involves being proactive in performing the right activity the right way the first time, and continuing to perform it to the required level. In logistics, that could translate into short, predictable transit times, certain levels of in-stock availability, and certain fill rates on customer orders.

Malcolm Baldrige National Quality Award

One reason that logistics has received more attention as a strategic function is the growing recognition given to it in the **Malcolm Baldrige National Quality Award.** This award, administered by the U.S. Department of Commerce, was designed to recognize organizations that have achieved an outstanding level of quality and competitive excellence in the global marketplace. Many organizations are using the award criteria to evaluate and improve their quality procedures, even if they do not intend to apply for the award.[27] The scoring criteria are shown in Table 1–3.

Twenty-five percent of the points used in judging applicants for awards are based on customer satisfaction. The "customer focus and satisfaction" category rates the company's knowledge of the customer, responsiveness, overall customer service systems, and ability to meet requirements and expectations.[28] Thus, an organization must have a good

---

[27]David Greisling, "Quality: How to Make It Pay," *Business Week,* Aug. 8, 1994, pp. 54–59.

[28]Lambert and Stock, *Strategic Logistics Management,* p. 19.

TABLE 1–3   Scoring the Baldrige Award, 1995 Criteria

1.0	Leadership (90 points)	
	1.1	Senior executive leadership (45)
	1.2	Leadership system and organization (25)
	1.3	Public responsibility and corporate citizenship (20)
2.0	Information and analysis (75 points)	
	2.1	Marketing of information and data (20)
	2.2	Competitive comparisons and benchmarks (15)
	2.3	Analysis and use of company-level data (40)
3.0	Strategic planning (55 points)	
	3.1	Strategy development (35)
	3.2	Strategy deployment (20)
4.0	Human resources development and management (140)	
	4.1	Human resource planning and evaluation (20)
	4.2	High-performance work systems (45)
	4.3	Employee education, training, and development (50)
	4.4	Employee well-being and satisfaction (25)
5.0	Process management (140)	
	5.1	Design and introduction of products and services (40)
	5.2	Process management: Product and service production and delivery (40)
	5.3	Process management: Support services (30)
	5.4	Management of supplier performance (30)
6.0	Business results (250)	
	6.1	Product and service quality results (75)
	6.2	Company operational and financial results (130)
	6.3	Supplier performance results (45)
7.0	Customer focus and satisfaction (250 points)	
	7.1	Customer and market knowledge (30)
	7.2	Customer relationship management (30)
	7.3	Customer satisfaction determination (30)
	7.4	Customer satisfaction results (100)
	7.5	Customer satisfaction comparison (60)
Total points = 1,000		

Source: *Malcolm Baldrige National Quality Award 1995 Criteria* (Milwaukee, WI: ASQC, 1995), p. 20.

logistics system and include logistics in its strategic planning process to score well in this major area.

ISO 9000 Programs   The **ISO 9000** (International Organization for Standardization) series is an internationally recognized certification program whereby the quality processes of firms are audited to verify whether they have well-documented and effective quality processes in place. It was born in Europe in 1987 in an effort to support trade between countries and companies.[29]

---

[29]James R. Evans and William M. Lindsay, *The Management and Control of Quality,* 2nd ed. (St. Paul, MN: West, 1993), pp. 412–15.

Just-in-Time

The Implications of JIT on Logistics

Just-in-time (JIT) is an inventory management philosophy aimed at reducing waste and redundant inventory by delivering products, components, or materials just when an organization needs them. As will be discussed in Chapters 9 and 10, JIT has profound implications on logistics systems. JIT requires close coordination of demand needs among logistics, carriers, suppliers, and manufacturing. JIT also represents a tremendous opportunity for the logistics function to contribute to the organization's success by reducing inventory while simultaneously maintaining or improving customer service levels. Thus, JIT represents an important trend in inventory management that will be discussed throughout this text. Applications of JIT principles to the retail and grocery sectors are discussed below in relation to quick response and efficient consumer response.

Quick Response

Quick response (QR) is a retail sector strategy which combines a number of tactics to improve inventory management and efficiency, while speeding inventory flows. Most QR is between manufacturer and retailer only. When fully implemented, QR applies JIT principles throughout the entire supply chain, from raw material suppliers through ultimate customer demand.

The concept works by combining electronic data interchange (EDI) with bar coding technology, so that the customer sales are tracked immediately. This information can be passed on to the manufacturer, who can then notify its raw material suppliers, and schedule production and deliveries as required to meet replenishment needs. This allows inventory reductions while speeding response time, lowering the number of out-of-stock products, and reducing handling and obsolescence. While QR began in the textile and apparel industry, it is now being applied by many industries in the retail sector. The grocery industry has begun an adaptation of this approach, called efficient consumer response, as discussed in the next section.

Cross-Docking

QR has had a major impact on distribution operations. Rather than "warehousing" product, distribution centers are now charged with "moving" the product through quickly. This frequently entails **cross-docking,** whereby the inbound product is unloaded, sorted by store, and reloaded onto trucks destined for a particular store, without ever being warehoused. As a result of QR, Mercantile Stores has reduced the number of distribution centers it owns from 12 to 8.[30]

Creating Floor-Ready Merchandise with Logistics

To further improve retail efficiency, some suppliers are shipping goods prehung and preticketed. This concept, known as "floor-ready merchandise," is growing in popularity. As noted by Randy Burnette, director of QR for Mercantile, "Our strategy and goal is to maximize the portion of business that is floor ready."[31] One retail executive commented that merchandise routinely spends an additional three days in the distribution center (DC) if it does not have retail price tickets and the proper hangers.[32] Floor-ready merchandise may lead to a reduction in the number of DCs, and processing time can be greatly reduced.

---

[30]Gary Robins, "Less Work, More Speed," *Stores,* Mar. 1994, p. 24.
[31]Ibid., p. 26.
[32]Susan Reda, "Floor-Ready Merchandise," *Stores,* Apr. 1994, p. 41.

Technology

Quick Response, Canadian Style

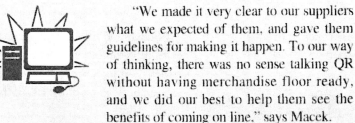

Executives at Toronto-based Hudson's Bay Company left the pioneering spirit to U.S. retailers when it came to developing quick response technology. They sat on the sidelines watching and learning from their U.S. counterparts for years.

Then, in late 1991 the decision was made to implement QR technology. Hudson's Bay executives quickly made up for lost time. Everything from UPC codes to floor-ready processes were set up and put into effect in less than two years. Ironically, as U.S. retailers and manufacturers hammer out guidelines for floor-ready merchandise today, they're looking to their neighbors to the north for tips.

According to Peggy Macek, director of merchandise systems at Hudson's Bay Company, getting suppliers to comply with the various standards, including floor-ready merchandise processing, involves a lot of partnering and understanding, and a bit of clout and coercion as well.

Computer technology allows for easy and accurate inventory control.

"We made it very clear to our suppliers what we expected of them, and gave them guidelines for making it happen. To our way of thinking, there was no sense talking QR without having merchandise floor ready, and we did our best to help them see the benefits of coming on line," says Macek.

"There were suppliers who balked initially, but we're the largest retailer in Canada. They quickly came to the conclusion that you can't fight city hall."

No doubt, the fact that The Bay cut off one of its largest suppliers for one month for refusing to comply with standards sent a clear message to Canadian manufacturers.

Currently, the retailer requires suppliers to price merchandise prior to shipping. Hangers have been standardized by merchandise type, and shipping cartons are moving through the DC [distribution center] without being opened.

While the Canadian retail scene is quite different from that in the United States—fewer retailers and manufacturers are more spread out, for example—the benefits realized by The Bay are significant.

"We're saving millions of dollars in distribution functions," reports Macek. "We used to have five distribution centers. Now, because of the technology that's been implemented and the speed with which we can push goods through the pipeline, we were able to shut down three DCs."

In the past, it took as long as two to three weeks for product to get from the DC to the selling floor at The Bay. Today, product bound for stores in Toronto and Montreal is usually on the selling floor within a day or two of arriving at the DC. Stores located in more remote areas of the country can have product on the selling floor five to six days after arrival at the DC.

Hudson's Bay Company, the oldest retailer in North America, had total sales in excess of $5 billion in 1993. The retailer operates 102 full-line department stores called The Bay, and a discount store division known as Zellers.

Source: *Stores*, Apr. 1994, p. 42.

Efficient Consumer Response

Efficient consumer response (ECR) combines several logistics strategies in an effort to improve the competitiveness of the grocery industry by cutting waste in the supply chain. It is the grocery industry's answer to QR.[33] ECR includes the following strategies:[34]

Strategies of Efficient Consumer Response

1. Widespread implementation of electronic data interchange up and down the supply chain, both between suppliers and manufacturers, manufacturers and distributors, and distributors and customers.
2. Greater use of point-of-sale data obtained by greater and more accurate use of bar coding.
3. Cooperative relationships between manufacturers, distributors, suppliers, and customers.
4. Continuous replenishment of inventory and flow through distribution.
5. Improved product management and promotions.

By applying the fourth point, continuous replenishment and flow through distribution, inventory is managed on a just-in-time basis, rather than stockpiled in warehouses and distribution centers. Product is cross-docked, whereby it is unloaded at one dock, broken down into store-sized shipments, and reloaded on trucks to go directly to the stores. Thus, cooperation and coordination are very important to ensure proper sequencing of truck loading and unloading, as well as the proper product mix. The belief is that the potential exists to reduce pipeline inventory by up to 40 percent.[35]

A key feature of ECR that distinguishes it from QR is the emphasis on moving away from the grocery industry's "deal mentality." Cooperation is required among industry participants to move away from the heavy use of promotional strategies. Such strategies encourage grocers to "stockpile" or forward buy product due to promotions such as a temporary low price or "buy two, get one free" deals. This creates excessive inventory in the supply chain, and reduces the number of times inventory turns over each year.

The ECR strategy was developed to offset some of the pressure on the grocery industry by mass merchandisers like Wal-Mart, and Warehouse clubs. It will be referred to throughout the text.

Logistics as a Competitive Weapon

Logistics Can Create a Competitive Advantage

Logistics may be the best source of competitive advantage for a firm because it is less easily duplicated than other elements of the marketing mix: product, price, and promotion. Consider, for example, forming close, ongoing relationships with carriers or logistics service providers can help give the firm a distinct competitive advantage in speed to the customer, reliability, availability, or other customer service factors.[36]

---

[33]For an excellent example of such a program, see Joseph C. Andranski, "Foundations for Successful Continuous Replenishment Programs," *The International Journal of Logistics Management* 5, no. 1 (1994), pp. 1–8.

[34]Carol Casper, "ECR: Waiting to Move Center Stage?" *Industrial Distribution,* Feb. 1994, pp. 83–85.

[35]Ibid.

[36]Donald J. Bowersox, "The Strategic Benefits of Logistics Alliances," *Harvard Business Review* 68, no. 4 (July–Aug. 1990), pp. 36–42.

The power of logistics in achieving an organization's customer service goals and supporting customer satisfaction has received an increased amount of attention in the press.[37] Companies that understand and utilize the potential of logistics as a competitive weapon include logistics as a key component of their strategic planning process. In recognition of the key role of logistics in supporting strategic customer service initiatives, the logistics function of Levi Strauss and Company began reporting to marketing rather than operations in 1990. To support this, logistics began formal strategic planning for 1990.[38]

Accounting for Logistics Costs

Implementation and utilization of the integrated logistics concept requires total cost analysis to be effective. The focus of management should be to minimize total logistics costs for a given customer service level. Thus, it is important to understand the costs associated with the logistics trade-offs in Figure 1–5.

Activity-Based Costing

In general, accounting systems have not changed and adapted to accurately account for the many trade-offs inherent in logistics activity and logistics decision making. The availability of timely, accurate, and meaningful logistics information is relatively rare in practice. However, this is beginning to change as more organizations move into activity-based costing (ABC) systems to allocate costs to activities on a more accurate and meaningful basis.[39] Much work remains to be done in this area. Some of the issues associated with the use of ABC in logistics are presented in greater depth in Chapter 13.

In addition, accounting and management support systems that are flexible in nature are needed. Logistics professionals must be able to get the information required to make decisions as they arise. Not all logistics decisions can be anticipated in advance and prepared for in a regularly scheduled logistics report. Thus, accounting systems that provide easy access to real-time data are needed to support unanticipated decisions.

Logistics as a Boundary-Spanning Activity

Logistics Plays a Key Role throughout the Supply Chain

As we have described extensively in this chapter, the logistics function and the activities performed by logistics do not exist in isolation. Logistics plays a key role in activities throughout the supply chain, both within and outside the organization. Outside the organization, logistics interfaces with customers in the order processing, order fulfillment, and delivery cycles. Logistics also interfaces with carriers, warehousers, suppliers, and other third parties that play a role in the supply chain.

---

[37]See Ulf Casten Carlberg, "Information Systems Must Offer Customized Logistics and Increase Profitability," *Industrial Engineering* 26, no. 6 (June 1994), p. 23–30; Daniel Innis and Bernard J. La Londe, "Customer Service: The Key to Customer Satisfaction, Customer Loyalty and Market Share," *Journal of Business Logistics* 15, no. 1 (1994), pp. 1–28; and "Logistics Mandate Is Customer Satisfaction," *Transportation and Distribution* 34, no. 12 (Dec. 1993), pp. 28–30.

[38]Cooper et. al., *Strategic Planning for Logistics*, pp. 165–78.

[39]Terrance Lynn Pohlen, *The Effect of Activity-Based Cost on Logistics Management*, doctoral dissertation, Ohio State University, 1993; and David A. Chudik, "Activity Based Costing for Distribution Operations," *Annual Conference Proceedings of the Council of Logistics Management*, Washington, DC (Oct. 3–6, 1993), pp. 37–52.

Within the organization, logistics interfaces with virtually every functional area in some capacity. Logistics interfaces with finance in the planning process and in the analysis of capital expenditures on investments in building and equipment to support distribution, transportation, warehousing, information technology, and related issues.

Logistics interfaces with accounting in establishing logistics costs (transportation, distribution, storage) for various products, customers, and distribution channels. Logistics also requires information from accounting regarding budgets and actual expenditures.

As discussed earlier, the interaction of logistics with other marketing activities is extensive. Logistics plays an instrumental role in customer satisfaction by providing high levels of customer service through good product availability, reliable service, and efficient operations that keep prices competitive.

Logistics must work closely with production and operations in a number of capacities. First, logistics often receives order releases for materials from production, and it needs to ensure that the items required are ordered, transported, and received on a timely basis. Storage also may need to be arranged. Logistics often manages the flow of materials or work in process within the organization. Logistics also must work with production in terms of stocking and shipping the finished product as it is available.

Logistics should be involved with research and development, product engineering, packaging engineering, and related functions in the new product development process. This often occurs through logistics participation on a new product team. It is vital for the logistics area to be represented very early in the new product development process.[40] This is critical in terms of designing the proper distribution channel, anticipating needs for inventory buildup, ensuring the availability of materials for production, and properly configuring the packaging for maximum efficiency and production within the distribution channel.

An increasing number of organizations are using the team approach to facilitate communications, create buy-in from multiple functions, and to anticipate problems. Logistics should be an active participant on teams that deal with issues affecting the supply chain.[41]

Global Logistics

Many leading organizations are heavily involved in international markets through purchasing inputs to production, other importing, exporting, joint ventures, alliances, foreign subsidiaries and divisions, and other means. This creates a need for familiarity with global logistics and global logistics networks. This need is likely to continue in the future. The Ohio State University's study of logistics career patterns reported that the top-rated global trends that are expected to have an impact on the careers of logistics professionals are:

The Most Important Global Trends

• The growth of information technology (21 percent)

• Supply chain management (15 percent)

• Globalization (11 percent)

---

[40]Phillip R. Witt, *Cost Competitive Products* (Reston, VA: Reston Publishing, 1986).

[41]See "Brewing Up a Logistics Partnership," *Distribution* 92, no. 9 (Sept. 1993), p. 49; and "How Sears Leverages Its LTL," *Distribution* 91, no. 9 (Sept. 1993), p. 46.

FIGURE 1-6

Logistics responsibilities: Allocation of time and effort

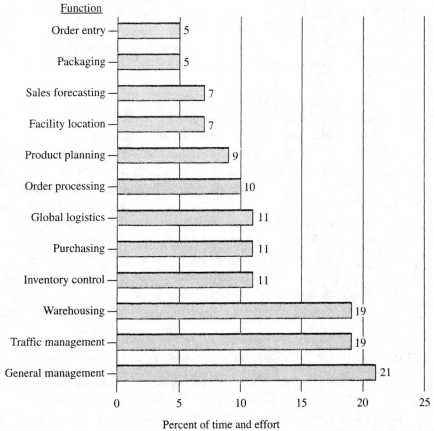

Source: James M. Masters and Bernard J. La Londe, *The 1996 Ohio State University Survey of Career Patterns in Logistics* (Columbus: The Ohio State University, 1996).

Increasing Skill Requirements

As suggested above, the demands on logistics professionals are increasing. As logisticians become increasingly involved in setting corporate strategy and other aspects of the strategic planning process, different skill sets are required in quality issues, global logistics, and improving relationships with third-party providers. One of the best sources of longitudinal data for trends in logistics careers has been the Logistics Career Patterns Study conducted annually by The Ohio State University. As shown in Figure 1-6, this study indicates that the greatest proportion of logistics time and effort is spent on general management issues.

A small percentage of time is spent on very repetitive issues such as order entry and packaging.[42] Information systems also are playing an increasingly important role in logistics, as discussed in the next section.

---

[42]James M. Masters and Bernard J. La Londe, *The 1996 Ohio State University Survey of Career Patterns in Logistics* (Columbus: The Ohio State University, 1996).

Logistics Information Systems

Information Is the Key to Integrated Logistics Management

Part of an organization's ability to use logistics as a competitive weapon is based on its ability to assess and adjust actual logistics performance real time. This means the ability to monitor customer demands and inventory levels as they occur, to act in a timely manner to prevent stockouts, and to communicate potential problems to customers. This requires excellent, integrated logistics information systems. These systems impact all of the logistics activities presented earlier, and must be integrated and take into account marketing and production activities. Such systems also must be integrated with other members of the supply chain, to provide accurate information throughout the channel from the earliest supplier through the ultimate customer.

Logistics information systems may link a variety of information technologies, as is the case with Wal-Mart. Wal-Mart uses EDI to communicate with suppliers, receiving information such as shipment, timing, quantities, and even invoicing. It uses bar coding to scan sales as customers make their purchases. The bar-coded information is thus captured at the point of sale. Wal-Mart then downloads the information to suppliers. Suppliers use these data to determine the orders they need to supply to Wal-Mart, rather than having Wal-Mart create the orders. This system provides suppliers with rapid feedback on sales, so that they can anticipate production requirements based on accurate, near real-time sales data. Wal-Mart also benefits because it no longer has to place orders with many suppliers, and it can keep its inventory levels to a minimum.

Outsourcing, Partnering, and Strategic Alliances

During the 1980s, many organizations began to recognize that they could not effectively and efficiently "do it all" themselves and still remain competitive. They began to look to third-party specialists to perform activities that were not a part of their "core competency." This activity is known as **outsourcing,** in which an organization hires an outside organization to provide a good or service that it traditionally had provided itself, because this third party is an "expert" in efficiently providing this good or service, while the organization itself may not be.

Outsourcing

Recently, outsourcing has been an area of growing interest and activity. Logistics outsourcing often involves third-party warehouses and use of public or contract transportation carriers. Outsourcing offers the opportunity for organizations to use the best logistics providers available to meet their needs.[43] Outsourcing may involve a partnership relationship or be ad hoc, on a transaction to transaction basis. Traditionally, such relationships have been arm's-length, with each party concerned only for its own welfare.[44]

Partnering

Managers in many firms are accepting the concept of partnering or establishing close, long-term working relationships with suppliers of goods or services, customers,

---

[43]Bernard J. La Londe, Martha C. Cooper and Thomas Noodeweir, *Customer Service: A Management Perspective,* (Oak Brook, IL: Council of Logistics Management, 1988), pp. 71–94.

[44]For an excellent discussion of outsourcing issues, see Arnold B. Maltz, "Outsourcing the Warehousing Function: Economics and Strategic Considerations," *Logistics and Transportation Review* 30, no. 2 (1994), pp. 245–66.

and third-party providers. This concept has been embraced by Bose Corporation, in the JIT II program. Bose uses the concept of an "in-plant," where key suppliers or service providers are actually on location at Bose's facility. Bose has such a relationship with Roadway Express, Inc. Bose states that this relationship creates efficiency between it and the carrier, creating improved communications, better service, and shared cost savings.[45]

Strategic Alliances

The most closely integrated partnerships are often referred to as **strategic alliances.** For a partnership to be a strategic alliance, it must be strategic in nature and must directly support one of the organization's distinctive competencies. Strategic alliances are rare in actual practice.

Technology

There has been a proliferation of technological developments in areas that support logistics. As discussed above, there have been major technological developments in the information systems area: EDI, bar coding, point-of-sale data, and satellite data transmissions are only a few examples. In addition, improvements in automated warehousing capabilities should be integrated into logistics plans for upgrading technology. Technology is having a profound effect on the way that logistics personnel interface with other functional areas, creating the ability to access more timely, accurate information. Combining information technology with automated warehousing reduces inherent human variability, creating an opportunity to improve customer service.

Green Marketing

Environmental Issues Are Becoming More Important

Environmental issues have been an area of growing concern and attention for businesses on a global scale. Transportation and disposal of hazardous materials are frequently regulated and controlled. In Europe, organizations are increasingly required to remove and dispose of packaging materials used for their products. These issues complicate the job of logistics, increasing costs and limiting options. Organizations are continually looking at reducing, reusing, and reapplying packaging materials, by-products of production, and obsolete items. Companies are substituting items that are more readily recyclable. Some have even gone so far as to begin designing products with disassembly specifically in mind.[46] These activities are covered in the term **green marketing.**

We have briefly summarized some of the current and future issues facing logistics professionals. These issues are recurring themes that will appear throughout this text.

Summary

In this chapter, we introduced the concept of logistics and described its development and relevance to the organization and economy as a whole. The concept of the systems

---

[45]William J. Warren, "JIT II Puts Bose a Little Ahead of the Cutting Edge," *American Shipper* 33, no. 12 (Dec. 1991), p. 47.

[46]"Manufacturing for Recovery," *Fortune,* Jan. 23, 1995, pp. 63–68ff.

Creative Solutions

Delivering the Goods

National Semiconductor, the world's 13th largest computer chip manufacturer began looking at how to increase logistical efficiency in the early 1990s in an effort to turn its profitability around. It discovered that it delivered 95 percent of its products within 45 days of the time they were ordered. While this was not satisfactory, the other 5 percent required as much as 90 days! Since the customers could not be sure which 5 percent would be late, they required 90 days worth of stock on everything. The system was overloaded with inventory.

After doing a profitability analysis, National cut 45 percent of its product line. To get the remaining

products to market on time, it simplified—going from 20,000 routes on 12 airlines, involving 10 warehouses, to 1 central facility in Singapore. To speed that product to market, it hired Federal Express to handle all of its sorting, shipping, and storage at its Singapore distribution center. This has resulted in major operating improvements. National can move products from factory to customer in four days or less. Distribution costs are down from 2.6 percent of revenues to 1.9 percent.

Source: Ron Henkoff. "Delivering the Goods," *Fortune*, Nov. 28, 1994, pp. 64–78.

approach was introduced and related to the role of logistics and its interface with marketing and other functions. The key role of logistics in customer service was emphasized. The systems approach was also related to the total cost concept and the principle of trade-offs as it relates to both the performance of logistics activity and the costs associated with such activity. The key logistics costs identified were customer service, inventory carrying costs, transportation, warehousing, order processing/information systems costs, and lot quantity costs.

We also examined the issue of logistics strategy, and the role of logistics in corporate strategy. This chapter closed with a summary of future challenges for logistics professionals. These challenges range from playing an active role in the strategic planning process to improving accounting information, information technology, and other types of technology and practices, such as TQM, JIT, QR, and ECR. The changing nature of logistics relationships, from team participation to forming partnering relationships with suppliers, was also explored.

There are many opportunities and challenges that face the logistics function in the future. We will begin to describe these in more depth in Chapter 2, which focuses on customer service.

Suggested Readings

Bowersox, Donald J.; Patricia J. Daugherty; Cornelia I. Dröge; Richard N. Germain; and Dale S.
    Rogers. *Logistical Excellence: It's Not Business as Usual.* Burlington, MA: Digital Press, 1992.
Heskett, James L. "Sweeping Changes in Distribution." *Harvard Business Review* 51, no. 2
    (Mar.–Apr. 1973), pp. 123–32.

Lambert, Douglas M. *The Development of an Inventory Costing Methodology: A Study of the Costs Associated with Holding Inventory.* Chicago: National Council of Physical Distribution Management, 1976.

Leenders, Michiel, and Harold E. Fearon. *Purchasing and Materials Management,* 11th ed. Burr Ridge, IL: Irwin/McGraw-Hill, 1997.

Mentzer, John T. "Managing Channel Relations in the 21st Century." *Journal of Business Logistics* 14, no. 1 (1993), pp. 27–41.

Smith, Peter A.; Jack Barry; Joseph L. Cavinato; John J. Coyle; Steven J. Dunn; and William Grenoble. *Logistics in Service Industries.* Oak Brook, IL: Council of Logistics Management, 1991.

Stock, James R. "Logistics Thought and Practice: A Perspective." *International Journal of Physical Distribution and Logistics Management* 20, no. 1 (1990), pp. 3–6.

———. *Reverse Logistics.* Oak Brook, IL: Council of Logistics Management, 1992.

Trunick, Perry A. "Logistics: An Agent for Change In the 90's." *Transportation and Distribution* 34, no. 11 (Nov. 1993), pp. 36–41.

Turner, J. R. "Integrated Supply Chain Management: What's Wrong with This Picture?" *Industrial Engineering* 25, no. 12 (Dec. 1993), pp. 52–55.

Questions and Problems

1. How do improvements in logistics productivity affect the economy as a whole, as well as the position of individual consumers?

2. How is logistics related to the marketing effort? Be sure to discuss customer service/customer satisfaction, integration of efforts, and cost and performance outputs.

3. What are the different types of utility? How does logistics directly or indirectly affect each one?

4. Why has logistics recently been receiving more attention as a strategic function of the organization?

5. What is meant by the profit leverage affect of logistics? What are the greatest cost savings opportunities for logistics?

6. Based on the examples shown in the text, what is the profit leverage effect of logistics in a firm with pretax profit of 5%? Of 10%? How could you use this information to get favorable attention for a logistics cost-saving effort?

7. Discuss the key challenges facing logistics today. What do you see as the greatest area of opportunity for logistics? Why?

8. How has the role and performance of logistics been enhanced by the growth of technology, particularly information technology? What do you see as key trends in the future?

9. Of the 14 areas of logistics responsibility, which do you believe will experience the most change in the next five years or so? Why?

THE DISTRIBUTION CHALLENGE!
PROBLEM: TORN IN THE U.S.A.

Call it the American dilemma: a company with long-range ideals that is required to show short-term results.

In order to satisfy the demanding financial community, a client of consultant Ernst & Young must demonstrate ever-improving earnings on a quarterly basis. At the same time, it must boost profitability by rapidly introducing new products. Virtually no lag is permitted, according to Stan Brown and Mike Brown, senior managers of Ernst & Young. Yet this relentless pressure is having a serious impact on the company's supply-chain performance.

One of this company's business units experiences a demand spike in sales during the last few days of each month. Up to half its monthly business might be transacted in that brief period. But the irregular pattern of supply and demand isn't the result of any oddities in the industry. It's purely an artificial situation, caused by the sales force scrambling for business at the end of each reporting period. Often that means artificially pulling demand forward to make sales targets. What's more, the erratic pace of sales leads to periods during which the company might not have enough inventory to fulfill demand.

Two problems result. One is that retailers are conditioned to order product only when promotions are provided, so they wait until then in hope of securing deep discounts. The other is that the seller's warehouse is overwhelmed by orders as it struggles to cope with a 150 percent utilization factor during a 24-hour period. Naturally, the warehouse is viewed by sales "as the bad guy, because it can't deliver," says Stan Brown.

The challenge: In a situation that is driven by the financial community—the demand for short-term profits—where is this company's leverage? What can it do to smooth out the flow of product without seriously compromising its profitability?

What Is Your Solution?

Source: "Distribution: The Challenge." *Distribution* 96, no. 4 (Apr. 1997), p. 76.

Customer Service

Chapter Outline

Chapter Objectives

- To define customer service.
- To show the central role that customer service plays in an organization's marketing and logistics efforts.
- To show how to calculate cost-revenue trade-offs.
- To illustrate how to conduct a customer service audit.
- To identify opportunities for improving customer service performance.

Introduction

In times of tough competition when many organizations offer similar products in terms of price, features, and quality, customer service differentiation can provide an organization with a distinct advantage over the competition.[1] Customer service represents the output of the logistics system as well as the "place" component of the organization's marketing mix. Customer service performance is a measure of how well the logistics system functions in creating time and place utility, with a focus on external customers.

The level of service provided to functions, such as marketing and production, affects the organization's ability to serve the needs of customers and will determine how well these functions communicate and interact with logistics on a day-to-day basis.[2] The level of customer service provided to customers determines whether the organization will retain existing customers and how many new customers it will attract.[3]

In virtually every industry today, from computers to clothing to cars, customers have a wide variety of choices. A company cannot afford to offend its customers. The customer service level that an organization provides has a direct impact on its market share, its total logistics costs and, ultimately, its overall profitability.

The Importance of Attracting and Retaining Customers

To illustrate, a key to corporate profitability is to successfully attract and retain customers. However, it has been estimated that the average customer turnover is between 10 and 30 percent for all U.S. companies.[4] If customer turnover could be reduced by 5 percent, bottom-line profitability could possibly increase significantly, perhaps by 60–95 percent annually.[5]

For these reasons, it is of the utmost importance that customer service be an integral part of the design and operation of all logistics systems.

Customer Service Defined

The definition of **customer service** varies across organizations. Suppliers and their customers can view the concept of customer service quite differently. In a broad sense, customer service is the measure of how well the logistics system is performing in providing time and place utility for a product or service. This includes activities such as the ease of checking stock, placing an order, and postsale support of the item.

Customer service is often confused with the concept of customer satisfaction. In contrast to customer service, **customer satisfaction** represents the customer's overall assessment of all elements of the marketing mix: product, price, promotion, and place. Thus, cus-

---

[1]"An Energized Process for Improving Customer Service," *NAPM Insights,* Apr. 1992, pp. 9–11; and Graham Sharman, "The Rediscovery of Logistics," *Harvard Business Review* 62, no. 5 (Sept.–Oct. 1984), pp. 71–79.

[2]Peter E. O'Reilly, "Getting to Know Them," *NAPM Insights,* May 1994, p. 8.

[3]Christopher Power, Lisa Driscoll, and Earl Bohn, "Smart Selling: How Companies Are Winning Over Today's Tougher Customer," *Business Week,* Aug. 3, 1992, p. 46.

[4]Toby B. Gooley, "How Logistics Drive Customer Service," *Traffic Management* 35, no. 1 (Jan. 1996), p. 46.

[5]Ibid.

tomer satisfaction is a broader concept that encompasses customer service. A thorough description of customer satisfaction can be found in many introductory marketing textbooks.[6]

Customer Service Can Be Viewed in Three Ways

In most organizations, customer service is defined in one or more ways, including (1) an activity or function to be managed, such as order processing or handling of customer complaints; (2) actual performance on particular parameters, such as the ability to ship complete orders for 98 percent of orders received within a 24-hour period; or (3) part of an overall corporate philosophy, rather than simply an activity or performance measures.[7] If an organization views customer service as a philosophy, it will likely have a formal customer service function and various performance measures.[8]

A Recent View of Customer Service

Customer service can be defined as:

Customer Service Defined

> . . . a process which takes place between the buyer, seller, and third party. The process results in a value added to the product or service exchanged. This value added in the exchange process might be short term as in a single transaction or longer term as in a contractual relationship. The value added is also shared, in that each of the parties to the transaction or contract are better off at the completion of the transaction than it was before the transaction took place. Thus, in a process view: Customer service is a process for providing significant value-added benefits to the supply chain in a cost-effective way.[9]

Successful implementation of the marketing concept requires that companies both win and retain customers. Too often, the emphasis is on winning new customers and gaining new accounts. But this is an extremely shortsighted approach for an ongoing business concern. Many business strategy textbooks used to say that "the objective of a firm is to make a profit," but this attitude is shifting. The objective of the firm is still to make a profit, but before that can take place, the firm needs to establish service policies and programs that will satisfy customers' needs and deliver them in a cost-efficient manner; that is, customer service.

Companies like L. L. Bean, Marriott, Procter & Gamble, Motorola, and Saturn Corporation have gained significant advantage in the marketplace by meeting and sometimes exceeding a customer's service expectations. Here are a few examples of how these firms and others have addressed customer service issues:

Customer Service Examples

- Marriott hotels regularly shares customer assessments with employees. Involving customers in the regular, formal evaluation process, allows Marriott to get employees committed to its focus on customer service.

---

[6]See, for example, Philip Kotler and Gary Armstrong, *Principles of Marketing,* 5th ed. (Englewood Cliffs, NJ: Prentice Hall, 1993).

[7]Bernard J. La Londe and Paul H. Zinszer, *Customer Service: Meaning and Measurement* (Chicago: National Council of Physical Distribution Management, 1976), pp. 156–59.

[8]For an overview of how customer service has been viewed during the previous 25 years, see, "A Compendium of Research in Customer Service," *International Journal of Physical Distribution and Logistics Management* 24, no. 4 (1994), pp. 1–68.

[9]Bernard J. La Londe, Martha C. Cooper, and Thomas G. Noordewier, *Customer Service: A Management Perspective* (Chicago: Council of Logistics Management, 1988), p. 5.

A customer service representative of Merck-Medco Managed Care fields a call, quickly accesses the patient's prescription information, and reminds the patient that a refill is due.

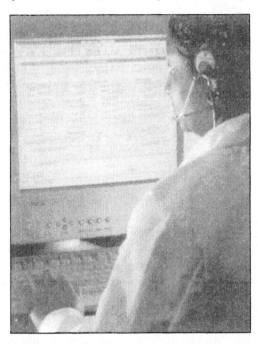

- Home Depot reviews home project tasks with customers to help improve the quality of its efforts.
- Printer Quad/Graphics sponsors a workshop twice a year. Customers meet the CEO, and employees escort them through plant facilities. The goal is to exchange information, so that the company and its employees are trained and oriented with respect to their roles in the service design and production activities.[10]

TQM and Customer Service

Do Customers Always Complain to Firms?

It is very expensive to win customers. Keeping customers should be a paramount concern. Determining what customers need in terms of service levels and delivering upon those needs in a cost-effective and efficient manner should be a key concern of the logistics function. A goal should be to "do it right the first time," to prevent complaints from ever occurring. A recent study indicates that for every customer that complains, as many as 19 simply choose to stop doing business with the organization, and usually tell their associates about their negative experience.[11]

However, the complainers have much to offer in terms of potential learning. They may alert the organization to a widespread problem which, if addressed, could reduce future complaints and help retain those "noncomplaining" customers who otherwise would

---

[10]How Companies Involve Customers," *Executive Report on Customer Satisfaction* 8, no. 9 (May 15, 1995), p. 7.

[11]George R. Walther, "Upside Down Marketing," Audio-Tech Business Book Summary 3, no. 5, section 1 (Mar. 1994), p. 4.

_____
Box 2–1

L. L. Bean: Customer Service Excellence

L. L. Bean is a catalog distributor of high-quality, durable outdoor clothing and sportswear. Located in Freeport, Maine, L. L. Bean has been widely noted as a leading company in providing excellent customer satisfaction and excellent customer service through its logistics/distribution operations.

L. L. Bean receives most of its orders by telephone. It needs to respond quickly and accurately to filling and shipping customer orders for products that vary a great deal in size and shape. As a result, orders are filled manually. One of the secrets to L. L. Bean's success is that, based on worker suggestions, it stocks high sales volume items close to packing stations. This minimizes excessive

movement of product, reducing order-filling time and improving efficiency.

L. L. Bean's performance is phenomenal. It boasts of a fill rate that averages 99.9 percent even during the Christmas season when it ships over 134,000 packages a day. As a result of its outstanding performance in distribution, many leading organizations, such as Xerox and Chrysler, have benchmarked L. L. Bean's logistics operations.

Source: Synthesized from Otis Port, John Carey, Kerin Kelly, and Stephanie Anderson. "Special Report: Quality," *Business Week*, Nov. 30, 1992, pp. 66–72; and Otis Port, "Beg, Borrow and Benchmark," *Business Week*, Nov. 30, 1992, pp. 74–75.

---

have simply walked away. In addition, if handled well, complaining customers actually become more loyal, and are nine times more likely to do business with that organization again in the future.[12]

Thus, quality in customer service, from initial dealings with the customer to proper handling of problems, is critical in achieving high levels of customer service. This in turn contributes to high levels of customer satisfaction.

Elements of Customer Service

Customer Service before, during, and after the Sale

The elements of customer service can be classified into three groups: pretransaction, transaction, and posttransaction elements. These groups are linked to the definitions of marketing which incorporate the notion of market transactions—before, during, and after the sale.[13] This conceptualization is depicted in Figure 2–1.

Pretransaction Elements.   The pretransaction elements of customer service tend to be related to the organization's policies regarding customer service, and can have a significant impact on customers' perceptions of the organization and their overall satisfaction. These elements are not all directly related to logistics. They must be formulated and in place before the organization can consistently implement and execute its customer service activities. Pretransaction elements include the following:

A Written Statement of Customer Service Policy Is Vital

1. **A written statement of customer service policy.** This policy would define service standards, which should be tied to customers' needs. It should include metrics for

_____
[12]Ibid.
[13]La Londe and Zinszer, *Customer Service,* pp. 272–82.

FIGURE 2–1

Elements of customer service

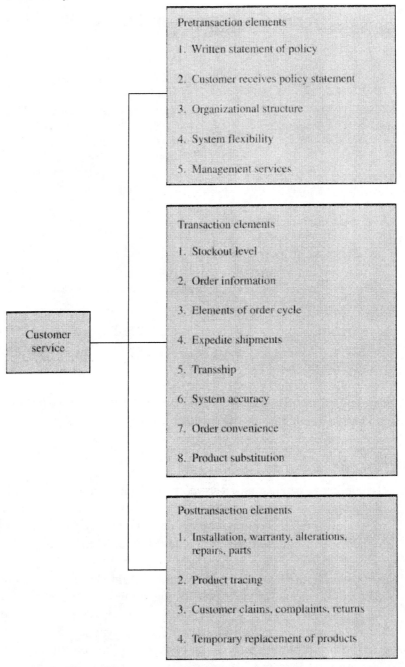

Source: Bernard J. La Londe and Paul H. Zinszer, *Customer Service: Meaning and Measurement* (Chicago: National Council of Physical Distribution Management, 1976), p. 281.

A ConAgra grocery products sales rep creates a greater market presence with more personal involvement at the store level.

tracking service performance and the frequency of reporting actual performance, and be measurable and actionable.

2. **Customers provided with a written statement of policy.** A written statement lets the customer know what to expect and helps to safeguard against unreasonable expectations. It should provide the customer with information about how to respond if expected service levels are not achieved by the firm.

refunds/
returns

Organizations Must Be Structured so that They Are Responsive to Customers

3. **Organization structure.** The organization structure best suited to ensure the achievement of customer service goals varies across organizations, but the senior logistics executive should be positioned at a high level and have high visibility within the firm. The structure should facilitate both internal and external communication of policies, performance, and corrective actions as needed. Customers should have easy access to individuals within the organization who can satisfy their needs and answer their questions. Imagine the frustration felt by a customer who has experienced a problem with product delivery or performance, who telephones the selling organization only to be put on hold, and transferred from one representative to another, continually reexplaining his or her entire problem! The customer may never call that organization again for anything.

4. **System flexibility.** Flexibility and contingency plans should be built into the system, which allow the organization to successfully respond to unforeseen events such as labor strikes, material shortages, and natural disasters such as hurricanes or flooding.

deliveries/
billing

5. **Management services.** Providing the customers with help in merchandising, improving inventory management, and ordering are examples of some of the services an organization may provide to its customers. These may be provided in the form of

training manuals, seminars, or one-on-one consultation. The services may be free of charge or fee based.

All of these pretransaction elements may be experienced by the customer outside of the normal order cycle. Decisions relating to the pretransaction elements tend to be relatively stable, long-term decisions that are changed infrequently. This provides some stability for the customer in terms of expectations.

Transaction Elements.   Transaction elements are the elements that are *normally* considered to be associated with customer service, and include the following:

How Much Inventory Should a Firm Have to Satisfy Customer Demand?

1. **Stockout level.** The stockout level measures product availability. Stockouts should be monitored by product and customer in order to better track potential problems. When stockouts occur, the organization should endeavor to maintain customer goodwill by offering a suitable substitute, drop-shipping from another location to the customer if possible, or expediting the shipment once the out-of-stock item arrives.

2. **Order information availability.** Customers' expectations regarding access to all types of information related to their orders have increased dramatically because of the availability of relatively inexpensive computing power. This includes information on inventory status, order status, expected or actual shipping date, and back-order status. Tracking back-order performance is important because customers pay close attention to problems and exceptions to delivery. Back-orders should be tracked by customer and by product type, so that recurring problems become visible and can be addressed in a timely fashion.

3. **System accuracy.** In addition to the ability to rapidly obtain a wide variety of data, customers expect that the information they receive about order status and stock levels will be accurate. Inaccuracies should be noted and corrected as quickly as possible. Continuing problems require major corrective action and a high level of attention. Errors are costly to correct for customers and suppliers in terms of time delays and paperwork created.

Order Cycle Defined

4. **Consistency of order cycle.** The order cycle is the total time from customer initiation of the order through receipt of the product or service by the customer. Thus, if a salesperson obtains an order from a customer and holds it for five days before entering the order, that adds five days to the order cycle time, even though those five days were invisible to the distribution center. Elements of the order cycle include placing the order, order entry if separate from placement, order processing, order picking and packing for shipment, transit time, and the actual delivery process. Customers tend to be more concerned with the consistency of lead times than with absolute lead time, so it is important to monitor actual performance in this regard and take corrective action if needed. However, with the increased emphasis on time-based competition, reducing total cycle time has received greater attention. This topic will be discussed later in this chapter.

5. **Special handling of shipments.** Special handling of shipments relates to any order that cannot be managed through the normal delivery system. This could happen because it needs to be expedited or has unique shipping requirements. The costs of such shipments are considerably higher than standard shipments. However, the cost of a lost customer could be higher still. The company should determine which customers or situations warrant special treatment and which do not.

6. **Transshipment.** Transshipments refer to shipping products between various distribution locations to avoid stockouts. For companies with multiple locations, some sort

FIGURE 2–2

Impact of product substitution on customer service levels

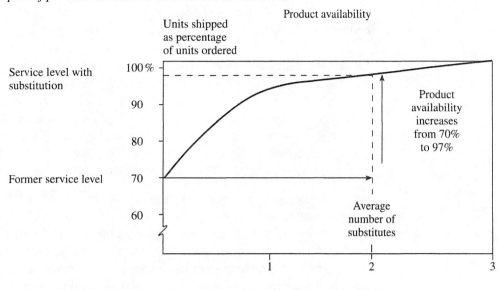

Number of acceptable substitutes

of policy should be in place concerning transshipments as opposed to back-ordering or drop-shipping directly to a customer from more than one location.

7. **Order convenience.** Order convenience refers to how easy it is for a customer to place an order. Customers prefer suppliers that are user-friendly. If forms are confusing, terms are not standardized, or the waiting time on hold on the telephone is long, customers may experience dissatisfaction. Order-related problems should be monitored and identified by talking directly with customers. Problems should be noted and corrected.

When Should Customers Be Offered Substitutes for Items That Are Not Available?

8. **Product substitution.** Product substitution occurs when the product that the customer ordered is not available, but is replaced by a different size of the same item or a different product that will perform just as well or better. Figure 2–2 illustrates that if a product currently has a 70 percent service level and one acceptable substitute that also has a 70 percent service level, a manufacturer can effectively raise its service level for that product to 91 percent. If the product has two acceptable substitutes, the in-stock availability becomes 97 percent! Thus, the ability to provide a customer with acceptable substitutes can significantly improve the firm's service level.

Developing Product Substitution Policies

The manufacturer should work with its customers to develop product substitution policies and should keep its customers informed of those policies. It is always a good idea to check with the customer before substituting one product for another. For example, if a custom furniture manufacturer orders one-gallon cans of lacquer, and the distributor is out of stock, the distributor may offer five-gallon units in their place. This may not be suitable because the furniture manufacturer may use only two gallons for each job and does not want to have partially used five-gallon containers of lacquer. However, if the distributor offers one-half-gallon cans at the same price per gallon, this may be a perfectly acceptable substitute to the customer.

47

The transaction elements of customer service often receive the most attention, because they are the most immediate and apparent to the customer. For example, in a recent survey of 1,300 companies, Ryder Systems found that 80 percent of respondents believed delivery of the product was as important as the quality of the product itself.[14]

Service after the Sale

Posttransaction Elements.   The posttransaction elements of customer service support the product or service after the customer has received it. Historically, this has tended to be the most neglected of the three groups of customer service elements, in part because a relatively small proportion of customers complain about poor service. However, retaining and satisfying current customers can be much more profitable than finding new customers. For example, Ford Motor Company estimated that "the lifetime value of a typical customer [is] $178,000."[15] Posttransaction elements include:

1. **Installation, warranty, repairs, and service parts.** These elements should be an important consideration in almost all purchases, especially purchases of capital equipment where such costs tend to far outweigh the cost of the purchased item itself.[16] These elements should receive the same attention and scrutiny as transaction elements.

2. **Product tracking.** Product tracking, also referred to as product tracing, is an important customer service element. For example, in order to inform consumers of potential problems, firms must be able to recall potentially dangerous products from the market once the potential hazard has been identified.

3. **Customer complaints, claims, and returns.** To resolve customer complaints, an accurate on-line information system is needed to process the data from the customer, monitor trends, and provide the customer with the most current information available. Logistics systems are designed to move products to customers, so the cost of nonroutine handling, particularly of small shipments such as customer returns, tends to be high. Customer returns go through the logistics process in reverse; hence the term **reverse logistics.**[17] Corporate policies should be established to handle these complaints as efficiently and effectively as possible.

Reverse Logistics

4. **Product replacement.** Depending on the item, having backup product temporarily available when the item is being serviced can be critical. For example, some automobile dealerships provide loaner cars to their customers at no charge while their cars are being serviced. This minimizes the inconvenience and may create a more loyal customer.

Importance of Customer Service for Gaining Strategic Advantage

Customer Service Is the Key Interface between Marketing and Logistics

Customer service is the output of the logistics system and is the key interface between the marketing and logistics functions, supporting the "place" element of the marketing

[14]"The Future of Transportation," advertisement in *Fortune*, Mar. 21, 1995.
[15]Walther, "Upside Down Marketing," p. 12.
[16]Lisa M. Ellram, *Total Cost Modeling in Purchasing* (Tempe, AZ: Center for Advanced Purchasing Studies, 1994), p. 10.
[17]Reverse logistics often refers to various environmental aspects such as disposal and recycling. However, the term is more encompassing and includes product recalls and product returns.

Technology

Delivery Speed Keeps Electronic Boutique at the Top of Its Game

"What moves faster than Sonic the Hedgehog?" Probably Electronics Boutique, the video game, computer software and hardware, and accessories retailer. The firm stocks between 2,500 and 3,500 SKUs in each of its 527 stores in the United States, United Kingdom, Canada, and Puerto Rico. Approximately 50 percent of its business occurs during the Christmas selling season. In a highly competitive industry, the firm has become a leader in fast order cycle times, rapid product replenishment, and customer service.

Especially important from a customer service perspective is that the peak sales period of a new video game occurs in the first two weeks after its introduction. This means that if Electronics Boutique

With 2,500 to 3,500 different products in a typical Electronics Boutique retail store, the logistics of providing the right combination of products and services requires the company to be a leader in fast order cycle times, and rapid product replenishment.

does not have the product in its stores, sales do not occur. "Miss the mark on getting a new release into the stores, and you've disappointed your customers, sending them across the mall to competitors such as Software Etc., Babbage's, or even Toys "Я" Us."

The firm does such a good job in getting new products on its shelves earlier than competitors that Sega selected Electronics Boutique as one of only three retailers to get advance release of the video game called "Saturn," a highly sought-after game during the 1995 Christmas season.

About two years ago, in a new 120,000 square-foot distribution center . . . which handles all replenishment and half of new release distribution, a technological revolution has been taking place. The center now runs on a computerized order management program that structures "putaway" of new receipts . . . Order picking is driven by a paperless pick system Rapistan Demag designed and installed two years ago. An As/400 computer generates pick orders for the stores, creating bar-code labels that are slapped on the three to five boxes each store receives daily, containing 15 to 90 titles each . . . Order pickers scan the bar codes, and LEDs at each pick site light up to indicate the number of pieces of each SKU to pick.

Each box contains the labels store personnel need for the goods in that box . . . When the day's delivery reaches the store, store personnel can rip open the key box with the hottest release and sell right out of the carton, if customers demand it, rather than wasting time unpacking and labeling a whole day's shipment. Store managers can check via computer what's in transit and which carton it's in.

Source: Laurie Joan Aron, "Delivery Speed Keeps Electronics Boutique at the Top of Its Game," *Inbound Logistics* 16, no. 1 (Jan. 1996), pp. 30–40.

mix. But even more important, customer service plays a significant role in developing and maintaining customer loyalty and ongoing satisfaction.

The product, pricing, and promotion elements of the marketing mix create value added for customers. However, when the performance of competitors is similar on these attributes, it is customer service that really brings the customer back.

Products and prices are relatively easy for competitors to duplicate. Promotional efforts also can be matched by competitors, with the possible exception of a well-trained and motivated sales force. The satisfactory service encounter, or favorable complaint resolution, is one important way that the organization can really distinguish itself in the eyes of the customer. Thus, logistics can play a key role in contributing to the organization's competitive advantage by providing excellent customer service.

How to Establish a Customer Service Strategy

An organization's entire marketing effort can be neutralized by poorly conceived or executed customer service policies. Yet customer service is often a neglected element of the marketing mix. As a result, customer service standards tend to be based on industry norms, historical practices, or management's judgment of what the customer wants, rather than what the customer really desires. Management often treats all customers the same, not recognizing that different customers want different levels and types of services.[18]

Service Policies Must Be Based on Customer Requirements

It is essential that a firm establish customer service policies based on customer requirements and supportive of the overall marketing strategy. What is the point of manufacturing a great product, pricing it competitively, and promoting it well, if it is not readily available to the consumer? At the same time, customer service policies should be cost efficient, contributing favorably to the firm's overall profitability.

Competitive Benchmarking

One popular method for setting customer service levels is to benchmark competitors' customer service performance. While it may be interesting to see what the competition is doing, this information has limited usefulness. In terms of what the customer requires, how does the firm know if the competition is focusing on the right customer service elements? Therefore, competitive benchmarking alone is insufficient.

Competitive benchmarking should be performed in conjunction with customer surveys that measure the importance of various customer service elements. Opportunities to close the "gaps" between customer requirements and the firm's performance can be identified. The firm can then target the primary customers of specific competitors while protecting its own key accounts from potential competitor inroads.

A number of methods have been suggested for establishing customer service strategies. Four have the greatest value:

1. Determining customer service levels based on customer reactions to stockouts at the retail level.
2. Cost/revenue trade-offs.

---

[18]Joseph Fuller, James O'Conor and Richard Rawlinson, "Tailored Logistics: The Next Advantage," *Harvard Business Review* 94, no. 3 (May–June 1994), pp. 87–94.

3. ABC analysis of customer service.
4. Customer service audits.

Each of these techniques is discussed below.

Customer Reactions to Stockouts

Most manufacturers do not sell exclusively to end users. Instead, they sell to wholesalers or other intermediaries who sell to the final customer. For this reason, it may be difficult for a manufacturer to assess the impact of stockouts on end users. For example, an out-of-stock situation at the manufacturer's warehouse does not necessarily mean an out-of-stock product at the retail level. One way to establish the desirable level of customer service at the retail level is to determine consumers' response to stockouts, which can include substituting another size of the same brand, switching brands, or perhaps going to a different store to buy the items. For most products, consumers will switch stores only if they believe that the product they desire is superior to or considerably less expensive than the available substitutes.

Stockouts Have Different Effects on Channel Members

To see how stockouts have a different effect at various levels of the channel of distribution, we can examine the infant formula industry. Most infant formula manufacturers do not advertise their products on national television, and generally limit the amount they spend on consumer-directed media advertising. They also limit the use of price promotion. Instead, they spend their marketing dollars on sample products to give to doctors and hospitals, who in turn give the product samples to new mothers. New mothers are often told not to switch brands because the baby develops a preference and may not adapt well to another brand. In addition, most mothers assume that their doctor would give them only the recommended products as samples. Thus, when the mother goes to the store to buy infant formula and the product is out of stock, she will go to a different store rather than risk switching products.

Understanding behavior at different levels in the channel is critical in formulating customer service strategies.[19] The penalty for being out of stock at a particular retail store is relatively low for the manufacturer of infant formula because the vast majority of customers will switch stores.

However, the penalty of running out of stock at a particular doctor or hospital is very high if, for example, it causes the doctor to switch from Mead Johnson's brand, Enfamil, to Ross Laboratories' brand, Similac. Mead Johnson will likely lose all the potential future business from mothers who give birth at that hospital and continue to feed their baby with Similac rather than Enfamil. Thus, the customer service implications are clear: Hospitals and doctors require a very high level of customer service, which may mean in-stock availability above 99 percent, and very short lead times of 24 to 48 hours.

The retailer also is likely to lose the sale if it is out of the customer's preferred brand of infant formula. The inventory position on an item such as infant formula, which would actually cause the customer to switch stores in case of a stockout, must be monitored

---

[19]See Larry W. Emmelhainz, Margaret A. Emmelhainz, and James R. Stock, "Logistics Implications of Retail Stockouts," *Journal of Business Logistics* 12, no. 2 (1991), pp. 129–42.

closely by the retailer. Frequent stockouts on such an item can cause customers to switch stores permanently.

When the manufacturer is aware of the implications of stockouts at the retail level, it can make adjustments in order cycle times, fill rates, transportation options, and other strategies that will result in higher levels of product availability in retail stores.

Sears and Whirlpool Establish Strategies to Avoid Stockouts

For some items, customers may be more willing to wait, even expecting to place a special order rather than have the item available in stock. For example, in the 1970s, Sears and Whirlpool conducted a study of customers and discovered that, in general, customers did not expect to take delivery of major appliances the same day they were purchased. Frequently, they were willing to wait five to seven days for the appliance, unless it was an emergency. This knowledge had major implications for the logistics system. Sears was required to have only floor models available for display purposes at the retail level and few if any appliances were required in inventory at their distribution centers (DCs).

Whirlpool used this knowledge to create and refine a new logistics approach. Appliances were manufactured and shipped to a large mixing warehouse in Marion, Ohio. Sears regional DCs were shipped products only when orders were received from Sears customers. Once there, they were cross-docked to a truck for delivery to the consumer. Using this system, Whirlpool was able to provide delivery of appliances to Sears consumers in 48 to 72 hours in most major U.S. markets.

For some products, consumers who face an out-of-stock situation on the particular stockkeeping unit (SKU) they desire will choose to switch brands or sizes. A **stockkeeping unit (SKU)** is an individual product that differs from other products in some way. The difference could be in size, color, scent, flavor, or some other relevant characteristic. If a customer switches to another size of the same product, the customer service level should be measured relative to the desired SKU and all substitutes. If a customer switches brands, then that manufacturer has lost a sale today; in addition, the customer may come to prefer the new brand, so that significant future sales are lost as well. The value of these lost sales is difficult to determine. As long as some sort of acceptable substitute is available to the customer, retailers are less concerned with this type of stockout because they have still made the sale.

If there are unplanned decreases in customer service levels because of labor strikes, materials shortages, or other factors, the company can look at sales "before," "during," and "after" such events to assess the impact of various levels of customer service on retail sales. This assessment is only relevant if the competitor's product was still available during the same period.

Cost/Revenue Trade-Offs

The total of logistics expenditures such as carrying inventory, transportation, and information/order processing can be viewed as the company's expenditures on customer service. Figure 2–3 illustrates the cost trade-offs and considerations required to implement an integrated logistics management concept. The objective is to provide the organization with the lowest total logistics costs, given a specific customer service level. While Figure 2–3 shows logistics issues as trade-offs, in some cases simultaneous improvement may occur in multiple areas, and the organization reduces its total cost while providing im-

Cost Trade-Offs in Integrated Logistics Management

FIGURE 2–3

Cost trade-offs required in a logistics system

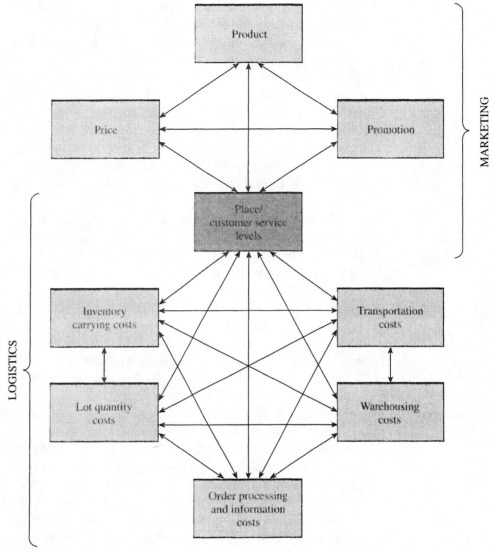

Marketing objective: Allocate resources to the marketing mix to maximize the long-run profitability of the firm.
Logistics objective: Minimize total costs given the customer service objective where: Total costs = Transportation costs + Warehousing costs + Order processing and information costs + Lot quantity costs + Inventory carrying costs.

Source: Adapted from Douglas M. Lambert, *The Development of an Inventory Costing Methodology: A Study of the Costs Associated with Holding Inventory* (Chicago: National Council of Physical Distribution Management, 1976), p. 7.

proved customer service. This is only possible by taking the perspective of the total system in the long run.

An Example of Cost Trade-Offs in Retailing

For example, if a major department store chain wishes to increase its retail in-stock levels to 98 percent, point-of-sale (POS) data that track actual sales by store and by SKU might be used. Thus, it has to invest in information technology such as in-store scanners of bar codes at each cash register and software to compile and analyze the data in addition to generating meaningful management reports. To maximize its leverage, the discount store chain also might want to invest in an **electronic data interchange (EDI)** system to provide rapid, two-way communication with its suppliers. Hypothetically, this could cost the chain roughly $200,000 per store. Thus, management appears to be making a trade-off: By investing in information technology, the store is increasing its costs to improve customer service levels.

If each dollar of additional sales revenue costs the company 60 cents in product costs, plus variable logistics and marketing expenses, the contribution margin is 40 percent. For each additional dollar of sales revenue, what sales need to be generated to break even? We can calculate the additional sales required to offset this investment by dividing the $200,000 investment by the 40 percent contribution margin. Thus, the company needs to increase sales by $500,000 per store, on average, to break even on this investment. If sales increase more than that, they will be ahead on this investment, achieving a positive return, rather than "trading off."

This decision would need to be evaluated considering how likely it is that each store would increase sales by $500,000 over some specified time period.[20] If current sales are $10 million per store per year, it would seem much more feasible to recover this investment in a timely manner than if sales are currently $2 million per store per year.

ABC Analysis/Pareto's Law

In Chapter 1, we used the abbreviation ABC for activity-based costing. Here, ABC analysis is used to denote a tool for classifying items or activities according to their relative importance. This concept also will be discussed in greater depth in conjunction with inventory management in Chapter 5.

ABC Analysis Described

The logic behind ABC classification is that some customers and products are more beneficial to a firm than others: beneficial in terms of profitability, sales revenues, segment growth rates, or other factors deemed important by corporate management. Using profitability as an example, the most profitable customer-product combinations should receive the most attention and, hence, higher customer service levels. Profitability should be measured according to a product's contribution toward fixed costs and profits.

Like ABC analysis, **Pareto's law** notes that many situations are dominated by relatively few critical elements. For example 80 percent of the bottlenecks in the logistics system may be caused by the failure of one carrier. This concept is also commonly referred to as the

The "80/20" Rule

80/20 rule. Table 2–1 illustrates how the importance of customers can be combined with the importance of products to establish customer service levels that are the most beneficial to a firm. This matrix can be interpreted as follows (using profitability as the relevant factor):

Customer-Product Contribution Matrix

1. Products in category A are the most profitable, followed by B, C, and D. The products in category A usually represent a small percentage of the firm's product line. The products in category D, on the other hand, are the least profitable and probably make up about 80 percent of the firm's product line.

---

[20]If the time period to recover the investment was greater than one year, the increased sales should be discounted to reflect the time value of money; that is, the concept that money received in the future is less valuable than money received today, or in the near term.

TABLE 2–1   A Customer-Product Contribution Matrix

	Product			
Customer Classification	*A*	*B*	*C*	*D*
I	1	2	6	10
II	3	4	7	12
III	5	8	13	16
IV	9	14	15	19
V	11	17	18	20

Source: Adapted from Bernard J. La Londe and Paul H. Zinszer, *Customer Service: Meaning and Measurement* (Chicago: National Council of Physical Distribution Management, 1976), p. 181.

TABLE 2–2   Making the Customer-Product Contribution Matrix Operational

Priority Range	*In-Stock Availability Standard (%)*	*Order Cycle Time Standard (Hours)*	*Order Completeness Standard (%)*
1–5	100%	48 hrs.	99%
6–10	95	72	97
11–15	90	96	95
16–20	85	120	93

Source: Adapted from Bernard J. La Londe and Paul H. Zinszer, *Customer Service: Meaning and Measurement* (Chicago: National Council of Physical Distribution Management, 1976), p. 182.

2. Customers in category I are the most profitable, but are few in number, maybe 5 to 10. Category V are the least profitable customers, accounting for the majority of the firm's customers.

3. The most profitable customer-product combination occurs when customers in category I buy products in category A. The next most profitable combines B products with category I customers, then category II customers with A products, and so on. Management will use some logical approach in ranking the various customer and product combinations. An example of one such approach is illustrated in Table 2–1.

An organization can use the data in Table 2–1 in setting customer service policies, as illustrated in Table 2–2. For example, the standards for customer-product combinations in priority range 1–5 may be 100 percent in-stock product availability, 48 hours' order cycle time, and 99 percent of all orders shipped complete (i.e., no partial shipments).

Again, if profitability is the relevant measure of customer and product importance, this method recognizes the need to provide the most profitable customers with the highest service levels in order to encourage customer loyalty and thus repeat business. Those less-profitable accounts can be made more attractive to the firm by reducing the service levels, which makes them less costly to service and therefore more profitable.

Consistency of Service Is Important Irrespective of the Service Level

A lower level of customer service does not mean that the service provided is less consistent. In other words, whatever the service level, 100 percent consistency of service is provided whenever possible. Consistency is important to all customers, irrespective of size or type. However, the important issue is that it is usually less expensive for a firm to deliver lower levels of customer service (e.g., lead time) with high consistency than it is to provide higher levels of service with low consistency; for example, a 72-hour order cycle time with high consistency is less expensive to the provider firm than a 48-hour order cycle time with low consistency.

As a generic example, it may be possible for a firm to develop several strategies that allow it to reduce its logistics costs while providing an acceptable level of customer service. Generally, the longer the order cycle time, the less inventory a firm must carry. As we will see later in this book, less inventory increases a firm's profits through reductions in inventory carrying costs. Also, it may be possible to obtain lower rates when transportation carriers are given more time to deliver products. As long as consistent service is provided to customers, most firms can plan ahead, knowing that order cycle times will be longer.

Gillette Implements a Multieschelon Customer Service Program

The principle is illustrated by Gillette, a global producer of razors and other personal care products. Gillette requires that small, **less-than-truckload (LTL)** customer orders be received by a certain day and time to be processed that week. These orders are then pooled and shipped with other orders destined for a particular geographical area. This is referred to as scheduled delivery.

The benefit of this approach is that Gillette can fill a truck, which lowers its transportation cost. It also reduces the absolute transit time and the variability in transit time, because the truck is going to one general area and dropping off products, or delivering to a regional carrier in the market for local delivery, rather than having many stops in dispersed areas. If customers miss the order deadline, they are given the option of waiting until the next week or having their order shipped LTL. Most opt to wait, for the cost and service reasons mentioned above.

The key to developing a customer-product contribution matrix that meets the needs of both the customer and the firm is knowing how customers define service, identifying which service components are most important, and determining how much customer service to provide. Customer service audits are often conducted to obtain this information prior to a firm establishing any kind of policy relating to customer-product profitability and customer service levels.

The Customer Service Audit

A customer service audit is used as a means of evaluating the level of service a company is providing and as a benchmark for assessing the impact of changes in customer service policies. The objectives of the audit are to (1) identify critical customer service elements, (2) identify how performance of those elements is controlled, and (3) assess the quality and capabilities of the internal information system.

Objectives of a Customer Service Audit

The audit typically includes four distinct stages:

- External customer service audit.
- Internal customer service audit.

- Identifying opportunities and methods for improvement.
- Establishing customer service levels.

Each of these stages is discussed below. While the stages tend to occur sequentially, there is some overlap between stages.

The External Customer Service Audit.   The external audit should be the starting point in an overall customer service audit, one that examines both internal and external factors. The key goals of the external audit are to:

Goals of an External Customer Service Audit

- Identify the elements of customer service that customers believe are important in their buying decision.
- Determine the customer's perception of the service being offered by the firm and each major competitor.

The first step is to determine which service elements the customer perceives as important. This should be accomplished using an interview format with a sample of the firm's customers. Interviewing can provide insights into customer service issues of which the firm may otherwise be unaware. Some of the key customer service elements to a retailer assessing a manufacturer might be the consistency of order cycle time, absolute length of the order cycle, whether the supplier uses EDI, the number of orders shipped complete, back-order policies of the firm, billing procedures, and backhaul policies. Because many service variables differ by industry, it is important to survey customers in order to establish their service requirements.

The Marketing Function Must Be Included in the Audit Process

It is beneficial to involve the marketing function in the external customer service audit for a number of reasons. First, marketing often has the major decision-making authority in terms of making customer service trade-offs within the marketing mix. Also, the marketing function can provide useful insights into a better understanding of customer needs and the incorporation of the most relevant issues in the design of any instruments used to collect customer data. A high level of involvement will create buy-in, so that more support will be provided by the marketing function when it later implements the audit findings.

If the organization does not have a corporate market research department to assist in the customer service audit, it could hire an outside research firm or consultant, or contact a local university where an undergraduate or MBA class, a professor, or doctoral candidate may be willing to carry out such research. Using an outside party often increases the response rate and reduces the response bias.

Once the important customer service elements have been identified, the next major step is to develop a questionnaire to gain feedback from a statistically valid and representative group of the firm's customers.

Using a Questionnaire to Obtain Customer Feedback

The questionnaire is used to determine the relative importance of various customer service elements, other marketing mix elements, and measures of the perceived performance of the firm and its major competitors on each element. Ideally, the organization would like to perform very well on those elements that customers and potential customers evaluate as the most important. This enables management to develop strategies by customer segments while considering the strengths and weaknesses of specific competitors.

It is important that the questionnaire ask about customers' relative market share with each supplier, as well as their overall perception/satisfaction with their supplier(s). This will allow the firm to examine the relationship between its sales and its performance as perceived by customers.

The questionnaire also should explore customers' expected levels of performance on key issues now and in the future. Demographic data will allow the firm to assess perceived performance differences according to geographical region, customer type, and other relevant dimensions.

For best results and validity, the questionnaire should be pretested with a small sample of customers to ensure that no critical issues have been missed and that customers are able to understand and answer the questions.

The External Audit Enables the Firm to Identify Service Problems and Opportunities

The results obtained from the customer service survey can reveal both opportunities and potential problems. The variables that receive the highest importance ratings from customers should be the focus of analysis and action. For example, if a firm scores significantly higher than competitors on key ratings, it could use those findings in their promotional mix—and perhaps generate increased sales revenues. If an organization scores significantly lower than competitors on important service variables or big gaps exist between desired performance and actual performance, it faces potentially significant problems. Without some corrective action, market share could erode if competitors take advantage of a firm's weaknesses.

Importance Ratings Cannot Be Used Alone

It would appear that the variables that receive the highest ratings should play the greatest role in share of business. However, this may not always be the case for a number of reasons:

- All of an industry's major suppliers may be performing at "threshold" levels or at approximately equal levels, which makes it difficult to distinguish among suppliers.

- Variables for which there are significant variances in vendor performance may be better predictors of market share than the variables described above.

- Customers may rate a variable as extremely important, but there may be few or no suppliers providing satisfactory levels of service for that variable. Such variables offer opportunities to provide differential service in the marketplace.

- A variable may be rated low in importance with a low variance in response. In addition, there may be no single supplier providing adequate service levels. Therefore, customers do not recognize the advantages of superior service for that variable. If one supplier improved performance, it could lead to gains in market share.[21]

The organization should look simultaneously at the importance of various elements and its position relative to competing suppliers. If customers perceive the supplier's performance to be poor on some attributes relative to management's beliefs on organization performance, management should determine whether it is measuring the firm's perfor-

---

[21]Jay U. Sterling and Douglas M. Lambert, "Establishing Customer Service Strategies within the Marketing Mix," *Journal of Business Logistics* 8, no. 1 (1987), pp. 1–30.

Corrective Actions Resulting from the Service Audit

mance the same way that customers are and, if not, adjust measurements to align with customer measures.

If the actual performance is better than customers believe it to be, management should determine how to educate customers and to inform them of actual performance. This might include providing the sales force with monthly or quarterly performance reports by customer that salespeople would review with each of their accounts.

The internal customer service audit can be conducted while the external customer service audit is occurring.

The Internal Customer Service Audit.   The internal customer service audit reviews the firm's current service practices. This provides a benchmark for assessing the impact of changes in customer service levels. As such, the internal customer service audit should address the following issues:

Internal Audit Questions

- How is customer service currently measured within the firm?
- What are the units of service measurement?
- What are the service performance standards or objectives?
- What is the current level of attainment: results versus objectives?
- How are these measures derived from the firm's information and/or the order processing systems?
- What is the internal customer service reporting system?
- How do each of the functional areas of the business (e.g., logistics, marketing) perceive customer service?
- What are the relationships between these functional areas in terms of communication and control?[22]

Goal of the Internal Audit

The major goal of the internal audit is to measure gaps between the firm's service practices and customer requirements. Customers' perceptions of current service levels also should be determined, because they may perceive service as worse than it really is. If that is the case, customers' perceptions should be the focus of change through education and promotion, rather than changing the firm's service levels.

Another key area to assess in the internal customer service audit is the communication flows from the customer to the company, and communication flows within the company, including the measurement and reporting of service performance. Communication is a major factor in determining how well customer service–related issues are understood. Without excellent internal communications, customer service tends to be reactive and problem focused, rather than proactive.[23]

Communication between the customer and the organization relates primarily to the order-ship-receive cycle. The seven major issues are order entry, postorder entry inquiry/ change, delivery, postdelivery reports of any shipment-related problems, billing, post-billing discrepancies, and payment-related issues. The audit can help determine the effectiveness of the communications.

---

[22]Ibid., p. 52.
[23]La Londe and Zinszer, *Customer Service*, p. 168.

Management Interviews Are a Good Source of Information

Management interviews are an important source of information. Interviews should be conducted with managers responsible for all logistics activities and activities with which logistics interacts, such as accounting/finance, sales/marketing, and production. The interviews should examine:

- Definition of responsibilities.
- Size and organizational structure.
- Decision-making authority and process.
- Performance measurements and results.
- Definition of customer service.
- Management's perception of how customers define customer service.
- Company plans to alter or improve customer service.
- Intrafunctional communications.
- Interfunctional communications.
- Communications with key contacts such as consumers, customers, transportation carriers, and suppliers.

In addition, management should give its assessment of customer service measurement and reporting. This should include not only assessment of how current systems measure performance, but also how the firm interfaces with customers on service-related issues.

Identifying Potential Solutions. The external service audit enables management to identify problems with the firm's customer service and marketing strategies. Used in combination with the internal service audit, it may help management adjust these strategies and vary them by segment in order to increase profitability. But if management wants to use such information to develop customer service and marketing strategies for optimal profitability, it must use these data to benchmark against competitors.

The most meaningful competitive benchmarking occurs when customer evaluations of competitors' performance are compared with each other and with customers' evaluations of the importance of supplier attributes. Once management has used this type of analysis to determine opportunities for gaining a competitive advantage, every effort should be made to identify best practice; that is, the most cost-effective use of technology and systems regardless of the industry in which it has been successfully implemented. Noncompetitors are much more likely to share their knowledge and, through such contacts, it is possible to uncover potential opportunities.[24]

A Methodology for Competitive Benchmarking

A methodology for competitive benchmarking can be demonstrated from the data contained in Table 2–3. The analysis involves a comparison of the performance of the major manufacturers in the office furniture industry. The first step is to generate a table with evaluations of the level of importance for each of the variables and the performance

---

[24]For more information on this approach, see Douglas M. Lambert and Arun Sharma, "A Customer-Based Competitive Analysis for Logistics Decisions," *International Journal of Physical Distribution and Logistics Management* 20, no. 1 (1990), pp. 17–24.

TABLE 2–3 **Importance and Performance of Office Furniture Manufacturers on Selected Customer Service Attributes**

| | | | Overall Importance—All Dealers | | Dealer Evaluations of Manufacturers | | | | | | | | | | | | |
| | | | | | Mfr. 1 | | Mfr. 2 | | Mfr. 3 | | Mfr. 4 | | Mfr. 5 | | Mfr. 6 | |
Rank	Variable Number	Variable Description	Mean	SD	Mean	SD	Mean	SD	Mean	SD	Mean	SD	Mean	SD	Mean	SD
1	9	Ability of manufacturer to meet promised delivery date (on-time shipments)	6.4	0.8	5.9	1.0	4.1	1.6	4.7	1.6	6.6	0.6	3.7	1.8	3.3	1.6
2	39	Accuracy in filling orders (correct product is shipped)	6.4	0.8	5.6	1.1	4.7	1.4	5.0	1.3	5.8	1.1	5.1	1.2	4.4	1.5
3	90	Competitiveness of price	6.3	1.0	5.1	1.2	4.9	1.4	4.5	1.5	5.4	1.3	4.4	1.5	3.6	1.8
4	40	Advance notice on shipping delays	6.1	0.9	4.6	1.9	3.0	1.6	3.7	1.7	5.1	1.7	3.0	1.7	3.1	1.7
5	94	Special pricing discounts available on contract/project quotes	6.1	1.1	5.4	1.3	4.0	1.7	4.1	1.6	6.0	1.2	4.7	1.5	4.5	1.8
6	3	Overall manufacturing and design quality of product relative to the price range involved	6.0	0.9	6.0	1.0	5.3	1.3	5.1	1.2	6.5	0.8	5.2	1.3	4.8	1.5
7	16	Updated and current price data, specifications, and promotion materials provided by manufacturer	6.0	0.9	5.7	1.3	4.1	1.5	4.8	1.4	6.3	0.9	4.9	1.7	4.3	1.9
8	47	Timely response to requests for assistance from manufacturer's sales representative	6.0	0.9	5.2	1.7	4.6	1.6	4.4	1.6	5.4	1.6	4.2	2.0	4.3	1.7

continued

TABLE 2–3 *continued*

Dealer Evaluations of Manufacturers

Rank	Variable Number	Variable Description	Overall Importance— All Dealers Mean	SD	Mfr. 1 Mean	SD	Mfr. 2 Mean	SD	Mfr. 3 Mean	SD	Mfr. 4 Mean	SD	Mfr. 5 Mean	SD	Mfr. 6 Mean	SD
9	14	Order cycle consistency (small variability in promised versus actual delivery; that is, vendor consistently meets expected date)	6.0	0.9	5.8	1.0	4.1	1.5	4.8	1.4	6.3	0.9	3.6	1.7	4.4	1.7
10	4b	Length of promised order cycle (lead) times (from order submission to delivery) for base line/in-stock ("quick ship") product	6.0	1.0	6.1	1.1	4.5	1.4	4.9	1.5	6.2	1.1	4.3	1.7	3.7	2.0
11	54	Accuracy of manufacturer in forecasting and committing to estimated shipping dates on contract/project orders	6.0	1.0	5.5	1.2	4.0	1.6	4.3	1.4	6.3	1.1	3.8	1.7	3.5	1.6
12	49a	Completeness of order (% of line items eventually shipped complete)—made-to-order product (contract orders)	6.0	1.0	5.5	1.2	4.3	1.2	4.7	1.3	6.0	1.1	4.4	1.4	4.0	1.6
43	45	Free WATS line provided for entering orders with manufacturer	5.3	1.5	3.6	2.5	4.8	2.0	3.4	2.6	3.5	2.6	2.0	1.5	3.8	1.9
50	33a	Price range of product line offering (e.g. low, medium, high price levels) for major vendor	5.0	1.3	4.4	1.5	4.6	1.6	5.1	1.5	5.2	1.4	4.3	1.6	3.9	1.6
101	77	Store layout planning assistance from manufacturer	2.9	1.6	4.2	1.7	3.0	1.5	3.4	1.6	4.7	1.6	3.0	1.4	3.4	1.2

Note: Mean (average score) based on a scale of 1 (not important) through 7 (very important).

Source: Adapted from Jay U. Sterling and Douglas M. Lambert, "Customer Service Research: Past, Present and Future," *International Journal of Physical Distribution and Materials Management* 19, no. 2 (1989), p. 19.

evaluations of all firms within the industry. The next step is to compare the importance score of each service attribute to customer evaluations of each manufacturer's performance.

Table 2–3 shows that one of the most important attributes identified by customers, "ability to meet promised delivery date," received a score of 6.4 (out of 7.0) in overall importance. Manufacturer 1's perceived performance of 5.9 is significantly less than the mean importance score of 6.4 as well as the perceived performance of manufacturer 4 (6.6). Therefore, manufacturer 1 must improve its performance to meet customer requirements and achieve competitive parity.

The variable "advance notice on shipping delays," rated 6.1 in overall importance, presents a different situation. None of the manufacturers were perceived to be meeting customer expectations. Therefore, if manufacturer 1 wished to improve its performance in this area, it could use this as a source of performance differentiation compared with that of its competitors, and perhaps gain a competitive advantage.

On the other hand, the variable "free inward WATS [Wide-Area Telecommunications Service] telephone lines for placing orders with manufacturers" was ranked as 43rd in overall importance. No manufacturer received a high evaluation for its performance on this service. This indicated that customers did not perceive the advantages of this attribute because the service was not presently available from any manufacturer. If a competitor were to change its order entry procedures to allow customers the ability to telephone their orders without cost, then two things could happen: (1) Customers would likely change their opinion of the advantages of this capability and consequently increase their perceptions of the importance of free WATS service; (2) the supplier that first introduced this service could achieve a definite, long-term competitive advantage.

Indeed, this is precisely what happened in the office furniture industry. One of the major manufacturers implemented an on-line, interactive order entry system utilizing free inward WATS service. Within three years, this capability became a norm for all of the major firms in the industry. Therefore, when looking for ways to improve customer service, it is equally critical to look at both important and relatively unimportant services because conditions change over time.

This highlights the notion that customers may not really know what they want because it has never been offered to them. By improving on performance of current parameters, companies are sentenced to "keeping up with the competition." Yet, history shows that the real winners are those who see an opportunity first and stake out a leadership position, taking on risk on investing in the future before it arrives.[25] It is the unexploited, unserved market that holds real growth opportunities.

Service Performance Standards and the Measurement of Performance

Establishing Customer Service Levels.   The final steps in the audit process are the actual establishment of service performance standards and the ongoing measurement of performance. Management must set target service levels for segments based on factors such as the type of customer, geographic area, channel of distribution, and product line. It must communicate this information to all employees responsible for implementing service

---

[25]Gary Hamel and C. K. Prahalad, "Seeing the Future First," *Fortune,* Sept. 5, 1994, pp. 64–70.

policies while also developing compensation programs that encourage employees to reach the firm's customer service objectives. Formal reports that document performance are a necessity.

Finally, management must repeat the process periodically to ensure that the firm's customer service policies and programs reflect current customer needs. The collection of customer information over time is the most useful element in guiding overall corporate strategy and the specific strategies of the various functional areas within the firm.

Developing and Reporting Customer Service Standards

Once management has determined which elements of customer service are most important, it must develop standards of performance. Designated employees should regularly report results to the appropriate levels of management. Customer service performance can be measured and controlled by:

Measuring and Controlling Customer Service Performance

- Establishing quantitative standards of performance for each service element.
- Measuring actual performance for each service element.
- Analyzing variance between actual services provided and the standard.
- Taking corrective action as needed to bring actual performance into line.[26]

Customer cooperation is essential for the company to obtain information about speed, dependability, and condition of the delivered product. To be effective, customers must be convinced that service measurement and monitoring will help improve future service. Whirlpool does extensive measurement of ERX, with which it has formed a partnership to improve its customer service. This relationship is discussed in Box 2–2.

Figure 2–4 contains a number of possible measures of service performance. The emphasis any firm places on individual elements must be based on what customers believe is important. Service elements such as inventory availability, meeting delivery dates, order status, order tracing, and back-order status require good communication between firms and their customers.

Automated Order Processing Improves Customer Service

Order processing offers significant potential for improving customer service because many companies have not kept pace with technological developments in that field. Consider the possibilities for improved communications if customers can either phone their orders to customer service representatives who have CRTs or input orders on their own computer terminals. Immediate information on inventory availability can be provided and product substitution can be arranged when a stockout occurs. Customers also can be given target delivery dates for their orders.

Figure 2–5 gives examples of customer service standards. The standards chosen should be those that best reflect what customers actually require, rather than what management thinks they need. Designated employees should measure and compare service

---

[26]William H. Hutchinson, Jr., and John F. Stolle, "How to Manage Customer Service," *Harvard Business Review* 46, no. 6 (Nov.–Dec. 1968), pp. 85–96; and Fuller, O'Conor, and Rawlinson, "Tailored Logistics," pp. 87–94.

Box 2–2

Whirlpool and ERX: Partners in Customer Service

In the early 1990s, Whirlpool Corporation, a leading manufacturer of major household appliances, became concerned about the low levels of on-time delivery performance to its dealers. It desired improved customer service, but believed that an outside expert would be able to do a better job. After all, it saw its own core competency in manufacturing high-quality, reliable appliances. Thus, Whirlpool was looking for an organization that could provide it with full logistics service for its finished product—from warehousing to final delivery and setup.

To meet Whirlpool's needs, a joint venture was established with Mark VII, Inc., and Elston Richards Warehousing Company, forming ERX. ERX obtained six of the eight Quality Express locations. Quality Express is a national delivery network designed to serve over 10,000 retailers and 50,000 construction sites. This system involves eight regional distribution centers which hold inventory. Inventory is then shipped to one of 48 locations *only* as needed to fill orders. Thus, the locations do not hold inventory, but serve as cross-docking sites. Whirlpool is responsible for all of the fixed distribution center costs and the leases for the trucks. It wants ERX

to focus on customer service, not assets. To better meet customers' needs and lower customers' inventory requirements, Whirlpool decreased its minimum order quantity from about a third of a truckload to five or six pieces. Now customers place smaller, more frequent orders. This levels demand considerably, which makes it much easier for Whirlpool to plan its own production and inventory needs. Thus, Whirlpool can focus on what it does best: manufacturing.

ERX is an important link to customer service and customer satisfaction. The delivery drivers unload the trucks and can handle returns, claims, and even reimburse the dealer. They also can unload and uncarton the product. Customer service also has improved in more tangible ways. Order cycle time has been reduced from over five days to one day in most cases, and two days in remote areas. On-time delivery has gone from 85 percent to over 99 percent, and damage has been reduced. This innovative relationship has benefited both Whirlpool and ERX.

Source: From Jay U. Sterling, "Managing Long-Term Partnership Alliances: How to Succeed and Fail," *Proceedings of the Annual Conference of the Council of Logistics Management*, Oct. 16–19, 1994, pp. 301–11.

performance to the standard, and report this information to management on a regular and timely basis.

The firm's order processing and accounting information systems can provide much of the information necessary for developing a customer-product contribution matrix and meaningful customer service management reports. We will discuss some of these important interfaces in Chapter 3, "Logistics Information Systems."

Impediments to an Effective Customer Service Strategy

Many companies have ineffective or inconsistent customer service strategies, policies, or programs. Sometimes even the best of firms may have difficulty in overcoming the various barriers or impediments that can hinder the implementation of successful customer service processes.

Examples of Customer Service Impediments

Failing to target specific market segments based on the services they require can be a costly mistake. Management sometimes hesitates to offer different levels of *customer service* for fear of violating antitrust laws. Service differentials are often viewed much like price

FIGURE 2–4

Possible measures of customer service performance

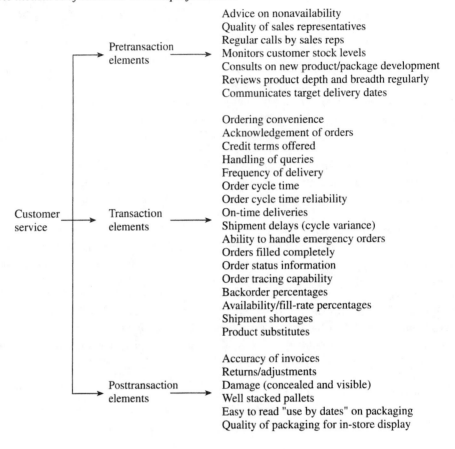

FIGURE 2–5

Examples of customer service standards

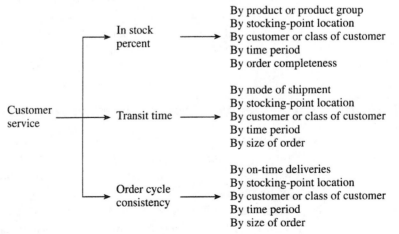

differentials that must be cost justified. However, most firms do not have the necessary cost information to do so.[27] Nevertheless, management can segment markets based on customers' evaluations of the importance of marketing services and can obtain the necessary financial data to determine the costs of serving such markets through a variety of research techniques.

Salespeople Can Create Unrealistic Customer Expectations

Salespeople can create unrealistic customer service expectations by promising faster delivery of orders to "make the sale." But most customers value reliability and consistency in filling orders more than speed of delivery. Consequently, attempting to decrease the order cycle on an ad hoc basis typically increases transportation costs resulting from the need to expedite shipments. Order-assembly costs can rise because of the disruption of normal work flows that occur in "rush" situations. Also, the so-called domino effect might occur. When salespeople override customer service policies on shipping dates, lead times, shipping points, modes of transportation, and units of sale, they disrupt the orders of other customers and cause an increase in logistics costs throughout the system.[28]

A firm's customer service standards and performance expectations are affected substantially by the competitive environment and perceived traditional industry practices. Consequently, it is vital that management understands industry norms, expectations, and the costs required to provide high levels of customer service.

Evidence suggests, however, that many firms do not measure the cost-effectiveness of service levels and have no effective way of determining competitive service levels. Information is fed back into the company through a sales organization that is frequently concerned with raising service levels or through industry anecdotes and outraged customers. The net result of this information feedback is that firms may overreact to imprecise cues from the marketplace or even from within their own firms.[29]

Considering the vast sums of money firms spend on research and development and advertising, it makes little sense for a company not to adequately research the levels of customer service necessary for profitable long-range business development.

Finally, the economic environment of the 1980s and 1990s has caused top management to push for higher inventory turnover rates. As highlighted in the press, this is still a major source of effort today.[30] This emphasis may lead to lower levels of customer service.

Global Customer Service Issues

The global perspective focuses on seeking common market demands worldwide, rather than cutting up world markets and treating them as separate entities with very different product needs.[31] On the other hand, different parts of the world have different service

---

[27]See Ellram, *Total Cost Modeling in Purchasing.*

[28]Douglas M. Lambert, James R. Stock, and Jay U. Sterling, "A Gap Analysis of Buyer and Seller Perceptions of the Importance of Marketing Mix Attributes," in *Enhancing Knowledge Development in Marketing,* ed. William Bearden et al. (Chicago: American Marketing Association, 1990), p. 208.

[29]La Londe, Cooper, and Noordewier, *Customer Service,* p. 29.

[30]Shawn Tully, "Raiding a Company's Hidden Cash," *Fortune,* Aug. 22, 1994, pp. 82–87.

[31]Martin Christopher, "Customer Service Strategies for International Markets," *Annual Proceedings of the Council of Logistics Management* (Oak Brook, IL: Council of Logistics Management, 1989), p. 327.

Global

Surviving and Thriving in an Era of Unprecedented Change: A Japanese Case Study

Japan's entire wholesaling industry is under extreme pressure these days, pushing companies like Ryoshoku, the country's second largest food wholesaler, to reinvent themselves. Economic conditions are driving retail price discounting, large format retail stores are emerging, discount chains are growing more popular, and market power is shifting to consumers and retailers. These factors are turning wholesalers' attention to meeting demands for lower supply chain costs.

Further complicating the picture, large retailers have increased the amount of direct trade between themselves and large manufacturers, in some cases squeezing out the wholesaler altogether. The American transplant, Toys "Я" Us Japan, has been a highly visible pioneer in reducing costs through bypassing traditional wholesaling channels and purchasing directly from the manufacturer. Moreover, large retailers have invested in point-of-sale data capture and analysis capabilities, reducing their reliance on wholesalers for these services. To meet these challenges and to maintain and increase market share, leading wholesalers are strengthening and expanding value-added services . . . particularly emphasizing information services, retail support, and logistics.

Faced with these changes and prospects for continued distribution system restructuring in Japan,

Ryoshoku is positioning itself to thrive in these uncertain times. Aiming to bridge the gap between manufacturers and retailers . . . it is developing market-based transfer/consolidation centers to provide its retail customers with frequent and efficient full-truckload, multiple-vendor deliveries to stores. This combined delivery service is designed to offer the same flexible small-lot, just-in-time service demanded by stores without all the inefficiencies, let alone the traffic congestion and pollution problems, of unconsolidated deliveries. Ryoshoku has invested in nine regional distribution centers to provide flexible unit picking and order assembly services.

To provide these sophisticated and constantly evolving logistics services, Ryoshoku has set up an independent logistics organization that has equal status as the marketing, sales, and information systems groups. Leveraging the company's strong culture of innovation and technology, the new logistics organization is pursuing efficient consumer response (ECR)–based partnerships along the supply chain and expanding information systems links to retailer storefronts and suppliers' operations.

Source: David Frentzel, "Surviving and Thriving in an Era of Unprecedented Change: Case Studies of Four Agile Japanese Companies," *Logistics!* a publication of Mercer Management Consulting (Fall 1995), pp. 11–12.

needs related to information availability, order completeness, expected lead times, and so on.[32] In addition, the local congestion, infrastructure, communications, and time differences may make it impossible to achieve high levels of customer service. The service provided by market should match local customer needs and expectations to the greatest degree possible.

---

[32]For some global examples, see Mauro Caputo and Valeria Mininno, "Internal, Vertical and Horizontal Logistics Integration in Italian Grocery Distribution," *International Journal of Physical Distribution and Logistics Management* 26, no. 9 (1996), pp. 64–90; Jae-Il Kim, "Logistics in Korea: Current State and Future Directions," *International Journal of Physical Distribution and Logistics Management* 26, no. 10 (1996), pp. 6–21; and Andrei N. Rodnikov, "Logostics in Command and Mixed Economies: The Russian Experience," *International Journal of Physical Distribution and Logistics Management* 24, no. 2 (1994), pp. 4–14.

Coca-Cola Services Japan and the United States

For example, Coca-Cola provides very different types of service in Japan than in the United States. Coca-Cola delivery drivers in Japan focus on providing merchandising in supermarkets, help in processing bills in small "mom and pop" operations, and respond to signals from communication systems in vending machines, so that time is not wasted delivering to full machines.[33] This creates the most efficient and effective customer service policy, rather than simply duplicating domestic patterns worldwide. The latter strategy could be both ineffective and expensive.

Improving Customer Service Performance

Effective Customer Service Strategies Require a Thorough Understanding of Customers and the Service Process

The levels of customer service a firm achieves often can be improved through one or more of the following actions: (1) thoroughly researching customer needs, (2) setting service levels that make realistic trade-offs between revenues and expenses, (3) making use of the latest technology in order processing systems, and (4) measuring and evaluating the performance of individual logistics activities.

An effective customer service strategy *must* be based on an understanding of how customers define *service*. The internal and external customer service audits previously discussed were utilized to obtain customer inputs into service strategies, plans, and programs. As described above, Coca-Cola has identified the distinctive logistics needs of its customers.[34]

Once the firm has determined their customers' view of service, management must select a customer service strategy that advances the firm's objectives for long-term profits, return on investment, or other relevant measures of performance. The optimum level of customer service is the one that obtains and retains the most profitable customers.

Order processing systems can have a major impact on customer service levels and perceptions (see Chapter 3). Many firms have antiquated order processing systems. The primary benefit of automating them is to reduce the order cycle time. Given that most customers prefer a consistent delivery cycle to a shorter one, it usually is unnecessary—even unwise—to reduce the order cycle time for customers. But by using the additional time internally for planning, the company can achieve savings in transportation, warehousing, inventory carrying costs, production planning, and purchasing.

Automation improves customer service by providing the following benefits to the customer:

- Better product availability.
- More accurate invoices.
- The ability to lower safety stock levels and their associated inventory carrying costs.
- Improved access to information on order status.

---

[33]Fuller, O'Conor, and Rawlinson, "Tailored Logistics," p. 88.

[34]For a discussion of logistics competitive advantage, see Ronald Henkoff, "Deliveriing the Goods," *Fortune,* Feb. 28, 1994, pp. 64–78.

In short, automated order processing systems enhance the firm's ability to perform all of the transaction and posttransaction elements of customer service. The benefits of improved logistics systems are demonstrated by the following example:

P&G and Wal-Mart Improve Customer Service

Procter & Gamble (P&G) now receives daily data by satellite on Wal-Mart's Pampers (disposable diapers) sales and forecasts and ships orders automatically. As a result, Wal-Mart can maintain smaller inventories and still cut the number of times it runs out of Pampers. And P&G has increased its proportion of on-time deliveries to 99.6 percent from 94 percent. P&G has gone from being a vendor that was maybe the least desirable to deal with to one of the most desirable. The results have been astonishing. P&Gs volume at Wal-Mart grew by more than 40 percent, or by more than $200 million.[35]

Finally, the development of an effective customer service program requires the establishment of customer service standards that do the following:

Customer Service Standards Are Necessary

- Reflect the customer's point of view.
- Provide an operational and objective measure of service performance.
- Provide management with cues for corrective action.[36]

Management also should measure and evaluate the impact of individual logistics activities—transportation, warehousing, inventory management, production planning, purchasing, and order processing—on customer service. Designated employees should report achievements regularly to the appropriate levels of management. Management should compare actual performance to standards and take corrective action when performance is inadequate. For management to be successful and efficient, a firm needs timely information. It also is necessary to hold individuals accountable for their performance because information alone does not guarantee improved decision making.

The success of a firm is no longer based exclusively on selling products; instead it is the value-added services provided that can create a differential and sustainable competitive advantage.[37] Logistics can be an important source of such service-based advantage.

Summary

This chapter opened with a definition of customer service. Although the importance of the individual elements of customer service varies from company to company, we reviewed the common elements that are of concern to most companies. We also saw the necessity for a customer service strategy consistent with corporate and marketing strategies. The successful implementation of the integrated logistics management concept depends on management's knowledge of the costs associated with different system designs, and of the relationship between system design and customer service levels. We saw how management can obtain better knowledge of the costs and revenues associated with different levels of customer service, and how it can implement cost/service trade-offs.

[35]Zachary Schiller, "Stalking the New Consumer," *Business Week,* Aug. 28, 1989, p. 62.
[36]La Londe and Zinszer, *Customer Service,* p. 180.
[37]Rahul Jacob, "Why Some Customers Are More Equal than Others," *Fortune,* Sept. 19, 1994, pp. 215–24.

Creative Solutions

Quality in Logistics

Total quality principles and tools have been woven into the very fabric of how we do business at Procter & Gamble. In my view, two of the most powerful aspects of total quality within P&G have been in process improvement and measurement systems.

Process improvement taught us that all parts of logistics are interrelated processes, not stand-alone functions. In response to this, P&G completely reorganized the company, creating a new organization—Product Supply. We broke down the traditional organizational hierarchy of manufacturing, engineering, distribution, and purchases. This has had a tremendous positive effect on the way we interact with each other and on how we view our work.

We also introduced measurement systems to virtually every process within Product Supply. For example, all over the world, P&G employees are measuring customer satisfaction through tracking of "perfect orders." Total order management, as we know it, monitors our logistics performance from the time an order is generated until it is billed to the customer.

This quality thinking is building a high degree of reliability throughout our entire delivery system. These measures are included in our carrier performance standards and shared openly with our carriers. This helps them gain a clear understanding of our strategies and what is expected from them. The top carriers soon develop their own measures and present this to us on a regular basis.

We have learned that data are the most powerful tools we have. Without data, you are just another person with an opinion.

Source: Dennis M. Whan, "Quality in Logistics," *Transportation and Distribution* 34, no. 7 (July 1993), p. 33.

The customer service audit is a method of determining the existing service levels, determining how performance is measured and reported, and appraising the impact of changes in customer service policy. Firms should conduct both internal and external service audits. Surveys are one means of finding out what management and customers view as important aspects of customer service.

Although customer service may represent the best opportunity for a firm to achieve a sustainable competitive advantage, many firms implement customer service strategies that are simply duplicates of those implemented by their major competitors. The audit framework represented in this chapter can be used by management to collect and analyze customer and competitive information.

We saw that there are some common roadblocks to an effective customer service strategy as well as some ways to improve performance. In the next chapter, we will present the influence of information technology on the efficiency and effectiveness of the logistics function.

Suggested Readings

Anderson, Eugene W.; Claes Fornell; and Donald R. Lehmann. *Economic Consequences of Providing Quality and Customer Satisfaction,* Report No. 93–112. Boston: Marketing Science Institute, 1993.

Byrne, Pat. "Improve the Customer Service Cycle." *Transportation and Distribution* 33, no. 6 (June 1993), pp. 66–67.

Catalano, Doug, and Bill Read. "Customer Service: A Process Approach." *Perspectives,* a publication of CSC Consulting (1994), pp. 1–7.

"A Compendium of Research in Customer Service." *International Journal of Physical Distribution and Logistics Management* 24, no. 4 (1994), pp. 1–68.

Copacino, William. "A New Way to Look at Your Customers." *Traffic Management* 30, no. 4 (Apr. 1994), pp. 29–30.

"An Energized Process for Improving Customer Service." *NAPM Insights,* Apr. 1992, pp. 9–11.

Frentzel, David. "Needs-Based Customer Segmentation." *Japan Institute of Logistics System Journal,* May–June 1995, pp. 49–53.

Fuller, Joseph; James O'Conor; and Richard Rawlinson. "Tailored Logistics: The Next Advantage." *Harvard Business Review* 94, no. 3 (May–June 1994), pp. 87–94.

Harrington, Lisa. "Logistics Unlocks Customer Satisfaction." *Transportation and Distribution* 36, no. 5 (May 1995), pp. 41–44.

Henkoff, Ronald. "Delivering the Goods." *Fortune,* Feb. 28, 1994, pp. 64–78.

Jacob, Rahul. "Why Some Customers Are More Equal than Others," *Fortune,* Sept. 19, 1994, pp. 215–24.

Kyj, Myroslaw J. "Customer Service as a Competitive Tool." *Industrial Marketing Management* 16 (1987), pp. 225–30.

La Londe, Bernard J., and Martha C. Cooper. *Partnerships in Providing Customer Service: A Third-Party Perspective.* Oak Brook, IL: Council of Logistics Management, 1989.

La Londe, Bernard J.; Martha C. Cooper; and Thomas G. Noordewier. *Customer Service: A Management Perspective.* Oak Brook, IL: Council of Logistics Management, 1988.

Lewis, James P. "Think like Your Customers." *Transportation and Distribution* 34, no. 7 (July 1993), pp. 26–28.

Mathe, Herve, and Roy D. Shapiro. "Managing the Service Mix: After Sale Service for Competitive Advantage." *The International Journal of Logistics Management* 1, no. 1 (1990), pp. 44–50.

Pine, B. Joseph, II; Don Peppers; and Martha Rogers. "Do You Want to Keep Your Customers Forever?" *Harvard Business Review* 95, no. 2 (Mar.–Apr. 1995), pp. 103–14.

Power, Christopher; Lisa Driscoll; and Earl Bohn. "Smart Selling: How Companies Are Winning Over Today's Tougher Customer." *Business Week,* Aug. 3, 1992, p. 46.

Sharma, Arun; Dhruv Grewal; and Michael Levy. "The Customer Satisfaction/Logistics Interface." *Journal of Business Logistics* 16, no. 2 (1995), pp. 1–21.

Sterling, Jay U., and Douglas M. Lambert. "Customer Service Research: Past, Present and Future." *International Journal of Physical Distribution and Materials Management* 19, no. 2 (1989), pp. 3–23.

_____. "Establishing Customer Service Strategies within the Marketing Mix." *Journal of Business Logistics.* 8, no. 1 (1987), pp. 1–30.

Walther, George R. "Upside Down Marketing." Audio-Tech Business Book Summaries 3, no. 5, sect. 1 (Mar. 1994), p. 4.

Questions and Problems

1. Customer service can be defined as an activity, a performance measure, or a corporate philosophy. What are the advantages and disadvantages of each of these types of definitions? How would you define customer service?

2. Explain the importance of the pretransaction, transaction, and posttransaction elements of customer service.

3. Explain why customer service should be integrated with other components of the marketing mix when management develops the firm's marketing strategy.

4. Explain how ABC analysis can be used to improve the efficiency of the customer service activity.

5. Why is the customer service audit important when establishing a firm's customer service strategy?

6. Why does automation of the order processing system represent such an attractive opportunity for improving customer service? How is this service improvement accomplished?

7. What are some ways that management can improve the firm's customer service performance?

8. Why is it important to use pretransaction, transaction, and posttransaction customer service elements to identify and develop customer service measures? Discuss specific examples of measures in each category.

THE DISTRIBUTION CHALLENGE!
PROBLEM: A CHILLING DILEMMA

The company is a maker of lightweight commercial air-conditioning units, the kind that goes on the roofs of strip malls or restaurants. We'll call it Arctic Atmospheres, Inc. Approximately 85 percent of its sales are replacement models, which means that the company relies heavily on repeat customers.

An air conditioner usually breaks down with little or no warning. Often the customer's livelihood depends on finding a replacement within a day or two—never mind who the provider is. "It's like an earthquake," notes Bob Sabath, vice president of Mercer Management Consulting. "You know it's going to happen in the next five years—you just don't know if it's tomorrow."

Arctic Atmospheres brought in Mercer Management to help optimize the company's distribution network and revive sales. At the time it had 16 distribution centers and warehouses around the country, stocking 45 different models.

Mercer's first idea was to shrink the network to four or five strategically placed warehouses, each with extensive inventory. That would have chopped 22 percent off Arctic's costs, but would have made rapid delivery tough. An Arctic vice president of marketing argued that the company should go in the opposite direction and expand to 24 locations with a full range of products. That would have been prohibitively expensive.

In the end, Arctic's solution combined local availability with minimal stocks. Which way did the company go?

What Is Your Solution?

Source: "Distribution: The Challenge," *Distribution* 95, no. 8 (Aug. 1996), p. 104.

CHAPTER
4
Inventory Concepts

Chapter Outline

Chapter Objectives

- To examine how the basic concepts of inventory management are applied.
- To illustrate how to calculate safety stocks.
- To show how production policies influence inventory levels.
- To demonstrate how inventories and customer service levels are interrelated.

Introduction

Inventory is a large and costly investment. Better management of corporate inventories can improve cash flow and return on investment. Nevertheless, most companies (retailers, wholesalers, and manufacturers) suffer through periodic inventory rituals; that is, crash inventory-reduction programs are instituted every year or so. However, the lack of comprehensive understanding of inventory management techniques and trade-offs often causes customer service levels to drop, so the programs are abandoned.[1]

Obviously, a better approach to inventory management is necessary. This chapter will provide the reader with the knowledge required to improve the practice of inventory management.

Basic Inventory Concepts

In this section, we will consider basic inventory concepts such as the reasons for holding inventory and various types of inventory.

Why Hold Inventory?

Inventory Serves Five Purposes

Formulation of an inventory policy requires an understanding of the role of inventory in production and marketing. Inventory serves five purposes within the firm: (1) It enables the firm to achieve economies of scale, (2) it balances supply and demand, (3) it enables specialization in manufacturing, (4) it provides protection from uncertainties in demand and order cycle, and (5) it acts as a buffer between critical interfaces within the channel of distribution.

Large Quantities Provide Several Advantages

Economies of Scale.   Inventory is required if an organization is to realize economies of scale in purchasing, transportation, or manufacturing. For example, ordering large quantities of raw materials or finished goods inventory allows the manufacturer to take advantage of the per unit price reductions associated with volume purchases. Purchased materials have a lower transportation cost per unit if ordered in large volumes. This lower per unit cost results because less handling is required; for example, an order of 1 unit usually requires the same administrative handling as 1,000 units, and truckload and full railcar shipments receive lower transportation rates than smaller shipments of less-than-truckload (LTL) or less-than-carload (LCL) quantities.

Finished goods inventory makes it possible to realize manufacturing economies. Plant utilization is greater and per unit manufacturing costs are lower if a firm schedules long production runs with few line changes. Manufacturing in small quantities leads to short production runs and high changeover costs.[2]

---

[1]Hau L. Lee and Corey Billington provide an excellent overview of key issues in inventory management in, "Managing Supply Chain Inventory: Pitfalls and Opportunities," *Sloan Management Review* 33, no. 3 (Spring 1992), pp. 65–73.

[2]With newer manufacturing technology, some companies have been able to lower changeover costs by reducing the time and effort required to make the machine adjustments to accommodate producing smaller quantities of each product.

The production of large quantities, however, may require that some of the items be carried in inventory for a significant period of time before they can be sold. The production of large quantities also may prevent an organization from responding quickly to stockouts, since large production runs mean that items are produced less frequently. The cost of maintaining this inventory must be "traded off" against the production savings realized.

Although frequent production changeovers reduce the quantity of inventory that must be carried and shorten the lead time that is required in the event of a stockout, they require time that could be used for manufacturing a product. In addition, at the beginning of a production run, the line often operates less efficiently due to fine-tuning the process and equipment settings.

Cost Trade-Offs

When a plant is operating at or near capacity, frequent line changes that create machine downtime may mean that contribution to profit is lost because there is not enough product to meet demand. In such situations, the costs of lost sales and changeovers must be compared to the increase in inventory carrying costs that would result from longer production runs. To respond to this, many companies, such as Honda of America Manufacturing, have made a major effort toward reducing changeover times.[3] This allows production of small lots, eliminating the penalty of higher setup costs.

Seasonal Inventories

Balancing Supply and Demand. Seasonal supply or demand may make it necessary for a firm to hold inventory. For example, a producer of a premium line of boxed chocolates experiences significant sales volume increases at Christmas, Valentine's Day, Easter, and Mother's Day. The cost of establishing production capacity to handle the volume at these peak periods would be substantial. In addition, substantial idle capacity and wide fluctuations in the workforce would result if the company were to produce to meet demand when it occurs. The decision to maintain a relatively stable workforce and produce at a somewhat constant level throughout the year creates significant inventory buildup at various times during the year, but at a lower total cost to the firm. The seasonal inventories are stored in a freezer warehouse that was built adjacent to the plant.

On the other hand, demand for a product may be relatively stable throughout the year, but raw materials may be available only at certain times during the year (e.g., producers of canned fruits and vegetables). This makes it necessary to manufacture finished products in excess of current demand and hold them in inventory.

Specialization. Inventory makes it possible for each of a firm's plants to specialize in the products that it manufactures. The finished products can be shipped to field warehouses where they are mixed to fill customer orders. The economies that result from the longer production runs and from savings in transportation costs more than offset the costs of additional handling. Companies such as Whirlpool Corporation have found significant cost savings in the operation of consolidation warehouses that allow the firm to specialize manufacturing by plant location. The specialization by facility is known as **focused factories.**[4]

---

[3]This information was obtained from David Curry, purchasing administrator of Honda of America Manufacturing.

[4]For a good description of "focused factories," see W. Skinner, "The Focused Factory," *Harvard Business Review* 52, no. 3 (May–June 1974), pp. 113–21.

Protection from Uncertainties. Inventory is held as protection from uncertainties; that is, to prevent a stockout in the case of variability in demand or variability in the replenishment cycle. Raw materials inventories in excess of those required to support production can result from speculative purchases made because management expects a price increase or supply shortage, perhaps due to a potential strike. Another reason to hold raw materials inventory is to maintain a source of supply. Regardless of the reason for maintaining inventory, the costs of holding the inventory should be compared to the savings realized or costs avoided by holding it.

Work-in-Process Inventory

Work-in-process inventory is often maintained between manufacturing operations within a plant to avoid a shutdown if a critical piece of equipment were to break down, and to equalize flow, since not all manufacturing operations produce at the same rate. The stockpiling of work-in-process within the manufacturing complex permits maximum economies of production without work stoppage. Increasingly, organizations are focusing on rebalancing production processes to minimize or eliminate the need for work-in-process inventory. This is supportive of JIT manufacturing initiatives, presented in Chapters 9 and 10.

Inventory Planning Is Essential

Inventory planning is critical to successful manufacturing operations because a shortage of raw materials can shut down the production line or lead to a modification of the production schedule; these events may increase expenses or result in a shortage of finished product. While shortages of raw materials can disrupt normal manufacturing operations, excessive inventories can increase inventory carrying costs and reduce profitability. Organizations are working closely with suppliers and carriers to improve supply reliability, allowing a reduction in the amount of raw materials held to cover delivery uncertainty. Internal performance metrics may influence inventory investment, as shown in the General Mills example in the Creative Solutions box at the end of this chapter.

Balanced Inventory

Finally, finished goods inventory can be used as a means of improving customer service levels by reducing the likelihood of a stockout due to unanticipated demand or variability in lead time. If the inventory is balanced, increased inventory investment will enable the manufacturer to offer higher levels of product availability and less chance of a stockout. A balanced inventory is one that contains items in proportion to expected demand.

Inventory as a Buffer. Inventory is held throughout the supply chain to act as a buffer for the following critical interfaces:

- Supplier-procurement (purchasing)
- Procurement-production
- Production-marketing
- Marketing-distribution
- Distribution-intermediary
- Intermediary-consumer/user

Inventory Is Held throughout the Supply Chain

Because channel participants are separated geographically, it is necessary for inventory to be held throughout the supply chain to successfully achieve time and place utility (see Chapter 1). Figure 4–1 shows the typical inventory positions in a supplier-manufacturer-

FIGURE 4–1

The logistics flow

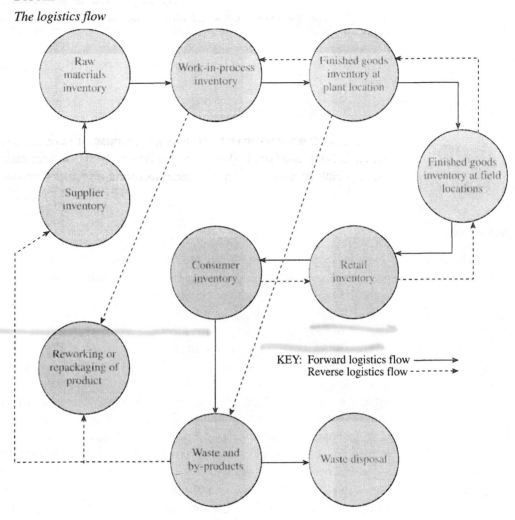

intermediary-consumer supply chain. Raw materials must be moved from a source of supply to the manufacturing location where they will be input into the manufacturing process. In many cases, work-in-process inventory will be necessary at the plant.

Once the manufacturing process has been completed, product must be moved into finished goods inventory at plant locations. The next step is the strategic deployment of finished goods inventory to field locations, which may include corporate-owned or leased distribution centers, public warehouses, wholesalers' warehouses, retail chain distribution centers, or delivery directly to the retail location. Inventory is then positioned to enable customer purchase. Similarly, the customer maintains an inventory to support individual or institutional consumption.

All of these product flows are the result of a decision by the ultimate consumer or user to purchase the product. The entire process depends on the information flow from the customer to the firm and to the firm's suppliers. Communication is an integral part of a logistics system because no product flows until information flows.

Reverse Logistics

It is often necessary to move a product backward through the channel for a number of reasons. For example, a customer may return a product because it is damaged, or a manufacturer may need to recall a product because of defects. This is referred to as "reverse logistics."[5]

Finally, another aspect that promises to become a bigger factor in the future is the disposition of wastes and by-products. One specific example involves "bottle laws," such as those enacted in Michigan, Vermont, Oregon, and Iowa. As sensitivity to litter from packaging and concern over resource utilization increase, environmentalists and concerned citizens in other states—if not nationwide—are likely to push for such laws. These laws are being applied to a wide variety of packaging materials in Europe.

Types of Inventory

Inventories Can Be Classified Based on Why They Exist

Inventories can be classified based on the reasons for which they are accumulated. The categories of inventories include cycle stock, in-transit inventories, safety or buffer stock, speculative stock, seasonal stock, and dead stock.

Cycle Stock.   Cycle stock is inventory that results from replenishment of inventory sold or used in production. It is required in order to meet demand under conditions of certainty; that is, when the firm can predict demand and replenishment times (lead times). For example, if the rate of sales for a product is a constant 20 units per day and the lead time is always 10 days, no inventory beyond the cycle stock would be required. While assumptions of constant demand and lead time remove the complexities involved in inventory management, let's look at Figure 4–2 for an example to clarify the basic inventory principles. The example shows three alternative reorder strategies.

Since demand and lead time are constant and known, orders are scheduled to arrive just as the last unit is sold. Thus, no inventory beyond the cycle stock is required. The average cycle stock in all three examples is equal to half of the order quantity. However, the average cycle stock will be 200, 100, or 300 units depending on whether management orders in quantities of 400 (part A), 200 (part B), or 600 (part C), respectively.

In-Transit Inventories.   In-transit inventories are items that are en route from one location to another. They may be considered part of cycle stock even though they are not available for sale or shipment until after they arrive at the destination. For the calculation of inventory carrying costs, in-transit inventories should be considered as inventory at the place of shipment origin since the items are not available for use, sale, or subsequent reshipment.

Holding Inventory in Excess of Demand

Safety or Buffer Stock.   Safety or buffer stock is held in excess of cycle stock because of uncertainty in demand or lead time. Average inventory at a stockkeeping

---

[5]See Ronald Kopicki, Michael J. Berg, and Leslie Legg, *Reuse and Recycling— Reverse Logistics Opportunities* (Oak Brook, IL: Council of Logistics Management, 1993); and James R. Stock, *Reverse Logistics* (Oak Brook, IL: Council of Logistics Management, 1992).

FIGURE 4–2

The effect of reorder quantity on average inventory investment with constant demand and lead time

A. Order quantity of 400 units

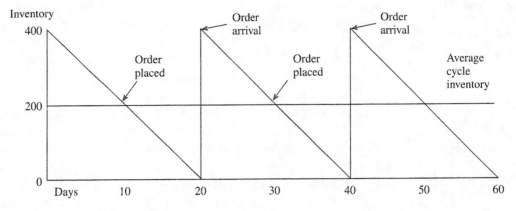

B. Order quantity of 200 units

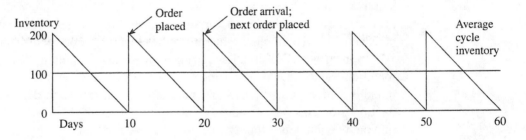

C. Order quantity of 600 units

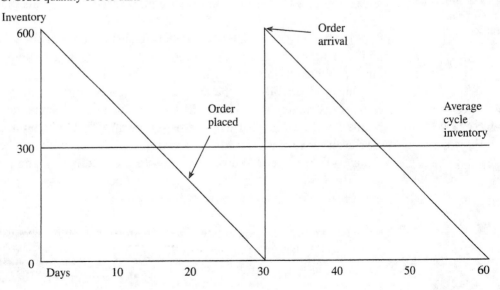

location that experiences demand or lead time variability is equal to half the order quantity plus the safety stock.

Inventory Levels Where Lead Times Are Constant but Demand Is Variable

In Figure 4–3, for example, the average inventory would be 100 units if demand and lead time were constant. But if demand was actually 25 units per day instead of the predicted 20 units per day with a 10-day lead time, inventory would be depleted by day 8 (200/25). Since the next order would not arrive until day 10 (order was placed on day zero), the company would be out of stock for two days. At 25 units of demand per day, this would be a stockout of 50 units in total. If management believed that the maximum variation in demand would be plus or minus 5 units, a safety stock of 50 units would prevent a stockout due to variation in demand. This would require holding an average inventory of 150 units (100 units average inventory + 50 units safety stock).

Inventory Levels Where Demand Is Constant but Lead Times Are Variable

Now consider the case in which demand is constant but lead time can vary by plus or minus two days (part B of Figure 4–3). If the order arrives 2 days early, the inventory on hand would be equal to a 12-day supply, or 240 units, since sales are at a rate of 20 units per day and 40 units would remain in inventory when the new order arrived. However, if the order arrived 2 days late, on day 12—which is a more likely occurrence—the firm would experience stockouts for a period of 2 days (40 units). If management believed that shipments would never arrive more than two days late, a safety stock of 40 units would ensure that a stockout due to variation in lead time would not occur if demand remained constant. This would require holding an average inventory of 140 units.

In most business situations, management must be able to deal with variability in demand and lead time. Forecasting is rarely accurate enough to predict demand, and demand is seldom, if ever, constant. In addition, transportation delays and supplier and production problems make lead time variability a fact of life. Consider part C of Figure 4–3, in which demand uncertainty (part A) and lead time uncertainty (part B) are combined.

Inventory Levels When Demand and Lead Times Are Variable

Combined uncertainty is the worst of all possible worlds. In this case, demand is above forecast by the maximum, 25 units instead of 20 units per day, and the incoming order arrives two days late. The result is a stockout period of four days at 25 units per day. If management wanted to protect against the maximum variability in both demand and lead time, the firm would need a safety stock of 100 units. This policy (no stockouts)would result in an average inventory of 200 units.

Good Forecasting Results in Less Safety Stock

In sum, variability in the order cycle requires safety stock. Since holding safety stock costs firms money, managers will try to reduce or eliminate variability. Forecasting can be used to better predict demand, resulting in less safety stock. Utilizing transportation carriers that provide consistent on-time deliveries will reduce lead time variability. Today, this concept is known as **time-definite delivery.** The goal is not necessarily to have the fastest delivery, but the most dependable, allowing safety stock reduction and the ability to plan more accurately.[6]

Speculative Stock.   Speculative stock is inventory held for reasons other than satisfying current demand. For example, materials may be purchased in volumes larger than necessary in order to receive quantity discounts, because of a forecasted price increase or mate-

---

[6]Helen L. Richardson, "Trust Time-Definite, Reduce Inventory," *Transportation and Distribution* 35, no. 1 (Jan. 1994), pp. 41–44.

FIGURE 4–3

Average inventory investment under conditions of uncertainty

A. With variable demand

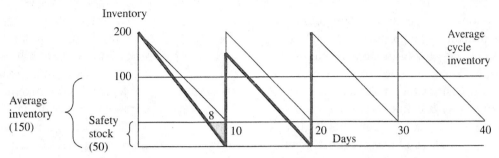

B. With variable lead time

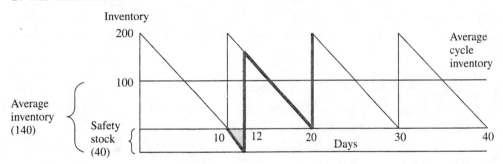

C. With variable demand and lead time

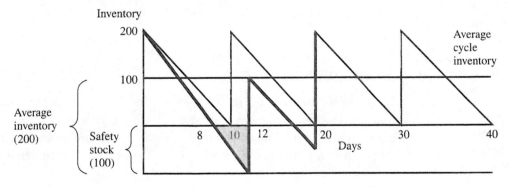

rials shortage, or to protect against the possibility of a strike. Production economies also may lead to the manufacture of products at times other than when they are in demand.

Seasonal Stock. Seasonal stock is a form of speculative stock that involves the accumulation of inventory before a seasonal period begins. This often occurs with agricultural products and seasonal items. The fashion industry also is subject to seasonality with new fashions coming out many times a year. The back-to-school season is a particularly important time. See the Global box for a presentation of how Benetton tries to take some of the guess work out of demand for fashions.

Global

Benetton Uses Postponement to Improve Global Inventory Management

The concept of postponement—delaying commitment of the product to its final form until the last possible moment—can be an outstanding technique for responding to variability in customer demand. Benetton has only one distribution center—in Castrette, Italy—to serve stores in 120 countries. Benetton produces its most popular styles as "gray" goods, or undyed garments. When it sees what the actual demand pattern is for a certain sweater or pair of leggings by color, it can dye the gray goods quickly and speed them off to market. That way, Benetton doesn't end up with too many aqua sweaters and not enough black sweaters. This allows Benetton to minimize its inventory while meeting customer demand and reducing end-of-season markdowns. Since it has only one distribution center and ships reorders based on actual demand, inventory is less likely to be located where it is not needed.

Source: Carla Rapoport and Justin Martin, "Retailers Go Global," *Fortune*, Feb. 20, 1995, pp. 102–8.

Dead Stock.   Dead stock refers to items for which no demand has been registered for some specified period of time. Dead stock might be obsolete throughout a company or only at one stockkeeping location. If it is the latter, the items may be transshipped to another location to avoid the obsolescence penalty or mark down at their current location. An example of a company that has created a business by selling dead stock is J. C. Whitney Company. It sells parts for automobiles that are no longer produced, after the auto manufacturers get rid of their replacement part inventories. A company like Whitney sells them at higher prices (low volume, high margin).

J. C. Whitney Company Makes Money from Selling Dead Stock

Basic Inventory Management

Objectives of Inventory Management

Inventory is a major use of working capital. Accordingly, the objectives of inventory management are to increase corporate profitability through improved inventory management, to predict the impact of corporate policies on inventory levels, and to minimize the total cost of logistics activities while meeting customer service requirements.

Measures of Inventory Management Effectiveness

Methods of Decreasing Inventory-Related Costs

The key measure of effective inventory management is the impact that inventory has on corporate profitability. Effective inventory management can improve profitability by lowering costs or supporting increased sales.

Measures to decrease inventory-related costs include reducing the number of backorders or expedited shipments, purging obsolete or dead stock from the system, or improving the accuracy of forecasts. Transshipment of inventory between field warehouses and small-lot transfers can be reduced or eliminated by better inventory planning. Better

For most firms, dead stock is something to be avoided. However, for the J. C. Whitney Company, dead stocks of old, obsolete automobile parts have been turned into a business opportunity. Antique car restorers, old car enthusiasts, and automobile repair shops purchase many hard-to-find parts from J. C. Whitney because they aren't readily available elsewhere.

inventory management can increase the ability to control and predict how inventory investment will change in response to management policy.

Inventory Turnover   Inventory turnover is another measure of inventory performance. It is measured as:

$$\frac{\text{Annual dollar sales volume at cost}}{\text{Average dollar inventory investment}}$$

All else being equal, a higher number is preferred, indicating that inventory moves through the firm's operations quickly, rather than being held for an extensive period. For example, an item with annual sales of $500,000 valued at cost and an average inventory

Motorola combines EDI and JIT to reduce paperwork and dramatically increase inventory management performance.

investment of $100,000, would have a turnover of five times. Turnover should not be used as the only measure of inventory effectiveness, but should be combined with other measures that reflect customer service issues.

Fill Rate
Increased sales are often possible if high levels of inventory lead to better in-stock availability and more consistent service levels. Fill rate is a common measure of the customer service performance of inventory. As presented in Chapter 2, "Customer Service," fill rate is often presented as the percentage of units available when requested by the customer. A 96 percent fill rate means that 4 percent of requested units were unavailable when ordered by the customer. Low inventory levels can reduce fill rates, hurting customer service and creating lost sales. The Technology box presents some of the inventory measurements used by Motorola's Information Systems Group in reengineering its inventory management processes.

Finally, total cost integration should be the goal of inventory planning; that is, management must determine the inventory level required to achieve least total cost logistics, given the required customer service objectives.

Impact of Demand Patterns on Inventory Management

Whether inventory is "pulled" or "pushed" through a system and whether the demand is "dependent" or "independent" has implications for inventory management methods.

Pull versus Push Systems
Pull versus push systems are distinguished by the way the company's production is driven. If a company waits to produce products until customers demand it, that is a pull system. Customer demand "pulls" the inventory. If a firm produces to forecast or anticipated sales to customers, that is a "push" system. The firm is "pushing" its inventory into the market in anticipation of sales.

Technology

Reengineering Inventory Management
at Motorola's Information Systems Group (ISG)

Motorola ISG recently revamped its inventory processes by combining EDI with JIT. In addition to drastically reducing the amount of paperwork in the procurement process, ISG is enjoying the following improvements in inventory performance:

- Reduced supplier cycle time from an average of six days to one, decreasing cycle stock needs.
- Reduced warehouse space by over 50 percent.
- Reduced total inventory by more than one-third.
- Eliminated the two-to-three-day lag between order receipt at ISG's warehouse and delivery to the production floor.
- Reduced raw material replenishment time from 40 days to 6 days.

ISG began its improved inventory management process by using EDI to reduce the order cycle times of its raw material suppliers thereby reducing inventory. With this accomplished, ISG added "auto order," to automatically release purchase orders when inventory reached a certain level. The next step was adding point-of-use delivery of materials directly to the location where the materials are used in manufacturing. This step reduced lead times and the buffer inventory between ISG's warehouse and production facilities.

Motorola ISG's next step is to move this system into place with its customers. This should further help ISG and its customers to reduce finished goods inventory and to speed up product lead times.

Source: Adapted from Joseph N. Salemi, "Just-in-Time EDI," *EDI World*, Jan. 1995, pp. 20–23.

Independent versus Dependent Demand

Independent versus dependent demand inventory focuses on whether the demand for an item depends on demand for something else. An independent demand item is a finished good, while dependent demand items are the raw materials and components that go into the production of that finished good. The demand for raw materials or components is "derived" based on the demand for the finished good. The need for dependent demand items doesn't have to be forecast; it can be calculated based on the production schedule of the finished good. The need for production of the finished good may be forecast or based on customer demand/orders.

Inventory managers must determine how much inventory to order and when to place the order. To illustrate the basic principles of reorder policy, let's consider inventory management under conditions of certainty. In reality, the more common situation is inventory management under uncertainty, but the management process will be similar in both instances.

Inventory Management under Conditions of Certainty

Components of Ordering Costs

Replenishment policy under conditions of certainty requires the balancing of ordering costs against inventory carrying costs.[7] For example, a policy of ordering large quantities

---

[7]When the supplier pays the freight cost.

infrequently may result in inventory carrying costs in excess of the savings in ordering costs. Ordering costs for products purchased from an outside supplier typically include (1) the cost of transmitting the order, (2) the cost of receiving the product, (3) the cost of placing it in storage, and (4) the cost of processing the invoice for payment.

In restocking its own field warehouses, a company's ordering costs typically include (1) the cost of transmitting and processing the inventory transfer, (2) the cost of handling the product if it is in stock, or the cost of setting up production to produce it, and the handling cost if the product is not in stock, (3) the cost of receiving at the field location, and (4) the cost of documentation. Remember that only direct out-of-pocket expenses should be included in ordering costs. Inventory carrying costs will be explained in detail in Chapter 5.

Economic Order Quantity.   The best ordering policy can be determined by minimizing the total of inventory carrying costs and ordering costs using the **economic order quantity (EOQ)** model. The EOQ is a "concept which determines the optimal order quantity on the basis of ordering and carrying costs. When incremental ordering costs equal incremental carrying costs, the most economic order quantity exists. It does not optimize order quantity and thus the shipment quantity, on the basis of total logistics costs, but only ordering and carrying costs."[8]

Two questions seem appropriate in reference to the example in Figure 4–2:

1. Should we place orders for 200, 400, or 600 units, or some other quantity?
2. What is the impact on inventory if orders are placed at 10-, 20-, or 30-day intervals, or some other time period? Assuming constant demand and lead time, sales of 20 units per day, and 240 working days per year, annual sales will be 4,800 units.[9] If orders are placed every 10 days, 24 orders of 200 units will be placed. With a 20-day order interval, 12 orders of 400 units are required. If the 30-day order interval is selected, 8 orders of 600 units are necessary. The average inventory is 100, 200, and 300 units, respectively. Which of these policies would be best?

Cost Trade-Offs in Calculating the EOQ

The cost trade-offs required to determine the most economical order quantity are shown graphically in Figure 4–4. By determining the EOQ and dividing the annual demand by it, the frequency and size of the order that will minimize the two costs are identified.

The EOQ Formula

The EOQ in units can be calculated using the following formula:

$$EOQ = \sqrt{\frac{2PD}{CV}}$$

where
   P = The ordering cost (dollars per order)
   D = Annual demand or usage of product (number of units)
   C = Annual inventory carrying cost (as a percentage of product cost or value)
   V = Average cost or value of one unit of inventory

---

[8]Kenneth B. Ackerman, *Words of Warehousing* (Columbus, OH: K. B. Ackerman Company, 1992), p. 28.
   [9]For this example, it was assumed that the plant was closed for four weeks each year. In an industrial application, we would use the actual number of working days for the firm in question.

FIGURE 4–4

Cost trade-offs required to determine the most economical order quantity

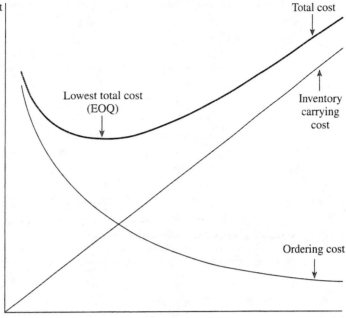

Now, using the EOQ formula, we will determine the best ordering policy for the situation described in Figure 4–2:

P = $40
D = 4,800 units
C = 25 percent
V = $100 per unit

$$EOQ = \sqrt{\frac{2(\$40)(4,800)}{(25\%)(100)}}$$

$$= \sqrt{\frac{384,000}{25}}$$

$$= 124 \text{ units}$$

If 20 units fit on a pallet, then the reorder quantity of 120 units would be established. This analysis is shown in Table 4–1.

The EOQ model has received significant attention and use in industry, but it is not without its limitations. The simple EOQ model is based on the following assumptions:

Assumptions of the EOQ Model

1. A continuous, constant, and known rate of demand.
2. Constant and known replenishment or lead time.
3. Constant purchase price independent of the order quantity or time.
4. Constant transportation cost independent of the order quantity or time.
5. The satisfaction of all demand (no stockouts are permitted).

TABLE 4–1   Cost Trade-Offs Required to Determine the Most Economical Order Quantity

Order Quantity	Number of Orders (D/Q)	Ordering Cost P × (D/Q)	Inventory Carrying Cost ½ Q × C × V	Total Cost
40	120	$4,800	$500	$5,300
60	80	3,200	750	3,950
80	60	2,400	1,000	3,400
100	48	1,920	1,250	3,170
120	40	1,600	1,500	3,100
140	35	1,400	1,750	3,150
160	30	1,200	2,000	3,200
200	24	960	2,500	3,460
300	16	640	3,750	4,390
400	12	480	5,000	5,480

6. No inventory in transit.
7. Only one product in inventory or at least no interaction between products (independent demand items).
8. An infinite planning horizon.
9. No limit on capital availability.

It would be very unusual to find a situation where demand and lead time are constant, both are known with certainty, and costs are known precisely. However, the simplifying assumptions are of great concern only if policy decisions will change as a result of the assumptions made. The EOQ solution is relatively insensitive to small changes in the input data.

Referring to Figure 4–4, one can see that the EOQ curve is relatively flat around the solution point. This is often referred to as the "bathtub effect." Although the calculated EOQ was 124 units (rounded to 120), an EOQ variation of 20 or even 40 units does not significantly change the total cost (see Table 4–1).

Adjusting the EOQ for Volume Transportation Rates and Quantity Discounts

Adjustments to the EOQ.   Typical refinements that must be made to the EOQ model include adjustments for volume transportation rates and for quantity discounts. The simple EOQ model did not consider the impact of these two factors. The following adjustment can be made to the EOQ formula so that it will consider the impact of quantity discounts and or freight breaks:[10]

$$Q^1 = 2\frac{rD}{C} + (1 - R)Q^0$$

---

[10]See Robert G. Brown, *Decision Rules for Inventory Management* (New York: Holt, Rinehart & Winston, 1967), pp. 205–6.

Inventory Management

Chapter Outline

Chapter Objectives

- To explore how inventory investment influences corporate profit performance.
- To demonstrate how inventory management contributes to least total cost logistics.
- To calculate inventory carrying costs.
- To present ways to recognize poor inventory management.
- To illustrate methods to improve inventory management.
- To show how profit performance can be improved by systems that reduce inventories.

Introduction

Inventories Represent the Largest Investment for Many Firms

Inventories represent the largest single investment in assets for many manufacturers, wholesalers, and retailers. Inventory investment can represent over 20 percent of the total assets of manufacturers, and more than 50 percent of the total assets of wholesalers and retailers (see Table 5–1). Competitive markets of the past 20 years have led to a proliferation of products as companies have attempted to satisfy the needs of diverse market segments. Customers have come to expect high levels of product availability. For many firms, the result has been higher inventory levels.

With the growing popularity of just-in-time (JIT) manufacturing, the reduction of product life cycles, and an increased emphasis on time-based competition, firms who hold large amounts of inventory have been much criticized. However, as we will present in this chapter, inventory does serve some very important purposes. But carrying excessive levels of inventory is costly. Organizations frequently do not identify or capture all of the many costs associated with holding inventory.

Inventories Must Compete with Other Capital Investments for Available Funds

Since capital invested in inventories must compete with other investment opportunities available to the firm, and because of the out-of-pocket costs associated with holding inventory, the activity of inventory management is extremely important. Management must have a thorough knowledge of inventory carrying costs to make informed decisions about logistics system design, customer service levels, the number and location of distribution centers, inventory levels, where to hold inventory and in what form, transportation modes, production schedules, and minimum production runs. For example, ordering in smaller quantities on a more frequent basis will reduce inventory investment, but may result in higher ordering costs and increased transportation costs.

It is necessary to compare the savings in inventory carrying costs to the increased costs of ordering and transportation to determine how the decision to order in smaller quantities will affect profitability. See the Global box for an explanation of how one company centralized its global inventory to save money and improve performance. A determination of inventory carrying costs also is necessary for new product evaluation, the evaluation of price deals/discounts, make-or-buy decisions, and profitability reports. It is thus imperative to accurately measure a firm's inventory carrying costs.

Financial Aspects of Inventory Strategy

The quality of inventory management and the inventory policies a firm sets have a significant impact on corporate profitability and the ability of management to implement its customer service strategies at least total cost logistics.

Inventory and Corporate Profitability

Inventory Represents a Significant Portion of a Firm's Assets

Inventory represents a significant portion of a firm's assets. Consequently, excessive inventory levels can lower corporate profitability in two ways: (1) net profit is reduced by out-of-pocket costs associated with holding inventory, such as insurance, taxes, storage, obsolescence, damage, and interest expense, if the firm borrows money specifically to finance

TABLE 5–1   Selected Financial Data for Manufacturers, Wholesalers, and Retailers ($ millions)

Companies	Sales	Net Profits	Net Profits as a Percent of Sales	Total Assets	Inventory Investment	Inventories as a Percent of Assets
Manufacturers						
Abbott Laboratories	$ 11,013.0	$1,882.0	17.1%	$ 11,125.6	$ 1,238.0	11.1%
Campbell Soup	7,678.0	802.0	10.4	6,632.0	739.0	11.1
Clorox	2,217.8	222.1	10.0	2,178.9	138.9	6.4
Dresser Industries	6,561.5	257.5	3.9	5,150.2	913.6	17.7
Ford Motor	146,991.0	4,446.0	3.0	262,876.0	6,656.0	2.5
General Electric	79,179.0	7,280.0	9.2	272,402.0	4,473.0	1.6
General Mills	5,416.0	476.4	8.8	3,294.7	395.5	12.0
Goodyear Tire & Rubber	13,112.8	101.7	0.8	9,671.8	1,774.0	18.3
Harris Corp.	3,659.3	178.4	4.9	3,206.7	544.1	17.0
Honeywell	7,311.6	402.7	5.5	5,493.3	937.6	17.1
3M	14,236.0	1,526.0	10.7	13,364.0	2,264.0	16.9
Newell	2,872.8	256.5	8.9	3,005.1	509.5	17.0
Pfizer	11,306.0	1,929.0	17.1	14,667.0	1,589.0	10.8
Sara Lee	18,624.0	916.0	4.9	12,602.0	2,807.0	22.3
Xerox	19,521.0	1,206.0	6.2	26,818.0	2,676.0	10.0
Wholesalers and retailers						
Baxter International	5,438.0	669.0	12.3%	7,596.0	883.0	11.6%
Bergen Brunswig	9,942.7	73.5	0.7	2,489.8	1,221.0	49.0
Dayton Hudson	25,371.0	463.0	1.8	13,389.0	3,031.0	22.6
Fleming Companies	16,486.7	26.7	0.2	4,055.2	1,051.0	25.9
Kmart	31,437.0	(220.0)	(0.7)	14,286.0	6,354.0	44.5
Nordstrom	4,453.1	147.5	3.3	2,702.5	719.9	26.6
Sears, Roebuck	38,236.0	1,271.0	3.3	36,167.0	4,646.0	12.8
Super Value Stores	16,486.3	166.4	1.0	4,183.5	1,092.0	26.1
Wal-Mart Stores	106,147.0	3,056.0	2.9	39,501.0	15,897.0	40.2
Winn-Dixie	12,955.5	255.6	2.0	2,648.6	1,179.0	44.5

Source: These data are 1996 fiscal year financial results gathered from a number of public sources.

Global

Changing Inventory Holding Patterns to Improve Performance at Atlas Copco Tools

A change is taking place in distribution today: a movement away from "chains" of stocking locations to planned or centralized delivery systems that rely on an excellent information system to provide coordination. Atlas Copco Tools, a Swedish manufacturer of pneumatic hand tools, had two central distribution centers and more than 50 regional warehouses and subsidiaries in approximately 50 countries throughout the world. Each of these locations held inventory. Unfortunately, none seemed to hold the right inventory because:

- Product availability at sales subsidiaries averaged 70 percent.
- Lead time from the central distribution centers to the customer was two weeks.
- Lead time from production to central distribution centers was between 12 and 20 weeks.
- Capital tied up in inventory was 30 percent of annual sales revenue.

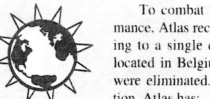

To combat this unsatisfactory performance, Atlas reconfigured its system, moving to a single central distribution center located in Belgium. All other stock points were eliminated. As a result of centralization, Atlas has:

- Reduced inventory by one-third.
- Reduced operating costs by $4 million a year.
- Substantially reduced its distribution labor force.
- Reduced average lead time within Europe from two weeks to 24–72 hours.

Thus, considering the trade-off between holding a great deal of inventory at multiple locations and centralizing distribution, Atlas found it could be more successful if it centralized.

Source: Philip B. Schary and Tage Skjøtt-Larsen, *Managing the Global Supply Chain* (Copenhagen: Handelshøjskolens. Forlag, 1995), pp. 225–28.

inventories; and (2) total assets are increased by the amount of the inventory investment, which decreases asset turnover, or the opportunity to invest in other more productive assets is foregone. In any case, the result is a reduction in return on net worth.

Inventory and Least Total Cost Logistics

Least total cost logistics is achieved by minimizing the total of the logistics costs illustrated in Figure 5–1 for a specified level of customer service. However, successful implementation of cost trade-off analysis requires that adequate cost data be available to management. Management should not set inventory levels and inventory turnover policies arbitrarily, but do so with full knowledge of inventory carrying costs, total logistics system costs, and necessary customer service policies.

Inventory Costs Impact Many Logistics Activities

The cost of carrying inventory has a direct impact not only on the number of warehouses that a company maintains, but on all of the firm's logistics policies, including stockouts and associated customer service costs. Inventory carrying costs are being traded off

FIGURE 5–1

Costs trade-offs required in a logistics system

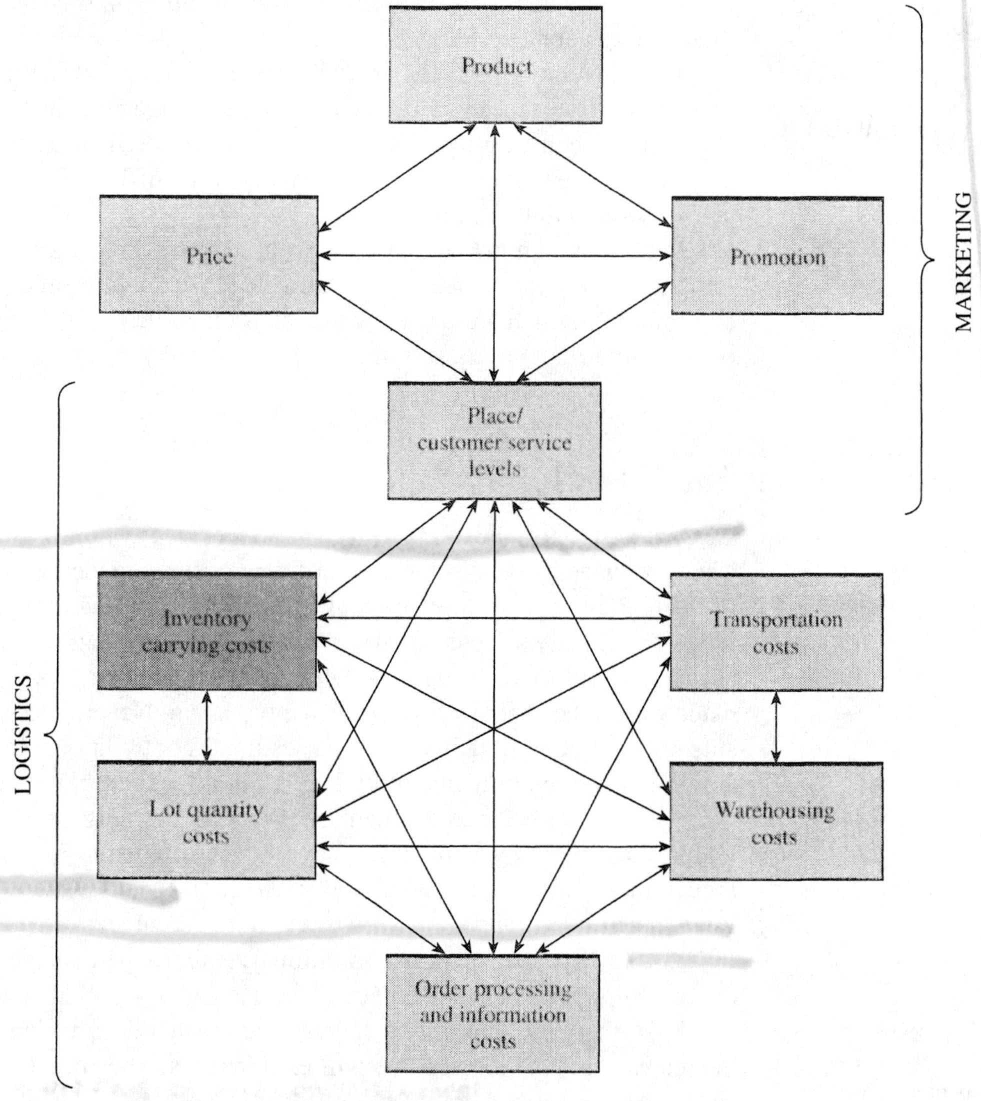

Marketing objective: Allocate resources to the marketing mix to maximize the long-run profitability of the firm.
Logistics objective: Minimize total costs, given the customer service objective, where Total costs = Transportation costs + Warehousing costs + Order processing and information costs + Lot quantity costs + Inventory carrying costs.

Source: Adapted from Douglas M. Lambert, *The Development of an Inventory Costing Methodology: A Study of the Costs Associated with Holding Inventory* (Chicago: National Council of Physical Distribution Management, 1976), p. 7.

If high inventory cost they will make less product but ship faster to make up for difference

if low inventory (can) cost they will make more product so its readily available but ship slower

with other logistics costs, such as transportation and customer service. For example, given the same customer service level, firms with low inventory carrying costs will likely hold more inventory and use slower modes of transportation, such as railroads, because this provides the least total cost logistics.

High inventory carrying costs likewise result in a reduction in inventory investment and require faster means of transportation, such as motor or air carriers to minimize total costs while achieving the desired customer service level. Thus, without an accurate assessment of the costs of carrying inventory, it is difficult for a company to implement logistics policies that minimize costs.

In addition, knowledge of the cost of carrying inventory is required to accurately determine economic manufacturing quantities, economic order quantities, and sales discounts, all of which are usually calculated on the basis of estimated costs in the majority of companies that use these formulas.[1]

Inventory Carrying Costs

Inventory carrying costs are those costs associated with the amount of inventory stored. They are made up of a number of different cost components and generally represents one of the highest costs of logistics.[2] The magnitude of these costs and the fact that inventory levels are directly affected by the configuration of the logistics system shows the need for accurate inventory carrying cost data. Without such data, appropriate trade-offs cannot be made within the organization or the supply chain. Nevertheless, most managers who consider the cost of holding inventory use estimates or traditional industry benchmarks.

We have seen how inventory levels can affect corporate profit performance and have discussed the need for assessment of inventory carrying costs in logistics system design. Unfortunately, many companies have never calculated inventory carrying costs, even though these costs are both real and substantial. When inventory carrying costs are calculated, they often include only the current interest rate plus expenditures such as insurance and taxes. Many managers use traditional textbook percentages or industry averages. All of these approaches have problems.

Do Interest Rates Reflect the True Costs of Capital?

First, there are only a few special circumstances in which the current interest rate is the relevant cost of money (we will explore these shortly). Traditional textbook percentages also have serious drawbacks.

Most of the carrying cost percentages presented in published sources between 1951 and 1997 were about 25 percent. If 25 percent was an accurate number in 1951, how could it be accurate in 1997, when the prime interest rate fluctuated between 3 and 20 percent during that period?

There also is the method of using inventory carrying costs that are based on "benchmarking" with industry averages. For the most part, businesspeople seem to find comfort

---

[1] We described these formulas in Chapter 4, "Inventory Concepts."

[2] This section draws heavily from Douglas M. Lambert, *The Development of an Inventory Costing Methodology: A Study of the Costs Associated with Holding Inventory* (Chicago: National Council of Physical Distribution Management, 1976).

in such numbers, but many problems are inherent with this practice. For example, would the logistics executive of a cosmetics manufacturer want to compare his or her firm to Avon, a company that sells its products door to door; Revlon, a company that sells its products through major department stores; or—even worse—use an average of the two companies? The last approach would compare the executive's firm to a nonentity—no company at all.

Even if two companies are very similar in terms of the manufacture and distribution of their products, the availability of capital may lead to two different inventory strategies; that is, one firm may experience shortages of capital—capital rationing—while the other may have an abundance of cash. If capital is short, the cost of money for inventory decisions may be 35 percent pretax, which is the rate of return the company is earning on new investments. If capital is plentiful, the cost of money may be 8 percent pretax, which is the interest rate the company is earning on its cash. If both of these companies are well managed, the company whose cost of money is 8 percent will have more inventory.

As presented above, the lower the cost of money, the more attractive it is to increase inventory levels. The company with the 35 percent cost of money will have lower inventories by making different trade-offs such as incurring production setup costs more frequently, choosing more expensive transportation modes, or reducing customer service levels. Each company may have what represents least total cost logistics, and yet one may turn its inventories 6 times a year and the other 12 times. However, if either company were to change any component of its logistics system in order to match the other's performance, total costs could increase and return on net worth could decrease.

Calculating Inventory Carrying Costs

Inventory Carrying Costs Should Include Only Those Costs That Vary with the Quantity of Inventory

Because each company faces a unique operating environment, each company should determine its own logistics costs and strive to minimize the total of these costs, given its customer service objectives. *Inventory carrying costs should include only those costs that vary with the quantity of inventory* and that can be categorized into the following groups: (1) capital costs, (2) inventory service costs, (3) storage space costs, and (4) inventory risk costs. The elements to be considered in each of these categories are identified in Figure 5–2.

Capital Costs on Inventory Investment.   Holding inventory ties up money that could be used for other types of investments. This holds true for both internally generated funds and capital obtained from external sources, such as debt from banks and insurance companies or from the sale of common stock. Consequently, the company's **opportunity cost of capital,** the rate of return that could be realized from some other use of the money, should be used to accurately reflect the true cost involved. Virtually all companies seek to reduce inventory because management recognizes that holding excessive inventory provides no value added to the firm. The company must consider what rate of return it is sacrificing on the cash invested in inventory.

Some companies differentiate among projects by categorizing them according to risk and looking for rates of return that reflect the perceived level of risk. For example, management could group projects into high-, medium-, and low-risk categories. High-risk

FIGURE 5–2

Normative model of inventory carrying cost methodology

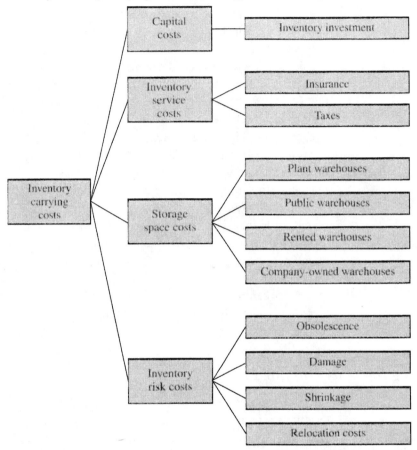

Source: Douglas M. Lambert, *The Development of an Inventory Costing Methodology: A Study of the Costs Associated with Holding Inventory* (Chicago: National Council of Physical Distribution Management, 1976), p. 68.

projects, such as investments in new products or technology, may have a desired rate of return of 25 percent after tax. Investment in new product inventory should reflect that higher perceived risk level.

Medium-risk projects may be required to obtain an 18 percent after-tax return while low-risk projects, which may include such investments as warehouses, private trucking, and inventory of established, stable product lines, might be expected to achieve an after-tax return of 10 percent. Keep in mind that all inventory carrying cost components must be stated in pretax numbers because all of the other costs in the trade-off analysis, such as transportation and warehousing, are reported in pretax dollars.

In some very special circumstances, such as the fruit-canning industry, short-term financing may be used to finance the seasonal buildup of inventories. Fruit must be packaged as it is harvested to meet all customer demand through the end of the next growing season. In this situation, the inventory buildup is short term and the actual cost of borrowing is the acceptable cost of money.

Once management has established the cost of money, it must determine the out-of-pocket (cash) value of the inventory for which the inventory carrying cost is being calculated. For wholesalers or retailers, the out-of-pocket value of the inventory is the current replacement cost of the inventory, including any freight costs paid, or the current market price if the product is being phased out. For manufacturers, the relevant cost is only the cost directly associated with producing the inventory and making it available for sale. Thus, it is necessary to know whether the company is using direct costs to determine the inventory value or using some form of absorption costing.

Direct Costing

Direct costing is a method of cost accounting based on separating costs into fixed and variable components. For management planning and control purposes, the fixed-variable cost breakdown provides more information than that obtained from current financial statements designed for external reporting. Under direct costing, the fixed costs of production are excluded from inventory values. Therefore, inventory values more closely reflect the out-of-pocket cost of their replacement. With **absorption costing** (otherwise known as full costing or full absorption costing), the traditional approach used by most manufacturers, fixed manufacturing overhead is included in the inventory value.

Absorption Costing

In addition to the distinction between direct costing and absorption costing, companies may value inventories based on actual costs or standard costs. Thus, there are four distinct costing alternatives:

1. **Actual absorption costing** includes actual costs for direct material and direct labor, plus predetermined variable and fixed manufacturing overhead.

2. **Standard absorption costing** includes predetermined direct material and direct labor costs, plus predetermined variable and fixed manufacturing overhead.

3. **Actual direct costing** includes actual costs for direct material and direct labor, plus predetermined variable manufacturing overhead; it excludes fixed manufacturing overhead.

4. **Standard direct costing** includes predetermined costs for direct material and direct labor, plus predetermined variable manufacturing overhead; it excludes fixed manufacturing overhead.[3]

The preceding material on methods of inventory valuation supports the conclusion that using industry averages for inventory carrying costs is not a good policy. This is so because the various component percentages may not be calculated using comparable inventory valuation systems.

The situation is complicated even further if one considers the various methods of accounting for inventory for tax purposes. Most manufacturing companies use one of the following three methods:

FIFO

1. **First-in, first-out (FIFO).** Stock acquired earliest is assumed to be sold first, leaving stock acquired more recently in inventory.

---

[3]Students who want to read more about direct and absorption costing and the methods of accounting for inventory should refer to Charles T. Horngren, George Foster, and Srikant M. Datar, *Cost Accounting: A Managerial Emphasis,* 9th ed. (Englewood Cliffs, NJ: Prentice Hall, 1997); or John G. Burch, *Cost and Management Accounting: A Modern Approach* (St. Paul, MN: West, 1994).

FIGURE 5–3

Inventory positions in the logistics system

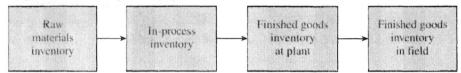

Assumption: A one-time increase (decrease) in finished goods inventory results in a one-time increase (decrease) in raw materials purchased.

LIFO

Average Cost

2. **Last-in, first-out (LIFO).** Sales are made from the most recently acquired stock, leaving items acquired in the earliest time period in inventory.
3. **Average cost.** This method could be a moving average in which each new purchase is averaged with the remaining inventory to obtain a new average price, or a weighted average in which the total cost of the opening inventory plus all purchases is divided by the total number of units.

For the purposes of calculating inventory carrying costs, it is immaterial whether the company uses LIFO, FIFO, or average cost for inventory valuation. To determine the value of the inventory for calculating carrying costs, multiply the number of units of each product in inventory by the standard or actual direct (variable) costs of manufacturing (or purchasing) the product and moving it to the storage location.

The current manufacturing or purchase costs are relevant for decision making because these are the costs that will be incurred if inventories are increased. Likewise, if products are held in field locations, the transportation cost incurred to move them there and the variable costs of moving them into storage become part of the cost of inventory. These costs are in addition to direct labor costs, direct material costs, and the variable manufacturing overhead.

The implicit assumption is that a reduction in finished goods inventory will lead to a corresponding reduction in inventory throughout the system (see Figure 5–3). That is, a one-time reduction in finished goods inventory results in a one-time reduction in raw materials purchases, as inventory is pushed back through the system.

In summary, inventory requires capital that could be used for other corporate investments; by having funds invested in inventory, a company forgoes the rate of return that it could obtain in such investments. Therefore, the company's opportunity cost of capital should be applied to the investment in inventory. The cost of capital should be applied to the out-of-pocket cost investment in inventory.

Inventory Service Costs. **Inventory service costs** are comprised of ad valorem (personal property) taxes and fire and theft insurance paid as a result of holding the inventory. Taxes vary depending on the state in which inventories are held. Tax rates can range from zero in states where inventories are exempt to as much as 20 percent of the assessed value. In general, taxes vary directly with inventory levels. Many states exempt inventories from taxation if they are placed into storage for subsequent shipment to customers in another state. With proper planning, a company can minimize this component when establishing a warehousing network. The cost of extra movement from a tax-exempt state, to the state where the product will be consumed must be considered in trade-off analysis.

Insurance rates are not strictly proportional to inventory levels because insurance is usually purchased to cover a certain value of product for a specified time period. Nevertheless, an insurance policy will be revised periodically based on expected inventory level changes. In some instances, an insurance company will issue policies in which premiums are based on the monthly amounts insured. Insurance rates depend on the materials used in the construction of the storage building, its age, and considerations such as the type of fire prevention equipment installed.

The actual dollars spent on insurance and taxes during the past year can be calculated as a percentage of that year's inventory value and added to the cost-of-money component of the carrying cost. If budgeted figures are available for the coming year, they can be used as a percentage of the inventory value based on the inventory plan—the forecasted inventory level—in order to provide a future-oriented carrying cost. In most cases, there will be few if any significant changes from year to year in the tax and insurance components of the inventory carrying cost.

Costs Associated with Warehousing

Plant Warehouse Costs

Public Warehouse Costs

Storage Space Costs.   Storage space costs relate to four general types of facilities: (1) plant warehouses, (2) public warehouses, (3) rented or leased (contract) warehouses, and (4) company-owned (private) warehouses.

Plant warehouse costs are primarily fixed. If any costs are variable, they are usually variable with the amount of product that moves through the facility, **throughput,** and not with the quantity of inventory stored. If some variable costs, such as the cost of taking inventory or any other expenses, change with the level of inventory, management should include them in inventory carrying costs. Fixed charges and allocated costs are not relevant for inventory policy decisions. If the firm can rent out the warehouse space or use it for some other productive purpose instead of using it for storing inventory, an estimate of the appropriate opportunity costs would be appropriate.

Public warehouse costs are usually based on the amount of product moved into and out of the warehouse (handling charges) and the amount of inventory held in storage (storage charges). In most cases, handling charges are assessed when the products are moved into the warehouse and storage charges are assessed on a periodic basis (e.g., monthly). Usually, the first month's storage must be paid when the products are moved into the facility. In effect, this makes the first month's storage a handling charge since it must be paid on every case of product regardless of how long it is held in the warehouse.

The use of public warehouses is a management policy decision because it may be the most economical way to provide the desired level of customer service without incurring excessive transportation costs. For this reason, handling charges, which represent the majority of costs related to the use of public warehouses, should be considered as throughput costs; that is, they should be thought of as part of the warehousing cost category of the cost trade-off analysis, and not part of inventory carrying costs. Only charges for *warehouse storage* should be included in inventory carrying costs because these are the public warehouse charges that will vary with the level of inventory.

Where a throughput rate (handling charge) is given based on the number of inventory turns, it is necessary to estimate the storage cost component by considering how the

Inventory control in a food manufacturing plant storage facility.

throughput costs per case will change if the number of inventory turns changes. Of course, the public warehouse fees that a company pays when its inventory is placed into field storage should be included in the value of its inventory investment.

Rented or leased warehouse space is normally contracted for a specified period of time. The amount of space rented is based on the maximum storage requirements during the period covered by the contract. Thus, warehouse rental charges do not fluctuate from day to day with changes in the inventory level, although rental rates can vary from month to month or year to year when a new contract is negotiated. Most costs, such as rent payment, the manager's salary, security costs, and maintenance expenses, are fixed in the short run. But some expenses, such as warehouse labor and equipment operating costs, vary with throughput. During the term of the contract, few if any costs vary with the amount of inventory stored.

All of the costs of leased warehouses could be eliminated by not renewing the contract and are therefore a relevant input for logistics decision making. However, operating costs that do not vary with the quantity of inventory stored, such as those outlined in the preceding paragraph, should not be included in the carrying costs. Rather, these costs belong in the warehousing cost category of the cost trade-off analysis. The inclusion of fixed costs, and those that are variable with throughput in inventory carrying costs, has no conceptual basis. Such a practice is simply incorrect and will result in erroneous decisions.

Private Warehouse Costs

The costs associated with *company-owned* or **private warehouses** are primarily fixed, although some may vary with throughput. All operating costs that can be eliminated by closing a company-owned warehouse or the net savings resulting from a change to public warehouses should be included in warehousing costs, not inventory carrying costs. Only those costs that vary with the quantity of inventory belong in inventory carrying costs. Typically, these costs are negligible in company-owned warehouses.

In most warehouses, the costs associated with order picking, put-away, and inventory control are significant because of the labor necessary to perform these tasks. Most of these costs vary with throughput and not inventory levels.

Inventory Risk Costs.   Inventory risk costs vary from company to company, but typically include charges for (1) obsolescence, (2) damage, (3) shrinkage, and (4) relocation of inventory.

Cost of Obsolescence   **Obsolescence cost** is the cost of each unit that must be disposed of at a loss because it can no longer be sold at a regular price. In essence, it is the cost of holding products in inventory beyond their useful life. Obsolescence cost is the difference between the original cost of the unit and its salvage value, or the original selling price and the reduced selling price if the price is lowered (marked down) to move the product. Generally, obsolescence costs are buried in the "cost of goods manufactured" account or the "cost of goods sold" account instead of being shown as a separate item on profit-and-loss statements. Consequently, managers may have some difficulty arriving at this figure. However, it is a relevant cost of holding inventory, especially as product life cycles decrease.

Damage Costs   **Damage costs** incurred during shipping should be considered a throughput cost, since they will continue regardless of inventory levels. Damage attributed to a public warehouse operation is usually charged to the warehouse operator if it is above a specified maximum amount. Damage is often identified as the net amount after claims.

Shrinkage Costs   **Shrinkage costs** have become an increasingly important problem for American businesses. Many authorities think inventory theft is a more serious problem than cash embezzlement. Theft is far more common, involves far more employees, and is hard to control. Shrinkage also can result from poor record keeping, or shipping wrong products or quantities to customers. In the case of agricultural products, natural ores, or similar items that are shipped in bulk, shrinkage may result from loss in weight or spillage that occurs during transportation and handling. However, shrinkage costs may be more closely related to company security measures than inventory levels, even though they definitely will vary with the number of warehouse locations. Thus, management may find it more appropriate to assign some or all of these costs to the warehouse locations than to the amount of inventory.

Relocation Costs

Relocation costs are incurred when inventory is transshipped from one warehouse location to another to avoid obsolescence. For example, products that are selling well in the Midwest may not be selling on the West Coast. By shipping the products to the location where they will sell, the company avoids the obsolescence cost but incurs additional transportation costs. Transshipments to avoid obsolescence or markdowns are the result of having too much inventory, and the cost should be included in inventory carrying costs. Often, transshipment costs are not reported separately, but are simply included in transportation costs. In such cases, a managerial estimate or a statistical audit of freight bills can isolate the transshipment costs.

The frequency of these types of shipments will determine which approach is more practical in any given situation. That is, if such shipments are rare, the percentage component of the carrying cost will be very small and a managerial estimate should suffice. The Technology box describes how one firm misused technology in relocating product, and actually increased its inventory expense!

In some cases, firms may incur transshipment costs as a result of inventory stocking policies. For example, if inventories are set too low in field locations, stockouts may occur and may be rectified by shipping product from the nearest warehouse location that has the items in stock. The transportation costs associated with transshipment to avoid stockouts are a result of decisions that involve trade-offs among transportation costs, warehousing costs, inventory carrying costs, or stockout costs. They are transportation costs and should not be classified as inventory carrying costs.

Because managers do not always know just how much of the costs of damage, shrinkage, and relocation are related to the amount of inventory held, they may have to determine mathematically if a relationship exists. For example, a cost for damage may be available, but the amount of this cost attributed to the volume of inventory may be unknown.

Damage can be a function of such factors as throughput, general housekeeping, the quality and training of management and labor, the type of product, the protective packaging used, the material handling system, the number of times that the product is handled, how it is handled, and the amount of inventory (which may lead to damage as a result of overcrowding in the warehouse). To say which of these factors is most important and how much damage each one accounts for is extremely difficult.

Even an elaborate reporting system may not yield the desired results, as employees may try to shift the blame for the damaged product. The quality of damage screening during the receiving function, and the possible hiding of damaged product in higher inventories until inventories are reduced, may contribute to the level of damage reported, regardless of the cause.

FIGURE 5–5

Annual inventory carrying costs compared to inventory turnovers

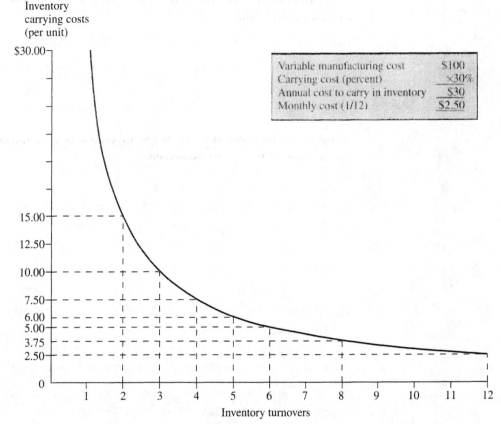

Variable manufacturing cost	$100
Carrying cost (percent)	×30%
Annual cost to carry in inventory	$30
Monthly cost (1/12)	$2.50

Source: Jay U. Sterling and Douglas M. Lambert, "Segment Profitability Reports: You Can't Manage Your Business without Them," unpublished manuscript, 1992.

Symptoms of Poor Inventory Management

This section deals with how to recognize improper management of inventories. Recognition of problem areas is the first step in determining where opportunities exist for improving logistics performance. If a firm is experiencing continuing problems associated with inventory management, a change in processes or systems may be in order.

The following symptoms may be associated with poor inventory management:

Symptoms Associated with Poor Inventory Management

1. Increasing numbers of back-orders.
2. Increasing dollar investment in inventory with back-orders remaining constant.
3. High customer turnover rate.
4. Increasing number of orders canceled.
5. Periodic lack of sufficient storage space.
6. Wide variance in turnover of major inventory items between distribution centers.

7. Deteriorating relationships with intermediaries, as typified by dealer cancellations and declining orders.

8. Large quantities of obsolete items.

In many instances inventory levels can be reduced by one or more of the following steps:

Methods for Reducing Inventory Levels

1. Multiechelon inventory planning. ABC analysis is an example of such planning.
2. Lead time analysis.
3. Delivery time analysis. This may lead to a change in carriers or negotiation with existing carriers.
4. Elimination of low turnover and/or obsolete items.
5. Analysis of pack size and discount structure.
6. Examination of procedures for returned goods.
7. Encouragement/automation of product substitution.
8. Installation of formal reorder review systems.
9. Measurement of fill rates by stockkeeping units (SKUs).
10. Analysis of customer demand characteristics.
11. Development of a formal sales plan and demand forecast by predetermined logic.
12. Expand view of inventory to include inventory management and information sharing at various levels in the supply chain.
13. Reengineering inventory management practices (include warehousing and transportation) to realize improvements in product flow.

In many companies, the best method of reducing inventory investment is to reduce order cycle time by using advanced order processing systems (see Chapter 3). If the order cycle currently offered to customers is satisfactory, the time saved in the transmittal, entry, and processing of orders can be used for inventory planning. The result will be a significant reduction in inventory.

Improving Inventory Management

Inventory management can be improved by using one or more of the following techniques: ABC analysis, forecasting, inventory models, and advanced order processing systems.

ABC Analysis

Pareto Principle

In his study of the distribution of wealth in Milan, Villefredo Pareto (1848–1923) found that 20 percent of the people controlled 80 percent of the wealth. The concept that critical issues, wealth, importance, and so on are concentrated among a few is termed **Pareto's law.** This applies in our daily lives—most of the issues we face have little importance, but a few are critical, long-term issues—and it certainly applies to inventory systems.[6]

---

[6]Richard B. Chase and Nicolas J. Aquilano, *Production and Operations Management,* 6th ed. (Burr Ridge, IL: Richard D. Irwin, 1992).

This type of ABC analysis should not be confused with activity based costing, also abbreviated as ABC (see Chapter 13). The logic behind ABC analysis is that 20 percent of the firm's customers or products account for 80 percent of the sales and perhaps an even larger percentage of profits. The first step in ABC analysis is to rank products by sales or, preferably, by contribution to corporate profitability if such data are available. The next step is to check for differences between high-volume and low-volume items that may suggest how certain items should be managed.

Inventory Levels Increase with the Number of Storage Locations

Inventory levels increase with the number of stockkeeping locations.[7] By stocking low-volume items at a number of logistics centers, the national demand for these products is divided by the number of locations. Each of these locations must maintain safety stock. If one centralized location had been used for these items, the total safety stock would be much lower. For example, if only one centralized warehouse is used and sales are forecast on a national basis, a sales increase in Los Angeles may offset a sales decrease in New York. However, safety stock is required to protect against variability in demand, and there is greater variability in demand when we forecast demand by regions. The total system inventory will increase with the number of field warehouse locations because the variability in demand must be covered at each location.

When a firm consolidates slow-moving items at a centralized location, transportation costs often increase. However, these costs may be offset by lower inventory carrying costs and fewer stockout penalties. Customer service can be improved through consolidation of low-volume items by decreasing the probability of experiencing a stockout. ABC analysis is a method for deciding which items should be considered for centralized warehousing.

An Example of ABC Analysis

At this point let's consider an example of ABC analysis.[8] An analysis of sales volume by product reveals that A items account for 5 percent of all items and contribute 70 percent to sales, B items account for 10 percent of items and add a further 20 percent to sales, while C items account for 65 percent of the remaining items but contribute only 10 percent to sales. The last 20 percent of the items have no sales whatsoever during the past year (see Figure 5–6). This statistical distribution is almost always found in companies' inventories.[9] The "degree of concentration of sales among items will vary by firm, but the shape of the curve will be similar."[10]

For A items, a daily or continuous review of inventory status might be appropriate; B items might be reviewed weekly while the C items should receive the least attention. Different customer service levels could be established for each category of inventory. An order fill rate of 98 percent might be set for A items, 90 percent for B items, and 85 percent for C items. This policy would result in an overall customer service level of 95 percent, as shown in Table 5–6. By focusing attention on the A items, management places greater emphasis on the products that contribute the most to sales and profitability.

---

[7]While average inventory at each facility decreases as the number of warehouse locations increases, total system inventory (all facilities) increases.

[8]This example is adapted from William C. Copacino, "Moving beyond ABC Analysis," *Traffic Management* 33, no. 3 (Mar. 1994), pp. 35–36; and Lynn E. Gill, "Inventory and Physical Distribution Management," in *The Distribution Handbook,* ed. James F. Robeson and Robert G. House (New York: Free Press, 1985), pp. 664–67.

[9]It is referred to as *log normal distribution.*

[10]Gill, "Inventory and Physical Distribution Management," p. 664.

Transportation

Chapter Outline

Chapter Objectives

- To examine transportation's role in logistics and its relationship to marketing.
- To describe alternative transport modes, intermodal combinations, and other transportation options.
- To examine the impact of deregulation on carriers and shippers.
- To examine the issues of transportation cost and performance measurement.
- To examine international dimensions of transportation.
- To identify major transportation management activities of carriers and shippers.
- To identify areas where computer technology is important.

Introduction

This chapter provides an overview of the transportation function and its importance to logistics. We will examine alternative transportation modes and intermodal combinations. We also describe key transportation management issues of shippers and carriers, transportation cost and performance measurement, and the role of computers.

Efficient transportation systems are the hallmark of industrialized societies. The transportation sector of most industrialized economies is so pervasive that we often fail to comprehend the magnitude of its impact on our way of life. In 1996, U.S. transportation expenditures were approximately $455 billion of the nation's total logistics costs, which were estimated to be $797 billion.[1]

U.S. Transportation Costs $455 Billion Yearly

Since 1970, the transportation sector has grown considerably. Figure 7–1 shows that since 1981, national freight transportation costs have been growing more slowly than the gross domestic product (GDP).[2]

FIGURE 7–1

Freight transportation outlays compared to GDP

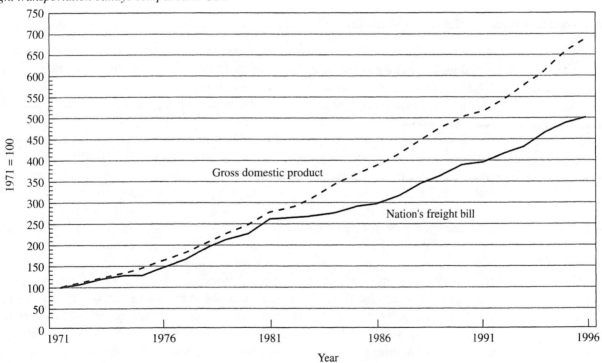

Source: Robert V. Delaney, "CLI's State of Logistics Annual Report," press conference at the National Press Club, Washington, DC (June 2, 1997), fig. 15.

---

[1]Robert V. Delaney, "CLI's State of Logistics Annual Report," press conference at the National Press Club, Washington, DC (June 2, 1997), p. 4.

[2]Deregulation of motor and rail transportation in 1980 resulted in transportation efficiencies.

Time and Place Utility

**Transportation
Provides Value-Added
through Place Utility**

Transportation physically moves products from where they are produced to where they are needed. This movement across space or distance adds value to products. This value-added is often referred to as **place utility.**

Time utility is created by warehousing and storing products until they are needed. Transportation is also a factor in time utility; it determines how fast and how consistently a product moves from one point to another. This is known as **time-in-transit** and *consistency of service,* respectively.

If a product is not available at the precise time it is needed, there may be expensive repercussions, such as lost sales, customer dissatisfaction, and production downtime, when the product is being used in the manufacturing process. Transportation service providers such as CSX, Federal Express (FedEx), Leaseway Transportation, Ryder Integrated Logistics, and United Parcel Service (UPS) have achieved success because they are able to provide consistent time-in-transit and thus increase the time and place utility of their customers' products.

Transportation/Logistics/Marketing Interfaces

Transportation moves products to markets that are geographically separated and provides added value to customers when the products arrive on time, undamaged, and in the quantities required. In this way, transportation contributes to the level of customer service, which is one of the cornerstones of customer satisfaction: an important component of the marketing concept.

Because transportation creates place utility and contributes to time utility—both of which are necessary for successful marketing efforts—the availability, adequacy, and cost of transportation impact business decisions seemingly unrelated to managing the transportation function itself; that is, what products should be produced, where should they be sold, where should facilities be located, and where should materials be sourced?

**For Many Firms
Transportation Is the
Largest Logistics
Cost**

Transportation is one of the largest logistics costs and may account for a significant portion of the selling price of some products. Low value-per-pound products such as basic raw materials (e.g., sand and coal) are examples. Transportation costs for computers, business machines, and electronic components may be only a small percentage of the selling price. Generally, the efficient management of transportation becomes more important to a firm as inbound and outbound transportation's share of product cost increases. Even with high-value products, expenditures for transportation are important although the percentage of selling price may be low, primarily because the total cost of transportation in absolute terms is significant.

Factors Influencing Transportation Costs and Pricing

In general, factors influencing transportation costs/pricing can be grouped into two major categories: product-related factors and market-related factors.

Product-Related Factors.   Many factors related to a product's characteristics influence the cost/pricing of transportation. They can be grouped into the following categories:

1. Density.
2. Stowability.
3. Ease or difficulty of handling.
4. Liability.

Density

Density refers to a product's weight-to-volume ratio. Items such as steel, canned foods, building products, and bulk paper goods have high weight-to-volume ratios; they are relatively heavy given their size. On the other hand, products such as electronics, clothing, luggage, and toys have low weight-to-volume ratios and thus are relatively lightweight given their size. In general, low-density products—those with low weight-to-volume ratios—tend to cost more to transport on a per pound (kilo) basis than high-density products.

Stowability

Stowability is the degree to which a product can fill the available space in a transport vehicle. For example, grain, ore, and petroleum products in bulk have excellent stowability because they can completely fill the container (e.g., railcar, tank truck, pipeline) in which they are transported. Other items, such as automobiles, machinery, livestock, and people, do not have good stowability, or cube utilization. A product's stowability depends on its size, shape, fragility, and other physical characteristics.

Ease or Difficulty of Handling

Related to stowability is the *ease or difficulty of handling* the product. Difficult-to-handle items are more costly to transport. Products that are uniform in their physical characteristics (e.g., raw materials and items in cartons, cans, or drums) or that can be manipulated with materials-handling equipment require less handling expense and are therefore less costly to transport.

Liability

Liability is an important concern. Products that have high value-to-weight ratios are easily damaged, and are subject to higher rates of theft or pilferage, cost more to transport. Where the transportation carrier assumes greater liability (e.g., with computer, jewelry, and home entertainment products), a higher price will be charged to transport the product.

Other factors, which vary in importance depending on the product category, are the product's hazardous characteristics and the need for strong and rigid protective packaging. These factors are particularly important in the chemical and plastics industries.

Market-Related Factors.   In addition to product characteristics, important market-related factors affect transportation costs/pricing. The most significant are:

1. Degree of intramode and intermode competition.
2. Location of markets, which determines the distance goods must be transported.
3. Nature and extent of government regulation of transportation carriers.
4. Balance or imbalance of freight traffic into and out of a market.
5. Seasonality of product movements.
6. Whether the product is transported domestically or internationally.

Each of these factors affects the costs and pricing of transportation. These topics will be examined later in this chapter. In addition, there are important service factors that need to be considered.

Transportation Impacts Customer Service

Customer service is a vital component of logistics management. While each activity of logistics management contributes to the level of service a company provides to its customers, the impact of transportation on customer service is one of the most significant. The most important transportation service characteristics affecting customer service levels are:

- Dependability—consistency of service.
- Time-in-transit.
- Market coverage—the ability to provide door-to-door service.
- Flexibility—handling a variety of products and meeting the special needs of shippers.
- Loss and damage performance.
- Ability of the carrier to provide more than basic transportation service (i.e., to become part of a shipper's overall marketing and logistics programs).

Each mode of transport—motor, rail, air, water, and pipeline—has varying service capabilities. In the next section, we will examine each mode in terms of its economic and service characteristics.

Carrier Characteristics and Services

Any one or more of five transportation modes—motor, rail, air, water, and pipeline—may be selected to transport products. In addition, intermodal combinations are available: rail-motor, motor-water, motor-air, and rail-water. Intermodal combinations offer specialized or lower cost services not generally available when a single transport mode is used. Other transportation options that offer a variety of services to shippers include freight forwarders, shippers' associations, intermodal marketing companies (or shippers' agents), third-party logistics service providers, parcel post, and air express companies.

Motor

The motor carrier, or trucking industry, is comprised of $121 billion (52 percent) for private fleets, $66 billion (29 percent) for-hire truckload, $23 billion (10 percent) package and express delivery, and $20 billion (9 percent) less-than-truckload shipments.[3] Motor carriers transport over 75 percent of the tonnage of agricultural products such as fresh and frozen meats, dairy products, bakery products, confectionery items, beverages, and consumer tobacco products. Many manufactured products are transported primarily by motor carriers, including amusement, sporting, and athletic goods; toys; watches and clocks; farm machinery; radios and television sets; carpets and rugs; clothing; drugs; and office **Motor Carriers Provide Fast and Reliable Service** equipment and furniture. Most consumer goods are transported by motor carrier. Motor carriage offers fast, reliable service with little damage or loss in transit.

Domestically, motor carriers compete with air for small shipments and rail for large shipments.[4] Efficient motor carriers can realize greater efficiencies in terminal, pickup,

---

[3]Delaney, "State of Logistics Annual Report," fig. 19.

[4]Smaller shipments transported by motor carriers are referred to as less-than-truckload (LTL), which is any quantity of freight weighing less than the amount required for the application of a truckload rate.

The dock area of the Food Marketing Division of SuperValu Stores in Ft. Wayne, Indiana, is where some of the 750 truckloads representing 1,600 shipments leave weekly to serve the division's 220 diverse retailer customers.

and delivery operations, which enables them to compete with air carriers on **point-to-point service**[5] for any size shipment if the distance involved is 500 miles or less.

Motor carriers compete directly with railroads for truckload (TL) shipments that are transported 500 miles or more. However, rail is the dominant mode when shipment sizes exceed 100,000 pounds. Motor carriers dominate the market for smaller shipments.[6]

The average length of haul for motor carriers is approximately 500 miles. Some national carriers have average hauls that are much longer while some intracity carriers may average only a few miles. LTL shipments are generally shorter hauls than TL shipments, but significant variability exists.

Motor Carriers Are Flexible and Versatile

Motor carriers are very flexible and versatile. The flexibility of motor carriers is made possible by a network of over 4 million miles of roads, thus enabling them to offer point-to-point service between almost any origin-destination combination. This gives motor carriers the widest market coverage of any mode. Motor carriers are versatile because they can transport products of varying sizes and weights over any distance.

Virtually any product can be transported by motor carriers, including some that require carrier equipment modifications.. Their flexibility and versatility have enabled them

---

[5]Point-to-point service refers to a single transport mode picking products up at origin and delivering them to their final destination. No additional transport modes are necessary.

[6]Shipments transported by motor carriers are referred to as truckload (TL) and less-than-truckload (LTL). When the terms were first developed, truck capacities were near 10,000 pounds, so this became the "norm" for designating the break point between a TL and LTL shipment. A TL amount was 10,000 pounds or more, while a LTL shipment was anything less than 10,000 pounds. Because the physical capacity of trucks has increased over the years, the amount that can be transported by truck has grown considerably. Today, LTL is any quantity of freight weighing less than the amount required for the application of a truckload rate.

to become the dominant form of transport (based on the amount of freight transported as measured in dollars) in the Americas and in many other parts of the world. Many motor carriers, particularly those involved in just-in-time programs, operate on a scheduled timetable. This results in very short and reliable transit times.

The amount of freight transported by motor carriers has steadily increased over the years. Motor carriage has become an important part of the logistics networks of most firms because the characteristics of the motor carrier industry are more compatible than other transport modes with the service requirements of the firms' customers. As long as it can provide fast, efficient service at rates between those offered by rail and air, the motor carrier industry will continue to prosper.

Baxter Healthcare, a large hospital supply company, presently outsources its truck-load transportation in order to utilize its carrier's expertise and efficiency, and to stream-line its operations (see Box 7–1).

Rail

In countries such as Austria, the People's Republic of China, and the former republics of the Soviet Union and Yugoslavia, rail is the dominant mode of transport. In the United States, most of the freight (in dollar terms) once shipped by rail has been shifted to motor carriers. Some traffic has been lost to water and pipeline carriers, which compete with railroads for bulk commodities. However, railroads carry the largest share of inter-city ton-miles and in 1995, this total was 1,276 billion ton-miles, or 18.29 million railcar loadings.[7] A ton-mile is one ton of freight moving a distance of one mile.

Railroads have an average length of haul of approximately 763 miles.[8] While rail service is available in almost every major metropolitan center in the world and in many smaller communities, the rail network is not nearly as extensive as the highway network.

Rail Lacks the Versatility and Flexibility of Motor Carriers

Rail transport lacks the versatility and flexibility of motor carriers because it is limited to fixed track facilities. As a result, railroads—like air, water, and pipeline transport—provide terminal-to-terminal service rather than point-to-point service unless companies have a rail siding at their facility, in which case service would be point to point.

Rail Costs Are Low

Rail transport generally costs less (on a weight basis) than air and motor carriage.[9] For many shipments, rail does not compare favorably with other modes on loss and damage ratios. Compared to motor carriers, it has disadvantages in terms of transit time and frequency of service, although railroads have improved significantly in these areas since deregulation of the U.S. rail industry in 1980.

Many trains travel on timetable schedules, but depart less frequently than motor carriers.[10] If a shipper has strict arrival and departure requirements, motor carriers usually

---

[7]"TM News Capsule," *Traffic Management* 35, no. 2 (Feb. 1996), p. 14.

[8]*Railroad Facts* (Washington, DC: Association of American Railroads, 1993), p. 3.

[9]In some transportation lanes and markets, motor carriers have been very price competitive with rail. In a few instances, motor carriers have been able to match or even undercut the rates charged by railroads.

[10]For a discussion of scheduled railroad service, see Peter Bradley, "It's about Time!" *Traffic Management* 34, no. 12 (Dec. 1995), pp. 37–39.

Box 7–1

Outsourcing Truckload Fleet Helps Baxter Healthcare Cut Supply Chain Costs

As the world's leading manufacturer and distributor of hospital and medical-related products, Baxter Healthcare of Deerfield, Illinois, is caught squarely in the middle of the ongoing overhaul of the U.S. health care system. To come out on top of this massive industry reengineering, Baxter relies on its logistics partners for help in streamlining its total medical supply chain, adding value, and cutting costs. In several important areas of its business, Baxter relies on outsourcing partners to handle the entire activity.

One partner is Schneider National/Schneider Dedicated. In 1993, Schneider took over Baxter's inbound truckload fleet operation. That operation provided inbound transport of 25 percent of the company's truckload shipments to production plants and replenishment centers. Baxter Healthcare made the decision to outsource its over-the-road private fleet (90 units at that time) in the summer of 1993. "When we stepped back and looked at the fleet," recalls Timothy Houghton, director of corporate transportation for Baxter Healthcare, "we decided that running a truckload (TL) carrier was not a core competency for us. We realized we couldn't possibly compete with national TL carriers.

"Our company philosophy," notes Houghton, "is that if we're not the number one or number two player in every market we service, then we get out of it. That's part of our commitment to taking cost out of the health care chain."

Leveraging Volumes

Houghton's analysis of Baxter's total inbound volumes indicated that the company not only was inefficient in its TL fleet operations, but also was not leveraging its inbound volumes with its for-hire carriers.

"We're a high-volume TL shipper, but we were using more than 100 truckload carriers—in addition to our private fleet—to handle inbound movements. We weren't leveraging our potential buying power," Houghton says.

"We also were spending an inordinate amount of time trying to keep track of and manage all those carriers."

To resolve this situation, Baxter first identified those lanes which could operate as closed loops (with full front-and-back-hauls), segregated them, and gave that business to Schneider Dedicated. "We operate about 95 units in our dedicated fleet, and have a loaded-mile factor of 94 percent," the distribution executive reports.

Then, the company concentrated the remaining 75 percent of its inbound TL business with a handful of core carriers, thereby obtaining better rates and service.

Schneider's tightly focused dedicated operation serves only those lanes where fully loaded round trips are possible. As a result, the operation is extremely cost effective, undercutting regular for-hire truckload rates by 15–25 percent, according to Houghton. At the same time, Schneider provides the high-quality service Baxter needs to keep its production plants running smoothly.

Greater Flexibility

Cost savings aren't the only benefit Baxter realizes from its Schneider operation. The new arrangement offers much more flexibility. "We were locked into the number of units and number of drivers," recalls Houghton. Dedicated contract carriage solved these problems, allowing Baxter complete flexibility to adjust fleet size to company demand. For example, if the company needs 10 additional units for the last two weeks in June, Houghton simply notifies Schneider and the units are slotted. "With the Schneider arrangement," says Houghton, "we get the best of all possible worlds."

In little more than a year, Schneider Dedicated saved Baxter 25 percent.

Source: *Outsourced Logistics Report*, Special Preview Issue, 1994, pp. 1–2.

TOFC and COFC Services

have a competitive advantage over railroads. Some of this rail disadvantage may be overcome through the use of trailer-on-flatcar (TOFC) or container-on-flatcar (COFC) service, which offer the economy of rail or water movements combined with the flexibility of trucking. TOFC and COFC eliminate much of the inventory penalty associated with rail transportation. Most logistics executives refer to TOFC and COFC as piggyback service.

Truck trailers or containers are delivered to the rail terminals, where they are loaded on flatbed railcars. Containers may be single or double stacked; that is, one or two containers on a single railcar.[11] At the destination terminal, they are off-loaded and delivered to the consignee, the customer who receives the shipment. We will examine these services in greater detail later in this chapter.

Railroads suffer in comparison to motor carriers in equipment availability. Railroads use their own as well as each other's railcars, and at times this equipment may not be located where it is most needed. Railcars may be unavailable because they are being loaded, unloaded, moved within railroad sorting yards, or undergoing repair. Other cars may be standing idle or lost within the vast rail network.

Recent Developments Aid Rail Utilization

A number of developments in the rail industry have helped to overcome some of these utilization problems. Advances have included computer routing and scheduling; the upgrading of equipment, roadbeds, and terminals; improvements in railcar identification systems; railcars owned or leased by the shipper; and the use of **unit trains** or dedicated through-train service between major metropolitan areas (i.e., nonstop shipments of one or a few shippers' products).[12]

Railroads own most of their car fleet, with the remainder leased or owned by shippers. Shippers that own or lease cars are typically heavy users of rail transport and are especially sensitive to railcar shortages that occur because of unique market or competitive conditions.

During the late 1980s, railroads recaptured some of the traffic previously lost to trucks, pipelines, and water carriers. The relative energy-efficiency advantage of railroads over motor carriers, deregulation of the rail industry, and the continuing trend toward consolidation through mergers and acquisitions hold promise for a brighter future for this transport mode.

Air

Domestically, air carriers transport less than 1 percent of ton-mile traffic in the United States. Revenues of scheduled air carriers from movement of freight were about $16 billion in 1993, but this represented only a small percentage of the total U.S. freight bill.[13]

Air Freight Is Used Primarily as a Premium Service

Although increasing numbers of shippers are using air freight for regular service, most view air transport as a premium, emergency service because of its higher cost. But when an item must be delivered to a distant location quickly, air freight offers the

---

[11]Helen L. Richardson, "Shippers and Carriers Win with Doublestack," *Transportation and Distribution* 30, no. 12 (Nov. 1989), pp. 22–24.

[12]Unit trains are trains of great length carrying a single product in one direction. Commodities transported by unit trains have included coal, grains, U.S. mail, automobiles, fruits, and vegetables.

[13]U.S. Bureau of the Census, *Statistical Abstract of the United States: 1995,* 115th ed. (Washington, DC: U.S. Government Printing Office, 1995), p. 625.

quickest time-in-transit of any transport mode. For most shippers, however, these time-sensitive shipments are relatively few in number or frequency.

Modern aircraft have cruising speeds of 500 to 600 miles per hour and are able to travel internationally. The average length of haul domestically is more than 800 miles, although international movements may be thousands of miles.[14]

For most commercial airlines, freight is incidental to passenger traffic, and is carried on a space-available basis. United Airlines led the way in cargo revenue for passenger airlines in 1995, with $757 million, followed closely by Northwest Airlines with $751 million.[15]

To a great extent, domestic air freight competes directly with motor carriers, and to a much lesser degree with rail carriers. Where countries are separated by large expanses of water, the major competitor for international air freight is water carriage.

Air carriers generally handle high-value products. Air freight usually cannot be cost-justified for low-value items, because the high price of air freight would represent too large a percentage of the product cost. Customer service considerations may influence the choice of transport, but only if service issues are more important than cost issues.

Air transport provides frequent and reliable service and rapid time-in-transit, but terminal and delivery delays and congestion may appreciably reduce some of this advantage. On a point-to-point basis over short distances, motor transport often matches or outperforms the total transit time of air freight. It is the *total* transit time that is important to the shipper rather than the transit time from terminal to terminal.

Despite the limitations of air carriers, the volume of air freight has grown over the years and it shows continuing growth even in the face of higher rates. Undoubtedly, as customers demand higher levels of service and as international shipments increase, air freight will have a potentially greater role in the distribution plans of many firms.

Water

Water transportation can be broken down into several distinct categories: (1) inland waterway, such as rivers and canals, (2) lakes, (3) coastal and intercoastal ocean, and (4) international deep sea. In the United States, water carriage competes primarily with rail and pipeline, since the majority of commodities carried by water are semiprocessed or raw materials transported in bulk. It is concentrated in low-value items (e.g., iron ore, grains, pulpwood products, coal, limestone, and petroleum) where speed is not critical.

The Importance of Water Carriage Varies around the World

Other than in ocean transport, water carriers are limited in their movement by the availability of lakes, rivers, canals, or intercoastal waterways. Reliance on water carriage depends to a greater or lesser degree on the geography of the particular location. In the United States, for example, approximately 467 billion revenue freight ton-miles ($21 billion), or around 15 percent of the total intercity freight, is moved by water.[16] In northern and central Europe, water carriage is much more important because of the vast system of

---

[14]*Air Transport 1994*, p. 16.
[15]Marcia Jedd, "Shedding the Stepchild Image," *Distribution* 95, no. 8 (July 1996), p. 58.
[16]*Statistical Abstract of the United States: 1995*, p. 626.

Barge traffic on the Mississippi River near St. Louis, Missouri.

navigable waterways, the accessibility to major population centers provided by water routes, and the relatively shorter distances between origins and destinations. In the Netherlands, Belgium, and Luxembourg, waterways account for 20 percent of all freight transported.[17]

The average length of haul varies tremendously depending on the type of water transport. For international ocean movements, the length of haul can be many thousands of miles. Generally, water is the dominant mode in international shipping. Domestically, movements are of shorter lengths, depending on the length of navigable waterways and lakes.

Water carriage is perhaps the most inexpensive method of shipping high-bulk, low-value commodities. However, because of the inherent limitations of water carriers, it is unlikely that water transport will gain a larger role in domestic commerce, although international developments have made marine shipping increasingly important.

VLCCs

The development of **very large crude carriers (VLCCs),** or supertankers, has enabled marine shipping to assume a vital role in the transport of petroleum between oil-producing and oil-consuming countries. Because of the importance of energy resources to industrialized nations, water carriage will continue to play a significant role in the transportation of energy resources. In addition, container ships have greatly expanded the use of water transport for many products.

Many domestic and most international shipments involve the use of containers. The shipper in one country places cargo into an owned or leased container at its facility or at

---

[17]Kevin A. O'Laughlin, James Cooper, and Eric Cabocel, *Reconfiguring European Logistics Systems* (Oak Brook, IL: Council of Logistics Management, 1993), p. 38.

point of origin.[18] Then the container is transported by rail or motor carriage to a water port for loading onto a container ship. After arrival at the destination port, it is unloaded and tendered to a rail or motor carrier in that country and subsequently delivered to the customer or consignee. The shipment leaves the shipper and arrives at the customer's location with no or minimal handling of the items within the container.

Containers Are Important in Global Commerce

The use of containers in intermodal logistics reduces staffing needs, minimizes in-transit damage and pilferage, shortens time in transit because of reduced port turnaround time, and allows the shipper to take advantage of volume shipping rates.

The largest ocean water carriers are Sea-Land Service, Evergreen Line, Maersk, Hanjin Shipping, and APL Limited. These companies utilize both container and general cargo ships. The container ships are very large; newer vessels are able to carry the equivalent of 6,000 twenty-foot containers.[19] Often, a carrier will form alliances with other ocean carriers to maximize market coverage and customer service levels.[20] See the Global box on the birth of containers.

Pipeline

Pipelines are able to transport only a limited number of products, including natural gas, crude oil, petroleum products, water, chemicals, and slurry products.[21] Natural gas and crude oil account for the majority of pipeline traffic. Oil pipelines transport approximately 18.4 percent of all domestic intercity freight traffic measured in ton-miles. In Europe and Japan, pipeline movements are relatively insignificant, although in the Commonwealth of Independent States (CIS), large amounts of product are moved using this form of transport.[22]

There are over 440,000 miles of intercity pipeline in the United States. The average length of haul is under 500 miles except for the 800-mile Trans-Alaska Pipeline System.[23] Pipelines offer the shipper an extremely high level of service dependability at a relatively low cost. Pipelines are able to deliver their product on time because of the following factors:

Characteristics of Pipeline Transportation

- The flows of products within the pipeline are monitored and controlled by computer.

- Losses and damages due to pipeline leaks or breaks are extremely rare.

- Climatic conditions have minimal effects on products moving in pipelines.

---

[18]Containers typically are 8 feet high, 8 feet wide, and of various lengths (e.g., 53 ft., 48 ft., 45 ft., 40 ft., 20 ft.) and are compatible conventional motor or rail equipment. A common transport statistic is the TEU, a 20-foot container equivalent.

[19]Robert J. Bowman, "Stormy Weather," *Distribution* 95, no. 8 (July 1996), pp. 72, 74.

[20]Toby B. Gooley, "Will Mega-Alliances Mean Mega-Benefits for Shippers?" *Logistics Management* 35, no. 5 (May 1996), pp. 65A–69A.

[21]Slurry is usually thought of as a solid product that is suspended in a liquid, often water, which can then be transported easily.

[22]*Statistical Abstract of the United States: 1995,* p. 626; O'Laughlin, Cooper, and Cabocel, *Reconfiguring European Logistics Systems,* p. 72.

[23]Donald F. Wood and James C. Johnson, *Contemporary Transportation,* 4th ed. (New York: Macmillan, 1993), pp. 147, 152.

Global

The Birth of Containers

On April 26, 1996, an anniversary of some significance occurred for Sea-Land Service Inc. The company marked the 40th anniversary of its first sailing—and with it the birth of containerization. On April 26, 1956, a small former tanker called the *Ideal X* set sail from Port Newark in New

York Harbor with containers on board, bound for Texas. Now a unit of CSX Transportation, Sea-Land is one of the largest containerized shipping companies in the world.

Source: "Management Update," *Logistics Management* 35, no. 6 (June 1996), p. 3.

TABLE 7–1   Estimated Distribution of Intercity Freight Ton-Miles in the United States

Mode	1993 (billions of ton-miles)	Percentage of Total 1993	1980	1960	1940
Rail	1,183	38%	38%	44%	61%
Motor	871	28	22	22	10
Air	12	<1	<1	<1	<1
Inland waterway	467	15	16	17	19
Oil pipeline	572	18	24	17	10
Total	3,105	100%	100%	100%	100%

Source: U.S. Bureau of the Census, *Statistical Abstract of the United States: 1995,* 115th ed. (Washington, DC: U.S. Government Printing Office, 1995), p. 626.

• Pipelines are not labor-intensive; therefore, strikes or employee absences have little effect on their operations.

The advantages in cost and dependability that pipelines have over other transport modes have stimulated shipper interest in moving other products by pipeline. Certainly, if a product is or can be in liquid, gas, or slurry form, it can be transported by pipeline. As the costs of other modes increase, shippers may give additional consideration to pipelines as a mode of transport for nontraditional products.

Each mode transports a large amount of freight, as shown in Tables 7–1 (United States) and 7–2 (Europe). The particular mode a shipper selects depends on the characteristics of the mode coupled with the needs of the company and its customers. Table 7–3 summarizes the economic and service characteristics of the five basic modes of transport.

TABLE 7–2   European Freight Movements (in Billion Ton-Kilometers)—1989

	Road[a]	Rail[b]	Inland Waterway[b]	Sea-going	Inland Pipeline
European Community					
Belgium	31.0[c]	8.0[c]	5.3	—	1.0
Denmark	9.2[c]	1.7	0	2.0[c]	1.6[c]
FR of Germany	124.2	60.0[c]	54.0	0.6[c]	8.8[c]
France	116.7	52.3[c]	7.0[c]	—	31.0[c]
Greece	12.5[c]	0.6[c]	0	—	—
Irish Republic	4.0[c]	0.6[c]	—	—	—
Italy	165.0[c]	20.0[c]	0.1	36.0[c]	9.0[c]
Luxembourg	0.2[c]	0.7	0.4	0	—
Netherlands	22.1[c]	3.1	36.0	—	4.6
Portugal	12.05[c]	1.7	—	—	—
Spain	143	11.9	—	28.0[c]	4.8[c]
United Kingdom	134.3	17.0	0.3	56.2	9.1
Other Europe					
Austria	8.0[c]	11.2[c]	1.8[c,d]	0	5.3
Czechoslovakia	23.8	72.0	4.8[d]	0	9.0[c]
German DR[f]	16.9	59.0	2.3	—	4.3
Hungary	13.4	19.8	2.1[d]	0	3.4
Sweden	22.6[c]	19.2	0	8.0[c]	—
Switzerland	7.5[c]	8.2	0.1	0	1.1
Yugoslavia	25.0[c,e]	25.9	8.8	—	3.4
Rest of the World					
Japan	260.0[c]	23.0[c]	0	2405	—
United States	1.200.0[c]	1,500.0[c]	550.0[c]	900.0[c]	9205
Soviet Republics	510.0[c]	4,000.0[c]	239.6	—	1,422

[a]In vehicles above a size threshold which (for EC countries) may not exceed 3.5 tons net or 6 tons gross vehicle weight.

[b]Carried by national and foreign vehicles.

[c]Estimated from previous years.

[d]Transport by national shipping undertaken at home and abroad.

[e]For hire and reward only.

[f]Now unified with the Federal Republic of Germany

Source: Kevin A. O'Laughlin, James Cooper, and Eric Cabocel, *Reconfiguring European Logistics Systems* (Oak Brook, IL: Council of Logistics Management, 1993), p. 72.

Third Parties

Third parties are companies similar to channel intermediaries that provide linkages between shippers and carriers. Often, third parties do not own transportation equipment themselves; instead, they partner with a number of carriers who provide the necessary equipment to transport their shipments. There are several types of third parties, including

TABLE 7–3   Comparison of U.S. Domestic Transportation Modes

	Motor	*Rail*	*Air*	*Water*	*Pipeline*
Economic Characteristics					
Cost	Moderate	Low	High	Low	Low
Market coverage	Point-to-point	Terminal-to-terminal	Terminal-to-terminal	Terminal-to-terminal	Terminal-to-terminal
Degree of competition (number of competitors)	Many	Few	Moderate	Few	Few
Predominant traffic	All types	Low–moderate value, moderate high density	High value, low–moderate density	Low value, high density	Low value, high density
Average length of haul (in miles)	515	617	885	376 to 1,367	276 to 343
Equipment capacity (tons)	10 to 25	50 to 12,000	5 to 125	1,000 to 60,000	30,000 to 2,500,000
Service Characteristics					
Speed (time-in-transit)	Moderate to fast	Moderate	Fast	Slow	Slow
Availability	High	Moderate	Moderate	Low	Low
Consistency (delivery time variability)	High	Moderate	High	Low to moderate	High
Loss and damage	Low	Moderate	Low	Low to moderate	Low
Flexibility (adjustment to shipper's needs)	High	Moderate	Moderate to high	Low to moderate	Low

transportation brokers, freight forwarders (domestic and foreign), shippers' associations or cooperatives, intermodal marketing companies (shippers' agents), and third-party logistics service providers.

Transportation Brokers.   **Transportation brokers** are companies that provide services to both shippers and carriers by arranging and coordinating the transportation of products. They charge a fee to do so, which usually is taken as a percentage of the revenue collected by the broker from the shipper. The broker in turn pays the carrier.[24]

Functions of Transportation Brokers

Shippers with minimal traffic support, or no traffic department at all, can use brokers to negotiate rates, oversee shipments, and do many of the things the shipper may not be able to do because of personnel or resource constraints. In these instances, the broker partially replaces some of the firm's own traffic department. The broker does not completely replace the traffic function; it merely assumes some of the transportation functions.

---

[24]James C. Johnson and Kenneth C. Schneider, "Licensed Transportation Brokers: Their Joys and Frustration," *Transportation Journal* 34, no. 4 (Summer 1995), pp. 38–51.

Small- and medium-sized shippers are the major users of transportation brokers, although larger firms utilize them in smaller markets.

Freight Forwarders.   **Freight forwarders** purchase transport services from various carriers, although in some instances they own the equipment themselves. For example, the most successful air freight forwarders typically purchase and operate their own equipment, rather than relying on other air carriers. Freight forwarders consolidate small shipments from a number of shippers into large shipments moving into a certain region at a lower rate. Because of consolidation efficiencies, these companies can offer shippers lower rates than the shippers could obtain directly from the carrier.[25] Often, the freight forwarder can provide faster and more complete service because they are able to tender larger volumes to the carrier.

Functions of Freight Forwarders

Freight forwarders can be classified as domestic or international, depending on whether they specialize in shipments within a country or between countries. They can be surface or air freight forwarders. If they are involved in international shipments, freight forwarders will provide documentation services, which is especially vital for firms with limited international marketing experience.

Often, freight forwarders and transportation brokers are viewed similarly, but there are important differences:

Differences between a Freight Forwarder and a Transportation Broker

- A forwarder is the shipper to a carrier and the carrier to a shipper.
- A broker is neither shipper nor carrier, but an intermediary between the two.
- A forwarder can arrange for transportation of freight by any mode.
- A broker can arrange for freight transportation only by a motor carrier.
- A forwarder is exempt from federal government oversight.
- A broker must be licensed by the Surface Transportation Board.
- A forwarder is primarily liable to a shipper for cargo loss and damage.
- A broker is not usually liable for cargo loss and damage, although many do provide this coverage.[26]

Shippers' Associations.   In their operations, shippers' associations are much like freight forwarders, but they differ in terms of perception by regulatory authorities. A shippers' association can be defined as a nonprofit cooperative that consolidates small shipments into truckload freight for member companies.

Functions of Shippers' Associations

Shippers' associations primarily utilize motor and rail carriers for transport. Because small shipments are much more expensive to transport (on a per pound or per unit basis) than large shipments, companies band together to lower their transportation costs through consolidation of many small shipments into one or more larger shipments. The members of the shippers' association realize service improvements.

Shippers' associations also can handle truckload shipments by purchasing large blocks of flatbed railcars at discount rates. They then fill the available railcars with the

---

[25]Consolidation refers to taking a number of small shipments and combining them into a single larger shipment.

[26]Mitchell E. MacDonald, "Broker vs. Forwarder," *Traffic Management* 31, no. 6 (June 1992), p. 62.

trailers on flatcars (TOFCs) of member companies. Both parties benefit as a result. Shippers are charged lower rates than they could get by themselves (shipping in smaller quantities), while the railroads realize better equipment utilization and the economies of large, direct-route piggyback trains.

Functions of IMCs

Intermodal Marketing Companies (or Shippers' Agents).   **Intermodal marketing companies (IMCs),** or shippers' agents, act much like shippers' associations or cooperatives. They specialize in providing piggyback services to shippers and are an important intermodal link between shippers and carriers. As the use of intermodal transportation increases in the future, shippers' agents will grow in importance as they purchase large quantities of TOFC/COFC services at discount and resell them in smaller quantities.

Third-Party Logistics Service Providers.   This sector is growing very rapidly. As illustrated in Box 7–2, Sears (mass merchandise retailer) and Menlo Logistics (third-party logistics service provider) have established a mutually beneficial relationship; Menlo provides significant transportation support for Sears LTL 1.2 billion pounds of freight annually.[27]

The Use of Third Parties Is Increasing

With the increasing emphasis on supply chain management, more companies are exploring the third-party option. For some firms, dealing with one third-party firm who will handle all or most of their freight offers a number of advantages, including the management of information by the third party, freeing the company from day-to-day interactions with carriers, and having the third party oversee hundreds or even thousands of shipments. Activities such as freight payment and dedicated contract carriage have been administered by third parties for many years. However, additional transportation and logistics activities are being outsourced. In some instances, some comapnies have outsourced large parts of their logistics operations to third parties.

Brokers, freight forwarders, shippers' associations, intermodal marketing companies, and third-party logistics service providers can be viable shipping options for a firm in the same way that the five basic modes and intermodal combinations can. The logistics executive must determine the optimal combination of transport alternatives for his or her company.

In addition to the preceding alternatives, many companies find that other transport forms can be used to distribute their products. Small-package carriers such as Federal Express (FedEx), United Parcel Service (UPS), and parcel post are important transporters of many time-sensitive products. These entities use a combination of transport modes, especially air. The U.S. domestic air freight market consists of 60 percent express, 25 percent passenger carriers, and 15 percent mail. The growth rate in this sector has been robust, averaging about 10 percent a year.[28]

---

[27]Thomas A. Foster, "How Sears Leverages Its LTL," *Distribution* 91, no. 9 (Sept. 1992), pp. 46, 49–50. For additional examples of the use of third parties, see James Aaron Cooke, "Third Time's a Charm!" *Logistics Management* 35, no. 3 (Mar. 1996), pp. 85–87; James Aaron Cooke, "Three 'Takes' on Third Party," *Logistics Management* 35, no. 5 (May 1996), pp. 53–55; and Toby B. Gooley, "Why GM Pushed Inbound Shipments Back Out the Door," *Traffic Management* 34, no. 6 (June 1995), pp. 49–52.

[28]John Bell, "Express Meets Time-Definite," *Distribution* 95, no. 8 (July 1996), p. 62.

Box 7–2

How Sears Leverages Its LTL Transportation

No shipper has embraced the third-party logistics concept more completely than Sears. In 1990, the merchandising giant spun off its own transportation and logistics operations as a separate company called Sears Logistics Services (SLS) to handle the needs of the Sears Merchandising Group and to take on other customers.

SLS in turn has contracted with third-parties to handle certain operations involved with warehousing, intermodal operations, customs brokerage, and, most recently, less-than-truckload (LTL) transportation.

This relationship with Menlo Logistics, a subsidiary of Consolidated Freightways (CF), is designed to handle about 1.2 billion pounds of LTL traffic each year from Sears 4,000 suppliers to SLS's network of distribution centers, and a limited amount of outbound LTL to Sears catalog stores throughout the country.

"Our overall transportation strategy is to leverage our freight to the density economics of a limited number of carriers," says Jim Comerford, vice president of transportation for SLS.

"We realized our problem was similar to what faced an LTL carrier with terminals all over the country," said Comerford. "Since major LTL carriers are adept at dealing with networks operating up to 200 to 300 terminals, we decided it made sense to talk to LTL-oriented companies to solve our problem."

Menlo won the bid and started planning with SLS in November 1991. Menlo started managing the LTL operations in December, and by January 6, 1992, Menlo was in full charge of managing all of Sears LTL movements from 4,000 vendors to SLS locations all over the country.

Menlo's primary function is to manage all LTL operations. The CF family of carriers handle the majority of the freight. CF MotorFreight receives about 58 percent. The four Con-Way carriers share approximately 29 percent. Twenty-one carriers not affiliated with CF handle about 13 percent of the LTL freight.

Menlo brings LTL vendor shipments to Sears' five catalog merchandise centers (CMCs) and eight retail replenishment centers (RRCs) as well as selected outbound movement from SLS's 46 cross-docking centers (CDCs) to remote areas.

"It is their responsibility to get the best rate on the lane and to determine which carrier will handle what freight,"

says Comerford. Menlo's financial success depends on its getting the best rates, because it earns its money in this partnership by performing as a property broker licensed by the Interstate Commerce Commission. Menlo receives payment from SLS and pays the carriers. Anything left over is revenue for Menlo. Menlo has four people at SLS headquarters in Itasca, Illinois, running the LTL operations.

The Menlo partnership results in a number of operational advantages for SLS, as shown below.

Twelve Ways SLS and Menlo Improve Logistics Performance

1. Increase land density by adjusting vendor shipping schedules.
2. Improve vendor packaging and shipping characteristics.
3. Find ways to avoid accessorial charges; that is, additional charges of carriers for services such as box car loading/unloading, transit stop-off, inspection, repackaging, etc.
4. Produce videotapes to teach SLS employees how to handle outbound loading better.
5. Train carrier employees so they know how to deal with SLS.
6. Use CF imaging technology to prepare proof of deliveries and handle claims.
7. Use EDI to create a paperless environment.
8. Have Menlo review Hazmat documentation to comply with all regulations without overdocumenting shipments.
9. Adjust SLS shipping zones to the operating boundaries of CF MotorFreight to improve efficiency of serving vendors.
10. Have Menlo help SLS inventory and dispose of trailers no longer needed for the terminal freight handling operation.
11. Gain carriers' commitment to stage trailers at RRCs.
12. Develop compatible logistics programs with large vendors unwilling to participate in Sears' freight collect program.

Source: Thomas A. Foster, "How Sears Leverages Its LTL," *Distribution* 91, no. 9 (Sept. 1992), pp. 46, 49–50.

Small-Package Carriers

For companies such as electronics firms, catalog merchandisers, cosmetic companies, and textbook distributors, small-package carriers can be important transportation options. During 1995, six million shipments were sent by means of small-package carriers. Growth rates for this transport sector are expected to average 10 to 15 percent per year.[29]

Shipping with the U.S. Postal Service

Parcel Post.   The U.S. Postal Service provides both surface and air parcel post services to companies shipping small packages. The advantages of parcel post are low cost and wide geographical coverage, both domestically and internationally. Disadvantages include specific size and weight limitations, variability in transit time, higher loss and damage ratios than other forms of shipment, and inconvenience because packages must be prepaid and deposited at a postal facility. Mail-order houses are probably the most extensive users of parcel post service.

Federal Express Transports 2.2 Million Packages Every Day

Air Express Companies.   Characterized by high levels of customer service, the air express industry has significantly expanded since its inception in 1973. The Federal Express Corporation, one of the best-known examples of an air express company, illustrates how the concept of supplying rapid transit with very high consistency has paid off. In 1995, FedEx had worldwide revenues of $9.4 billion (profits of $298 million). This represented 2.2 million daily express packages, transported on 496 aircraft, and supported by 35,900 vehicles and more than 94,000 employees.[30] Because some firms need to transport certain products quickly, the air express industry is able to offer overnight (or second day) delivery of small parcels to many locations throughout the world.

Many carriers have experienced a drop in order quantities as their customers aim to reduce inventory by ordering more frequently and in smaller quantities. This has increased the demand for air express–type services.[31] Competition is fierce among the "giants" of the industry, including FedEx, UPS, TNT Worldwide, Airborne Express, and DHL Airways.[32] As long as there is a need to transport products quickly and with very high levels of consistency, the air express companies will continue to provide a valuable service for many shippers.

Intermodal Services

In addition to the five basic modes of transport, a number of intermodal combinations are available to the shipper. The more popular combinations are trailer-on-flatcar (TOFC) and container-on-flatcar (COFC). Intermodal movements combine the cost and/or service advantages of two or more modes in a single product movement.

---

[29]John Bell, "Expanding a Small World," *Distribution* 95, no. 8 (July 1996), p. 56.

[30]Federal Express, *1995 Annual Report,* p. 1.

[31]Helen L. Richardson, "Will Shrinking Shipments Shrink Profits?" *Transportation and Distribution* 36, no. 3 (Mar. 1995), p. 45.

[32]See Brian P. Analla and Marilyn M. Helms, "Worldwide Express Small Package Industry," *Transportation Quarterly* 50, no. 1 (Winter 1996), pp. 51–64; and "FedEx, UPS Set Sights on LTL Freight," *Logistics Management* 35, no. 6 (June 1996), pp. 45–47.

A truck chassis is positioned to receive a container from a doublestack train in Chicago, Illinois. The truck can move the cargo directly to a retail store or other user.

Piggyback (TOFC/COFC).   In piggyback service, a motor carrier trailer or a container is placed on a rail flatcar and transported from one terminal to another. Axles can be placed under the containers, so they can be delivered by a truck. At the terminal facilities, motor carriers perform the pickup and delivery functions. Piggyback service thus combines the low cost of long-haul rail movement with the flexibility and convenience of truck movement.

Since 1976 shippers have increased their use of piggyback service by 200 percent. In 1994 there were 8.1 million intermodal shipments, with 1995 and 1996 shipments approximating the same levels.[33] Figure 7–2 shows the shift in freight between highway and intermodal traffic.

Truck and rail partnerships to support intermodalism, such as the one begun in 1989 between the Santa Fe Railroad and J. B. Hunt Transportation Services, are relatively common.[34] The railroad carries freight on the long haul, and the trucking company picks up and delivers between the customer and railroad. Seventy-seven percent of intermodal users agree that such alliances have a positive impact on transportation options available to them.[35]

---

[33]Robert J. Bowman, "Hitting the Wall," *Distribution* 95, no. 8 (July 1996), p. 52.

[34]Mitchell E. MacDonald, "Intermodal Battles a Perception Problem," *Traffic Management* 29, no. 5 (May 1990), p. 32.

[35]Martha Spizziri, "Intermodal Overcomes the Obstacles," *Traffic Management* 33, no. 4 (Apr. 1994), pp. 39–42.

FIGURE 7–2

Freight shift to intermodal transportation

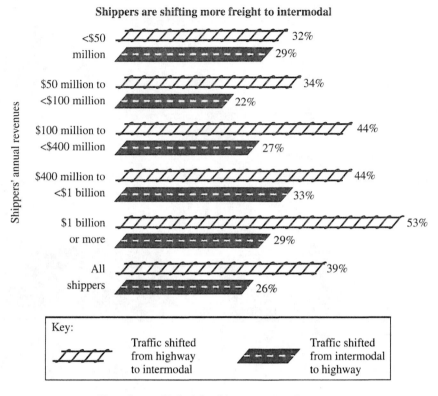

Shippers are shifting more freight to intermodal

<$50 million — 32% / 29%

$50 million to <$100 million — 34% / 22%

$100 million to <$400 million — 44% / 27%

$400 million to <$1 billion — 44% / 33%

$1 billion or more — 53% / 29%

All shippers — 39% / 26%

Shippers' annual revenues

Key:

Traffic shifted from highway to intermodal

Traffic shifted from intermodal to highway

More than a third of the shippers *surveyed diverted freight from highway to intermodal in 1993.*

Source: Adapted from Martha Spizziri, "Intermodal Overcomes the Obstacles," *Traffic Management,* 33, no. 3 (Apr. 1994), p. 39.

Roadrailers

Roadrailers.   An innovative intermodal concept was introduced in the late 1970s. **Roadrailers,** or trailertrains as they are sometimes called, combine motor and rail transport in a single piece of equipment. As shown in Figure 7–3, the roadrailer resembles a conventional motor carrier (truck) trailer. However, the trailer has both rubber truck tires and steel rail wheels. Over highways, tractor power units transport the trailers in the normal way, but instead of placing the trailer on a flatcar for rail movement, the wheels of the trailer are retracted and the trailer rides directly on the rail tracks.

The advantages of this intermodal form of transport are that rail flatcars are not required and that the switching time to change wheels on the trailer is less than loading and unloading the trailer from the flatcar. The major disadvantages of roadrailers are the added weight of the rail wheels, which reduces fuel efficiency and results in higher movement costs in addition to the higher cost of the equipment. The disadvantages have tended to outweigh the advantages, resulting in very low usage of this intermodal option. If technology improvements can reduce the cost of this transport option, usage is likely to increase.

FIGURE 7–3

Selected forms of intermodal transportation

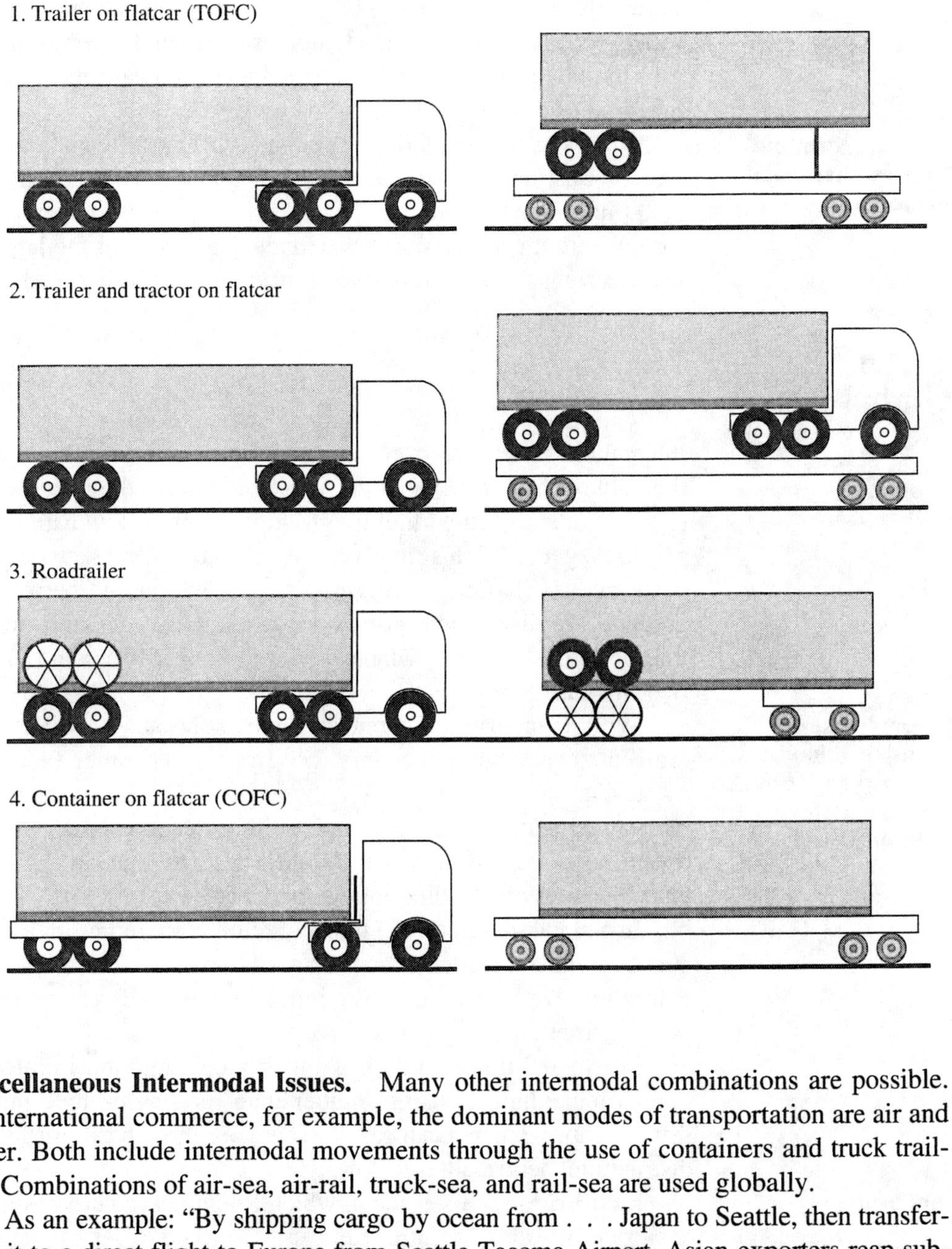

1. Trailer on flatcar (TOFC)

2. Trailer and tractor on flatcar

3. Roadrailer

4. Container on flatcar (COFC)

Miscellaneous Intermodal Issues.   Many other intermodal combinations are possible. In international commerce, for example, the dominant modes of transportation are air and water. Both include intermodal movements through the use of containers and truck trailers. Combinations of air-sea, air-rail, truck-sea, and rail-sea are used globally.

As an example: "By shipping cargo by ocean from . . . Japan to Seattle, then transferring it to a direct flight to Europe from Seattle-Tacoma Airport, Asian exporters reap substantial benefits. They can cut their transit times from 30 days for all-water service to about 14 days, and slash freight costs by up to 50 percent compared with all-air service."[36]

---

[36]Toby B. Gooley, "Air Freight Hits the Rails," *Logistics Management* 35, no. 3 (Mar. 1996), p. 112A.

Between 1980 and 1995, intermodal freight movements increased steadily, often at double-digit growth rates.[37] While that growth rate has now plateaued, intermodal movements by carriers and intermodal marketing companies (IMCs) continue to be important means of transporting products domestically and internationally. While overall industry growth may have stabilized, many shippers and carriers are exploring expanded usage of this form of transport.

Briggs & Stratton Utilizes Intermodal Transport

Briggs & Stratton Corporation, a $1 billion Milwaukee-based manufacturer of internal combustion engines used in lawn tractors, mowers, and other equipment, exports 2,000 intermodal containers a year. The company makes just-in-time deliveries to Europe, where it competes against Honda. Because intermodal service has become more reliable, Briggs & Stratton is able to meet tight delivery schedules.[38]

Global Issues

International freight transportation can involve any of the five basic modes of transportation, although air and water carriage are perhaps the most important. Motor and rail carriage are the most important freight movements *within* nations.

Managers of firms involved in international markets must be aware of the services, costs, and availability of transport modes within and between the countries where their products are distributed. For example, air and water transportation directly compete for transoceanic shipments. Management must consider many factors when it compares the two alternatives.

International Transportation Is More Expensive Than Domestic Transportation

Within countries, differences can exist because of taxes, subsidies, regulations, government ownership of carriers, geography, and other factors. Because of government ownership or subsidies to railroads in Europe, rail service benefits from newer or better maintained equipment, track, and facilities. Japan and Europe utilize water carriage to a much larger degree than the United States or Canada due to the length and favorable characteristics of coastlines and inland waterways.

In general, international transportation costs represent a much higher fraction of merchandise value than domestic transportation costs. This is primarily due to the longer distances involved, administrative requirements, and related paperwork that must accompany international shipments.[39]

Intermodal transportation is much more common in international movements. Even though rehandling costs are higher than for single-mode movements, cost savings and service improvements can result. There are three basic forms of international intermodal distribution, described as follows:

Landbridge

Landbridge is a service in which foreign cargo crosses a country en route to another country. For example, European cargo en route to Japan may be shipped by ocean to the

---

[37]Peter Bradley, "Intermodal Falls Off the Fast Tract," *Traffic Management* 35, no. 2 (Feb. 1996), p. 26.

[38]"Special Report: Think Global, Go International," *International Business* 6, no. 3 (Mar. 1993), p. 61.

[39]Paul S. Bender, "International Logistics," in *The Distribution Management Handbook,* ed. James A. Tompkins and Dale Harmelink (New York: McGraw-Hill, Inc., 1994), pp. 8.5–8.6.

Figure 7–4

International distribution shipping options

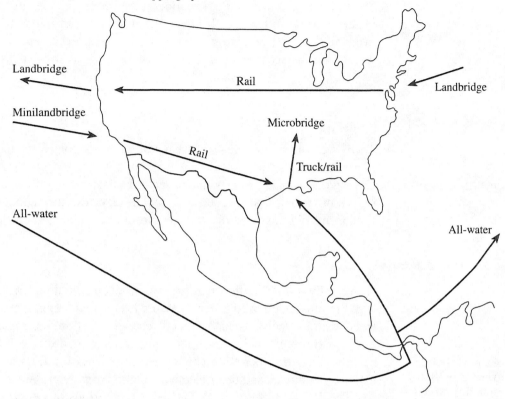

Source: David L. Anderson, "International Logistics Strategies for the Eighties," *Proceedings of the Twenty-Second Annual Conference of the National Council of Physical Distribution Management,* 1984, p. 363. Used by permission of the Council of Logistics Management.

East Coast of the United States, then moved by rail to the West Coast, and from there shipped by ocean to Japan.

Minilandbridge   **Minilandbridge (MLB)** (also called *minibridge*) is a special case of landbridge, where foreign cargo originates or terminates at a point within the United States.

Microbridge   **Microbridge** is a relatively new service being provided by ports on the West Coast. In contrast with minibridge, this service provides door-to-door rather than port-to-port transportation. The big advantage of microbridge is that it provides a combined rate, including rail and ocean transportation, in a single tariff that is lower than the sum of the separate rates (see Figure 7–4).[40]

A comparison of single-mode and intermodal movements between the Far East and the U.S. East Coast demonstrates the advantages of the latter. If we compare an all-water movement with a minilandbridge movement for comparable shipments, the costs are

[40]Paul S. Bender, "The International Dimension of Physical Distribution Management," in *The Distribution Handbook,* ed. James A. Robeson and Robert G. House (New York: Free Press, 1985), pp. 791–92.

approximately the same. But MLB is significantly faster, thus offering the opportunity to reduce order cycle times and to improve customer service levels.

In making traffic and transportation decisions, the logistics manager must know and understand the differences between the domestic and international marketplace. Modal availability, rates, regulatory restrictions, service levels, and other aspects of the transportation mix may vary significantly from one market to another.

Regulatory Issues

There are two major areas of transportation regulation: economic and safety. All freight movements are subject to safety regulation, but not all are subject to economic regulation. The regulation of the transportation sector has had an enormous impact on the logistics activities of carriers and shippers. We will briefly describe economic and safety regulation, legal forms of transportation, and the impact of deregulation on shippers and carriers.

Forms of Regulation

Transportation Is Governed by Both Economic and Safety Regulations

Historically, transportation regulation has developed along two lines. The first, and perhaps the most publicized in recent years, is *economic* regulation. Economic regulation affects business decisions such as mode/carrier selection, rates charged by carriers, service levels, and routing and scheduling. *Safety* regulation deals with labor standards, working conditions for transportation employees, shipment of hazardous materials, vehicle maintenance, insurance, and other elements relating to public safety.

The 1970s, 1980s, and 1990s have been periods of **deregulation** in North America, Europe, and elsewhere throughout the world. At the same time, safety regulation has been increasing in terms of its scope and breadth. In the United States, all transport modes are regulated (economic and safety) by the Department of Transportation (DOT) and are subject to a variety of laws such as the Occupational Safety and Health Act (OSHA) of 1970, the Hazardous Materials Transportation Uniform Safety Act (1990), and the National Environmental Policy Act (1969). An important part of the responsibilities of a logistics or transportation executive is to keep abreast of regulatory changes because of their potential impact on the firm's operations.

U.S. Transportation Modes Have Mostly Been Deregulated

In recent years, the role of various U.S. transportation agencies in administering the regulatory environment has changed. Since the early 1970s, the trend has been toward decreasing economic regulation of transportation. Four of the five basic modes of transport have been deregulated at the federal level.

Transportation is also regulated at the state level. It is beyond the scope of this book to examine the myriad of state regulations that exist, but carriers and shippers must be familiar with all regulations in states where they operate.

Legally Defined Forms of Transportation

In addition to classifying alternative forms of transportation by mode, carriers can be classified on the basis of the four legal forms: common, contract, exempt, and private carriers. The first three forms are for-hire carriers, and the last is owned by a shipper. **For-hire carriers** transport freight belonging to others and are subject to various federal, state, and local statutes and regulations. For the most part, private carriers transport their own goods and supplies in their own equipment and are exempt from most regulations, except for those dealing with safety and taxation.

Deregulation has reshaped how logistics executives view the transport modes, particularly the legal forms of transportation. In principle, these legal designations no longer exist because of deregulation. For example, the distinction between common and contract motor carriers was eliminated by the Trucking Industry Regulatory Reform Act of 1994 (TIRRA). However, the terms are used within the industry and do provide some guidance with respect to transportation type.

Common Carriers

Common Carriers. **Common carriers** offer their services to any shipper to transport products, at published rates, between designated points. To operate legally, they must be granted authority from the appropriate federal regulatory agency. With deregulation, common carriers have significant flexibility with respect to market entry, routing, and pricing. Common carriers must offer their services to the general public on a nondiscriminatory basis; that is, they must serve all shippers of the commodities which their equipment can feasibly carry. A significant problem facing common carriers is that the number of customers cannot be predicted with certainty in advance. Thus, future demand is uncertain. The result has been that many common carriers have entered into contract carriage.

Contract Carriers

Contract Carriers. A **contract carrier** is a for-hire carrier that does not hold itself out to serve the general public; instead, it serves a limited number of shippers under specific contractual arrangements. The contract between the shipper and the carrier requires the carrier to provide a specified transportation service at a specified cost. In most instances, contract rates are lower than common carrier rates because the carrier is transporting commodities it prefers to carry for cost and efficiency reasons. An advantage is that transport demand is known in advance.

Exempt Carriers

Exempt Carriers. An **exempt carrier** is a for-hire carrier that transports certain products such as unprocessed agricultural and related products (e.g., farm supplies, livestock, fish, poultry, and agricultural seeds). Carriers of newspapers also are given exempt status. The exempt status was originally established to allow farmers to transport their products using public roads; however, it has been extended to a wider range of products transported by a variety of modes. In addition, local cartage firms operating in a municipality or a "commercial zone" surrounding a municipality are exempt.

Generally, exempt carrier rates are lower than common or contract carriage rates. Because very few commodities are given exempt status, the exempt carrier is not a viable form of transport for most companies. In reality, because transportation deregulation has eliminated pricing regulations, almost all carriers can be considered exempt from pricing restrictions.

Private Carriers

Private Carriers. A **private carrier** is generally not for-hire and is not subject to federal economic regulation. Private carriage means that a firm is providing transportation primarily for its own products. As a result, the company must own or lease the transport equipment and operate its own facilities. From a legal standpoint, the most important factor distinguishing private carriage from for-hire carriers is the restriction that the transportation activity must be incidental to the primary business of the firm.

Private carriage has had an advantage over other carriers because of its flexibility and economy. The major advantages of private carriage have been related to cost and service. With deregulation, common and contract carriage can often provide excellent service levels at reasonable costs. Later in this chapter, we will examine the private versus for-hire transportation decision and discuss more fully the pros and cons of private carriage.

Impact of Deregulation

Economic Deregulation Has Been the Trend

The degree to which the transportation sector has been regulated has varied over the years. Since 1977, the trend in the United States has been toward less economic regulation. Airlines were the first transport mode to be extensively deregulated, with the amendment of the Federal Aviation Act in 1977 followed by the passage of the Airline Deregulation Act of 1978. Railroads and motor carriers were next, with the passage of the Staggers Rail Act and the Motor Carrier Act, both in 1980. In 1984, the Shipping Act partially deregulated ocean cargo carriers. Further deregulation occurred through the Negotiated Rates Act of 1993, Trucking Industry Regulatory Reform Act (TIRRA) of 1994, Federal Aviation Administration Authorization Act of 1994 (including Section 601 that affected motor carriers), and the ICC Termination Act of 1995.

Deregulation of the major transportation modes has had a significant impact on motor, rail, air, and water carriers, and the shippers who use their services. Freight transportation has moved into a new age. The next decade promises to be an exciting time for carriers and shippers. We will begin by examining the motor carrier industry.

Motor Carrier Act of 1980

Motor.   The Motor Carrier Act of 1980 substantially reduced the amount of economic regulation of interstate trucking. The act specifically addressed restrictions on market entry, routing, *intercorporate* hauling, contract carriage, rates, and transportation brokers.

As a result of this legislation, motor carriers have had to be cost-efficient in order to survive. For example, in the less-than truckload (LTL) market between 1980 and 1989, approximately one-half of the largest motor carriers declared bankruptcy. The shakeout of unprofitable and inefficient motor carriers that characterized the first 10 years after deregulation (1980–1989) has passed and, since 1990, the motor carrier industry has exhibited much more stability.

As a by-product of a more competitive environment, there have been significant developments in the offerings of rates and services. Rates for truckload (TL) and LTL have declined since 1984. Energy costs and other factors may cause these rates to increase, but the trend will likely continue downward (or perhaps stabilize) over the long term. Deregulation removed constraints on motor carriers' product, service, and price offerings, and new price and service trade-offs emerged. As mentioned previously, significant additional deregulation has occurred during the 1990s.

Let's look more closely at this legislation.

Warehousing

Chapter Outline

Chapter Objectives

- To show why warehousing is important in the logistics system.
- To identify the major types or forms of warehousing.
- To examine the primary functions of warehousing.
- To compare public and private warehousing from a financial perspective.
- To identify the factors that affect the size and number of warehouses.
- To examine the warehouse site selection decision from macro- and microperspectives.
- To describe the factors that affect warehouse layout and design.
- To describe global warehousing issues.
- To provide an overview of the importance of productivity and accounting/control issues in warehouse management.

Introduction

Warehousing Links Producers and Customers

Warehousing is an integral part of every logistics system. There are an estimated 750,000 warehouse facilities worldwide, including state-of-the-art, professionally managed warehouses, as well as company stockrooms, garages, self-store facilities, and even garden sheds.[1] Warehousing plays a vital role in providing a desired level of customer service at the lowest possible total cost (see Figure 8–1). Warehousing activity is an important link between the producer and the customer. Over the years, warehousing has developed from a relatively minor facet of a firm's logistics system to one of its most important functions.

We can define **warehousing** as that part of a firm's logistics system that stores products (raw materials, parts, goods-in-process, finished goods) at and between point of origin and point of consumption, and provides information to management on the status, condition, and disposition of items being stored. The term **distribution center (DC)** is sometimes used, but the terms are not identical. **Warehouse** is the more generic term.

Warehouses and Distribution Centers Are Not the Same

Warehouses store all products, DCs hold minimum inventories and predominantly high-demand items. Warehouses handle most products in four cycles [receive, store, ship, and pick], DCs handle most products in two: receive and ship. Warehouses perform a minimum of value-added activity, DCs perform a high percentage of value adding, including possible final assembly. Warehouses collect data in batches, DCs collect data in real-time. Warehouses focus on minimizing the operating cost to meet shipping requirements, DCs focus on maximizing the profit impact of meeting customer delivery requirements.[2]

With an increasing interest in improving inventory turns and reducing time to market, the role of distribution increasingly focuses on filling orders rapidly and efficiently.

Effective warehouse management involves a thorough understanding of the functions of warehousing, the merits of public versus private warehousing, and the financial and service aspects of warehousing decisions. Managers need knowledge of the methods that can improve warehousing performance and a strategy for locating warehousing facilities at optimal locations.

Strategic versus Operational Warehousing Decisions

Warehousing decisions may be strategic or operational. *Strategic* decisions deal with the allocation of logistics resources over an extended time in a manner consistent and supportive of overall enterprise policies and objectives. They can take either long-range or project-type forms.

An example of a long-range strategic decision is the choice of a logistics system design. A project-type decision might deal with consolidation of branch warehouses into a regional distribution center. Other examples of typical strategic questions include the following:

- Should warehousing be owned, leased, rented, or some combination of these?
- Should the warehousing functions be "spun off"; that is, contracted out to a third-party provider?
- Should the company install new materials handling equipment or continue to hire more labor?

---

[1]Richard J. Sherman, "The Warehouse Systems Market: Fragmented or Segmented?" *The Report on Supply Chain Management,* June 1996, p. 3.

[2]Richard L. Dawe, "Reengineer Warehousing," *Transportation and Distribution* 36, no. 1 (Jan. 1995), p. 102.

FIGURE 8–1

Cost trade-offs required in a logistics system

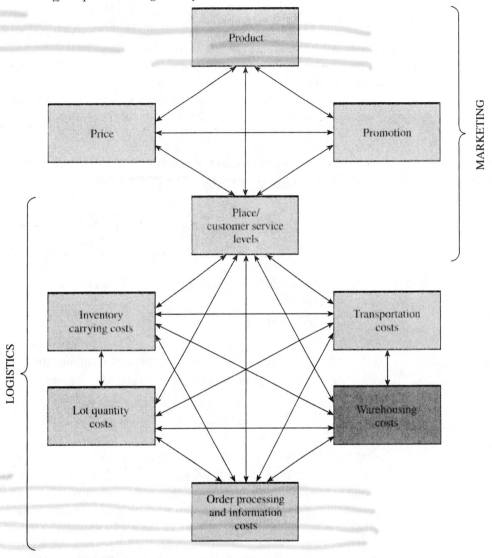

Marketing objective: Allocate resources to the marketing mix to maximize the long-run profitability of the firm.
Logistics objective: Minimize total costs given the customer service objective where Total costs = Transportation costs + Warehousing costs + Order processing and information costs + Lot quantity costs + Inventory carrying costs.

Source: Adapted from Douglas M. Lambert, *The Development of an Inventory Costing Methodology: A Study of the Costs Associated with Holding Inventory* (Chicago, IL: National Council of Physical Distribution Management, 1976), p. 7.

Operational decisions are used to manage or control logistics performance. Typically, these decisions are routine in nature and involve time spans of one year or less. They relate to the coordination and performance of the logistics system. For example, a warehouse manager would be concerned with how to best utilize labor in the shipping department. Due to the short time horizon involved, these decisions have more certainty than strategic decisions.

Nature and Importance of Warehousing

Warehousing has traditionally provided storage of products (referred to as inventory) during all phases of the logistics process. Two basic types of inventories can be placed into storage: (1) raw materials, components, and parts (physical supply); and (2) finished goods (physical distribution). Also, there may be inventories of goods-in-process and materials to be disposed of or recycled, although in most firms these constitute only a small portion of total inventories.

Why do companies hold inventories in storage? Traditionally, the warehousing of products has occured for one or more of the following reasons:

Why Should a Firm Have Inventories?

1. Achieve transportation economies.
2. Achieve production economies.
3. Take advantage of quantity purchase discounts and forward buys.
4. Maintain a source of supply.
5. Support the firm's customer service policies.
6. Meet changing market conditions (e.g., seasonality, demand fluctuations, competition).
7. Overcome the time and space differentials that exist between producers and consumers.
8. Accomplish least total cost logistics commensurate with a desired level of customer service.
9. Support the just-in-time programs of suppliers and customers.
10. Provide customers with a mix of products instead of a single product on each order.
11. Provide temporary storage of materials to be disposed of or recycled (i.e., reverse logistics).

Several Uses of Warehousing.   Figure 8–2 identifies some of the uses of warehousing in both the physical supply and physical distribution systems. Warehouses can be used to support manufacturing, to mix products from multiple production facilities for shipment to a single customer, to breakbulk or subdivide a large shipment of product into many smaller shipments to satisfy the needs of many customers, and to combine or consolidate a number of small shipments into a single higher-volume shipment.[3]

Warehousing is used increasingly as a "flow-through" point rather than a "holding" point, or even bypassed (e.g., scheduled deliveries direct to customers), as organizations increasingly substitute information for inventory, purchase smaller quantities, and use warehouses as "consolidation points" to receive purchased transportation rates and service levels.

Pull versus Push Systems in Warehousing

The traditional method [of distribution] is a push system. Production plans are based on capabilities and capacities of the plant, and product is produced in the expectation that it will sell. When it is produced faster than it can be sold, it is stockpiled at plant warehouses. If sales cannot be accelerated, then the plant will be slowed down until supply moves into balance with

---

[3]An exhaustive listing of logistics definitions is given in Joseph L. Cavinato, ed., *Transportation-Logistics Dictionary,* 3rd ed. (Washington, DC: International Thomson Transport Press, 1989).

FIGURE 8–2

Uses of warehousing in physical supply and physical distribution

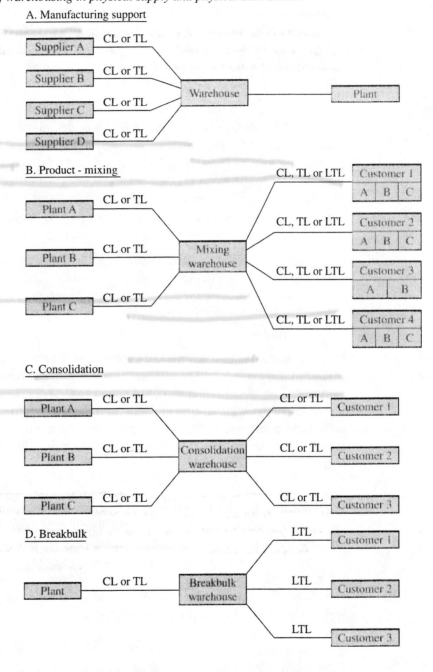

A. Manufacturing support

B. Product - mixing

C. Consolidation

D. Breakbulk

demand. In this system, warehousing serves to absorb excess production. Today's pull system depends on information. It is based on a constant monitoring of demand. . . . With a pull system, there is no need for a reservoir. Instead, the warehouse serves as a flow-through center, offering improved service by positioning inventory closer to the customer.[4]

---

[4]Kenneth B. Ackerman, "Push versus Pull," *Warehousing Forum* 11, no. 7 (June 1996), p. 3.

LTL—less than truckload

Manufacturing Support.   In supporting manufacturing operations, warehouses often play the important role of inbound consolidation points for the receipt of shipments from suppliers. As shown in Figure 8–2, part A, firms order raw materials, parts, components, or supplies from various suppliers, who ship truckload (TL) or carload (CL) quantities to a warehouse located in close proximity to the plant. Items are transferred from the warehouse to the manufacturing plant(s).

Product Mixing

Product Mixing.   From a physical distribution or outbound perspective, warehouses can be used for product mixing, outbound consolidation, or breakbulk. Product mixing (see Figure 8–2, part B) often involves multiple plant locations (e.g., plant A, plant B, and plant C) that ship products (e.g., products A, B, and C) to a central warehouse. Each plant manufactures only a portion of the total product offering of the firm. Shipments are usually made in large quantities (TL or CL) to the central warehouse, where customer orders for multiple products are combined or mixed for shipment.

**Outbound
Consolidation**

Consolidation.   When a warehouse is used for outbound consolidation (see Figure 8–2, part C), TL or CL shipments are made to a central facility from a number of manufacturing locations. The warehouse consolidates or combines products from the various plants into a single shipment to the customer.

**Breakbulk
Warehouses**

Breakbulk.   Breakbulk warehouses (see Figure 8–2, part D) are facilities that receive large shipments of product from manufacturing plants. Several customer orders are combined into a single shipment from the plants to the breakbulk warehouse. When the shipment is received at the warehouse, it is broken down into smaller LTL shipments which are sent to customers in the geographical area served by the warehouse. As illustrated in Box 8–1, breakbulk operations are sometimes carried out by using transportation innovations rather than warehousing.

**Relationships
between
Warehousing and
Transportation**

Warehousing and Transportation.   Transportation economies are possible for both the physical supply system and the physical distribution system. In the case of physical supply, small orders from a number of suppliers may be shipped to a consolidation warehouse near the source of supply; in this way, the producer can achieve a TL or CL shipment to the plant, which normally is situated at a considerably greater distance from the warehouse. The warehouse is located near the sources of supply so that the LTL rates apply only to a short haul, and the volume rate is used for the long haul from the warehouse to the plant.

Warehouses are used to achieve similar transportation savings in the physical distribution system. In the packaged goods industry, manufacturers often have multiple plant locations, with each plant manufacturing only a portion of the company's product line. Such plants are often referred to as *focused factories.*

Usually, these companies maintain a number of **field warehouse** locations from which mixed shipments of the entire product line can be made to customers. Shipments

---
Box 8–1

Warehousing in the High-Fashion Goods Industry

Fashion is a very perishable commodity . . . a hot-selling fashion item is a loser . . . unless it is on the selling floor precisely when it is most in fashion. In some cases, that can be as little as 7 to 10 days.

Saks Fifth Avenue operates 69 stores served by two distribution centers. One is in Yonkers, New York, close to Saks's flagship store on New York City's Fifth Avenue. The second is in Ontario, California, well situated to serve the trendy Southern California market.

Neither of these operations is in any sense a warehouse . . . Items generally move through these centers on a 24-hour turnaround. There is an emphatic realization . . . that every hour that a rack of $800 dresses sits in a distribution center can represent a lost sale and lost profit.

Speedy transit starts at the beginning of the pipeline. About 80 percent of Saks's imported items move into one of these centers by air freight. Imports move to one of the distribution centers based on the region where they originate: Yonkers handles the European imports and Ontario covers the Far East.

Items are exchanged between the two centers by air freight, with a dedicated flight in each direction between New York and Los Angeles every business day.

The distribution centers then serve their local stores with a combination of air freight and trucking.

Source: Bruce Vail, "Logistics, Fifth Avenue Style," *American Shipper* 36, no. 8 (Aug. 1994), p. 49.

---

from plants to field warehouses are frequently made by rail in full carload quantities of the products manufactured at each plant. Orders for customers, comprised of various items in the product line, are shipped by truck at TL or LTL rates. The use of field warehouses results in lower transportation costs than direct shipments to customers. Savings are often significantly larger than the increased costs resulting from warehousing and the associated increase in inventory carrying costs.

Relationships between Warehousing and Production

Warehousing and Production.   Short production runs minimize the amount of inventory held throughout the logistics system by producing quantities near to current demand, but they carry increased costs of setups and line changes.[5] If a plant is operating near or at capacity, frequent line changes may leave the manufacturer unable to meet product demand. If so, the cost of lost sales—the lost contribution to profit on unrealized sales—could be substantial.

On the other hand, the production of large quantities of product for each line change results in a lower per unit cost on a full-cost basis and more units for a given plant capacity. However, long production runs lead to larger inventories and increased warehouse requirements. Consequently, production cost savings must be balanced with increased logistics costs in order to achieve least total cost.

---

[5]These costs can vary widely and depend on the level of technology employed in the manufacturing process. Newer, high-tech production equipment can be changed from one product to another with little downtime and very little cost.

Traditionally, warehousing was necessary if a company was to take advantage of quantity purchase discounts on raw materials or other products. Not only is the per unit price lower as a result of the discount, but if the company pays the freight, transportation costs will be less on a volume purchase because of transportation economies. Similar discounts and savings can accrue to manufacturers, retailers, and wholesalers. Once again, however, those savings must be weighed against the added inventory costs incurred as a result of larger inventories.

Increasingly, companies operating with a JIT manufacturing philosophy are negotiating with their suppliers to receive cumulative quantity discounts. Thus, they receive the lower rate based on total yearly order volume rather than individual order size.

Holding inventories in warehouses may be necessary to maintain a source of supply. For example, the timing and quantity of purchases is important in retaining suppliers, especially during periods of shortages. It may be necessary to hold an inventory of items that are in short supply as a result of damage in transit, vendor stockouts, or a strike against one of the company's suppliers.

Warehousing and Customer Service

Warehousing and Customer Service.   Customer service policies, such as a 24-hour delivery standard, may require a number of field warehouses in order to minimize total costs while achieving the standard. Changing market conditions may make it necessary to warehouse product in the field, primarily because companies are unable to accurately predict consumer demand and the timing of retailer or wholesaler orders. By keeping some excess inventory in field warehouse locations, companies can respond quickly to meet unexpected demand. In addition, excess inventory allows manufacturers to fill customer orders when shipments to restock the field warehouses arrive late.

Warehousing and Least Total Cost Logistics

Warehousing and Least Total Cost Logistics.   The majority of firms utilize warehousing to accomplish least total cost logistics at some prescribed level of customer service, considering the trade-offs shown in Figure 8–1. Factors that influence a firm's warehousing policies include:

- The industry.
- The firm's philosophy.
- Capital availability.
- Product characteristics such as size, perishability, product lines, substitutability, and obsolescence rates.
- Economic conditions.
- Competition.
- Seasonality of demand.
- Use of just-in-time programs.
- Production process in use.[6]

[6]For a discussion of many of the changes taking place in business which are affecting the roles of warehousing in logistics, see Kenneth B. Ackerman, "21st Century Business Theory and Warehouse Operations," *Warehousing Forum* 10, no. 6 (May 1995), pp. 1–2; and "Warehousing: Coping with the Challenge of Change," *Modern Materials Handling* 50, no. 6 (May 1995), pp. 12–13.

Types of Warehousing

In general, firms have a number of warehousing alternatives. Some companies may market products directly to retail customers (called **direct store delivery**), thereby eliminating warehousing in the field. Mail-order catalog companies, for example, utilize warehousing only at a point of origin, such as sales headquarters or plant.

Cross-Docking

Cross-Docking.   Another alternative is to utilize cross-docking concepts, whereby warehouses serve primarily as "distribution mixing centers." Product arrives in bulk and is immediately broken down and mixed in the proper range and quantity of products for customer shipment. In essence, the product never enters the warehouse. This topic will be described more fully in the next section.

Cross-docking is becoming popular among retailers, who can order TL, then remix and immediately ship to individual store locations. Products usually come boxed for individual stores from the supplier's location. For example, Laney & Duke, Hanes's third-party warehousing company in Jacksonville, Florida, tickets merchandise, places it on hangers, and boxes it up for individual Wal-Mart stores to replace items sold. The trailer leaves Jacksonville for the Wal-Mart DC where product is cross-docked to trucks for stores. At stores, the boxes are opened and garments are immediately ready to hang on display racks.

Most firms warehouse products at some intermediate point between plant and customers. When a firm decides to store product in the field, it faces two warehousing options: rented facilities, called *public warehousing,* or owned or leased facilities, called *private warehousing.*

Contract Warehousing

Contract Warehousing.   Another option exists, termed **contract warehousing,** which is a variation of public warehousing. Contract warehousing is an arrangement between the user and provider of the warehousing service. It has been defined as:

> . . . a long-term mutually beneficial arrangement which provides unique and specially tailored warehousing and logistics services exclusively to one client, where vendor and client share the risks associate with the operation. [There is a] focus on productivity, service and efficiency, not the fee and rate structure itself.[7]

Firms must examine important customer service and financial considerations to choose between public and private warehousing. For example, operating costs for a public warehouse tend to be higher because the warehouse will attempt to operate at a profit; it may also have selling and advertising costs. However, a firm makes no initial investment in facilities when it uses public warehousing. From a customer service perspective, private warehousing can generally provide higher service levels because of its more specialized facilities and equipment, and its better familiarity with the firm's products, customers, and markets.

---

[7]Kenneth B. Ackerman, "Contract Warehousing—Better Mousetrap, or Smoke and Mirrors?" *Warehousing Forum,* 8 no. 9 (Aug. 1993), p. 1; see also William G. Sheehan, "Contract Warehousing: The Evolution of an Industry," *Journal of Business Logistics* 10, no. 1 (1989), p. 31; and Thomas W. Speh, et al., *Contract Warehousing: How It Works and How to Make It Work Effectively* (Oak Brook, IL: Warehousing Education and Research Council, 1993).

The two options must be examined closely. In some instances, innovative public warehouses can provide higher levels of service owing to their expertise and strong competitive drive to serve the customer.[8]

Types of Public Warehouses

Public Warehouses.   There are many types of public warehouses, including: (1) general merchandise warehouses for manufactured goods, (2) refrigerated or cold storage warehouses, (3) bonded warehouses, (4) household goods and furniture warehouses, (5) special commodity warehouses, and (6) bulk storage warehouses. Each type provides users with a broad range of specialized services.

General Merchandise Warehouse.   The *general merchandise warehouse* is probably the most common form. It is designed to be used by manufacturers, distributors, and customers for storing almost any kind of product.

Refrigerated Warehouses.   *Refrigerated or cold storage warehouses* provide a temperature-controlled storage environment. They tend to be used for preserving perishable items such as fruits and vegetables. However, a number of other items (e.g., frozen food products, some pharmaceuticals, photographic paper and film, and furs) require this type of facility.

Bonded Warehouses

Bonded Warehouses.   Some general merchandise or special commodity warehouses are known as **bonded warehouses.** These warehouses undertake surety bonds from the U.S. Treasury and place their premises under the custody of an agent of the Treasury. Goods such as imported tobacco and alcoholic beverages are stored in this type of warehouse, although the government retains control of the goods until they are distributed to the marketplace. At that time, the importer must pay customs duties to the Internal Revenue Service. The advantage of the bonded warehouse is that import duties and excise taxes need not be paid until the merchandise is sold, so that the importer has the funds on hand to pay these fees.

Household Goods Warehouses

Household Goods Warehouses.   *Household goods warehouses* are used for storage of personal property rather than merchandise. The property is typically stored for an extended period as a temporary layover option. Within this category of warehouses, there are several types of storage alternatives. One is the open storage concept. The goods are stored on a cubic-foot basis per month on the open floor of the warehouse. Household goods are typically confined to this type of storage. A second kind of storage is private room or vault storage, where users are provided with a private room or vault to lock in and secure goods. A third kind, container storage, provides users with a container into which they can pack goods. Container storage affords better protection of the product than open storage.

Special Commodity Warehouses

Special Commodity Warehouses.   *Special commodity warehouses* are used for particular agricultural products, such as grains, wool, and cotton. Ordinarily each of these warehouses handles one kind of product and offers special services specific to that product.

---

[8]For a brief overview of the three general types of warehousing (private, public, and contract), see American Warehouse Association, "Three Warehousing Choices: Private, Public, and Contract," *Logistics Today* 1, no. 2 (1993), pp. 1–3.

**Bulk Storage
Warehouses**

Bulk Storage Warehouses.   *Bulk storage warehouses* provide tank storage of liquids and open or sheltered storage of dry products such as coal, sand, and chemicals. These warehouses may provide services such as filling drums from bulk or mixing various types of chemicals with others to produce new compounds or mixtures.

Warehousing Operations: Three Functions

Warehousing serves an important role in a firm's logistics system. In combination with other activities, it provides the firm's customers with an acceptable level of service. The obvious role of warehousing is to store products, but warehousing also provides break-bulk, consolidation, and information services. These activities emphasize product flow rather than storage.

Fast and efficient movement of large quantities of raw materials, component parts, and finished goods through the warehouse, coupled with timely and accurate information about the products being stored, are the goals of every logistics system. These goals have received increasing attention from the top management of many organizations (see Box 8–2).

**Three Functions of
Warehousing**

Warehousing has three basic functions: movement, storage, and information transfer. Recently, the movement function has been receiving the most attention as organizations focus on improving inventory turns and speeding orders from manufacturing to final delivery (see Figure 8–3).

Movement

The movement function can be further divided into several activities, including:

- Receiving
- Transfer or putaway
- Order picking/selection
- Cross-docking
- Shipping[9]

The *receiving* activity includes the actual unloading of products from the transportation carrier, the updating of warehouse inventory records, inspection for damage, and verification of the merchandise count against orders and shipping records.

Transfer or *putaway* involves the physical movement of the product into the warehouse for storage, movement to areas for specialized services such as consolidation, and movement to outbound shipment. Customer *order selection* or *order picking* is the major movement activity and involves regrouping products into the assortments customers desire. Packing slips are made up at this point.

Cross-docking bypasses the storage activity by transferring items directly from the receiving dock to the shipping dock (see Figure 8–4). A pure cross-docking operation would avoid putaway, storage, and order picking. Information transfer would become paramount because shipments require close coordination.

---

[9]See James A. Tompkins et al., *Facilities Planning,* 2nd. ed. (New York: John Wiley, 1996), pp. 389–450.

Box 8–2

How Moore Keeps Its Operations in Top Form

A Canadian corporation headquartered in Toronto, Moore Business Forms and Systems manufactures custom business forms and documents. Corporate sales in 1994 topped $2.3 billion.

To serve customers in the United States, Moore operates 18 U.S. distribution centers. Although some 75 percent of products are shipped directly from the factory to the purchaser, another 25 percent go into storage for later shipment.

Moore developed six critical measurements designed to maximize warehouse efficiency and effectiveness while maintaining a high level of customer service. The six-element program (referred to as the RSVP program) consists of the following:

1. *Safety*—zero safety incidents or accidents; the OSHA employee logbooks that report accidents are used for evaluation.
2. *Shipping Errors*—zero shipping errors in the firm's pick and pack activities (i.e., ship exactly what was ordered to the customer); financial statement information indicates whether orders have been filled completely.
3. *On-Time Shipments*—delivery of freight precisely when requested because customers are operating JIT operations; warehouse records on shipping performance are used for evaluation.

4. *Customer Problems*—customer feedback is periodically requested for every shipment, and summary statistics are compiled for management review.
5. *Cost per Line Shipped*—based on the number of items shipped in a period, the company came up with a cost per line and measures that expense against a preestablished objective; financial statements and the firm's computerized inventory system measure costs in this area.
6. *Total Warehouse Expenses*—an overall measure of warehouse efficiency which determines whether workers kept warehousing costs in line with company standards and projections.

At the end of each quarter, Moore measures each warehouse's performance against the criteria and issues bonuses to the employees, managers, and directors. During 1994, more than a third of the warehouses met all six objectives. At the end of the year, 99.6 percent of Moore's customers rated their service level as good or better.

Source: James Aaron Cooke, "How Moore Keeps Its Operations in Top Form," *Traffic Management* 34, no. 9 (Sept. 1995), pp. 23–27.

Cross-docking has become commonplace in warehousing because of its impact on costs and customer service. For example, approximately 75 percent of food distribution involves the cross-docking of products from supplier to retail food stores.[10] Eliminating the transfer or putaway of products reduces costs and the time goods remain at the warehouse, thus improving customer service levels.[11]

---

[10]"Grocery Warehouses Turn to Cross-Docking," *Traffic Management* 34, no. 2 (Feb. 1995), p. 77-S.

[11]A large literature overviews cross-docking. The interested reader is directed to the following sources: Tom Andel, "Define Cross-Docking before You Do It," *Transportation and Distribution* 35, no. 11 (Nov. 1994), pp. 93–98; *Cross-Docking in the '90s,* Monograph Series no. M0020 (Raleigh, NC: Tompkins Associates, n.d.); Lisa Harrington, "Cross-Docking Takes Costs Out of the Pipeline," *Distribution* 92, no. 9 (Sept. 1993), pp. 64–66; "Implementing a Cross-Docking Program," *Distribution Center Management* 30, no. 5 (May 1995), p. 3; and James T. Westburgh, "Cross-Docking in the Warehouse—An Operator's View," *Warehousing Forum* 10, no. 9 (Aug. 1995), pp. 1–3.

FIGURE 8–3

Typical warehouse functions and flows

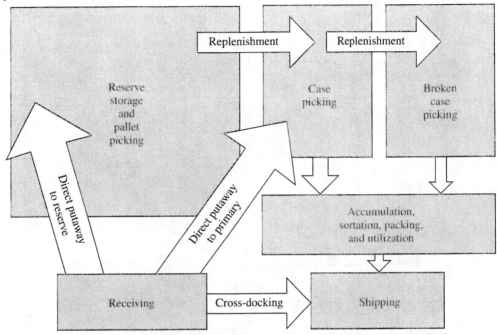

Source: James A. Tompkins et al., *Facilities Planning,* 2nd ed. (New York: John Wiley, 1996), p. 392.

Cross-docking should be considered as an option by firms meeting two or more of the following criteria:

When Should Cross-Docking Be Considered?

- Inventory destination is known when received.
- Customer is ready to receive inventory immediately.
- Shipment to fewer than 200 locations daily.
- Daily throughput exceeds 2,000 cartons.
- More than 70 percent of the inventory is conveyable.
- Large quantities of individual items received by firm.
- Inventory arrives at firm's docks prelabeled.
- Some inventory is time sensitive.
- Firm's distribution center is near capacity.
- Some of the inventory is prepriced.[12]

Shipping, the last movement activity, consists of product staging and physically moving the assembled orders onto carrier equipment, adjusting inventory records, and checking orders to be shipped. It can consist of sortation and packaging of items for specific customers. Products are placed in boxes, cartons, or other containers, placed on pallets, or shrinkwrapped (i.e., the process of wrapping products in a plastic film), and are marked with information necessary for shipment, such as origin, destination, shipper, consignee, and package contents.

[12]"Receiving Is Where Efficiency Starts," *Modern Materials Handling* 50, no. 5 (Mid-Apr. 1995), p. 9.

FIGURE 8-4

Two examples of cross-docking

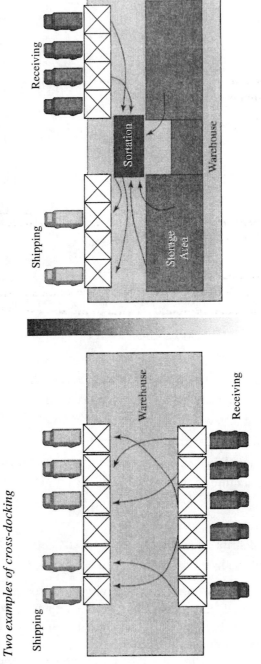

Under a cross-docking system, palletloads can be moved directly across the warehouse floor from receiving to shipping (left). Boxes, however, first must pass through a sortation system (right).

Source: James Aaron Cooke, "Cross-Docking Rediscovered," *Traffic Management* 33, no. 11 (Nov. 1994), p. 51.

Storage

Temporary Storage

Storage, the second function of warehousing, can be performed on a temporary or a semipermanent basis. *Temporary storage* emphasizes the movement function of the warehouse and includes only the storage of product necessary for basic inventory replenishment. Temporary storage is required regardless of the actual inventory turnover. The extent of temporary inventory storage depends on the design of the logistics system and the variability experienced in lead time and demand. A goal of cross-docking is to utilize only the temporary storage function of the warehouse.

Semipermanent Storage

Semipermanent storage is the storage of inventory in excess of that required for normal replenishment. This inventory is referred to as buffer or safety stock. The most common conditions leading to semipermanent storage are (1) seasonal demand, (2) erratic demand, (3) conditioning of products such as fruits and meats, (4) speculation or forward buying, and (5) special deals such as quantity discounts.

Information Transfer

Information transfer, the third major function of warehousing, occurs simultaneously with the movement and storage functions. Management always needs timely and accurate information as it attempts to administer the warehousing activity. Information on inventory levels, throughput levels (i.e., the amount of product moving through the warehouse), stockkeeping locations, inbound and outbound shipments, customer data, facility space utilization, and personnel is vital to the successful operation of a warehouse. Organizations are relying increasingly on computerized information transfer utilizing electronic data interchange (EDI) and bar coding to improve both the speed and accuracy of information transfer.

In spite of numerous attempts by firms to reduce the flow of paperwork, the amount of paperwork is still significant. For this reason and many others, management in many firms has attempted to automate the clerical function whenever possible. The developments in electronic communications have been instrumental in reducing the clerical activities in all aspects of warehousing.

Successful completion of all of the warehousing activities already mentioned eliminates the need for *checking.* However, errors and mistakes do occur within any warehouse operation, usually making it necessary to conduct a check of previous activities. In some instances, this activity can be minimized in operations where employees are empowered to perform quality control at their respective levels within the warehouse. This activity may be performed by teams, instead of individuals.

It is important to eliminate any inefficiencies in movement, storage, and information transfer within the warehouse. These can occur in a variety of forms:

Examples of Warehousing Inefficiencies

- Redundant or excessive handling.
- Poor utilization of space and cube.
- Excessive maintenance costs and downtime due to obsolete equipment.
- Dated receiving and shipping dock conditions.
- Obsolete computerized information handling of routine transactions.

The competitive marketplace demands more precise and accurate handling, storage, and retrieval systems, as well as improved packaging and shipping systems. It is vital for a warehouse operation to have the optimal mix of manual and automated handling systems. These issues are presented in more depth in Chapter 9. The next section compares and contrasts private and public warehousing.

Public versus Private Warehousing

One of the most important warehousing decisions a company makes is whether to use public (rented) or private (owned or leased) facilities. To make the proper decision from a cost and service standpoint, the logistics executive must understand the advantages and disadvantages, as well as the financial implications, of each alternative.[13]

Contract warehousing is a variant of public warehousing in which the organization has a contractual relationship to utilize a certain amount of space and services in a facility or facilities over a set time period. This arrangement gives the warehouser more stability and certainty in making investments and planning for the future.

Advantages and Disadvantages of Public Warehousing

Advantages.   The benefits that may be realized if a firm uses public warehouses rather than privately owned or leased warehouses include: (1) conservation of capital: (2) the ability to increase warehouse space to cover peak requirements; (3) reduced risk; (4) economies of scale; (5) flexibility; (6) tax advantages; (7) specific knowledge of costs for storage and handling; and (8) potential minimization of labor disputes.

Conservation of Capital

Conservation of Capital.   One of the major advantages of public warehouses is that they require no capital investment from the user. The user avoids the investment in buildings, land, and materials handling equipment, as well as the costs of starting up the operation and hiring and training personnel.

Adjusts for Seasonality

Use of Space to Meet Peak Requirements.   If a firm's operations are subject to seasonality, the public warehouse option allows the user to rent as much storage space as needed to meet peak requirements. A private warehouse, on the other hand, has a constraint on the maximum amount of product that can be stored because it cannot be expanded in the short term. Also, it is likely to be underutilized during a portion of each year. Since most firms experience variations in inventory levels because of seasonality in demand or production, sales promotions, or other factors, public warehousing offers the distinct advantage of allowing storage costs to vary directly with volume.

Reduced Risk

Reduced Risk.   Companies normally plan for a distribution facility to have a life span of 20 to 40 years. By investing in a private warehouse, management assumes the risk that

---

[13]See James Aaron Cooke, "Getting the Right Fit," *Traffic Management* 34, no. 2 (Feb. 1995), Warehousing and Distribution Supplement, pp. 78–80.

changes in technology or in the volume of business will make the facility obsolete. With public warehousing, the user firm can switch to another facility in a short period of time, often within 30 days.

Economies of Scale

Economies of Scale.   Public warehouses are able to achieve economies of scale that may not be possible for some firms. Because public warehouses handle the requirements of a number of firms, their volume allows the employment of a full-time warehousing staff. In addition, building costs are nonlinear, and a firm pays a premium to build a small facility. Additional economies of scale can be provided by using more expensive, but more efficient, materials handling equipment and by providing administrative and other expertise.

Public warehouses often can offer a number of specialized services more economically than a private warehouse. These specialized services include the following:

• Broken-case handling, which is breaking down manufacturers' case quantities to enable orders for less-than-full-case quantities to be filled.

• Packaging of manufacturers' products for shipping. Exel Logistics, a public warehousing and logistics services firm, has performed a variation of this service for the California Growers Association. Product was shipped to the Atlanta distribution center in "brights"—cans without labels—and the labels were put on the product at the warehouse as orders were received from customers.

• Consolidation of damaged and recalled products for shipment to the manufacturer in carload or truckload quantities. In addition to the documentation and prepacking that may be necessary, the public warehouse can perform the *reworking* (repair, refurbishing) of damaged product.

• Equipment maintenance and service.

• Stock spotting of product for manufacturers with limited or highly seasonal product lines. **Stock spotting** involves shipping a consolidated carload of inventory to a public warehouse just prior to a period of maximum seasonal sales.

• A breakbulk service whereby the manufacturer combines the orders of different customers in a particular market and ships them at the carload or truckload rate to the public warehouse. There the individual orders are separated and local delivery is provided.

Economies of scale result from the consolidation of small shipments with those of noncompetitors who use the same public warehouse. The public warehouse consolidates orders of specific customers from the products of a number of different manufacturers on a single shipment. This results in lower shipping costs and reduced congestion at the customer's receiving dock. Customers who pick up their orders at the public warehouse are able to obtain the products of several manufacturers with one stop, if the manufacturers all use the same facility.

Greater Flexibility

Flexibility.   Another major advantage offered by public warehouses is flexibility. Owning or holding a long-term lease on a warehouse can become a burden if business conditions necessitate changes in locations. Public warehouses require only a short-term contract and, thus, short-term commitments. Short-term contracts available from public warehouses make it easy for firms to change field warehouse locations because of changes in the marketplace (e.g., population shifts), the relative cost of various transport modes, volume of a product sold, or the company's financial position.

In addition, a firm that uses public warehouses does not have to hire or lay off employees as the volume of business changes. A public warehouse provides the personnel required for extra services when they are necessary, without having to hire them on a full-time basis.

Tax Advantages   *Tax Advantages.*   In some states, a firm can have an advantage if it does not own property in the state. Ownership means that the firm is doing business in the state and is thus subject to various state *taxes.* These taxes can be substantial. If the company does not currently own property in a state, it may find it advantageous to use a public warehouse.

Some states do not charge property taxes on inventories in public warehouses; this tax shelter applies to both regular warehouse inventories and storage-in-transit inventories. A **free-port** provision enacted in some states allows inventory to be held for up to one year, tax-free. The manufacturer pays no real estate tax. The public warehouse pays real estate taxes and includes this cost in its warehouse rates, but the cost is smaller on a per unit throughput basis because the cost is allocated among all of the clients using the public warehouse.

Knows Exact Warehousing Costs   *Knowledge of Exact Storage and Handling Costs.*   When a company uses a public warehouse, it knows the exact storage and handling costs because it receives a bill each month. The user can forecast costs for different levels of activity because the costs are known in advance. Firms that operate their own facilities often find it extremely difficult to determine the fixed and variable costs of warehousing precisely.

A public warehouse may be very flexible and adaptable in terms of meeting an organization's special requirements. For example, PRISM Team Services, a San Francisco area warehouser in the food industry, emphasizes value-added services such as just-in-time delivery, plant production support, and export shipping.[14]

Can Minimize Labor Disputes   *Insulation from Labor Disputes.*   The courts have ruled that a labor union does not have the right to picket a public warehouse when the union is involved in a labor dispute with one of the customers of that warehouse. Thus, using a public warehouse has the advantage of insulating the manufacturer's distribution system from a labor dispute.

Disadvantages.   A number of disadvantages are associated with the use of public warehousing.

Communication Problems   *Communication Problems.*   Effective communication may be a problem with public warehouses because not all computer terminals and systems are compatible. A warehouse operator may hesitate to add another terminal for only one customer. In addition, the lack of standardization in contractual agreements makes communication regarding contractual obligations difficult.

---

[14]Ann Saccamano, "California Warehouse Operator Emphasizes Tailored Services, sans Bells and Whistles," *Traffic World,* May 8, 1995, pp. 66–67.

Lack of Specialized Services

Lack of Specialized Services.   The space or specialized services desired may not always be available in a specific location. Many public warehouse facilities provide only local service and are of limited use to a firm that distributes regionally or nationally. A manufacturer that wants to use public warehouses for national distribution may find it necessary to deal with several different operators and monitor several contractual agreements.

Space May Not Be Available

Shortage of Space.   Public warehousing space may not be available when and where a firm wants it. Shortages of space do occur periodically in selected markets, which can have an adverse affect on the logistics and marketing strategies of a firm.

Advantages and Disadvantages of Private Warehousing

Advantages.   The advantages associated with private warehousing will now be described.

Degree of Control

Control.   In private warehousing, the company that owns the goods can exercise a greater degree of control. The firm has direct control of and responsibility for the product until the customer takes possession or delivery, which allows the firm to integrate the warehousing function more easily into its total logistics system.

Flexibility

Flexibility.   With warehouse control comes a greater degree of flexibility to design and operate the warehouse to fit the needs of customers and the characteristics of the product. Companies with products requiring special handling or storage may not find public warehousing feasible. The firm must utilize private warehousing or ship the product directly to customers. The warehouse can be modified through expansion or renovation to facilitate product changes, or it can be converted to a manufacturing plant or branch office location.

Less Costly over the Long Term

Less Costly.   Private warehousing can be less costly over the long term. Operating costs can be 15 to 25 percent lower if the company achieves sufficient throughput or utilization. The generally accepted industry norm for the utilization rate is 75 to 80 percent. If a firm cannot achieve at least 75 percent utilization, it generally would be more appropriate to use public warehousing.

Better Use of Human Resources

Better Use of Human Resources.   By employing private warehousing, a firm can make better use of its human resources. There is greater care in handling and storage when the firm's own workforce operates the warehouse. Some public warehouses allow their clients to use their own employees in the handling and storage of products. The company can utilize the expertise of its technical specialists.

Tax Benefits

Tax Benefits.   A company also can realize tax benefits when it owns its warehouses. Depreciation allowances on buildings and equipment reduce taxes payable.

Sears services its U.S. retail stores with several large distribution centers located strategically throughout the country.

Intangible Benefits

Intangible Benefits.   There may be certain intangible benefits associated with warehouse ownership. When a firm distributes its products through a private warehouse, it can give the customer a sense of permanence and continuity of business operations. The customer sees the company as a stable, dependable, and lasting supplier of products. However, customers are more concerned with on-time delivery of products and remote warehousing sites can provide similar service levels if managed properly. The Creative Solutions box at the end of the chapter shows how Lincoln Electric achieved better distribution and thus better service for its customers through its distribution centers.

Disadvantages.   A number of disadvantages are associated with the use of private warehousing.

Lack of Flexibility

Lack of Flexibility.   Many experts feel that the major drawback of private warehousing is the same as one of its main advantages—flexibility. A private warehouse may be too costly because of its fixed size and costs. Regardless of the level of demand the firm experiences, the size of the private warehouse is restricted in the short term. A private facility cannot expand and contract to meet increases or decreases in demand. When demand is low, the firm must still assume the fixed costs as well as the lower productivity linked to unused warehouse space. The disadvantage can be minimized if the firm is able to rent out part of its space.

If a firm uses only private warehouses, it loses flexibility in its strategic location options. If a company cannot adapt to rapid changes in market size, location, and preferences it may lose a valuable business opportunity. Customer service and sales could fall if a private warehouse cannot adapt to changes in the firm's product mix.

Financial Constraints   ***Financial Constraints.***   Because of the high costs involved, many firms are simply unable to generate enough capital to build or buy a warehouse. A warehouse is a long-term, often risky investment (which later may be difficult to sell because of its customized design). The hiring and training of employees, and the purchase of materials handling equipment makes start-up a costly and time-consuming process. And, depending on the nature of the firm, return on investment may be greater if funds are channeled into other profit-generating opportunities.

Rate of Return   ***Rate of Return.***   A further consideration in the decision is the rate of return that the private warehouse alternative will provide. At a minimum, the investment in a corporate-owned warehouse should generate the same rate of return as the firm's other investments. Most companies find it advantageous to use some combination of public and private warehousing. Private warehouses are used to handle the basic inventory levels required for least cost logistics in markets where the volume justifies ownership. Public warehouses are used where volume is insufficient to justify ownership or to store peak requirements.

Public warehouses typically charge on the basis of cases, pallets, or hundredweight stored or handled. When the volume of activity is sufficiently large, public warehousing charges exceed the cost of a private facility, making ownership more attractive.[15]

Facility Development

One of the more important decisions a logistics executive faces is how to develop an optimal warehousing network for the firm's products and customers. Such a decision encompasses a number of significant elements. Management must determine the size and number of warehouses, and ascertain their location. Each warehouse must be laid out and designed properly in order to maximize efficiency and productivity.

Size and Number of Warehouses

Two issues that must be addressed are the size and number of warehouse facilities. These are interrelated decisions because they typically have an inverse relationship; that is, as the *number* of warehouses increases, the average *size* of a warehouse decreases.

Size of a Warehouse.   Many factors influence how large a warehouse should be. First, it is necessary to define how size is measured. In general, size can be defined in terms of

---

[15]For a discussion of these and other issues concerning public and private warehousing, as well as criteria to consider in selecting between the various warehousing options, see Cooke, "Getting the Right Fit," pp. 78–80; James Aaron Cooke, "How to Pick a Public Warehouse," *Traffic Management,* Jan. 1994, Warehousing and Distribution Supplement pp. 14–16; C. Alan McCarrell, "Monitoring Public Warehouses," *Warehousing Forum* 8, no. 4 (Mar. 1993), pp. 1–4; Hugh L. Randall, "Contact Logistics: Is Outsourcing Right for You?" in *The Logistics Handbook,* ed. James F. Robeson and William C. Copacino (New York: Free Press, 1994), pp. 508–16; and William G. Sheehan, "Criteria for Judging a Public Warehouse," *Warehousing Forum* 11, no. 5 (Apr. 1996), p. 3.

square footage or cubic space. Most public warehouses still use square footage dimensions in their advertising and promotional efforts.

Unfortunately, square footage measures ignore the capability of modern warehouses to store merchandise vertically. Hence, the cubic space measure was developed. Cubic space refers to the total volume of space available *within* a facility. It is a much more realistic size estimate than square footage because it considers more of the available usable space in a warehouse. Some of the most important factors affecting the size of a warehouse are:

**Factors Affecting
Warehouse Size**

- Customer service levels.
- Size of market or markets served.
- Number of products marketed.
- Size of the product or products.
- Materials handling system used.
- Throughput rate.
- Production lead time.
- Economies of scale.
- Stock layout.
- Aisle requirements.
- Office area in warehouse.
- Types of racks and shelves used.
- Level and pattern of demand.

As a company's service levels increase, it typically requires more warehousing space to provide storage for higher levels of inventory. As the market served by a warehouse increases in number or size, additional space is required. When a firm has multiple products or product groupings, especially if they are diverse, it needs larger warehouses to maintain at least minimal inventory levels of all products. In general, greater space requirements are necessary when products are large; production lead time is long; manual materials handling systems are used; the warehouse contains office, sales, or computer activities; and demand is erratic and unpredictable.

**Warehouse Size Is
Related to the
Materials Handling
Equipment Used**

To illustrate, consider the relation of warehouse size to the type of materials handling equipment used.[16] As Figure 8–5 shows, the type of forklift truck a warehouse employs can significantly affect the amount of storage area necessary to store product. Because of different capabilities of forklift trucks, a firm can justify the acquisition of more expensive units when it is able to bring about more effective utilization of space. The four examples in Figure 8–5 show that warehouse layout and warehouse handling systems, one of the topics described in Chapter 9, are intertwined.

The simplest type of forklift truck, the counterbalanced truck, requires aisles that are 10 to 12 feet wide. At $30,000, it is the least expensive forklift. The turret truck requires aisles only 5 to 7 feet wide to handle the same amount of product, but it costs $65,000 or

---

[16]Examples can be found in Clyde E. Witt, "Multi-Million Dollar Facelift for Exchange Service," *Material Handling Engineering* 43, no. 8 (Aug. 1988), pp. 47–53; "How to Implement Robotic Palletizing," *Material Handling Engineering* 43, no. 7 (July 1988), pp. 61–64; and Clyde E. Witt, "Publisher Creates Textbook Case for Distribution," *Material Handling Engineering* 43, no. 3 (Mar. 1988), pp. 41–47.

FIGURE 8–5

Narrow-aisle trucks can reduce floor space

Type of truck	Deep reach	Turret	Reach-fork	Counter-balanced
Area required	5,550 sq. ft.	3,070 sq. ft.	6,470 sq. ft.	10,000 sq. ft.
Aisle width	102 inches	66 inches	96 inches	144 inches
Floor space saved	45%	70%	33%	———

Source: James Aaron Cooke, "When to Choose a Narrow-Aisle Lift Truck," *Traffic Management* 28, no. 12 (Dec. 1989), p. 55.

more.[17] The warehouse decision maker must examine the cost trade-offs for each of the available systems, and determine which alternative is most advantageous from a cost-service perspective.

Demand Fluctuations Impact Warehouse Size

Demand also has an impact on warehouse size. Whenever demand fluctuates significantly or is unpredictable, inventory levels generally must be higher. This results in a need for more space and thus a larger warehouse. All the warehousing space need not be private. Many firms utilize a combination of private and public warehousing. Figure 8–6 shows the relationship between demand and warehouse size.

The hypothetical firm depicted in Figure 8–6 utilizes private warehousing to store 36,000 units of inventory. This results in full utilization of its facilities all year, with the exception of July and August. For months when inventory requirements exceed private warehousing space, the firm rents short-term storage space from one or more public warehouses. In essence, the firm develops private facilities to accommodate a maximum level of inventory of 36,000 units.

Inventory velocity (as measured by turnover) and the maximization of "direct deliveries" to customers (bypassing a regional or wholesaler's warehouse) can have a great impact on the size of a warehouse. Whirlpool Corporation developed a computer program to simulate these two characteristics, as well as the cubic warehousing space requirements of its total channel network, including wholesale distributors. The company calculated the square footage required for each of its factory-controlled and wholesale warehouses. It added space to the base requirements of each of its major product categories in order to

---

[17]See Edward H. Frazelle and James M. Apple, Jr., "Materials Handling Technologies," in *The Logistics Handbook,* ed. James F. Robeson and William C. Copacino, (New York: Free Press, 1994), p. 560.

Figure 8–6

The relationship of demand to warehouse size

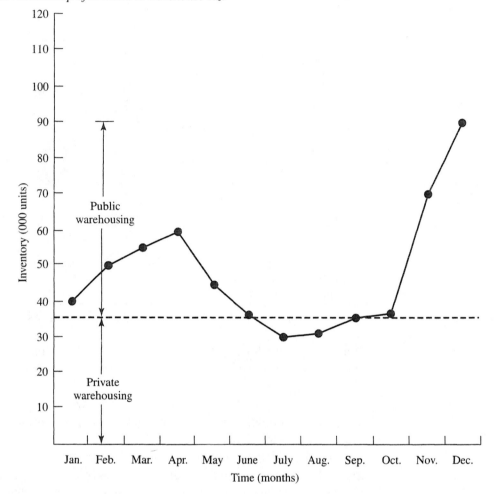

provide for aisles and docks, and unused (empty) vertical and horizontal storage bays. By manipulating planned sales volumes, inventory turns, and orders shipped directly to dealers, Whirlpool was able to accurately project future warehousing needs.[18]

Four Factors Influence the Number of Warehouses

Number of Warehouses.   Four factors are significant in deciding on the number of warehousing facilities: cost of lost sales, inventory costs, warehousing costs, and transportation costs. Figure 8–7 depicts these cost areas except for cost of lost sales.

Cost of Lost Sales

Cost of Lost Sales.   Although lost sales are extremely important to a firm, they are the most difficult to calculate and predict, and they vary by company and industry. If the **cost of lost sales** appeared in Figure 8–7, it would generally slope down and to the right. The degree of slope, however, would vary by industry, company, product, and customer.

---

[18]Illustration provided by Professor Jay U. Sterling, University of Alabama, and former director of logistics planning for Whirlpool Corporation.

FIGURE 8–7

Relationship between total logistics cost and the number of warehouses

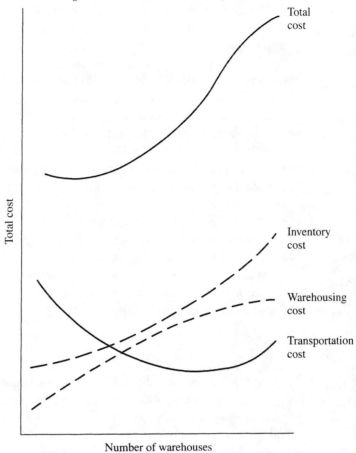

The remaining components of Figure 8–7 are more consistent across firms and industries.

Inventory Costs

Inventory Costs.   Inventory costs increase with the number of facilities because firms usually stock a minimum amount (e.g., safety stock) of all products at every location, although some companies have specific warehouses dedicated to a particular product or product grouping. This means that both slow and fast turnover items are stocked; thus, more total space is required.

Warehousing Costs

Warehousing Costs.   Warehousing costs increase, because more warehouses mean more space to be owned, leased, or rented, but they decrease after a number of warehouses are brought on-line, particularly if the firm leases or rents space. Public and contract warehouses often offer quantity discounts when firms acquire space in multiple locations.

Transportation Costs

Transportation Costs.   Transportation costs initially decline as the number of warehouses increase, but they eventually curve upward if too many facilities are employed owing to the combination of inbound and outbound transportation costs. A firm must be concerned with the total delivered cost of its products, not simply the cost of moving products to warehouse locations. In general, the use of fewer facilities means lower inbound transport costs due to bulk shipments from the manufacturer or supplier.

After the number of warehouses increases to a certain point, the firm may not be able to ship its products in such large quantities and may have to pay a higher rate to the transportation carrier. Local transportation costs for delivery of products from warehouses to customers may increase because of minimum charges that apply to local cartage.

If the cost of lost sales is not included, the slopes shown in Figure 8–7, taken together, indicate that fewer warehouses are better than many warehouses. However, customer service is a critical element of a firm's marketing and logistics systems. In general, if the cost of lost sales is very high, a firm may wish to expand its number of warehouses or use scheduled deliveries. There are always cost-service trade-offs. Management must determine the optimal number of warehouses given the desired customer-service level.

Value of Computers.   Computers can help minimize the firm's number of warehouses by improving warehouse layout and design, inventory control, shipping and receiving, and the dissemination of information. Coupled with more efficient warehouses, the substitution of information for inventories tends to reduce the number of warehouses needed to service a firm's customers. In essence, the more responsive the logistics system, the less need there is for warehousing.

Location Analysis

Where Is the Best Place to Locate a Warehouse?

Where would be the best place to build a warehouse that would service the greatest number of U.S. consumers? Bloomington, Indiana, would be closer, on average, to the U.S. population than any other location.[19] If a firm wished to locate facilities closest to its potential customers, using one or more warehouses in their logistics network, a number of sites would be possible. Table 8–1 identifies the best locations given various warehouse configurations.

The site-selection decision can be approached from macro and micro perspectives. The macro perspective examines the issue of where to locate warehouses geographically within a general area so as to improve the sourcing of materials and the firm's market offering (improve service and/or reduce cost). The micro perspective examines factors that pinpoint specific locations within the large geographic areas.

Macro Approaches.   In one of the best-known macro approaches to warehouse location, Edgar M. Hoover, an American location theorist, identified three types of location strategies: (1) market positioned, (2) production positioned, and (3) intermediately positioned.[20] The **market-positioned strategy** locates warehouses nearest to the final customer. This maximizes customer service levels and enables a firm to utilize transportation economies—TL and CL shipments—from plants or sources to each warehouse location.

Market-Positioned Warehouses

---

[19]"10 Best Warehouse Networks for 1997," Chicago Consulting Information Sheet, undated.

[20]Edgar M. Hoover, *The Location of Economic Activity* (New York: McGraw-Hill, 1948), p. 11.

2 LEAN LOGISTICS

No other area of business operations involves the complexity or spans the geography of logistics. All around the globe, 24 hours of every day, 7 days a week, during 52 weeks a year, logistics is concerned with getting products and services where they are needed at the precise time desired. It is difficult to visualize accomplishing any marketing, manufacturing, or international commerce without logistics. Most consumers in highly developed industrial nations take a high level of logistical competency for granted. When they purchase goods—at a retail store, over the telephone, or via the Internet—they expect product delivery will be performed as promised. In fact, their expectation is for timely, error-free logistics every time they order. They have little or no tolerance for failure to perform.

Although logistics has been performed since the beginning of civilization, implementing best practice logistics is one of the most exciting and challenging operational areas of supply chain management. Because logistics is both old and new, we choose to characterize the rapid change taking place in best practice as a renaissance.

Logistics involves the management of order processing, inventory, transportation, and the combination of warehousing, materials handling, and packaging, all integrated throughout a network of facilities. The goal of logistics is to support procurement, manufacturing, and market distribution operational requirements. Within a firm the challenge is to coordinate functional competency into an integrated operation focused on servicing customers. In the broader supply chain context, operational synchronization is essential with customers as well as material and service suppliers to link internal and external operations as one integrated process.

Lean logistics refers to the superior ability to *design and administer systems to control movement and geographical positioning of raw materials, work-in-process, and finished inventories at the lowest total cost.* To achieve lowest total cost means that financial and human assets committed to logistics must be held to an absolute minimum. It is also necessary to hold direct operational expenditures as low as possible. The combination of resources, skills, and systems required to achieve lean logistics are challenging to integrate, but once achieved, such integrated competency is difficult for competitors to replicate. Industry Insight 2-1 illustrates how Dell Computers has used lean logistics principles to gain competitive advantage.

This chapter focuses on the contribution of lean logistics to integrated supply chain management. First, cost and service are emphasized. Next, the logistics value proposition is developed. Then traditional business functions that combine to create the logistical process are reviewed. Finally, the importance of logistical synchronization to supply chain integration is highlighted in terms of performance cycle structure and dynamics.

The Logistics of Business Is Big and Important

It is through the logistical process that materials flow into the manufacturing capacity of an industrial nation and products are distributed to consumers. The recent growth in global commerce and the introduction of e-commerce have expanded the size and complexity of logistical operations.

Logistics adds value to the supply chain process when inventory is strategically positioned to achieve sales. Creating logistics value is costly. Although difficult to measure, most experts agree that the annual expenditure to perform logistics in the United States was approximately 10.1 percent of the $9.96 billion Gross National Product (GNP) or $1.006 billion.[1] Expenditure for transportation in 2000 was $590 billion, which represented 58.6 percent of total logistics cost. As further illustrated in Table 2-1, the logistics of business is truly big business!

Despite the sheer size of logistical expenditure, the excitement of lean logistics is not cost containment or reduction. The excitement generates from understanding how select firms use logistical competency to achieve competitive advantage. Firms that

---

[1]Robert V. Delaney, Twelfth Annual "State of Logistics Report," presented to the National Press Club, Washington, DC, June 4, 2001.

INDUSTRY INSIGHT 2-1 DELL GOES TO THE EXTREME

According to industry legend, Henry Ford's manufacturing philosophy was "You can have any color you want as long as it's black." The manufacturing strategy that has fostered unprecedented success for Dell Computers is the exact opposite of Ford's mindset: "Build every order to order." Essentially, it spawns the ultimate manufacturing oxymoron: mass customization.

The critical component to facilitate mass customization is a logistics program built upon a concept of "extreme warehousing" and a superior software platform. Ryder Integrated Logistics, a subsidiary of Ryder Systems, Miami, Florida, houses supplier-owned inventory for Dell at locations in Austin, Texas, and Nashville, Tennessee. The Austin facility is fed by 50 global suppliers and the Nashville site is fed by 60 vendors worldwide.

"Dell requires suppliers to respond with order fulfillment within two hours. The only way suppliers can meet this expectation is to utilize our logistics management," explains Dave Hanley, director of business development for Ryder. "Dell maintains less than six days of inventory, and turns work-in-process approximately 264 times annually. The company uses our services to minimize investment in inventory, and to abolish 'dead space,' or 'nonproductive storage areas.'"

"We replenish to kanbans and maintain a working inventory at the production facility," Hanley says. "Dell does an incredible job of estimating what products will be selling, and different products peak at various times. Laptops are big now and business machines are more popular in the first quarter of the year than in the last."

Currently, Ryder has responsibility for the inventory from the time it arrives at its facilities until it delivers to Dell. Hanley is confident that incorporating Ryder's processes and logistics management across all inbound shipments from suppliers, beginning at every point of origin, would bring tremendous additional value to Dell.

While he acknowledges Dell is the master of execution in manufacturing, Hanley says the software used by Ryder to manage the extreme warehousing requirements is one of the computer manufacturer's "top three critical success factors."

The software had to satisfy many requirements—from open architecture to a scalable platform that would grow with Dell. The solution has done precisely that, expanding with the Austin facility as it grew from 12,000 square feet in 1997 to more than 600,000 square feet by 1999.

"Extreme warehousing demands fast response and critical management," says Hanley. "There's a live customer waiting for the order, and a mistake today means a disappointed customer in just two days."

This rapid fulfillment doesn't allow recovery time for mistakes, so the WMS has to execute perfectly and flawlessly on every order, he notes.

Source: Anonymous, "Dell Goes to the Extreme," *Inbound Logistics,* January 2000, p. 122.

have developed world-class logistical competency enjoy competitive advantage as a result of providing important customers superior service. Leading logistical performers typically implement information technology capable of monitoring global logistical activity on a real time basis. Such technology identifies potential operational breakdowns and facilitates corrective action prior to delivery service failure. In situations where timely corrective action is not possible, customers can be provided advance notification of developing problems, thereby eliminating the surprise of an unavoidable service failure. In many situations, working in collaboration with customers and suppliers, corrective action can be taken to prevent operational shutdowns or costly customer service failures. By performing at above industry average with respect to inventory availability, speed and consistency of delivery, and operational efficiencies, logistically sophisticated firms are ideal supply chain partners.

TABLE 2-1   U.S. Logistics Costs, 1980–2000 ($ Billions Except GDP)

Year	Nominal GDP ($ Trillion)	Values of All Business Inventory	Percent of Inventory Carrying Rate	Inventory Carrying Costs	Transpor- tation Costs	Admini- strative Costs	Total U.S. Logistics Cost	Logistics (% of GDP)
1980	$ 2.80	692	31.8	220	214	17	451	16.1
1981	3.13	747	34.7	259	228	19	506	16.2
1982	3.26	760	30.8	234	222	18	474	14.5
1983	3.54	758	27.9	211	243	18	472	13.3
1984	3.93	826	29.1	240	268	20	528	13.4
1985	4.21	847	26.8	227	274	20	521	12.4
1986	4.45	843	25.7	217	281	20	518	11.6
1987	4.74	875	25.7	225	294	21	540	11.4
1988	5.11	944	26.6	251	313	23	587	11.5
1989	5.44	1005	28.1	282	329	24	635	11.7
1990	5.80	1041	27.2	283	351	25	659	11.4
1991	5.99	1030	24.9	256	355	24	635	10.6
1992	6.32	1043	22.7	237	375	24	636	10.1
1993	6.64	1076	22.2	239	396	25	660	9.9
1994	7.05	1127	23.5	265	420	27	712	10.1
1995	7.40	1211	24.9	302	441	30	773	10.4
1996	7.81	1240	24.4	303	467	31	801	10.3
1997	8.32	1280	24.5	314	503	33	850	10.2
1998	8.79	1323	24.4	323	529	34	886	10.1
1999	9.30	1379	24.1	332	554	35	921	9.9
2000	9.96	1485	25.4	377	590	39	1006	10.1

Source: Robert V. Delaney, Twelfth Annual "State of Logistics Report," presented to the National Press Club, Washington, DC, June 4, 2001.

The Logistical Value Proposition

Thus far it has been established that logistics should be managed as an integrated effort to achieve customer satisfaction at the lowest total cost. Here we add that the modern challenge is to create *value*. In this section, the elements of the logistical value proposition, service, and cost minimization are discussed in greater detail.

Service Benefits

Almost any level of logistical service can be achieved if a firm is willing to commit the required resources. In today's operating environment, the limiting factor is economics, not technology. For example, a dedicated inventory can be maintained in close geographical proximity to a major customer. A fleet of trucks can be held in a constant state of delivery readiness. To facilitate order processing, dedicated communications can be maintained on a real time or Internet-enabled basis between a customer and a supplier's logistical operation. Given this high state of logistical readiness, a product or component could be delivered within minutes of identifying a customer requirement. Availability is even faster when a supplier agrees to consign inventory at a customer's facility, eliminating the need to perform logistical operations when a product is needed. The logistics to support consignment are completed in advance of the customer's need for the product. While such extreme service commitment might constitute a sales manager's dream, it is costly and typically not necessary to support most market distribution and manufacturing operations.

The key strategic issue is how to outperform competitors in a cost-effective manner. If a specific material is not available when required for manufacturing, it may force a plant shutdown resulting in significant cost, potential lost sales, and even the loss of a major customer's business. The profit impact of such failures is significant. In contrast, the profit impact of an unexpected 1- or 2-day delay in delivering products to replenish warehouse inventory could be minimal or even insignificant in terms of impact on overall operational performance. In most situations, the cost/benefit impact of logistical failure is directly related to the importance of service to the customer. The more significant the service failure impact upon a customer's performance, the greater is the priority placed on error-free logistical performance.

Creation and basic logistical performance is measured in terms of availability, operational performance, and service reliability.[2] The term *basic logistics service* describes the level of service a firm provides all established customers.

Availability involves having inventory to consistently meet customer material or product requirements. The traditional paradigm has been the higher inventory availability, the greater is the required inventory amount and cost. Information technology is providing new ways to achieve high inventory availability for customers without correspondingly high capital investment. Information that facilitates availability is critical to achieving lean logistics performance.

Operational performance deals with the time required to deliver a customer's order. Operational performance involves delivery *speed* and *consistency*. Naturally, most customers want fast delivery. However, fast delivery is of limited value if inconsistent from one order to the next. A customer gains little benefit when a supplier promises next-day delivery but, more often than not, delivers late. To achieve smooth operations, firms typically focus on service consistency first and then seek to improve delivery speed. Other aspects of operational performance are also important. A firm's operational performance can be viewed in terms of its *flexibility* to accommodate unusual and unexpected customer requests. Another aspect of operational performance is frequency of malfunction and, when such malfunction occurs, the required recovery time. Few firms can perform perfectly all the time. It is important to estimate the likelihood of something going wrong. *Malfunction* is concerned with the probability of logistical performance involving failures, such as damaged products, incorrect assortment, or inaccurate documentation. When such malfunctions occur, a firm's logistical competency can be measured in terms of *recovery time*. Operational performance is concerned with how a firm handles all aspects of customer requirements, including service failure, on a day in and day out basis.

Service reliability involves the *quality* attributes of logistics. The key to quality is accurate measurement of availability and operational performance. Only through comprehensive performance measurement is it possible to determine if overall logistical operations are achieving desired service goals. To achieve service reliability, it is essential to identify and implement inventory availability and operational performance measurements. For logistics performance to continuously meet customer expectations, it is essential that management be committed to continuous improvement. Logistical

---

[2]These basic measures of customer service are more fully developed in Chapter 3.

quality does not come easy; it's the product of careful planning supported by employee training, operational dedication, comprehensive measurement, and continuous improvement. To improve service performance, goals need to be established on a selective basis. Some products are more critical than others because of their importance to the customer and their relative profit contribution.

The level of basic logistical service should be realistic in terms of customer expectations and requirements. In most cases, firms confront situations wherein customers have significantly different purchase potential. Some customers require unique or special value-added services. Thus, managers must realize that customers are different and that services provided must be matched to accommodate unique requirements and purchase potential. In general, firms tend to be overly optimistic when committing to average or basic customer service performance. Inability to consistently meet an unrealistically high basic service target might result in more operating and customer relationship problems than if less ambitious goals had been attempted from the outset. Unrealistic across-the-board service commitments can also dilute a firm's capability to satisfy special requirements of high potential customers.

Cost Minimization

The focus of lean logistics can be traced to relatively recent developments of total costing theory and practice. In 1956, a classic monograph describing airfreight economics provided a new perspective concerning logistical cost.[3] In an effort to explain conditions under which high-cost air transport could be justified, Lewis, Culliton, and Steele conceptualized the total cost logistics model. Total cost was positioned to include *all* expenditures necessary to perform logistical requirements. The authors illustrated an electronic parts distribution strategy wherein the high variable cost of direct factory-to-customer air transport was more than offset by reductions in traditional inventory and field warehouse costs. They concluded that the least *total cost* logistical way to provide the desired customer service was to centralize inventory in one warehouse and make deliveries using air transportation.

This concept of total cost, although fundamentally basic, had not previously been applied to logistical operations. Probably because of the economic climate of the times and the radical departure in suggested practice, the total cost proposition generated a great deal of debate. The prevailing managerial practice, reinforced by accounting and financial control, was to focus attention on achieving the lowest possible cost for *each* individual function of logistics with little or no attention to integrated total cost. Managers had traditionally focused on minimizing functional cost, such as transportation, with the expectation that such effort would achieve the lowest combined costs. Development of the total cost concept opened the door to examining how functional costs interrelate and impact each other. Subsequent refinements provided a more comprehensive understanding of logistical cost components and identified the critical need for developing functional cost analysis and activity-based costing capabilities. However, the implementation of effective logistical process costing remains a new millennium challenge. Many long-standing practices of accounting continue to serve as barriers to fully implementing total cost logistical solutions.

---

[3]Howard T. Lewis, James W. Culliton, and Jack D. Steele, *The Role of Air Freight in Physical Distribution* (Boston, MA: Harvard University, 1956).

Logistics Value Generation

The key to achieving logistical leadership is to master the art of matching operating competency and commitment to key customer expectations and requirements. This customer commitment, in an exacting cost framework, is the **logistics value proposition.** It is a unique commitment of a firm to an individual or selected groups of its customers.

The typical enterprise seeks to develop and implement an overall logistical competency that satisfies customer expectations at a realistic total cost expenditure. Very seldom will either the lowest total cost or the highest attainable customer service constitute the fundamental logistics strategy. Likewise, the appropriate combination will be different for different customers. A well-designed logistical effort must have high customer response and capability while controlling operational variance and minimizing inventory commitment. And, most of all, it must have relevancy to specific customers.

Significant advances have been made in the development of tools to aid management in the measurement of cost/service trade-offs. Formulation of a sound strategy requires a capability to estimate operating cost required to achieve alternative service levels. Likewise, alternative levels of system performance are meaningless unless viewed in terms of overall business unit marketing, manufacturing, and procurement strategies.

Leading firms realize that a well-designed and well-operated logistical system can help achieve competitive advantage. In fact, as a general rule, firms that obtain a strategic advantage based on logistical competency establish the nature of their industry's competition. Industry Insight 2-2 illustrates industry leadership enjoyed by Cisco Systems as a result of logistical competency.

The Work of Logistics

In the context of supply chain management, logistics exists to move and position inventory to achieve desired time, place, and possession benefits at the lowest total cost. Inventory has limited value until it is positioned at the right time and at the right location to support ownership transfer or value-added creation. If a firm does not consistently satisfy time and place requirements, it has nothing to sell. For a supply chain to realize the maximum strategic benefit of logistics, the full range of functional work must be integrated. Decisions in one functional area will impact cost of all others. It is this interrelation of functions that challenges the successful implementation of integrated logistical management. Figure 2-1 provides a visual representation of the interrelated nature of the five areas of logistical work: (1) order processing; (2) inventory; (3) transportation; (4) warehousing, materials handling, and packaging; and (5) facility network. As described below, work related to these functional areas combines to create the capabilities needed to achieve logistical value.

Order Processing

The importance of accurate information to logistical performance has historically been underappreciated. While many aspects of information are critical to logistics operations, the processing of orders is of primary importance. Failure to fully understand this importance resulted from a failure to understand how distortion and dynamics impact logistical operations.

INDUSTRY INSIGHT 2-2 CISCO'S SINGLE ENTERPRISE STRATEGY

Cisco's sales were growing by 100 percent per year in the mid-90s. Employment was swelling to keep pace and supply chain costs were unacceptably high. Product life cycles continued to shorten. Demands for reliability, flexibility, and speed escalated at an alarming rate. To keep pace, Cisco undertook a wholesale revamping of its business processes, from design and forecasting to raw materials acquisition, production, distribution, and customer follow-up.

The creation of Cisco's global networked business model arose in multiple departments at the same time, out of a shared realization of the need for change. Within this model, Cisco views its supply chain as a fabric of relationships, rather than in a linear fashion. The goal was to transcend the internal focus of Enterprise Resource Planning (ERP) systems to embrace a networked supply chain of all trading partners. Primary goals were servicing the customer better, coping with huge growth, and driving down costs. Utilizing the Internet, it is pursuing a single enterprise strategy.

Today Cisco relies on five contract manufacturers for nearly 60 percent of final assembling and testing and 100 percent of basic production. Through strict oversight and a clear set of standards, Cisco ensures that every partner achieves the same high level of quality. All 14 of its global manufacturing sites, along with two distributors, are linked via a single enterprise extranet.

The quest for a single enterprise has tied Cisco to its suppliers in unprecedented ways. Product now flows from first- and second-tier suppliers without the documentation and notifications on which most supply chains rely. Instead of responding to specific work orders, contract manufacturers turn out components according to a daily build plan derived from a single long-term forecast shared throughout the supply chain. Items move either to Cisco or directly to its customers. Payment occurs automatically upon receipt; there are no purchase orders, invoices, or traditional acknowledgments.

In exchange for getting paid sooner, suppliers are required to aggressively attack their cost structures but not to the point where they can't make a profit. "It's not a partnership if you're putting the other guy out of business," says Barbara Siverts, manager of supply chain solutions within Cisco's Internet Business Solutions unit.

Cisco cites at least $128 million in annual savings from its single enterprise strategy. It has reduced time to market by 25 percent, while hitting 97 percent of delivery targets. Inventories have been cut nearly in half. Order cycle time has declined from 6 to 8 weeks 4 years ago to between 1 and 3 weeks now. Under a program known as dynamic replenishment, demand signals flow instantly to contract manufacturers. Inventories can be monitored by all supply chain partners on a real time basis.

Some 55 percent of product now moves directly from supplier to customer, bypassing Cisco altogether. This has removed several days from the order cycle. Direct fulfillment means reduced inventories, labor costs, and shipping expenses. Cisco pegs savings at $10 per unit, or around $12 million a year.

Working with UPS, Cisco took control of the outbound supply chain, allowing for time-definite delivery throughout Europe within 5 to 8 days, via a single point of contact. With Oracle's inventory control system hooked directly into UPS's logistics management system, Cisco now tracks product to destination on a real time basis. The extra measure of control allows it to intercept, reroute, or reconfigure orders on short notice. Through deferred delivery, Cisco ensures that a component won't arrive at the customer's dock until it's ready to be installed.

Cisco's outsourcing strategy took another step forward recently, with the decision to turn over shipping and warehousing functions to FedEx Corp. The air, ground, and logistics services provider will manage a merge-in-transit operation for direct shipment to end customers, resulting in the near elimination of Cisco-operated warehouses within 5 years.

Source: Robert J. Bowman, "At Cisco Systems, the Internet Is Both Business and Business Model," *Global Logistics & Supply Chain Strategies,* May 2000, pp. 28–38.

FIGURE 2-1

Integrated logistics

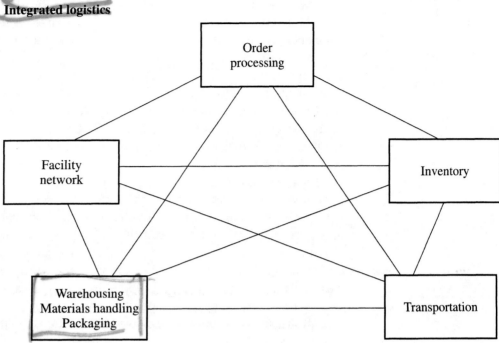

Current information technology is capable of handling the most demanding customer requirements. When desired, order information can be obtained on a real time basis.

The benefit of fast information flow is directly related to work balancing. It makes little sense for a firm to accumulate orders at a local sales office for a week, mail them to a regional office, process the orders as a batch, assign them to a distribution warehouse, and then ship them via air to achieve fast delivery. In contrast, data transmission or Web-based communication of orders direct from the customers' office combined with slower, less costly surface transportation may have achieved even faster overall delivery service at a lower total cost. The key objective is to balance components of the logistical system.

Forecasting and communication of customer requirements are the two areas of logistical work driven by information. The relative importance of each facet of operational information is directly related to the degree to which the supply chain is positioned to function on a responsive or anticipatory basis. The more responsive the supply chain design, the greater the importance is of accurate and timely information regarding customer purchase behavior. As established in Chapter 1, supply chains are increasingly reflecting a blend of responsive and anticipatory operations.

In most supply chains, customer requirements are transmitted in the form of orders. The processing of these orders involves all aspects of managing customer requirements from initial order receipt, delivery, invoicing, and collection. The logistics capabilities of a firm can only be as good as its order processing competency.

Inventory

The inventory requirements of a firm are directly linked to the facility network and the desired level of customer service. Theoretically, a firm could stock every item sold in every facility dedicated to servicing each customer. Few business operations can afford such a luxurious inventory commitment because the risk and total cost are prohibitive. The objective in inventory strategy is to achieve desired customer service with the minimum inventory commitment. Excessive inventories may compensate for deficiencies in basic design of a logistics system but will ultimately result in higher-than-necessary total logistics cost.

Logistical strategies should be designed to maintain the lowest possible financial investment in inventory. The basic goal is to achieve maximum inventory turn while satisfying service commitments. A sound inventory strategy is based on a combination of five aspects of selective deployment: (1) core customer segmentation, (2) product profitability, (3) transportation integration, (4) time-based performance, and (5) competitive performance.

Every enterprise that sells to a variety of different customers confronts uneven opportunity. Some customers are highly profitable and have outstanding growth potential; others do not. The profitability of a customer's business depends upon the products purchased, volume, price, value-added services required, and supplemental activities necessary to develop and maintain an ongoing relationship. Because highly profitable customers constitute the core market of every enterprise, inventory strategies need to focus on them. The key to effective logistical segmentation rests in the inventory priorities dedicated to support core customers.

Most enterprises experience a substantial variance in the volume and profitability across product lines. If no restrictions are applied, a firm may find that less than 20 percent of all products marketed account for more than 80 percent of total profit. While the so-called 80/20 rule or **Pareto principle** is common in business, management must avoid such outcomes by implementing inventory strategies based on fine-line product classification. A realistic assessment of the incremental value added by stocking low-profit or low-volume products is essential to avoiding excessive cost. For obvious reasons, an enterprise wants to offer high availability and consistent delivery of its most profitable products. High-level support of less profitable items, however, may be necessary to provide full-line service to core customers. The trap to avoid is high service performance on less profitable items that are typically purchased by fringe or noncore customers. Therefore, product line profitability must be considered when developing a selective inventory policy.

The product stocking plan at a specific facility has a direct impact upon transportation performance. Most transportation rates are based on the volume and size of specific shipments. Thus, it may be sound strategy to stock a sufficient range or assortment of products at a warehouse to be able to arrange consolidated shipments. The corresponding savings in transportation may more than offset the increased cost of holding the inventory.

A firm's degree of commitment to deliver products rapidly to meet a customer's inventory requirement is a major competitive factor. If products and materials can be delivered quickly, it may not be necessary for customers to maintain large inventories. Likewise, if retail stores can be replenished rapidly, less safety stock is required. The alternative to stockpiling and holding safety stock is to receive exact and timely inventory replenishment. While such time-based programs reduce customer inventory to absolute minimums, the savings must be balanced against other supply chain costs incurred as a result of the time-sensitive logistical process.

Finally, inventory strategies cannot be created in a competitive vacuum. A firm is typically more desirable to do business with, than competitors, if it can promise and perform rapid and consistent delivery. Therefore, it may be necessary to position inventory in a specific warehouse to gain competitive advantage even if such commitment increases total cost. Selective inventory deployment policies may be essential to gain a customer service advantage or to neutralize a strength that a competitor currently enjoys.

Material and component inventories exist in a logistical system for reasons other than finished product inventory. Each type of inventory and the level of commitment must be viewed from a total cost perspective. Understanding the interrelationship between order processing, inventory, transportation, and facility network decisions is fundamental to integrated logistics.

Transportation

Transportation is the operational area of logistics that geographically moves and positions inventory. Because of its fundamental importance and visible cost, transportation has traditionally received considerable managerial attention. Almost all enterprises, big and small, have managers responsible for transportation.

Transportation requirements can be satisfied in three basic ways. First, a private fleet of equipment may be operated. Second, contracts may be arranged with dedicated transport specialists. Third, an enterprise may engage the services of a wide variety of carriers that provide different transportation services on a per shipment basis. From the logistical system viewpoint, three factors are fundamental to transportation performance: (1) cost, (2) speed, and (3) consistency.

The **cost** of transport is the payment for shipment between two geographical locations and the expenses related to maintaining in-transit inventory. Logistical systems should utilize transportation that minimizes *total* system cost. This may mean that the least expensive method of transportation may not result in the lowest total cost of logistics.

Speed of transportation is the time required to complete a specific movement. Speed and cost of transportation are related in two ways. First, transport firms, capable of offering faster service, typically charge higher rates. Second, the faster the transportation service is, the shorter the time interval during which inventory is in-transit and unavailable. Thus, a critical aspect of selecting the most desirable method of transportation is to balance speed and cost of service.

Consistency of transportation refers to variations in time required to perform a specific movement over a number of shipments. Consistency reflects the dependability of transportation. For years, transportation managers have identified consistency as the most important attribute of quality transportation. If a shipment between two locations takes 3 days one time and 6 the next, the unexpected variance can create serious supply chain operational problems. When transportation lacks consistency, inventory safety stocks are required to protect against service breakdowns, impacting both the seller's and buyer's overall inventory commitment. With the advent of new information technology to control and report shipment status, logistics managers have begun to seek faster movement while maintaining consistency. Speed and consistency combine to create the quality aspect of transportation.

In designing a logistical system, a delicate balance must be maintained between transportation cost and service quality. In some circumstances low-cost, slow transportation is satisfactory. In other situations, faster service may be essential to achieving operating goals. Finding and managing the desired transportation mix across the supply chain is a primary responsibility of logistics.

Warehousing, Materials Handling, and Packaging

The first three functional areas of logistics—order processing, inventory, and transportation—can be engineered into a variety of different operational arrangements. Each arrangement has the potential to contribute to a specified level of customer service with an associated total cost. In essence, these functions combine to create a system solution for integrated logistics. The fourth functionality of logistics—warehousing, materials handling, and packaging—also represents an integral part of a logistics operating solution. However, these functions do not have the independent status of those previously discussed. Warehousing, materials handling, and packaging are an integral part of other logistics areas. For example, inventory typically needs to be warehoused at selected times during the logistics process. Transportation vehicles require materials handling for efficient loading and unloading. Finally, the individual products are most efficiently handled when packaged together into shipping cartons or other unit loads.

When distribution facilities are required in a logistical system, a firm can choose between the services of a warehouse specialist or operating their own facility. The decision is broader than simply selecting a facility to store inventory since many value-adding activities may be performed during the time products are warehoused. Examples of such activities are sorting, sequencing, order selection, transportation consolidation, and, in some cases, product modification and assembly.

Within the warehouse, materials handling is an important activity. Products must be received, moved, stored, sorted, and assembled to meet customer order requirements. The direct labor and capital invested in materials handling equipment is a significant element of total logistics cost. When performed in an inferior manner, materials handling can result in substantial product damage. It stands to reason that the fewer the times a product is handled, the less the potential exists for product damage and the overall efficiency of the warehouse is increased. A variety of mechanized and automated devices exist to assist materials handling. In essence, each warehouse and its materials handling capability represent a minisystem within the overall logistical process.

To facilitate handling efficiency, products in the form of cans, bottles, or boxes are typically combined into larger units. This larger unit, typically called the **master carton,** provides two important features. First, it serves to protect the product during the logistical process. Second, the master carton facilitates ease of handling, by creating one large package rather than a multitude of small, individual products. For efficient handling and transport, master cartons are typically consolidated into larger unit loads. The most common units for master carton consolidation are pallets, slip sheets, and various types of containers.

When effectively integrated into an enterprise's logistical operations, warehousing, materials handling, and packaging facilitate the speed and overall ease of product flow throughout the logistical system. In fact, several firms have engineered devices to move broad product assortments from manufacturing plants directly to retail stores without intermediate handling.

Facility Network

Classical economics neglected the importance of facility location and overall network design to efficient business operations. When economists originally discussed supply-and-demand relationships, facility location and transportation cost differentials were assumed either nonexistent or equal among competitors.[4] In business operations, however, the number, size, and geographical relationship of facilities used to perform logistical operations directly impacts customer service capabilities and cost. Network design is a primary responsibility of logistical management since a firm's facility structure is used to ship products and materials to customers. Typical logistics facilities are manufacturing plants, warehouses, cross-dock operations, and retail stores.

Network design is concerned with determining the number and location of all types of facilities required to perform logistics work. It is also necessary to determine what inventory and how much to stock at each facility as well as the assignment of customers. The facility network creates a structure from which logistical operations are performed. Thus, the network integrates information and transportation capabilities. Specific work tasks related to processing customer orders, warehousing inventory, and materials handling are all performed within the facility network.

The design of a facility network requires careful analysis of geographical variation. The fact that a great deal of difference exists between geographical markets is easy to illustrate. The 50 largest U.S. metropolitan markets in terms of population account for the majority of retail sales. Therefore, an enterprise marketing on a national scale must establish a logistical network capable of servicing prime markets. A similar geographic disparity exists in typical material and component part source locations. When a firm is involved in global logistics, issues related to network design become increasingly complex.

The importance of continuously modifying the facility network to accommodate change in demand and supply infrastructures cannot be overemphasized. Product assortments, customers, suppliers, and manufacturing requirements are constantly changing in a dynamic competitive environment. The selection of a superior locational network can provide a significant step toward achieving competitive advantage.

Logistical Operations

The internal operational scope of integrated logistics operations is illustrated by the shaded area of Figure 2-2. Information from and about customers flows through the enterprise in the form of sales activity, forecasts, and orders. Vital information is refined into specific manufacturing, merchandising, and purchasing plans. As products and materials are procured, a value-added inventory flow is initiated which ultimately results in ownership transfer of finished products to customers. Thus, the process is viewed in terms of two interrelated flows: inventory and information. While internal integrative management is important to success, the firm must also integrate across the supply chain. To be fully effective in today's competitive environment, firms must extend their enterprise integration to incorporate customers and suppliers. This extension reflects the position of logistics in the broader perspective of supply chain management. Supply chain integration is discussed later in this chapter (see Logistical Synchronization).

---

[4]Alfred Weber, *Theory of the Location of Industries,* transl. Carl J. Friedrich (Chicago, IL: University of Chicago Press, 1928); August Lösch, *Die Räumliche Ordnung der Wirtschaft,* (Jena: Gustav Fischer Verlag, 1940); Edgar M. Hoover, *The Location of Economic Activity* (New York, NY: McGraw-Hill Book Company, 1938); Melvin L. Greenhut, *Plant Location in Theory and Practice* (Chapel Hill, NC: University of North Carolina Press, 1956); Walter Isard, et. al., *Methods of Regional Analysis: An Introduction to Regional Science* (New York, NY: John Wiley & Sons, 1960); Walter Isard, *Location and Space Economy* (Cambridge, MA: The MIT Press, 1968); and Michael J. Webber, *Impact of Uncertainty on Location* (Cambridge, MA: The MIT Press, 1972).

FIGURE 2-2

Logistical integration

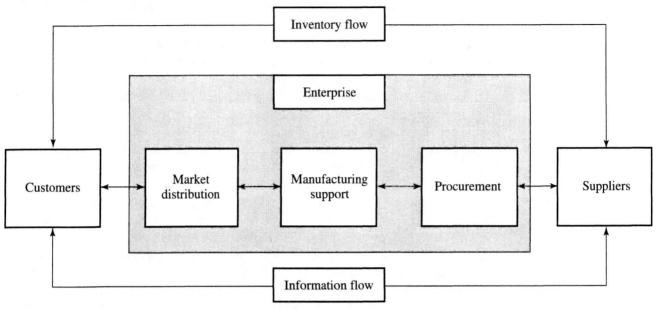

Inventory Flow

The operational management of logistics is concerned with movement and storage of materials and finished products. Logistical operations start with the initial shipment of a material or component part from a supplier and are finalized when a manufactured or processed product is delivered to a customer.

From the initial purchase of a material or component, the logistics process adds value by moving inventory when and where needed. Providing all goes well, materials and components gain value at each step of their transformation into finished inventory. In other words, an individual part has greater value after it is incorporated into a machine than it had as a part. Likewise, the machine has greater value once it is delivered to a customer.

To support manufacturing, work-in-process inventory must be properly positioned. The cost of each component and its movement becomes part of the value-added process. For better understanding, it is useful to divide logistical operations into three areas: (1) market distribution, (2) manufacturing support, and (3) procurement. These components are illustrated in the shaded area of Figure 2-2 as the combined logistics operational units of an enterprise.

Market Distribution

The movement of finished product to customers is **market distribution.** In market distribution, the end customer represents the final destination. The availability of product is a vital part of each channel participant's marketing effort. Even a manufacturer's agent, who typically does not own inventory, must be supported by inventory availability to perform expected marketing responsibilities. Unless a proper assortment of products is efficiently delivered when and where needed, a great deal of the overall marketing effort will be jeopardized. It is through the market distribution process that the timing and geographical placement of inventory become an integral part of marketing. To support the wide variety of marketing systems that exist in a highly commercialized nation, many different market distribution systems are available. All market distribution systems have one common feature: They link manufacturers, wholesalers, and retailers into supply chains to provide product availability.

Manufacturing Support

The area of **manufacturing support** concentrates on managing work-in-process inventory as it flows between stages of manufacturing. The primary logistical responsibility in manufacturing is to participate in formulating a master production schedule and to arrange for its implementation by timely availability of materials, component parts, and work-in-process inventory. Thus, the overall concern of manufacturing support is not how production occurs but rather *what, when,* and *where* products will be manufactured.

Manufacturing support is significantly different from market distribution. Market distribution attempts to service the desires of customers and therefore must accommodate the uncertainty of consumer and industrial demand. Manufacturing support involves movement requirements that are under the control of the manufacturing enterprise. The uncertainties introduced by random customer ordering and erratic demand that market distribution must accommodate are not typical in manufacturing operations. From the viewpoint of overall planning, the separation of manufacturing support from outbound market distribution and inbound procurement activities provides opportunities for specialization and improved efficiency. The degree to which a firm adopts a response strategy serves to reduce or eliminate the separation of manufacturing.

Procurement

Procurement is concerned with purchasing and arranging inbound movement of materials, parts, and/or finished inventory from suppliers to manufacturing or assembly plants, warehouses, or retail stores. Depending on the situation, the acquisition process is commonly identified by different names. In manufacturing, the process of acquisition is typically called *purchasing*. In government circles, acquisition has traditionally been referred to as *procurement*. In retailing and wholesaling, *buying* is the most widely used term. In many circles, the process is referred to as *inbound logistics*. For the purposes of this text, the term *procurement* will include all types of purchasing. The term *material* is used to identify inventory moving inbound to an enterprise, regardless of its degree of readiness for resale. The term *product* is used to identify inventory that is available for consumer purchase. In other words, materials are involved in the process of adding value through manufacturing whereas products are ready for consumption. The fundamental distinction is that products result from the value added to material during manufacture, sortation, or assembly.

Within a typical enterprise, the three logistics operating areas overlap. Viewing each as an integral part of the overall value-adding process creates an opportunity to capitalize on the unique attributes of each within the overall process. Table 2-2 provides a more exacting definition of the day-to-day work involved in each subprocess of logistics. The overall challenge of a supply chain is to integrate the logistical processes of participating firms in a manner that facilitates overall efficiency.

Information Flow

Information flow identifies specific locations within a logistical system that have requirements. Information also integrates the three operating areas. Within individual logistics areas, different movement requirements exist with respect to size of order, availability of inventory, and urgency of movement. The primary objective of information flow management is to reconcile these differentials to improve overall supply chain performance. It is important to stress that information requirements parallel the

---
TABLE 2-2   Specific Operating Concerns of Market Distribution, Manufacturing Support, and Procurement in Overall Logistics

---

Market Distribution

Activities related to providing customer service. Requires performing order receipt and processing, deploying inventories, storage and handling, and outbound transportation within a supply chain. Includes the responsibility to coordinate with marketing planning in such areas as pricing, promotional support, customer service levels, delivery standards, handling return merchandise, and life cycle support. The primary market distribution objective is to assist in revenue generation by providing strategically desired customer service levels at the lowest total cost.

Manufacturing Support

Activities related to planning, scheduling, and supporting manufacturing operations. Requires master schedule planning and performing work-in-process storage, handling, transportation, and sortation, sequencing and time phasing of components. Includes the responsibility for storage of inventory at manufacturing sites and maximum flexibility in the coordination of geographic and assembly postponement between manufacturing and market distribution operations.

Procurement

Activities related to obtaining products and materials from outside suppliers. Requires performing resource planning, supply sourcing, negotiation, order placement, inbound transportation, receiving and inspection, storage and handling, and quality assurance. Includes the responsibility to coordinate with suppliers in such areas as scheduling, supply continuity, hedging, and speculation, as well as research leading to new sources or programs. The primary procurement objective is to support manufacturing or resale organizations by providing timely purchasing at the lowest total cost.

---

actual work performed in market distribution, manufacturing support, and procurement. Whereas these areas contain the actual logistics work, information facilitates coordination of planning and control of day-to-day operations. Without accurate information the effort involved in the logistical system can be wasted.

Logistical information has two major components: planning/coordination and operations. The interrelationship of the two types of logistical information is illustrated in Figure 2-3. In-depth discussion of information technology is reserved for Part II, at which time the architecture of logistical information systems is developed in greater detail. The objective here is to introduce the framework that details information needed to manage integrated logistics.

Planning/Coordination

The overall purpose of planning/coordination is to identify required operational information and to facilitate supply chain integration via (1) strategic objectives, (2) capacity constraints, (3) logistical requirements, (4) inventory deployment, (5) manufacturing requirements, (6) procurement requirements, and (7) forecasting. Unless a high level of planning/coordination is achieved, the potential exists for operating inefficiencies and excessive inventory. The challenge is to achieve such planning/coordination across the range of firms participating in a supply chain to reduce duplication and unneeded redundancy.

The primary drivers of supply chain operations are **strategic objectives** derived from marketing and financial goals. These initiatives detail the nature and location of customers that supply chain operations seeks to match to the planned products and services. The financial aspects of strategic plans detail resources required to support inventory, receivables, facilities, equipment, and capacity.

FIGURE 2-3

Logistics information requirements

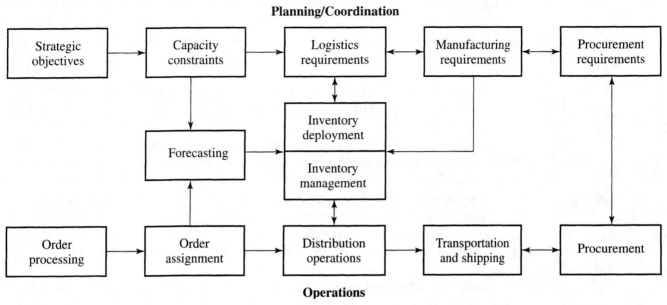

Capacity constraints identify internal and external manufacturing and market distribution limitations. Given strategic objectives, capacity constraints identify limitations, barriers, or bottlenecks within manufacturing and distribution facilities. It also helps identify when specific manufacturing or distribution work should be outsourced. To illustrate, whereas Kellogg owns the brand and distributes *Cracklin' Oat Bran,* all manufacturing is performed by a third party on a contract basis. The output of capacity constraint planning is time-phased objectives that detail and schedule facility utilization, financial resources, and human requirements.

Using inputs from forecasting, promotional scheduling, customer orders, and inventory status, **logistical requirements** identify the specific work facilities, equipment, and labor forces required to support the strategic plan.

Inventory deployment interfaces with inventory management between planning/ coordination and operations, as shown in Figure 2-3. The deployment plan details the timing of where inventory will be positioned to efficiently move inventory through the supply chain. From an information perspective, deployment specifies the *what, where,* and *when* for the logistics processes. From an operational viewpoint, inventory management is performed on a day-to-day basis.

In production situations, **manufacturing requirements** determine planned schedules. The traditional deliverable is a statement of time-phased inventory requirements that is used to drive Master Production Scheduling (MPS) and Manufacturing Requirements Planning (MRP). In situations characterized by a high degree of responsiveness, Advance Planning Systems (APS) are more commonly used to time-phase manufacturing.

Procurement requirements represent a time-sequenced schedule of material and components needed to support manufacturing requirements. In retailing and wholesaling establishments, purchasing determines inbound merchandise. In manufacturing situations, procurement arranges for arrival of materials and component parts from suppliers. Regardless of the business situation, purchasing information is used to coordinate decisions concerning supplier qualifications, degree of desired speculation, third-party arrangements, and feasibility of long-term contracting.

Forecasting utilizes historical data, current activity levels, and planning assumptions to predict future activity levels. Logistical forecasting is generally concerned with relatively short-term predictions. Typical forecast horizons are from 30 to 90 days. The forecast challenge is to quantify expected sales for specific products. These forecasts form the basis of logistics requirement and operating plans.

Operations

A second purpose of accurate and timely information is to facilitate logistical operations. To satisfy supply chain requirements, logistics must receive, process, and ship inventory. Operational information is required in six related areas: (1) order processing, (2) order assignment, (3) distribution operations, (4) inventory management, (5) transportation and shipping, and (6) procurement. These areas of information facilitate the areas of logistical work outlined in Figure 2-1 and the related discussion.

Order processing refers to the exchange of requirements information between supply chain members involved in product distribution. The primary activity of order management is accurate entry and qualification of customer orders. Information technology has radically changed the traditional process of order management.

Order assignment identifies inventory and organizational responsibility to satisfy customer requirements. The traditional approach has been to assign responsibility or planned manufacturing to customers according to predetermined priorities. In technology-rich order processing systems, two-way communication linkage can be maintained with customers to generate a negotiated order that satisfies customers within the constraints of planned logistical operations.

Distribution operations involve information to facilitate and coordinate work within logistics facilities. Emphasis is placed on scheduling availability of the desired inventory assortment with minimal duplication and redundant work effort. The key to distribution operations is to store and handle specific inventory as little as possible while still meeting customer order requirements.

Inventory management is concerned with information required to implement the logistics plan. Using a combination of human resources and information technology, inventory is deployed and then managed to satisfy planned requirements. The work of inventory management is to make sure that the overall logistical system has appropriate resources to perform as planned.

Transportation and **shipping** information directs inventory movement. In distribution operations, it is important to consolidate orders so as to fully utilize transportation capacity. It is also necessary to ensure that the required transportation equipment is available when needed. Finally, because ownership transfer often results from transportation, supporting transaction documentation is required.

Procurement is concerned with the information necessary to complete purchase order preparation, modification, and release while ensuring overall supplier compliance. In many ways information related to procurement is similar to that involved in order processing. Both forms of information exchange serve to facilitate operations that link a firm with its customers and suppliers.

The overall purpose of operational information is to facilitate integrated management of market distribution, manufacturing support, and procurement operations. Planning/coordination identifies and prioritizes required work and identifies operational information needed to perform the day-to-day logistics. The dynamics of supply chain synchronization is discussed next.

Logistical Operating Arrangements

The potential for logistical services to favorably impact customers is directly related to operating system design. The many different facets of logistical performance requirements make operational design a complex task as an operating structure must offer a balance of performance, cost, and flexibility. When one considers the variety of logistical systems used throughout the world to service widely diverse markets, it is astonishing that any structural similarity exists. But keep in mind that all logistical arrangements have two common characteristics. First, they are designed to manage inventory. Second, the range of alternative logistics systems is based on available technology. These two characteristics tend to create commonly observed operating arrangements. Three widely utilized structures are echelon, direct, and flexible.

Echelon

Classification of a logistical system as having an echeloned structure means that the flow of products typically proceeds through a common arrangement of firms and facilities as it moves from origin to final destination. The use of echelons usually implies that total cost analysis justifies stocking some level of inventory or performing specific activities at consecutive levels of the supply chain.

Echelon systems utilize warehouses to create inventory assortments and achieve consolidation economies associated with large-volume transportation shipments. Inventories positioned in warehouses are available for rapid deployment to customer requirements. Figure 2-4 illustrates the typical echeloned value chain.

Typical echelon systems utilize either break-bulk or consolidation warehouses. A break-bulk facility typically receives large-volume shipments from a variety of suppliers. Inventory is sorted and stored in anticipation of future customer requirements. Food distribution centers operated by major grocery chains and wholesalers are examples of break-bulk warehouses. A consolidation warehouse operates in a reverse profile. Consolidation is typically required by manufacturing firms that have plants at different geographical locations. Products manufactured at different plants are stored in a central warehouse facility to allow the firm to ship full-line assortments to customers. Major consumer product manufacturers are prime examples of enterprises using echeloned systems for full-line consolidation.

Direct

In contrast to inventory echeloning are logistical systems designed to ship products direct to customer's destination from one or a limited number of centrally located inventories. Direct distribution typically uses premium transport combined with information technology to rapidly process customer orders and achieve delivery performance. This

FIGURE 2-4

Echelon-structured logistics

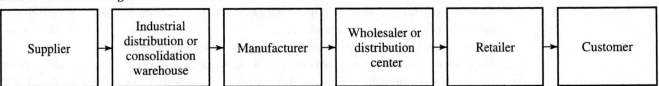

FIGURE 2-5

Echeloned and direct-structured logistics

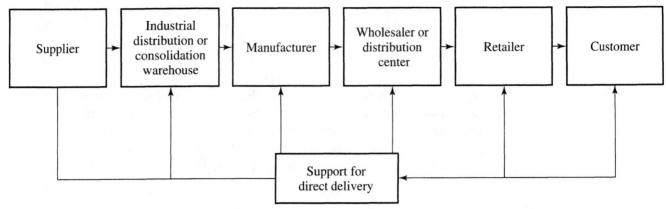

combination of capabilities, designed into the order delivery cycle, reduces time delays and overcomes geographical separation from customers. Examples of direct shipments are plant-to-customer truckload shipments, direct store delivery, and various forms of direct to consumer fulfillment required to support catalog and e-commerce shopping. Direct logistical structures are also commonly used for inbound components and materials to manufacturing plants because the average shipment size is typically large.

When the economics justify, logistics executives tend to desire direct alternatives because they reduce anticipatory inventories and intermediate product handling. The deployment of direct logistics is limited by high transportation cost and potential loss of control. In general, most firms do not operate the number of warehouses today that were common a few years ago and have been able to modify echelon structures to include direct logistics capabilities. Figure 2-5 illustrates direct logistics capability being added to an echeloned logistics structure.

Flexible

The ideal logistical arrangement is a situation wherein the inherent benefits of echeloned and direct structures are combined into a flexible logistics system. As noted in Chapter 1, anticipatory commitment of inventory should ideally be postponed as long as possible. Inventory strategies often position fast-moving products or materials in forward warehouses, while other, more risky or costly items, are stocked at a central location for direct distribution to customers. The basic service commitment and the order size economics determine the most desirable and economical structure to service a specific customer.

To illustrate, automobile replacement parts logistics typically distributes to customers utilizing a flexible logistics strategy. Specific parts are inventoried in warehouses located at various distances from dealers and retail outlets based on pattern and intensity of demand. As a general rule, the slower the part turnover is, the more erratic the demand is, and therefore the greater the benefit is of centralized inventory. The slowest or least demanded parts may only be stocked at one location that services customers throughout the entire world. Fast-moving parts that have more predictable demand are stocked in forward warehouses close to dealers to facilitate fast delivery.

A contrasting example is an enterprise that sells machine parts to industrial firms. The nature of this business supports a completely opposite flexible distribution strategy. To offer superior service to customers who experience machine failure and unexpected downtime, the firm stocks slow movers in all local warehouses. In contrast to the automotive firm, high-demand, fast-turnover parts in this industry can be accurately forecasted due to routine preventative maintenance. The least cost logistical methods for these fast movers are to ship direct from a centralized warehouse located adjacent to the parts manufacturing plant. These alternative logistics strategies, both of which use different flexible logistical capabilities, are justified based on unique customer requirements and intensity of competition confronted. The automotive manufacturer is the sole supplier of parts during the new car warranty period and must provide dealers rapid delivery of parts to promptly repair customer cars. Dealers require fast replenishment of parts inventory to satisfy customers while minimizing inventory investment. As cars grow older and the demand for replacement parts increases, alternative manufacturers enter the replacement parts market. During this highly competitive stage of the model's life cycle, rapid logistical response is required to be competitive. As a model ages, competition drops out of the shrinking aftermarket, leaving the original manufacturer as the sole supplier.

The industrial component supplier, in contrast to the automotive company, offers standard machine parts having a high degree of competitive substitutability. Whereas products used on a regular basis can be forecasted, slow or erratic demanded products are impossible to forecast. This enterprise forces a situation wherein customers measure suppliers in terms of how fast unexpected machine breakdowns can be remedied. Failure to perform to the level of customer expectation can open the door for a competitor to prove its capability.

Each enterprise faces a unique customer situation and can be expected to use a different flexible logistics strategy to achieve competitive superiority. The channel strategy that satisfies customer expectations at lowest attainable total cost typically utilizes a combination of echeloned and direct capabilities.

Beyond the basic channel structure, flexible capabilities can be designed into a logistical system by developing a program to service customers using alternative facilities. Flexible logistics capabilities can be designed to operate on an emergency or routine basis.

Emergency Flexible Structure

Emergency flexible operations are preplanned strategies to resolve logistical failures. A typical emergency occurs when an assigned shipping facility is out of stock or for some other reason cannot complete a customer's order. For example, a warehouse may be out of an item with no replenishment inventory scheduled to arrive until after the customer's specified order delivery date. To prohibit back-order or product cancellation, a contingency operating policy may assign the total order, or at least those items not available, for shipment from an alternative warehouse. The use of emergency flexible operation procedures is typically based on the importance of the specific customer or the critical nature of the product being ordered.

Routine Flexible Structure

A flexible logistics capability that has gained popularity as a result of improved communications involves procedures for serving specified customers developed as part of the basic logistical system design. The flexible logistics rules and decision scenarios specify alternative ways to meet service requirements, such as assignment of different shipping facilities. A strategy that exploits routine flexible operations may be justified in at least four different situations.

First, the customer-specified delivery location might be near a point of equal logistics cost or time for delivery from two different logistics facilities. Customers located at such points of indifference offer the supplying firm an opportunity to fully utilize available logistical capacity. Orders can be serviced from the facility having the best inventory positioning to satisfy customer requirements and the available capacity to achieve timely delivery. This form of flexible logistics offers a way to fully utilize system capacity by balancing workloads between facilities while protecting superior customer service commitments. The benefit is operating efficiency, which is transparent to the customer who experiences no service deterioration.

A second situation justifying routine flexible distribution is when the size of a customer's order creates an opportunity to improve logistical efficiency if serviced through an alternative channel arrangement. For example, the lowest-total-cost method to provide small shipment delivery may be through a distributor. In contrast, larger shipments may have the lowest total logistical cost when shipped factory direct to customers. Provided that alternative methods of shipment meet customer service expectations, total logistical cost may be reduced by implementing routine flexible policies.

A third type of routine flexible operations may result from a selective inventory stocking strategy. The cost and risk associated with stocking inventory require careful analysis to determine which items to place in each warehouse. With replacement parts, a common strategy mentioned earlier is to stock selected items in specific warehouses with the total line only being stocked at a central facility. In general merchandise retailing, a store or distribution center located in a small community may only stock a limited or restricted version of a firm's total line. When customers desire nonstocked items, orders must be satisfied from an alternative facility. The term *mother facility* is often used to describe inventory strategies that designate larger facilities for backup support of smaller restricted facilities. Selective inventory stocking by echelon level is a common strategy used to reduce inventory risk. The reasons for selective echelon stocking range from low product profit contribution to high per unit cost of inventory maintenance. One way to operationalize a fine-line inventory classification strategy is to differentiate stocking policy by system echelons. In situations following such classified stocking strategies it may be necessary to obtain advanced customer approval for split-order delivery. However, in some situations firms that use differentiated inventory stocking strategies are able to reconfigure customer orders for same time delivery, thereby making the arrangement customer transparent.

The *fourth* type of routine flexible operations results from agreements between firms to move selected shipments outside the established echeloned or direct logistics arrangements. Two special arrangements gaining popularity are flow through **cross-docks** and **service supplier arrangements.** A cross-dock operation involves multiple suppliers arriving at a designated time at the handling facility and is typically deployed in situations where storage and materials handling can be avoided. Inventory receipts are sorted across the dock and consolidated into outbound trailers for direct destination delivery. Cross-dock operations are growing in popularity in the food industry for building store-specific assortments and are common methods of continuous inventory replenishment for mass merchant and other retail stores.

Another form of routine flexible operations is to use integrated service providers to assemble products for delivery. This is similar to consolidation for transportation

FIGURE 2-6

Flexible direct echeloned structured logistics

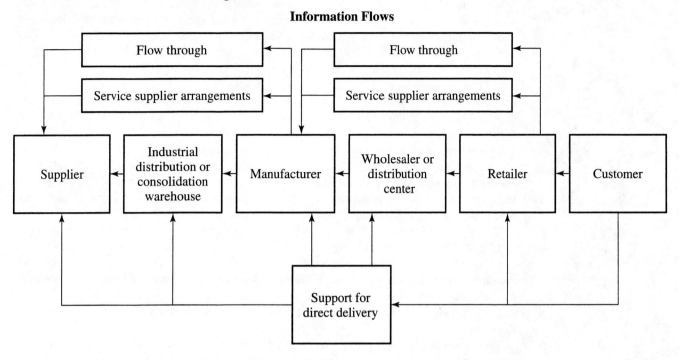

Information Flows

purposes discussed in the previous section of this chapter. However, as a form of flexible logistics, specialists are used to avoid storage and handling of slow-moving products through the mainstream of the echeloned logistics structure. Such service providers can also provide important value-added services. For example, Smurfit-Stone builds in-store point-of-sale displays for direct store delivery.

Figure 2-6 introduces flexibility to the logistical operating structures previously illustrated. A prerequisite to effective flexible operations is the use of information technology to monitor inventory status throughout the network and provide the capability to rapidly switch methods for handling customer orders. The use of flexible operations for emergency accommodation has a well-established track record. To a significant degree, an effective, flexible logistics strategy can substitute for the safety stock maintained in a traditional anticipatory-driven logistical system. As illustrated in Industry Insight 2-3, Biogen capitalized on flexible logistics and supply chain operations to secure a competitive edge.

The attractiveness of using integrated service providers is directly related to the designed flexibility of a firm's logistics strategy. If a firm elects to offer direct distribution, the services of highly reliable, fast transportation will be required. An echelon structure means that opportunities may exist for volume-oriented transportation and the services of firms that specialize in operating cross-docking facilities. A strategy that seeks the combined benefits of echeloned and direct logistics may be an ideal candidate for the integrated services of a third-party logistics specialist. It is important to keep in mind that the selected logistics strategy directly drives channel structure and relationships. To a significant degree, information technology is forcing reconsideration of long-standing practices regarding rigid ways of conducting business. These developments can be illustrated by an examination of managerial practices required to achieve internal and external integration of logistical operations.

INDUSTRY INSIGHT 2-3 BIOGEN UNCHAINED

When Biogen was founded in 1978, it had a simple, research-centered business model: its scientists would use biotechnology to discover compounds that might be used to create new drugs, and then it would license those compounds to big pharmaceutical companies. It had no need to build a manufacturing or distribution infrastructure because it didn't intend to actually produce drugs.

That business model was turned upside down in 1994 when the company received preliminary FDA approval to market Avonex, a breakthrough drug that could slow the progression of multiple sclerosis. Biogen suddenly had to find a way to get a product to customers quickly and dependably while building an efficient delivery system for the long term. The company embraced an entirely new way to organize and manage production and distribution. It would work with a network of partners to get its new product to market, becoming a virtual manufacturer.

The first step was to determine which tasks it would perform and which it would outsource. Biogen took a hard look at the four core tasks of drug production—bulk manufacturing, formulation, packaging, and warehousing and distribution—and determined that it could handle the bulk manufacturing at its existing facility. It would contract out everything else.

In choosing its partners, it looked for organizations that were big enough to accommodate rapid growth but small enough to give the Biogen account top priority. For formulation, which consisted of freeze-drying the drug and storing it at low temperatures, it chose Ben Venue Laboratories, a contract manufacturer in Ohio. Packaging Coordinators, a small but innovative company near Philadelphia, was given the job of packaging. And for warehousing and distribution, Biogen chose to partner with Amgen, which had a new distribution center in Louisville, Kentucky.

Biogen kept tight control over managing the network. It stationed some of its people at partners' sites, offered their staffs training and supervision, and installed new computer systems to manage the flow of shared information. It also set tough standards for the performance of the network, establishing world-class objectives for execution and quality and insisting on a goal of fulfilling every order without delay. The worst scenario would be to run out of the product. A shortage would not only hurt the patients who relied on the drug, but it would also undermine Biogen's profits. Because Avonex carried a high price—$1,000 for a month's supply—the cost of carrying inventory was tiny relative to the cost of a lost sale.

As the company waited for final FDA approval of Avonex, it worked with its partners to develop four detailed contingency plans for getting the drug to patients as quickly as possible.

Finally, at 11 AM on Friday, May 17, 1996, Biogen received FDA approval. The virtual organization worked seamlessly. The first shipments of Avonex reached pharmacy shelves within 35 hours—a new record for the pharmaceutical industry—and the drug was ready for dispensing by Monday morning. Within 6 months, Avonex had displaced Betaseron, another multiple sclerosis treatment drug introduced 3 years earlier, as the market leader, garnering more than 60 percent of new prescriptions.

The full value of the production and distribution network became apparent over time: between 1996 and 1999, the drug's production volume increased fivefold, and the virtual organization scaled up flawlessly to accommodate the growth. Avonex has never gone out of stock, and there have been no serious customer service problems or product recalls.

The outsourcing of key operational elements has enabled Biogen to achieve a competitive cost structure despite its limited production experience and small scale. It has also helped the company keep its fixed assets low, even when production volume increased dramatically. The required capital investment was modest relative to the size of the business, and much of the investment risk could be shared with partners.

Source: David Bovet and Joseph Martha, "Biogen Unchained," *Harvard Business Review,* May–June 2000, p. 28.

Logistical Synchronization

The previous discussion positioned logistics as an integrated management process within an individual firm. The challenge of supply chain management is to integrate operations across multiple firms that are jointly committed to the same value proposition. In an effort to facilitate logistical operations, supply chain participants must jointly plan and implement operations. Multifirm operational integration across a supply chain is referred to as **logistical synchronization.**

Logistical synchronization seeks to coordinate the flow of materials, products, and information between supply chain partners to reduce duplication and unwanted redundancy to an absolute minimum. It also seeks to reengineer internal operations of individual firms to create leveraged overall supply chain capability. Leveraged operations require a joint plan concerning the logistics work that each participating firm will perform and be held accountable for. At the heart of supply chain integration is the goal of leveraging member core competencies to achieve overall reduction of inventory dwell time.

As defined in Chapter 1, dwell time is the ratio of time inventory sits idle in comparison to the amount of time it is being productively moved to a desired location in the supply chain. To illustrate, a product or component stored in a warehouse is dwelling. In contrast, the same part moving in a transportation vehicle on the way to a customer is being productively deployed. Ideally, the shipment will arrive in a timely manner to be immediately used by the customer in a value-added process. The desire is to directly integrate inventory into the customer's value-adding process without product being placed in storage or otherwise restricting continuous movement. The benefits of synchronization serve to support the generalization that speed of performing a specific service or product movement is secondary to synchronizing the timing of supply with demand requirements.

Performance Cycle Structure

The performance cycle represents the elements of work necessary to complete the logistics related to market distribution, manufacturing, or support procurement. It consists of specific work ranging from identification of requirements to product delivery. Because it integrates various aspects of work, the performance cycle is the primary unit of analysis for logistical synchronization. At a basic level, information and transportation must *link* all firms functioning in a supply chain. The operational locations that are linked by information and transportation are referred to as **nodes.**

In addition to supply chain nodes and links, performance cycles involve inventory assets. Inventory is measured in terms of the **asset investment level** allocated to support operations at a node or while a product or material is in transit. Inventory committed to supply chain nodes consists of base stock and safety stock. Base stock is inventory held at a node and is typically one-half of the average shipment size received. Safety stock exists to protect against variance in demand or operational lead time. It is *at* and *between* supply chain nodes that work related to logistics is performed. Inventory is stocked and flows through nodes, necessitating a variety of different types of materials handling and, when necessary, storage. While a degree of handling and in-transit storage takes place within transportation, such activity is minor in comparison to that typically performed within a supply chain node, such as a warehouse.

Performance cycles become dynamic as they accommodate **input/output requirements.** The *input* to a performance cycle is demand, typically in the form of a work order that specifies requirements for a product or material. A high-volume supply chain will typically require a different and wider variety of performance cycles than a chain having fewer throughputs. When operating requirements are highly predictable or relatively low-volume throughput, the performance cycle structure required to provide supply chain logistical support can be simplified. The performance cycle structures required to support a large retail enterprise like Target or Wal★Mart supply chains are far more complex than the operating structure requirements of a catalog fulfillment company.

Supply chain *output* is the level of performance expected from the combined logistical operations that support a particular arrangement. To the extent that operational requirements are satisfied, the combined logistical performance cycle structure of the supply chain is effective in accomplishing its mission. Efficiency of a supply chain is a measure of resource expenditure necessary to achieve such logistical effectiveness. The effectiveness and efficiency of logistical performance cycles are key concerns in supply chain management.

Depending on the operational mission of a particular performance cycle in a supply chain structure, the associated work may be under the complete control of a single enterprise or may involve multiple firms. For example, manufacturing support cycles are often under the operational control of a single enterprise. In contrast, performance cycles related to market distribution and procurement typically involve multiple firms.

It is important to realize that transaction frequency and intensity will vary between performance cycles. Some performance cycles are established to facilitate a one-time purchase or sale. In such a case, the associated supply chain is designed, implemented, and abolished once the transaction is complete. Other performance cycles represent long-standing structural arrangements. A complicating fact is that any operation or facility in one logistical arrangement may simultaneously be participating in a number of other performance cycles. For example, the warehouse facility of a hardware wholesaler might regularly receive merchandise from multiple manufacturers and service competing retailers. Likewise, a motor carrier may participate in numerous different supply chains, spanning a wide variety of industries.

When one considers a supply chain of national or multinational scope that is involved in marketing a broad product line to numerous customers, engaging in basic manufacturing and assembly, and procuring materials and components on a global basis, the notion of individual performance cycles linking all participating firms' operations is difficult to comprehend. It is almost mind-boggling to estimate how many performance cycles exist in the supply chain structure of General Motors or IBM.

Regardless of the number and different missions of performance cycles a supply chain deploys to satisfy its logistical requirements, each must be individually designed and operationally managed. The fundamental importance of performance cycle design and operation cannot be overemphasized: *The logistics performance cycle is the basic unit of supply chain design and operational control. In essence, the performance cycle structure is the framework for implementation of integrated logistics across the supply chain.*

Figure 2-7 portrays an echeloned supply chain structure illustrating basic logistics performance cycles. Figure 2-8 illustrates a network of flexible performance cycles integrated in a multiecheloned structure.

Three points are important to understanding the architecture of integrated supply chain logistical systems. First, as noted earlier, the performance cycles are the fundamental unit for integrated logistics across the supply chain. Second, the performance cycle structure of a supply chain, in terms of link and nodal arrangement, is basically

FIGURE 2-7

Logistical performance cycles

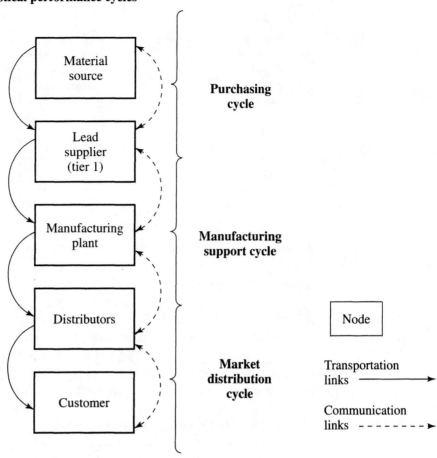

FIGURE 2-8

Multi-echeloned flexible logistical network

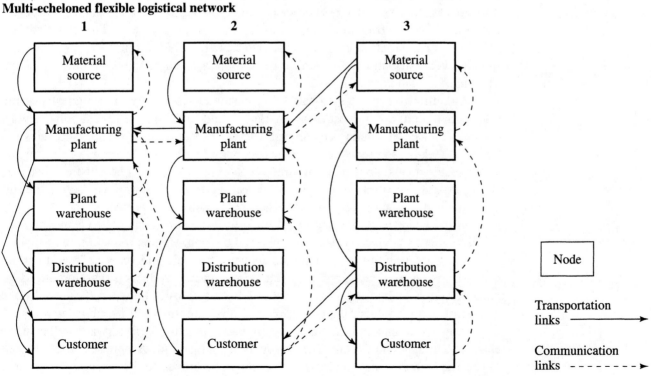

187

FIGURE 2-9

Basic market distribution performance cycle activities

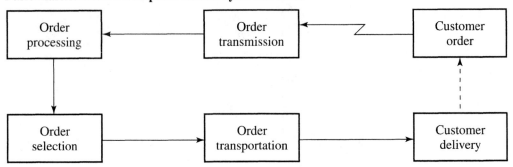

the same whether one is concerned with market distribution, manufacturing support, or procurement. However, considerable differences exist in the degree of control that an individual firm can exercise over a specific type of performance cycle. Third, regardless of how vast and complex the overall supply chain structure, essential interfaces and control processes must be identified and evaluated in terms of individual performance cycle arrangements and associated managerial accountability.

To better understand the importance of synchronization in supply chain integration, the similarities and differences in market distribution, manufacturing support, and procurement performance cycles are discussed and illustrated.

Market Distribution Performance Cycles

Market distribution operations are concerned with processing and delivering customer orders. Market distribution is integral to sales performance because it provides timely and economical product availability. The overall process of gaining and maintaining customers can be broadly divided into transaction-creating and physical-fulfillment activities. The transaction-creating activities are advertising and selling. The physical-fulfillment activities include (1) order transmission, (2) order processing, (3) order selection, (4) order transportation, and (5) customer delivery. The basic market distribution performance cycle is illustrated in Figure 2-9. From a logistical perspective, market distribution performance cycles link a supply chain with end customers. This interface can be conflictive.

Marketing is dedicated to satisfying customers to achieve the highest possible sales penetration. So, in most firms, marketing and sales impose liberal policies when it comes to accommodating customers. This may mean that marketing and sales will typically seek broad product assortments supported with high inventory or that all customer requirements, no matter how small or how profitable, will be satisfied. The marketing expectation is that zero logistical defect service will be achieved across the supply chain and customer-focused marketing efforts will be supported.

On the other hand, the traditional mindset in manufacturing is to achieve lowest possible unit cost, which typically is achieved by long, stable production runs. Continuous manufacturing processes maintain economy of scale and generate lowest per unit cost. Ideally, in continuous processing, a narrow line of products is mass-produced. Inventory serves to buffer and resolve the inherent conflict between these traditional marketing and manufacturing philosophies. The commitment of inventory to reconcile marketing and manufacturing has typically meant positioning it forward in the supply chain in anticipation of future sale. Products are shipped to warehouses based on forecasted requirements, acknowledging they might be moved to the wrong market and at the wrong time. The end result of such risky decisions is that critical inventory can be improperly deployed in an attempt to efficiently support customer service requirements. At this point, the important concept to keep in mind is that the market distribution performance cycle operates downstream in the supply chain forward from manufacturing and close to end customer. Inventories committed to market distribution, when correctly positioned, represent the maximum potential value that can be achieved by the logistical process.

The very fact that market distribution deals with customer requirements means that this facet of supply chain operations will be more erratic than either manufacturing support or procurement performance cycles. Attention to *how* customers order products is essential to reduce market distribution operational variance and simplify transactions. First, every effort should be made to improve forecast accuracy. Second, a program based on collaborative planning with customers should be initiated to reduce as much uncertainty as possible. Third, and finally, market distribution performance cycles should be designed to be as responsive as possible, which might include implementation of postponement strategies.

The key to understanding market distribution performance-cycle dynamics is to keep in mind that customers initiate the supply chain process when they order products. The agility and flexibility of response related to market distribution constitutes one of logistics' most significant competencies.

Manufacturing Support Performance Cycles

Manufacturing is the node in a supply chain that creates *form* value. To a significant degree, manufacturing efficiency depends on logistical support to establish and maintain an orderly and economic flow of materials and work-in-process inventory as required by production schedules. The degree of specialization required in market distribution and procurement can overshadow the importance of positioning and timing inventory movement to support manufacturing. Because customers and suppliers are not involved, manufacturing logistics is less visible than its counterparts.

The identification of manufacturing logistical support as a distinct operating area is a relatively new concept. The justification for focusing on performance cycles to support production is found in the unique requirements and operational constraints of flexible manufacturing strategies. To provide maximum flexibility, traditional manufacturing practices related to economy of scale are being reevaluated to accommodate quick product switchover and shorter production runs. Exacting logistical support between supply chain participants is required to perfect such time-sensitive manufacturing strategies. It is important to once again stress that the mission of logistical manufacturing support is to facilitate the *what, where,* and *when* of production, not the how. The goal is to support all manufacturing requirements in the most efficient manner.

Manufacturing support operations are significantly different than either market distribution or procurement. Manufacturing support logistics is typically captive within individual firms, whereas the other two performance areas must deal with the behavioral uncertainty across the supply chain. Even in situations when outsource contract manufacturing is used to augment internal capacity, overall control of a single enterprise is greater than in the other two operating areas. The benefits to be gained by exploitation of this control opportunity are the prime justification for treating manufacturing logistical support as a distinct operating area.

A recently introduced practice that is rapidly growing is to use **lead suppliers** to coordinate and facilitate the work of a group of related manufacturing suppliers. These related suppliers may produce similar or complementary products that are used to produce a subassembly that is part of a more complex product. The term *tier one* supplier is frequently used to describe the positioning of lead suppliers between a major manufacturer and suppliers of specific parts or components. The purpose of the lead supplier is to reduce the overall complexity of managing the supply chain. It is common for lead suppliers to be awarded contracts to perform subassembly operations, coordinate inbound movements, and oversee the work and quality of smaller suppliers. The lead supplier is delegated the responsibility of sorting, assembly, and sequencing subassemblies to support manufacturing. In such situations, the logistics of procurement and manufacturing are combined. The acronym JIT, which stands for Just-in-Time, evolved from an early effort at this type of supply chain synchronization by the Toyota Motor Car Company.[5]

Within a typical manufacturing organization, procurement has the responsibility to provide materials and outsourced manufactured components when and where needed. Once a firm's manufacturing operation is initiated, subsequent requirements for interplant movement of materials or semifinished products become the responsibility of manufacturing support. Manufacturing logistical support involves dock-to-dock movement and any intermediate storage required but typically does not include materials handling that is integral to in-plant assembly or production. When the manufacturing process is completed, finished inventory is allocated and deployed either directly to customers or to distribution warehouses for subsequent shipment to customers or customization. At the time of this movement, market distribution operations are initiated.

When a supply chain includes multiple plants that specialize in specific production activities, the manufacturing support system may contain a complex network of performance cycles. To the extent that specialized plants perform unique stages of production and fabrication prior to final assembly, numerous handlings and transfers may be required to complete the manufacturing process. It is the job of manufacturing logistics to perform this support process. In select situations, the complexity of manufacturing support may exceed that of market distribution or procurement.

Procurement Performance Cycles

Several activities or tasks are required to facilitate an orderly flow of materials, parts, or finished inventory along a supply chain: (1) sourcing, (2) order placement and expediting, (3) transportation, and (4) receiving. These activities, as illustrated in Figure 2-10, are required to complete the procurement process. Once materials, parts, or resale products are received, the subsequent storage, handling, and transportation requirements to facilitate either manufacturing or market distribution are appropriately provided by other performance cycles. Because of the focus on external supplies, this facet of procurement is referred to as *inbound logistics*. As shown in Industry Insight 2-4, Lands' End utilizes superior inbound logistics to achieve successful overall logistical performance.

With three important differences, the procurement performance cycle is similar to the market distribution cycle. First, delivery time, size of shipment, method of transport, and value of products involved are substantially different in procurement. Procurement often involves very large shipments, which may use barge, deep-water vessels, unit trains, and multiple truckloads for transport. Many materials and components

---

[5]See Richard J. Shonberger, *Japanese Manufacturing Techniques* (New York, NY: Macmillan Free Press, 1982); George C. Jackson, "Just in Time Production: Implications for Logistics Managers," *Journal of Business Logistics* 4, no. 2 (1983); and Richard J. Ackonberger, *Japanese Manufacturing Techniques, Nine Hidden Lessons in Simplicity* (New York, NY: The Free Press, 1982).

FIGURE 2-10

Procurement cycle activities

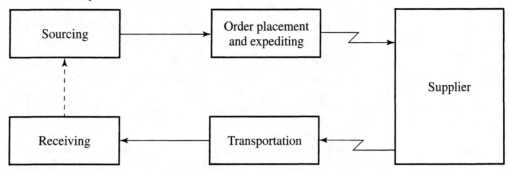

INDUSTRY INSIGHT 2-4 INBOUND OPERATIONS AT LANDS' END

Lands' End is one of the best-known mail-order companies because of its focus on high-quality merchandise, excellent product guarantees, and quick service. Serving a customer base of 6 million out of a 500,000 square foot distribution center in Dodgeville, Wisconsin, is not an easy task. Lands' End manages the extensive operation with two phone centers and 900 order operators. Much of its success is attributed to the company's inbound logistics system.

Lands' End works with some 250 suppliers that manufacture and merchandise products to meet specific, high-quality specifications. Furthermore, Lands' End has developed partnerships with inbound carriers as well. Lands' End produces 13 catalogs every year, which equates to one each month plus a special Christmas issue. Each catalog is filled with new products, seasonal items, and a variety of choices in clothing, luggage, bedding, and bath products.

To make this selection available, Lands' End sets strict operating goals for its procurement performance cycle. The main goal is to ensure that all merchandise offered in an upcoming catalog is available at the Dodgeville distribution center before final mailing of the catalog. This enables Lands' End to deliver customer orders within 24 hours, even on the first day the catalog arrives at the customer's home.

To achieve this goal, Lands' End concentrates on quality with its suppliers and carriers. In terms of supplier relations, Lands' End performs extensive quality inspection upon material receipt and sends teams to suppliers' facilities to assess their operations and offer suggestions for improvements. Furthermore, all suppliers are given a manual that explains Lands' End requirements and specifications for quality merchandise.

In terms of carriers, Lands' End controls all inbound transportation movements. This control allows it to develop partnership arrangements with key carriers to reduce costs by consolidating volumes and distances. In addition, Lands' End shares information by allowing electronic linkage between specific carriers and its Dodgeville distribution center.

Lands' End feels that its outbound success, achieved through a superior physical distribution system, is directly related to its successful inbound system. The efficient and cost-effective procurement process is maintained by concentrating on quality and partnerships with the inbound value chain.

Source: Deborah Catalano Ruriani, "Where Perfection Begins," *Inbound Logistics,* November 1992, pp. 20–23.

may be purchased internationally. While exceptions do exist, the typical goal in procurement is to focus on achieving inbound logistics at the lowest cost. The lower value of materials and parts in contrast to finished products means that a greater potential trade-off exists between cost of maintaining inventory in transit and time required to use low-cost modes of transport. Unless faced with an unexpected requirement, there is normally no benefit for paying premium rates for faster inbound transport. Therefore, performance cycles in purchasing are typically longer than those associated with market distribution of finished products.

Of course, for every rule there are exceptions. When high-value components are employed in manufacturing or in response-based business models, emphasis typically shifts to smaller purchases of exact requirements for arrival at precise times. Such precision logistics requires positive control. In such situations, the value of the material or component might justify the use of premium high-speed and reliable transportation delivery.

For example, a plant that manufacturers cake mix typically uses large quantities of flour in its production process. Since flour in bulk is relatively inexpensive, it makes sense for the firm to purchase flour in extremely large quantities that are shipped by rail. It would not make a lot sense to purchase small quantities, losing the bulk quantity price discount, and pay the high cost of small transportation shipments. In contrast, an automotive customizer buying electronic sunroofs might purchase on an as-required basis. Sunroof packages are significantly different for every car, and each package is relatively expensive. As such, the customizer is likely to order individual units to avoid holding inventory and be willing to pay premium transportation for fast delivery.

A second unique feature of purchasing is that the number of suppliers involved in a supply chain is typically less than the end-customer base it services. This difference was illustrated in Industry Insight 2-4. Lands' End has a customer base of over 6 million, but only deals with about 250 suppliers. In market distribution operations, each firm is only one of many participants in an overall supply chain. In contrast, the procurement performance cycle is usually more direct. Materials and parts are often purchased directly from either the original manufacturer or a specialized industrial wholesaler.

Finally, since the customer order processing cycle handles orders in response to customers' requirements, random ordering is a common situation in market distribution. In contrast, the procurement system initiates orders. The ability to determine when and where products are purchased serves to substantially reduce operational variance.

These three major differences in procurement, as contrasted to the market distribution order cycle, permit more orderly programming of logistical activities. The major uncertainty in procurement is the potential of price changes or supply discontinuity. A final feature of performance cycle synchronization critical to all facets of logistics is **operational uncertainty.**

Performance Cycle Uncertainty

A major objective of logistics in all operating areas is to reduce performance cycle uncertainty. The dilemma is that the structure of the performance cycle itself, operating conditions, and the quality of logistical operations all combine randomly to introduce operational variance.

Figure 2-11 illustrates the type and magnitude of variance that can develop in performance cycle operations. The performance cycle illustration is limited to finished goods inventory delivery. The time distributions, as illustrated, statistically reflect performance history for each task of a typical performance cycle. The diagram illustrates the minimum to maximum time historically required to complete each task and the related time distribution for the overall performance cycle. The vertical dashed line reflects the average time for performance of each task.

FIGURE 2-11

Performance cycle uncertainty

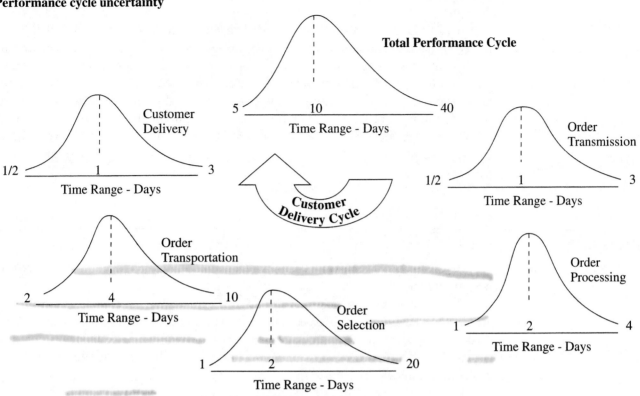

In terms of specific tasks, the variance results from the nature of the work involved. Order transmission is highly reliable when electronic transfer (EDI) or Web-based communications are used and more erratic when using telephone or routine mail. Regardless of the level of technology deployed, operational variance will occur as a result of daily changes in workload and resolution of unexpected events.

Time and variance related to order processing are a function of workload, degree of automation, and policies related to credit approval. Order selection, speed, and associated delay are directly related to capacity, materials handling sophistication, and human resource availability. When a product is out of stock, the time to complete order selection includes manufacturing scheduling. The required transportation time is a function of distance, shipment size, type of transport, and operating conditions. Final delivery to customers can vary depending on authorized receiving times, delivery appointments, workforce availability, and specialized unloading and equipment requirements.

In Figure 2-11 the history of total order-to-delivery time performance ranged from 5 to 40 days. The 5-day cycle reflects the unlikely event that each task is performed at the fastest possible time. The 40-day cycle represents the equally unlikely opposite extreme wherein each task required maximum time. The planned or target order-to-delivery cycle performance is to control combined variance so that actual operations meet a specific time goal as often as possible. Whenever actual performance is more or less than 10 days, managerial action may be necessary to satisfy customer requirements. Such expediting and de-expediting require extra resources and reduce overall logistical efficiency.

The goal of performance cycle synchronization is to achieve the planned time performance. Delayed performance at any point along the supply chain results in potential disruption of operations. Such delays require that safety stocks be established to cover variances. When performance occurs faster than expected, unplanned work will be required to handle and store inventory that arrives early. Given the inconvenience and expense of either early or late delivery, it is no wonder that logistics managers place a premium on operational consistency. Once consistent operations are achieved, every effort should be made to reduce the time required to complete the performance cycle to a minimum. In other words, shorter cycles are desirable because they reduce total assets deployed. However, speed is only a valid goal if it is consistent. Given consistency as the primary goal, faster order cycles reduce inventory risk and improve turn performance.

Summary

Logistics is the process that links supply chains into integrated operations. The cost of performing logistics is a major expenditure for most businesses.

Logistical service is measured in terms of availability, operational performance, and service reliability. Each aspect of service is framed in terms of customer expectations and requirements. Lean logistics is all about providing the essential customer service attributes at the lowest possible total cost. Such customer commitment, in an exacting cost framework, is the logistics value proposition.

The actual work of logistics is functional in nature. Facility locations must be established to form a network, information must be formulated and shared, transportation must be arranged, inventory must be deployed, and, to the extent required, warehousing, materials handling, and packaging activities must be performed. The traditional orientation was to perform each functional task as well as possible with limited consideration given to how one work area impacted another. Because the work of logistics is extremely detailed and complex, there is a natural tendency to focus on performing functions. While functional excellence is important, it must be supportive of overall logistical competency.

The functions of logistics combine into the three primary operational processes of market distribution, manufacturing support, and procurement. To achieve internal integration, the inventory and information flows between these areas must be coordinated.

In supply chain synchronization, the operational focus is the logistics performance cycle. The performance cycle is also the primary unit of analysis in logistical design. The performance cycle structure provides the logic for combining the nodes, levels, links, and allocation of assets essential to performing market distribution, manufacturing support, and procurement operations. Many similarities and a number of critical differences exist among performance cycles dedicated to these vital logistics operating areas. Fully understanding these similarities and differences is vital to planning and controlling overall supply chain integration. The basic proposition is that regardless of size and complexity, logistical integration is best understood and evaluated by the structure and dynamics of performance cycle.

The primary goal is to achieve consistency. The challenge is to design a supply chain capable of performing the required logistical work as rapidly but, even more important, as consistently as possible. Unexpected delays, as well as faster than expected performance, can combine to increase or decrease the elapsed time required to complete a performance cycle. Both early and late delivery are undesirable and unacceptable from an operational perspective.

Chapter 2 has developed some important foundations of the logistical discipline and how it creates value in a supply chain context. These insights regarding the nature of logistics work, the importance of achieving internal operational integration through managing inventory and information flow, viewing the performance cycle structure as the basic unit of analysis, and the management of operational uncertainty combine to form a logically consistent set of concepts essential to supporting supply chain management. Chapter 3 focuses on customer requirements that drive supply chain performance.

Challenge Questions

1. Illustrate a common trade-off that occurs between the work areas of logistics.
2. Discuss and elaborate on the following statement: "The selection of a superior location network can create substantial competitive advantage."
3. Why are market distribution operations typically more erratic than manufacturing support and procurement operations?
4. How has transportation cost, as a percentage of total logistics cost, tracked since 1980?
5. Describe the *logistics value proposition*. Be specific regarding specific customer accommodation and cost.
6. Describe the fundamental similarities and differences between procurement, manufacturing support, and market distribution performance cycles as they relate to logistical control.
7. Compare and contrast a performance cycle node and a link. Give an example of each.
8. How does the "quest for quality" affect logistical operations? Does the concept of total quality have relevancy when applied to logistics?
9. Discuss uncertainty as it relates to the overall logistical performance cycle. Discuss and illustrate how performance cycle variance can be controlled.
10. What is the logic of designing echeloned logistical structures? Can echeloned and direct structures be combined?

3   CUSTOMER ACCOMMODATION

While in some ways it's an insight into the obvious, it is important to establish initially that logistics contributes to an organization's success by accommodating customers' delivery and availability expectations and requirements. What is not so obvious, however, is what exactly is meant by the term *customer*. The supply chain management concept requires careful consideration of just what is meant by the term and realization that there are many different perspectives.

From the perspective of the total supply chain, the ultimate customer is the end user of the product or service whose needs or requirements must be accommodated. It has historically been useful to distinguish between two types of end users. The first is a **consumer,** an individual or a household who purchases products and services to satisfy personal needs. When a family purchases an automobile to be used for personal transportation, that family is the consumer of the supply chain. The second type is an

organizational end user. Purchases are made by organizations or institutions to allow an end user to perform a task or job in the organization. When a company buys an automobile for a sales person or buys tools to be used by an assembly worker in a manufacturing plant, the company is considered to be a customer and the salesperson or assembly worker is the end user of the supply chain's products. A supply chain management perspective demands that all firms in the supply chain focus on meeting the needs and requirements of end users, whether they are consumers or organizational end users.

Another perspective of customer exists for a specific firm within the supply chain. This perspective recognizes that intermediate organizations often exist between the firm and end users. Common terminology generally recognizes these organizations as **intermediate customers.** Thus, in the Procter & Gamble (P&G) supply chain that provides Tide laundry detergent to ultimate consumers, Kroger and Safeway supermarkets are intermediate customers; they purchase Tide from P&G for the purpose of reselling to ultimate consumers.

Finally, for a logistician, a customer is any delivery location. Typical destinations range from consumers' homes to retail and wholesale businesses to the receiving docks of manufacturing plants and distribution centers. In some cases the customer is a different organization or individual who is taking ownership of the product or service being delivered. In many other situations the customer is a different facility of the same firm or a business partner at some other location in the supply chain. For example, it is common for the logistics manager of a retail distribution center to think of the individual stores to be serviced as customers of the distribution center, even though the stores are part of the same organization.

Regardless of the motivation and delivery purpose, the customer being serviced is the focal point and driving force in establishing logistical performance requirements. It is critical to fully understand customer needs that must be accommodated in establishing logistical strategy. This chapter details the nature of various approaches to accommodating customer requirements. The first section presents the fundamental concepts that underlie customer-focused marketing, with consideration of how logistics fits into a firm's overall marketing strategy. The second section describes the nature of the outputs of the supply chain to end users and how these outputs must be structured to meet their requirements. The sections that follow expand upon increasing levels of sophistication in accommodating customers. These levels range from traditional notions of logistics customer service to satisfaction of customers by meeting their expectations to the ultimate in accommodation—helping customers be successful by meeting their business requirements.

Customer-Focused Marketing

The basic principles of customer-focused marketing have their roots in the **marketing concept**—a business philosophy that suggests that the focal point of a business's strategy must be the customers it intends to serve. It holds that for an organization to achieve its goals, it must be more effective than competitors in identifying specific customer needs and focusing resources and activities on accommodating these customer requirements. Clearly, many aspects of a firm's strategy must be integrated to accommodate customers, and logistics is only one of these. The marketing concept builds on four fundamental ideas: customer needs and requirements are more basic than products or services; different customers have different needs and requirements;

products and services become meaningful only when available and positioned from the customer's perspective, which is the focus of logistics strategies; and volume is secondary to profit.

The belief that customer needs are more basic than products or services places a priority on fully understanding what drives market opportunities. The key is to understand and develop the combination of products and services that will meet those requirements. For example, if customers only require a choice of three different colored appliances, it makes little sense to offer six colors. It also makes little sense to try to market only white appliances if color selection is important from a customer's perspective. The basic idea is to develop sufficient insight into basic needs so that products and services can be matched to these opportunities. Successful marketing begins with in-depth study of customers to identify product and service requirements.

The second fundamental aspect of the marketing concept is that there is no single market for any given product or service. All markets are composed of different segments, each of which has somewhat different requirements. Effective market segmentation requires that firms clearly identify segments and select specific targets. While a comprehensive discussion of market segmentation is beyond the scope of this text, it is important to note that customers' logistical requirements frequently offer an effective basis for classification. For example, a contractor building new homes may place an order for appliances several weeks before needed for installation, while a consumer buying a replacement for a broken appliance may require immediate availability and delivery. It is unlikely that a company can operate in every market segment or profitably fulfill every possible combination of customer requirements; thus careful matching of capabilities with specific segments is an essential aspect of the marketing concept.

For marketing to be successful, products and services must be available to customers. In other words, the third fundamental aspect of marketing is that customers must be readily able to obtain the products they desire. To facilitate purchase action, the selling firm's resources need to be focused on customers and product positioning. Four economic utilities add value to customers: *form, possession, time,* and *place.* The product's form is for the most part generated in the manufacturing process. For example, form utility results from the assembly of parts and components for a dishwasher. In the case of a service such as a haircut, form utility is accomplished with the completion of specified activities such as shampooing, cutting, and styling. Marketing creates possession by informing potential customers of product/service availability and enabling ownership exchange. Thus, marketing serves to identify and convey the attributes of the product or service and to develop mechanisms for buyer–seller exchange. Logistics provides time and place utility requirements. Essentially, this means that logistics must ensure that the product is available when and where desired by customers. The achievement of time and place requires significant effort and is expensive. Profitable transactions materialize only when all four utilities are combined in a manner relevant to customers.

The fourth aspect of the marketing concept is the focus on profitability as contrasted to sales volume. An important dimension of success is the degree of profitability resulting from relationships with customers, not the volume sold. Therefore, variations in all four basic utilities—form, possession, time, and place—are justified if a customer or segment of customers value and are willing to pay for the modification. Using the appliance example, if a customer requests a unique color option and is willing to pay extra, then the request can and should be accommodated, providing a positive contribution margin can be earned. The final refinement of marketing strategy is based on an acknowledgment that all aspects of a product/service offering are subject to modification when justifiable on the basis of profitability.

Transactional versus Relationship Marketing

Traditional marketing strategies focus on obtaining successful exchanges, or transactions, with customers to drive increases in revenue and profit. In this approach, termed **transactional marketing,** companies are generally oriented toward short-term interaction with their customers. The traditional marketing concept emphasizes accommodating customers' needs and requirements, something few business organizations would argue with. However, as practiced in many firms, the result is a focus on creating successful individual transactions between a supplier and its customers. Further, the practice of segmentation and target marketing generally results in rather large groupings of customers, each having somewhat similar needs and requirements. In this approach to marketing *undifferentiated, differentiated,* and *niche* strategies are common.

An undifferentiated strategy views all potential customers as if they are essentially the same. While the organization may go through the process of segmentation, it ultimately *averages* the customers' needs and then tries to design a product and process that will meet the needs of the average customer. This allows the firm to streamline its manufacturing, market distribution, logistics, and promotional efforts to obtain cost efficiencies. For many years, Coca-Cola had only one cola product, Regular Coke, which was intended to satisfy the needs of all cola drinkers. For many years UPS followed a similar one-size-fits-all strategy in parcel delivery. Customers benefit from low-cost operations but many may not be fully satisfied due to the supplier's inability to satisfy unique requirements.

In a differentiated strategy, a firm targets multiple market segments, serving each with a product/service and market distribution process matched to more specifically meet that segment's unique needs and requirements. Coca-Cola today offers Diet Coke, Caffeine-free Coke, Cherry Coke, etc. When Federal Express entered the market for parcel distribution, UPS responded by developing a capability to meet the needs of shippers who required more rapid and controlled delivery. The result was different offerings to different market segments. While a differentiated strategy increases organizational complexity and cost, it allows a firm to accommodate more specifically the requirements of different customer groups.

A niche strategy is frequently utilized by small firms or new companies that choose to target one segment out of the overall market by offering very precise services. In the soft drink industry, Jolt Cola exists for those few customers who desire high sugar and high caffeine content. In parcel delivery, several small firms focus on customers who require same-day delivery.

Paralleling the development of the supply chain management concept, there has been a shift in philosophy regarding the nature of marketing strategy. This shift has generally been acknowledged as **relationship marketing.** Relationship marketing focuses on the development of long-term relations with key supply chain participants such as end users, intermediate customers, and suppliers in an effort to develop and retain long-term preference and loyalty. Relationship marketing is based on the realization that in many industries it is more important to retain current customers and gain a larger share of their purchases than it is to go out and attempt to attract new customers.[1]

The ultimate in market segmentation and relationship marketing is to focus on the individual customer. This approach, referred to as *micromarketing* or *one-to-one marketing,* recognizes that each individual customer may indeed have unique requirements.

[1]Thomas O. Jones and W. Earl Sasser, Jr., "Why Satisfied Customers Defect," *Harvard Business Review,* November/December 1995, pp. 88–99.

For example, although Wal★Mart and Target are both mass merchandisers, their requirements in terms of how they desire to interact logistically with suppliers differ significantly. A manufacturer who wants to do business with both of these major retailers must adapt its logistical operations to the unique needs of each. The best way to ensure long-term organizational success is to intensely research and then accommodate the requirements of individual customers.[2] Such relationships may not be feasible with every customer. It is also true that many customers may not desire this close relationship with all suppliers. However, one-to-one relationships can significantly reduce transaction costs, better accommodate customer requirements, and move individual transactions into a matter of routine.

There are four steps involved in implementing a one-to-one marketing program. The first is to identify the individual customers for the company's products and services. As simple as this may seem, many companies still tend to think in terms of groups of customers rather than individual customers.

The second step is to differentiate the customers, both in terms of value to the organization and in terms of their unique requirements. Clearly, all customers do not represent the same potential sales volume or profitability. Successful one-to-one marketers focus their efforts on those customers who represent the greatest potential return. Understanding differential customer needs provides the foundation for customization of products and services.

The third step involves the actual interaction with customers with the goal of improving both cost-efficiency and effectiveness. For example, cost-efficiency might be improved by automating routine interactions such as order placement or requests for information. Effectiveness can be improved by understanding that each interaction with a customer occurs in the context of all previous interactions.

Ultimately, one-to-one marketing is operationalized in the fourth step, customizing the organization's behavior. The company must adapt some aspect of its behavior to the customer's individually expressed needs. Whether it means customizing a manufactured product or tailoring services, such as customer packaging or delivery, the production and/or service end of the business must be able to deal with a particular customer in an individual manner.[3] Industry Insight 3-1 describes how Square D, a manufacturer of electrical equipment, has implemented relationship and one-to-one marketing with its key customers.

Supply Chain Service Outputs

Understanding customer-focused marketing in a supply chain context requires consideration of the services actually provided to end customers. Bucklin presented a long-standing theory that specifies four generic service outputs necessary to accommodate customer requirements: (1) spatial convenience, (2) lot size, (3) waiting or delivery time, and (4) product variety and assortment.[4] As discussed above, different customers may have different requirements regarding such service outputs. It follows that different supply chain structures may be required to accommodate these differences.

---

[2]For a comprehensive discussion of the one-to-one approach, see Don Peppers and Martha Rogers, *The One-to-One Manager: Real World Lessons in Customer Relationship Management* (New York, NY: Doubleday, 1999).

[3]Don Peppers, Martha Rogers, and Bob Dorf, "Is Your Company Ready for One-to-One Marketing," *Harvard Business Review,* January/February 1999, pp. 151–60.

[4]Louis P. Bucklin, *A Theory of Distribution Channel Structure* (Berkeley, CA: IBER Special Publications, 1966).

INDUSTRY INSIGHT 3-1 GETTING A SQUARE D-EAL

At Square D Co., a Palatine, Illinois-based manufacturer of electrical control products and unit of Paris-based Schneider Electric, VP of Marketing Chris Curtis enthusiastically promotes Square D's marketing approach toward its strategic accounts. These accounts, such as Daimler-Chrysler and IBM Corp., are high profile and generate significant sales. Square D uses a Relationship Management Process or RMP to market its products to these accounts. RMP stresses creating one-to-one marketing partnerships in which Square D customers are provided with exactly the products and level of service they want.

For example, Scott Chakmak is Square D's director of strategic accounts—DaimlerChrysler and spends his working days in DaimlerChrysler's Kenosha, Wisconsin, plant. This proximity to the customer allows Square D's sales staff to become well acquainted with DaimlerChrysler's needs. Prior to Daimler's acquisition of Chrysler, Mr. Chakmak realized that Square D's team could ease the workload of Chrysler's engineers by helping with the design of a new engine assembly line. He suggested that his team oversee the design of the electrical control system of each machine to ensure conformity. The consistency of the design would reduce training time and make Chrysler's employees more versatile.

After more than 2 years, Chrysler finally agreed to Square D's proposal and put its supplier in charge of the project. Communicating via the Internet with more than 80 other contributing suppliers around the world, Square D completed the project in 27 months, significantly shorter than the industry standard of 36 months, according to Mr. Chakmak.

Since that first project, Square D has overseen similar projects for various DaimlerChrysler plants around the world. "The first project took 2 years to sell," recalls Mr. Chakmak. "It took 9 months to sell the next time. Then it was 30 days. Since then, it's basically been a handshake."

Ultimately, RMP is about customer segmentation. If customers don't want or require value-added services, Square D simply sells them the products they need. For other customers, value-added services can be customized to meet their specific product needs. These extra efforts can be quite worthwhile for Square D, enhancing its value as a supplier to a strategic customer. For example, Square D is now the sole supplier of power supply equipment to IBM Corp.

Square D must adhere to rigorous standards in handling strategic accounts. Square D and its sister Schneider brand, Modicon, sell to IBM approximately $11 million in electrical control products annually under a 3-year pact signed last year. This pact ensures that IBM receives volume discounting, standardization across plants, prompt shipping, available inventory for essential products, and responsive service.

Mr. Curtis sums up Square D's RMP approach as an evolution of the total quality management movement of the 1980s. Instead of the manufacturing process, RMP scrutinizes Square D's relationship with its customers to better accommodate individual requirements and improve channel success.

Source: Sean Callahan, "Getting a Square D-eal," *Advertising Age's Business Marketing,* January/February 2000, pp. 3, 35.

Spatial Convenience

Spatial convenience, the first service output, refers to the amount of shopping time and effort that will be required on the part of the customer. Higher levels of spatial convenience are achieved in a supply chain by providing customers with access to its products in a larger number of places, thus reducing shopping effort. Consider, for example, the household furniture industry. Some manufacturers utilize a structure that includes department stores, mass merchandisers, and numerous chain and independent furniture specialty stores. Ethan Allen, on the other hand, restricts brand availability to a limited number of authorized Ethan Allen retail stores. This difference in the level of spatial convenience has major implications for the overall supply chain structure and for the logistics cost incurred in the supply chain. It is also clear that some customers are willing to expend greater time and effort than others as they search for a desired product or brand.

Lot Size

The second service output is **lot size,** which refers to the number of units to be purchased in each transaction. When customers are required to purchase in large quantities, they must incur costs of product storage and maintenance. When the supply chain allows them to purchase in small lot sizes, they can more easily match their consumption requirements with their purchasing. In developed economies, alternative supply chains frequently offer customers a choice of the level of lot-size service output. For example, consumers who are willing to purchase paper towels in a 12- or 24-roll package may buy at Sam's Club or Costco. As an alternative, they may buy single rolls at the local grocery or convenience store. Of course, the supply chain that allows customers to purchase in small quantities normally experiences higher cost and therefore demands higher unit prices from customers.

Waiting Time

Waiting time is the third generic service output. Waiting time is defined as the amount of time the customer must wait between ordering and receiving products: the lower the waiting time, the higher the level of supply chain service. Again, alternative supply chains offer consumers and end users choices in terms of the amount of waiting time required. In the personal computer industry, a consumer may visit an electronics or computer specialty store, make a purchase, and carry home a computer with, literally, no waiting time. Alternatively, the customer may order from a catalog or via the Internet and wait for delivery to the home or office. In a general sense, the longer the waiting time required, the more inconvenient for the customer. However, such supply chains generally incur lower costs and customers are rewarded in the form of lower prices for their willingness to wait.

Product Variety

Product variety and **assortment** are the fourth service output. Again, different supply chains offer differing levels of variety and assortment to consumers and end users. Typical supermarkets are involved in supply chains that provide a broad variety of many different types of products and an assortment of brands, sizes, etc., of each type. In fact, supermarkets may have over 35,000 different items on the shelves. Warehouse stores, on the other hand, offer much less product variety or assortment, generally stocking in the range of 8000 to 10,000 items, and usually offer only one brand and size of an item. Convenience stores may stock only a few hundred items, offering little variety or assortment as compared to supermarkets.

Supply chains provide additional service outputs to their customers. In addition to the four generic service outputs discussed above, other researchers have identified services related to information, product customization, and after-sales support as critical to selected customers.[5] The point to keep in mind is that there is no such thing as a homogeneous market where all consumers desire the same services presented in the same way. They may differ in terms of which services are most important and in terms of the level of each of the services desired to accommodate their needs. For example,

---

[5]V. Kasturi Rangan, Meluia A. J. Menzies, and E. P. Maier, "Channel Selection for New Industrial Products: A Framework, Method, and Application," *Journal of Marketing* 56 (July 1992), pp. 72–3.

some consumers may require immediate availability of a personal computer while others feel that waiting 3 days for a computer configured to their exact requirements is preferable. Additionally, customers differ in terms of how much they are willing to pay for services. Since higher levels of service generally involve higher market distribution costs, organizations must carefully assess customer sensitivity to prices relative to their desire for reduced waiting time, convenience, and other service outputs.

This discussion of generic service outputs focuses primarily on consumer or organizational end users in a supply chain. It has important implications for how supply chains are ultimately configured, what types of participating companies may be included to satisfy service requirements, and the costs that are incurred in the process. Attention is now focused on more specific considerations of customer accommodation in a *logistical* context. Three levels of customer accommodation are discussed: customer service, customer satisfaction, and customer success.

Customer Service

The primary value of logistics is to accommodate customer requirements in a cost-effective manner. Although most senior managers agree that customer service is important, they sometimes find it extremely difficult to explain what it is and what it does. While common expressions of customer service include "easy to do business with" and "responsive to customers," to develop a full understanding of customer service, a more thorough framework is required.

Philosophically, customer service represents logistics' role in fulfilling the marketing concept. A customer service program must identify and prioritize all activities required to accommodate customers' logistical requirements as well as, or better than, competitors. In establishing a customer service program, it is imperative to identify clear standards of performance for each of the activities and measurements relative to those standards. In basic customer service programs, the focus is typically on the operational aspects of logistics and ensuring that the organization is capable of providing the seven rights to its customer: the *right* amount of the *right* product at the *right* time at the *right* place in the *right* condition at the *right* price with the *right* information.

It is clear that outstanding customer service adds value throughout a supply chain. The critical concern in developing a service strategy is: *Does the cost associated with achieving specified service performance represent a sound investment?* Careful analysis of competitive performance and customer sensitivity to service attributes is required to formulate a basic service strategy. In Chapter 2, the fundamental attributes of basic customer service were identified as availability, operational performance, and service reliability. These attributes are now discussed in greater detail.

Availability

Availability is the capacity to have inventory when desired by a customer. As simple as this may seem, it is not at all uncommon for an organization to expend considerable time, money, and effort to generate customer demand and then fail to have product available to meet customer requirements. The traditional practice in organizations is to stock inventory in anticipation of customer orders. Typically an inventory stocking plan is based on forecasted demand for products and may include differential stocking policies for specific items as a result of sales popularity, profitability, and importance of an item to the overall product line and the value of the merchandise.

While the detail of establishing inventory stocking policies is covered in Chapter 10, suffice it to say at this time that inventory can be classified into two groups: base stock determined by forecasted and planned requirements, and safety stock to cover unexpected variations in demand or operations.

It should be clear that achieving high levels of inventory availability requires a great deal of planning. In fact, the key is to achieve these high levels of availability for selected or core customers while minimizing overall investment in inventory and facilities. Exacting programs of inventory availability are not conceived or managed *on average;* availability is based on three performance measures: *stockout frequency, fill rate,* and *orders shipped complete.*

Stockout Frequency

A **stockout,** as the term suggests, occurs when a firm has no product available to fulfill customer demand. Stockout frequency refers to the probability that a firm will not have inventory available to meet a customer order. For example, a study of retail supermarkets revealed that at any point in time during a week, the average supermarket is out of stock of approximately 8 percent of the items planned to be on the shelves. It is important to note, however, that a stockout does not actually occur until a customer desires a product. The aggregation of all stockouts across all products is an indicator of how well a firm is positioned to provide basic service commitments in product availability. While it does not consider that some products may be more critical in terms of availability than others, it is the starting point in thinking about inventory availability.

Fill Rate

Fill rate measures the magnitude or impact of stockouts over time. Being out of stock does not affect service performance until a customer demands a product. Then it is important to determine that the product is not available and how many units the customer wanted. For example, if a customer wants 100 units of an item and only 97 are available, the fill rate is 97 percent. To effectively consider fill rate, the typical procedure is to evaluate performance over time to include multiple customer orders. Thus, fill rate performance can be evaluated for a specific customer, product, or for any combination of customers, products, or business segments.

Fill rate can be used to differentiate the level of service to be offered on specific products. In the earlier example, if all 100 products ordered were critical to a customer, then a fill rate of 97 percent could result in a stockout at the customer's plant or warehouse and severely disrupt the customer's operations. Imagine an assembly line scheduled to produce 100 automobiles that receives only 97 of its required brake assemblies. In situations where some of the items are not critical to performance, a fill rate of 97 percent may be acceptable. The customer may accept a back order or be willing to reorder the short items at a later time. Fill rate strategies need to consider customer requirements for products.

Orders Shipped Complete

The most exacting measure of performance in product availability is **orders shipped complete.** It views having everything that a customer orders as the standard of acceptable performance. Failure to provide even one item on a customer's order results in that order being recorded as *zero* in terms of complete shipment.

These three measures of availability combine to establish the extent to which a firm's inventory strategy is accommodating customer demand. They also form the basis to evaluate the appropriate level of availability to incorporate into a firm's basic logistical service program. High levels of inventory have typically been viewed as the means to increasing availability; however, new strategies that use information technology to identify customer demand in advance of actual customer orders have allowed some organizations to reach very high levels of basic service performance without corresponding increases in inventory. These strategies are discussed more fully in Chapter 10.

Operational Performance

Operational performance deals with the time required to deliver a customer's order. Whether the performance cycle in question is market distribution, manufacturing support, or procurement, operational performance is specified in terms of speed of performance, consistency, flexibility, and malfunction recovery.

Speed

Performance cycle speed is the elapsed time from when a customer establishes a need to order until the product is delivered and is ready for customer use. The elapsed time required for total performance cycle completion depends on logistical system design. Given today's high level of communication and transportation technology, order cycles can be as short as a few hours or may take several weeks or months.

Naturally, most customers want fast order cycle performance. Speed is an essential ingredient in many just-in-time and quick-response logistical strategies as fast performance cycles reduce customer inventory requirements. The counterbalance is that speed of service is typically costly: Not all customers need or want maximum speed if it means increased total cost. The justification for speed must be found in the positive trade-offs; that is, the only relevant framework for estimating the value of service speed is the customer's perceived benefits.

Consistency

Order cycle consistency is measured by the number of times that actual cycles meet the time planned for completion. While speed of service is important, most logistical managers place greater value on consistency because it directly impacts a customer's ability to plan and perform its own activities. For example, if order cycles vary, then a customer must carry safety stock to protect against potential late delivery; the degree of variability translates directly into safety stock requirements. Given the numerous activities involved in performance cycle execution there are many potential sources of inconsistency in performance (review Figure 2-11).[6]

The issue of consistency is fundamental to effective logistics operations as it is becoming increasingly common for customers to actually specify a desired date and even specify a delivery appointment when placing orders. Such a precise specification may be made taking into consideration a supplier's performance cycle but that is not always the case. In fact, customers frequently place orders far in advance of their need for product replenishment. In such situations, it is very difficult for customers to understand why failure to deliver as specified occurs. Their viewpoint of supplier consistency in operational performance is whether the supplier delivered at the specified date and time. In such situations the definition of consistency must be modified. It is no

---

[6]See Figure 2-11, p. 63.

longer sufficient to evaluate in terms of planned time, such as 4 days to complete the cycle. It is essential to determine whether the performance cycle was completed according to the customer's specification.

Flexibility

Flexibility involves a firm's ability to accommodate special situations and unusual or unexpected customer requests. For example, the standard pattern for servicing a customer may be to ship full-trailer quantities to a customer's warehouse. However, from time to time, the customer may desire to have shipments of smaller quantities made direct to individual retail locations. A firm's logistical competency is directly related to how well it is able to accommodate such unexpected circumstances. Typical events requiring flexible operations are: (1) modification to basic service agreements such as a change in ship-to location; (2) support of unique sales or marketing programs; (3) new-product introduction; (4) product recall; (5) disruption in supply; (6) one-time customization of basic service for specific customers or segments; and (7) product modification or customization performed while in the logistics system, such as price-marking, mixing, or packaging. In many ways the essence of logistical excellence rests in the ability to be flexible.

Malfunction Recovery

Regardless of how fine-tuned a firm's logistical operations, malfunctions will occur. The continuous performance of service commitments on a day-in, day-out basis is a difficult task. Ideally, adjustments can be implemented to prevent or accommodate special situations, thereby preventing malfunctions. For example, if a stockout of an essential item occurs at a distribution facility that normally services a customer, the item may be obtained from an alternative facility utilizing some form of expedited transportation. In such situations the malfunction may actually be transparent to the customer. While such transparent recoveries are not always possible, effective customer service programs anticipate that malfunctions and service breakdowns will occur and have in place contingency plans to accomplish recovery and measure compliance.

Service Reliability

Service reliability involves the combined attributes of logistics and concerns a firm's ability to perform all order-related activities, as well as provide customers with critical information regarding logistical operations and status. Beyond availability and operational performance, attributes of reliability may mean that shipments arrive damage-free; invoices are correct and error-free; shipments are made to the correct locations; and the exact amount of product ordered is included in the shipment. While these and numerous other aspects of overall reliability are difficult to enumerate, the point is that customers demand that a wide variety of business details be handled routinely by suppliers. Additionally, service reliability involves a capability and a willingness to provide accurate information to customers regarding operations and order status. Research indicates that the ability of a firm to provide accurate information is one of the most significant attributes of a good service program.[7] Increasingly, customers indicate that advanced notification of problems such as incomplete orders is more critical

---

[7]Donald J. Bowersox, David J. Closs, and Theodore P. Stank, *21st Century Logistics: Making Supply Chain Integration a Reality* (Oak Brook, IL: Council of Logistics Management, 1999).

than the complete order itself. Customers hate surprises! More often than not, customers can adjust to an incomplete or late delivery, if they have advanced notification.

The Perfect Order

The ultimate in logistics service is to do everything right and to do it right the first time. It is not sufficient to deliver a complete order but to deliver it late. Nor is it sufficient to deliver a complete order on time but to have an incorrect invoice or product damage incurred during the handling and transportation process. In the past, most logistics managers evaluated customer service performance in terms of several independent measures: fill rates were evaluated against a standard for fill; on-time delivery was evaluated in terms of a percentage of deliveries made on time relative to a standard; damage rates were evaluated relative to a standard for damage; etc. When each of these separate measures was acceptable relative to standard, overall service performance was considered acceptable.

Recently, however, logistics and supply chain executives have begun to focus attention on zero-defect or six-sigma performance. As an extension of Total Quality Management (TQM) efforts within organizations, logistics processes have been subjected to the same scrutiny as manufacturing and other processes in the firm. It was realized that if standards are established independently for customer service components, even if performance met standard on each independent measure, a substantial number of customers may have order-related failures. For example, if orders shipped complete, average on-time delivery, average damage-free delivery, and average correct documentation are each 97 percent, the probability that any order will be delivered with no defects is approximately 88.5 percent. This is so because the potential occurrence of any one failure combined with any other failure is $.97 \times .97 \times .97 \times .97$. The converse of this, of course, is that some type of problem will exist on as many as 11.5 percent of all orders.

The notion of the perfect order is that an order should be delivered complete, delivered on time, at the right location, in perfect condition, with complete and accurate documentation. Each of these individual elements must comply with customer specifications. Thus, complete delivery means all product the customer originally requested, on time means at the customer's specified date and time, etc. In other words, total order cycle performance must be executed with zero defects—availability and operational performance must be perfectly executed and all support activities must be completed exactly as promised to the customer. While it may not be possible to offer zero defects as a basic service strategy across the board to all customers, such high-level performance may be an option on a selective basis.

It is clear that the resources required to implement a perfect order platform are substantial. Extremely high fill rates require high inventory levels to meet all potential order requirements and variations. However, such complete service cannot be achieved based totally on inventory. One way of elevating logistics performance to at least near-zero defects is to utilize a combination of customer alliances, information technology, postponement strategies, inventory stocking strategies, premium transportation, and selectivity programs to match logistical resources to core customer requirements. Each of these topics is the subject of detailed discussion in subsequent chapters. Suffice it to say at this time that firms achieving superior logistical customer service are well aware of the challenge related to achieving zero defects. By having a low tolerance for errors, coupled with a commitment to resolve whatever discrepancies occur, such firms can achieve strategic advantage over their competitors. Industry Insight 3-2 describes the importance of achieving perfect order performance, as well as the difficulties in the emerging industry of consumer-delivered groceries.

Basic Service Platforms

To implement a basic service platform, it is necessary to specify commitment level to all customers in terms of availability, operational performance, and reliability. The fundamental question, "How much basic service should the system provide?" is not easy to answer.

The fact is that many firms establish their basic service platforms based on two factors. The first factor is competitor or *industry acceptable practice.* In most industries, levels of minimum and average service performance have emerged. These acceptable levels are generally well known by both the suppliers and the customers throughout the industry. It is not uncommon to hear logistics and supply chain executives speak of customer service commitments in terms of "doing as well as competition" or "beating our major competitors' performance." The second factor derives from the firm's overall *marketing strategy.* If a firm desires to differentiate from com-

INDUSTRY INSIGHT 3-2 GROCERIES DELIVERED TO YOUR DOORSTEP

Several grocers are attempting to offer greater convenience to customers by offering electronic order placement and home delivery. This simple concept is quite complex to implement effectively.

The most important factor influencing consumer-direct channel adoption and customer loyalty is the ability to consistently pick and deliver perfect orders. However, it is complex and expensive to structure a low-cost logistics system to provide these desired service levels.

Consumer-direct logistics focuses on fulfilling demand at the household level through consistent delivery of perfect orders as it ensures a continuous supply of product at the lowest possible cost. A dedicated fulfillment center is preferred for greater picking accuracy, order customization, fill rates, and operational flexibility, but produces significantly higher operating margins than a traditional grocery store model.

Product fulfillment is the highest direct cost of processing an order, due to the goal of a consistent perfect order. This process typically includes household-level customization in high-impact perishable and prepared meat categories that mandate different temperature controls and date-management practices. For example, some consumers prefer green bananas to yellow bananas or rare roast beef sliced thin to the standard sliced product. Given an average 60-item order and a 99 percent picking accuracy at the individual item level, only 55 percent of all orders would be perfectly filled. The operator's challenge is to incorporate household-level specification in a high-volume, scalable operating environment where customers are ordering electronically.

Delivery capabilities involve the physical logistics of moving products directly to the customer's home. Most providers unitize products from across three temperature zones into a secure container and load it into a multitemperature vehicle to maintain proper temperatures across the home-delivery chill chain.

Unique characteristics of the grocery business (e.g., number of items per order, customer preferences within a given SKU, temperature maintenance requirements for different products) emphasize the difficulty of designing a logistics system to deliver perfect orders to each customer every time.

Source: Frank F. Britt, "The Logistics of Consumer-Direct," *Progressive Grocer,* May 1998, p. 39.

petitors based on logistics competency, then high levels of basic service are required. If the firm differentiates on price, then it likely will commit to lower levels of logistical service due to the resources required and costs related to high-level commitment.

The fact is that even firms with a high level of basic customer service commitment generally do not take a total zero-defect approach across the board for all customers. The common service commitment is to establish internal performance standards for each service component. These standards typically reflect prevailing industry practice in combination with careful consideration of cost and resource commitments. Typical service standards such as 97 percent fill rate or delivery within 3 days may be established and then performance would be monitored relative to these internal standards. While it is generally assumed that this strategic approach results in accommodating customers as well as or better than competitors, it does not assure that customers are, in fact, satisfied with either the overall industry performance or even the performance of an organization that performs above industry standard. In fact, there is only one way to be sure customers are satisfied—*ask them.*

Customer Satisfaction

Customer satisfaction has long been a fundamental concept in marketing and business strategy. In building a customer satisfaction program, however, the first question that must be answered is, What does it mean to say that a customer is satisfied? The simplest and most widely accepted method of defining customer satisfaction is known as **expectancy disconfirmation.** Simply stated, if a customer's expectations of a supplier's performance are met or exceeded, the customer will be satisfied. Conversely, if perceived performance is less than what the customer expected, then the customer is dissatisfied. A number of companies have adopted this framework for customer satisfaction and follow a commitment to meet or exceed customers' expectations. In fact, many organizations have gone further by speaking in terms of *delighting* their customers through performance which exceeds expectations.

While this framework for customer satisfaction is relatively straightforward, the implications for building a customer service platform in logistics are not. To build this platform it is necessary to explore more fully the nature of customer expectations. What do customers expect? How do customers form these expectations? What is the relationship between customer satisfaction and customer perceptions of overall logistics service quality? Why do many companies fail to satisfy customers, and why are so many companies perceived as providing poor logistics quality? If a company satisfies its customers, is that sufficient? The following sections provide some answers to these critical questions.

Customer Expectations

It is clear that when customers transact business with a supplier they have numerous expectations, many of which revolve around the supplier's basic logistical service platform; that is, they have expectations regarding availability, operational performance, and service reliability. Frequently, they have in place formal programs to monitor suppliers' performance with respect to each of these dimensions of logistical performance. However, in a pioneering study of service expectations and service quality, Parasuraman, Zeithaml, and Berry identified a set of 10 categories of customer expectations,

---

TABLE 3-1   Customer Expectations Related to Logistical Performance

Reliability: Reliability is one of the aspects of the firm's basic service platform. In this context, however, reliability refers to performance of *all* activities as promised by the supplier. If the supplier promises next day delivery and delivery takes 2 days, it is perceived as unreliable. If the supplier accepts an order for 100 cases of a product, it implicitly promises that 100 cases will be delivered. The customer expects and is only satisfied with the supplier if all 100 are received. Customers judge reliability in terms of all aspects of the basic service platform. Thus, customers have expectations concerning damage, documentation accuracy, etc.

Responsiveness: Responsiveness refers to customers' expectations of the willingness and ability of supplier personnel to provide prompt service. This extends beyond mere delivery to include issues related to quick handling of inquiries and resolution of problems. Responsiveness is clearly a time-oriented concept and customers have expectations regarding suppliers' timely handling of all interactions.

Access: Access involves customer expectations of the ease of contact and approachability of the supplier. For example, is it easy to place orders, to obtain information regarding inventory or order status?

Communication: Communication means proactively keeping customers informed. Rather than waiting for customer inquiries concerning order status, customers have expectations regarding suppliers' notification of status, particularly if problems with delivery or availability arise. Customers do not like to be surprised, and advance notice is essential.

Credibility: Credibility refers to customer expectations that communications from the supplier are in fact believable and honest. While it is doubtful that many suppliers intentionally mislead customers, credibility also includes the notion of completeness in required communications.

Security: Security deals with customers' feelings of risk or of doubt in doing business with a supplier. Customers make plans based on their anticipation of supplier performance. For example, they take risk when they schedule production and undertake machine and line setups in anticipation of delivery. If orders are late or incomplete, their plans must be changed. Another aspect of security deals with customer expectations that their dealings with a supplier will be confidential. This is particularly important in supply chain arrangements when a customer has a unique operating agreement with a supplier who also services competitors.

Courtesy: Courtesy involves politeness, friendliness, and respect of contact personnel. This can be a particularly vexing problem considering that customers may have contact with numerous individuals in the organization ranging from sales representatives to customer service personnel to truck drivers. Failure by one individual may destroy the best efforts of all the others.

Competency: Competence is judged by customers in every interaction with a supplier and, like courtesy, can be problematic because it is perceived in every interaction. In other words, customers judge the competence of truck drivers when deliveries are made, warehouse personnel when orders are checked, customer service personnel when phone calls are made, and so forth. Failure by any individual to demonstrate competence affects customer perceptions of the entire organization.

Tangibles: Customers have expectations regarding the physical appearance of facilities, equipment, and personnel. Consider, for example, a delivery truck that is old, damaged, or in poor condition. Such tangible features are additional cues used by customers as indicators of a firm's overall performance.

Knowing the Customer: While suppliers may think in terms of groups of customers and market segments, customers perceive themselves as unique. They have expectations regarding suppliers' understanding their uniqueness and supplier willingness to adapt to their specific requirements.

---

each of which has implications for logistical management.[8] While their later research has focused on a reduced set of five determinants, Table 3-1 presents their original conceptualization with specific examples of logistical expectations that customers may have. These categories could, of course, be considered in the context of other marketing activities, such as expectations related to sales force performance.

---

[8]A. Parasuraman, Valerie Zeithaml, and Leonard L. Berry, "A Conceptual Model of Service Quality and Its Implications for Future Research," Report No. 84-106 (Cambridge, MA: Marketing Science Institute, 1984).

In a logistical and supply chain context, the notion of customer expectations is particularly complex because customers are usually business organizations made up of numerous functions and individuals.[9] Different personnel in a customer organization may prioritize the criteria of performance differently, or they may have different levels of expectation for the criteria. For example, some personnel may be most concerned with responsiveness and rapid handling of an inquiry regarding order status, while others may be more concerned with order completeness or meeting a delivery appointment. Meeting customer expectations requires an understanding of how these expectations are formed and the reasons many companies fail to meet those expectations.

Perceived Service Quality and Customer Satisfaction

Closely related to the concept of customer satisfaction is the concept of perceived service quality. Early on, one leading expert noted that *service quality* is "performance which results in customer satisfaction, or freedom from deficiency which avoids customer dissatisfaction."[10] In more recent research related specifically to logistics it was generalized that "The service quality approach is an attempt to understand customer satisfaction from the perspective of the differences between customer perceptions and actual service on various attributes."[11] While many authors do draw a distinction between customer satisfaction and service quality, the distinction is based primarily on the notion that satisfaction refers to a customer's evaluation of a single transaction, whereas service quality is an evaluation over multiple transactions. It is clear that the two concepts are sufficiently similar to warrant their being treated simultaneously.

A Model of Customer Satisfaction

Figure 3-1 provides a framework for understanding the process by which customers actually form their expectations of supplier performance. It also suggests that frequently a number of *gaps* exist which a supplier must overcome if it is to base its platform of customer accommodation on the satisfaction of customers.

There are several factors that influence customer expectations, both in terms of a prioritization of the criteria discussed above, as well as the level of expectation relative to each of the criteria. The first of these factors is very simply the customer's needs or requirements. At the heart of their own business strategies, customers have requirements, that depend on the performance of their suppliers. To a major extent, customers expect that these needs can and will be met by suppliers. Interestingly, however, customers' expectations are frequently not the same as their real requirements or needs. Previous supplier performance is a major factor influencing customer expectations. A supplier who consistently delivers on time will most likely be expected to deliver on time in the future. Similarly, a supplier with a poor record concerning performance will be expected to perform poorly in the future. It is important to note that previous performance experienced with one supplier may also influence the customer's expectation regarding other suppliers. For example, when Federal Express demonstrated the ability to deliver small packages on a next-day basis, many customers began to expect a similar performance capability from other suppliers.

---

[9]Logistics researchers have developed specific questionnaire scales to be used for assessment of satisfaction with logistics service. See, for example, John T. Mentzer, Daniel Flint, and John L. Kent, "Developing a Logistics Service Quality Scale," *Journal of Business Logistics* 20, no. 1 (1999), pp. 11–29.

[10]Joseph M. Juran, *Juran on Leadership for Quality: An Executive Handbook* (New York, NY: Free Press, 1980).

[11]John T. Mentzer, Daniel Flint, and John L. Kent, op. cit., p. 11.

FIGURE 3-1

Satisfaction and quality model

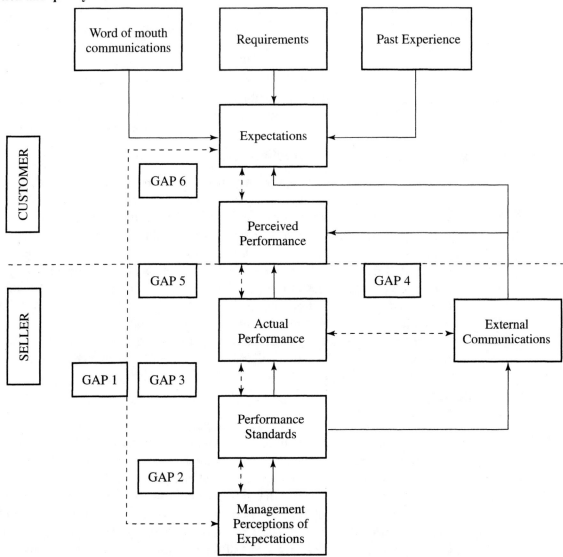

Source: Adapted from A. Parasuraman, Valerie Zeithaml, and Leonard L. Berry, "A Conceptual Model of Service Quality and Its Implications for Future Research," Report No. 84-106 (Cambridge, MA: Marketing Science Institute, 1984).

Related to a customer's perception of past performance is word-of-mouth. In other words, customers frequently communicate with one another concerning their experiences with specific suppliers. At trade and professional association meetings, the subject of suppliers is a common topic of discussion among executives. Much of the discussion may revolve around supplier performance capabilities. Such discussions help form individual customer expectations.

Perhaps the most important factor influencing customer expectations are the communications coming from the supplier itself. Promises and commitments made by sales personnel or customer service representatives, statements contained in marketing and promotional messages, even the printed policies and procedures of an organization represent communications that customers depend upon. These communications become a critical basis on which they form their expectations. The promise of meeting a delivery appointment or having full product availability becomes an expectation in the customer's mind. Indeed many suppliers may be guilty of setting themselves up for failure by overcommitting in an attempt to influence customer expectations.

Figure 3-1 also provides a framework for understanding what must be done by an organization to deliver customer satisfaction. The failure of many firms to satisfy their customers can be traced to the existence of one or more of the gaps identified in the framework.

Gap 1: Knowledge

The first and the most fundamental gap that may exist is between customers' real expectations and managers' perception of those expectations. This gap reflects management's lack of knowledge or understanding of customers. While there may be many reasons for this lack of understanding, it is clear that no beneficial customer satisfaction platform can be established without a thorough understanding of customer expectations, how they are prioritized, and how they are formed. Since sales typically has the major responsibility for customer interactions, knowledge regarding logistics expectations is often difficult to obtain.

Gap 2: Standards

Even if full understanding of customer expectations exists, it is still necessary to establish standards of performance for the organization. The standards gap exists when internal performance standards do not adequately or accurately reflect customer expectations. This is precisely the case in many organizations that develop their basic service platform based on examination of internal operating capabilities or on a superficial examination of competitive service performance.

Gap 3: Performance

The performance gap is the difference between standard and actual performance. If the standard is a fill rate of 98 percent, based on research with customers regarding their expectations, and the firm actually performs at 97 percent, a performance gap exists. It should be pointed out that many firms focus their efforts to improve satisfaction by eliminating the performance gap. It may be, however, that the dissatisfaction exists due to a poor understanding of customer expectations in the first place.

Gap 4: Communications

The role of communications in customer satisfaction cannot be overemphasized. As discussed previously, overcommitment, or promising higher levels of performance than can actually be provided, is a major cause of customer dissatisfaction. There should be no gap between what a firm is capable of doing and what customers are told about those capabilities.

Gap 5: Perception

It is true that customers sometimes perceive performance to be lower or higher than actually achieved. In logistics, many managers frequently lament, "We're only as good as the last order." Thus, although performance over a long time period has been very good, a late or incomplete or otherwise subpar delivery may result in a customer's expression of extreme dissatisfaction.

Gap 6: Satisfaction/Quality

The existence of any one or more of the above gaps leads to customer perception that performance is not as good as expected. In other words, these gaps result in customer dissatisfaction. When building a platform for delivering customer satisfaction, a firm must ensure that these gaps do not exist.

Increasing Customer Expectations

As an important component of TQM the notion of continuous improvement has been accepted by most organizations. As a corollary of continuous improvement, there has been a continued escalation of customers' expectations concerning supplier capabilities. Performance, which meets customer expectations one year, may result in extreme dissatisfaction next year as customers increase their expectations regarding acceptable performance levels.

To some extent, the increase in expectations can be traced to the dynamics of competition. As discussed previously, most industries traditionally have had explicit or implied levels of performance, which were considered to be adequate. If a firm wanted to be a serious competitor, it generally had to achieve these minimum industry service expectations. However, when one firm in the industry focuses on logistics as a core competency and provides higher performance levels, customers come to expect other suppliers to follow. Consider, for example, that after Federal Express introduced real time tracking of shipment status, UPS and other parcel delivery firms shortly followed suit.

Does achieving perfect order performance ensure that customers are satisfied? On the surface it would seem so. After all, if all orders are delivered with no defects, what basis exists for customers to be dissatisfied? Part of the answer to this question lies in the fact that perfect orders, as important as they are, deal with the execution of individual transactions and deliveries. Customer satisfaction is a much broader concept, dealing with many other aspects of the overall relationship between suppliers and customers. For example, a customer may continuously receive perfect orders but be dissatisfied with such aspects of the relationship as difficulty in obtaining information, long delays in response to inquiries, or even the perception that some supplier personnel do not treat the customer with proper courtesy and respect. Thus, satisfaction transcends operational performance to include aspects of personal and interpersonal relationships.

Limitations of Customer Satisfaction

Due to its explicit focus on customers, a commitment to satisfaction represents a step beyond a basic service platform in an organization's efforts to accommodate its customers. It is realistic to think that a firm satisfying customer expectations better than competitors will gain some competitive advantage in the marketplace. Nevertheless, it is important to realize some of the shortcomings and limitations of the customer satisfaction emphasis.

The first limitation is that many executives make a fundamental, yet understandable, mistake in their interpretation of satisfaction. In many organizations it is assumed that customers who are satisfied are also happy, maybe even delighted, with the suppliers' performance. That may or may not be the actual situation. It must be remembered that satisfaction is the customers' perception of actual performance in relation to expectation, not their requirements. Examination of Figure 3-2 may help explain this difference between satisfaction and happiness. The fact is that customers may have an expectation that a firm will not perform at a high level. If the customer has an expectation of a low level of performance and indeed perceives that the firm performs at this

FIGURE 3-2

Satisfaction is not the same as happiness

		Expectation		
		LO	MED	HI
	HI	Very Satisfied	Very Satisfied	Satisfied
Performance	**MED**	Very Satisfied	Satisfied	Dissatisfied
	LO	Satisfied	Dissatisfied	Dissatisfied

low level, it is clear that performance and expectation match. By definition, the customer is satisfied. The same is true at mid-level expectations and perceptions as well as high levels of each.

This notion that low levels of performance may be considered satisfactory can best be illustrated by example. Suppose a customer expects a supplier to provide, over time, a fill rate of 95 percent, or late deliveries 10 percent of the time, or damage of 2 percent. If the supplier in fact provides this level of performance, as is perceived by the customer, the customer is satisfied. Performance perceived to be poorer than the expectation level results in dissatisfaction. Is the satisfied customer necessarily happy about the supplier's fill rate or late deliveries? Of course not. While expectations may be met, indeed may be met as well as or better than competition, there is still no assurance that the customer will be happy. Even performance higher than that expected, while satisfying to customers, may not actually result in happiness. The focus on customer expectations ignores the fact that expectations are not the same as needs or requirements.

The second limitation to consider is actually related to the first: satisfied customers are not necessarily loyal customers. Even though their expectations are being met, satisfied customers may choose to do business with competitors. This can occur because they expect a competitor to perform at a higher level or at least as well as the organization in question. For many years, marketing and supply chain executives have assumed that satisfied customers are also loyal customers. Yet research has frequently shown that many customers, who report being satisfied that their expectations have been met, are likely to patronize and do business with competitors.[12]

A third limitation to customer satisfaction is that firms frequently forget satisfaction lies in the expectations and perceptions of individual customers. Thus, there is a tendency to aggregate expectations across customers and neglect the basic tenets of marketing strategy related to differences among customer segments as well as individual customers. Simply stated, what satisfies one customer may not satisfy other, much less all, customers.

Despite these limitations, customer satisfaction does represent a commitment beyond basic service to accommodate customers. It provides explicit recognition that the only way to ensure that customers are being accommodated is to focus on customers themselves. Firms that focus primarily on industry and competitor standards of basic service performance are much less likely to find that their customers are very satisfied or highly satisfied with their performance.

---

[12]Michael J. Ryan, Robert Raynor, and Andy Morgan, "Diagnosing Customer Loyalty Drivers," *Marketing Research* 11, no. 2 (Summer 1999), pp. 18–26.

TABLE 3-2   Evolution of Management Thought

Philosophy	Focus
Customer Service	Meet Internal Standards
Customer Satisfaction	Meet Expectations
Customer Success	Meet Customer Requirements

Note: Notice that the satisfaction model does not focus on *requirements.*

Customer Success

In recent years, some firms have discovered that there is another commitment that can be made to gain true competitive advantage through logistical performance. This commitment is based on recognition that a firm's ability to grow and expand market share depends on its ability to attract and hold the industry's most successful customers. The real key, then, to customer-focused marketing lies in the organization's using its performance capabilities to enhance the success of those customers. This focus on customer success represents major commitment toward accommodating customers. Table 3-2 summarizes the evolution that customer-focused organizations have experienced. Notice that a customer service focus is oriented toward establishment of internal standards for basic service performance. Firms typically assess their customer service performance relative to how well these internal standards are accomplished. The customer satisfaction platform is built on the recognition that customers have expectations regarding performance and the only way to ensure that customers are satisfied is to assess their perceptions of performance relative to those expectations.

Customer success shifts the focus from expectations to the customers' real requirements. Recall from the previous discussion that customer requirements, while forming the basis for expectations, are not the same as expectations. Requirements are frequently downgraded into expectations due to perceptions of previous performance, word-of-mouth, or communications from the firm itself. This explains why simply meeting expectations may not result in happy customers. For example, a customer may be satisfied with a 98 percent fill rate, but for the customer to be successful in executing its own strategy, a 100 percent fill rate on certain products or components may be necessary.

Achieving Customer Success

Clearly, a customer success program involves a thorough understanding of individual customer requirements and a commitment to focus on long-term business relationships having high potential for growth and profitability. Such commitment most likely cannot be made to all potential customers. It requires that firms work intensively with customers to understand requirements, internal processes, competitive environment, and whatever else it takes for the customer to be successful in its own competitive arena. Further, it requires that an organization develop an understanding of how it can utilize its own capabilities to enhance customer performance. Industry Insight 3-3 describes how the customer success philosophy developed at Dow Plastics, a division of Dow Chemical.

INDUSTRY INSIGHT 3-3 "WE DON'T SUCCEED UNLESS YOU DO"

In 1988, Dow hired the Anderson & Lembke ad agency, which is known for its cutting-edge creativity. Dow had just realigned its various plastics businesses into a single unit called Dow Plastics. Anderson & Lembke's tasks were to publicize the new entity and assist in its competitive positioning.

Dow's customers and its competitors' customers were surveyed. They ranked Dow a distant third behind industry leaders DuPont and GE Plastics. However, customers were unhappy with the service level they received from all three. "Vendors peddled resins as a commodity," says Hans Ullmark, president of Anderson & Lembke. "They competed on price and delivered on time, but gave no service."

These findings, confirmed by about 200 qualitative interviews, led to a positioning strategy that exceeded the standard customer service guarantee to promise customer success. This strategy, which began as a tag line for a division, grew in influence until it became the core of the parent company's mission statement: "We don't succeed unless you do."

It was concluded that whether a customer was using Dow plastics to manufacture grocery bags or complex aerospace applications, Dow Plastics needed to help them succeed in their markets. A campaign was developed which included print ads, direct-mail pieces, and supportive materials. The targeted communications promoted the different virtues of Dow Plastics' disparate products, but all carried the tag line "We don't succeed unless you do." This slogan and underlying philosophy tied the units together and created a brand identity for the division.

The campaigns were key in changing Dow Plastics from a sales-oriented company into a market-oriented company—from selling plastics to selling customer success. Dow has become the most preferred plastics supplier.

Dow's philosophy is so transformed that when a new product or market is encountered, they ask, "How does this fit in with 'We don't succeed unless you do'?"

Source: Nancy Arnott, "Getting the Picture," *Sales and Marketing Management,* June 1994, p. 74.

In many ways a customer success program requires a comprehensive supply chain perspective on the part of logistics executives. This is most easily explained by examining the relations depicted in Figure 3-3. The typical focus in basic service and satisfaction programs is that the firm attempts to meet standards and expectations of next-destination customers, whether they are consumers, industrial end users, or intermediate or even internal customers. How those customers deal with their customer is typically not considered to be a problem. A supply chain perspective and a customer success program explicitly recognize that logistics executives must alter this focus. They must understand the entire supply chain, the different levels of customer within that supply chain, and develop programs to ensure that next-destination customers are successful in meeting the requirements of customers down the supply chain. If all supply chain members adopt this perspective, then all members share in the success.

To ensure that a customer is successful may require a firm to reinvent the way a product is produced, market distributed, or offered for sale. In fact, collaboration between suppliers and customers to find potential avenues for success may result in the greatest breakthroughs in terms of redefining supply chain processes. The general topic of collaborative relationships and alliances is further developed in Chapter 4. It is enough to say here that such arrangements are not possible without significant amounts of information exchange between the involved businesses to facilitate an in-depth understanding of requirements and capabilities. However, one important way that many firms have responded to the challenges of customer success is through the development of value-added services.

FIGURE 3-3

Moving to customer success

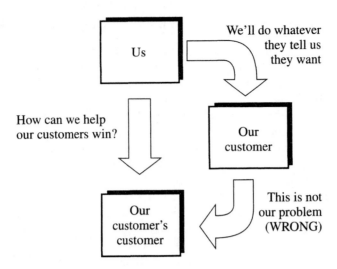

Value-Added Services

The notion of value-added service is a significant development in the evolution to customer success. By definition, **value-added services** refer to unique or specific activities that firms can jointly develop to enhance their efficiency and/or effectiveness. Value-added services help foster customer success. Because they tend to be customer-specific, it is difficult to generalize all possible value-added services.

When a firm becomes committed to value-added solutions for major customers, it rapidly becomes involved in customized or tailored logistics. It is doing unique things to enable specific customers to achieve their objectives. IBM's ability to produce and deliver customized personal computers and networks to individual customers is one example of adding value to a rather standard product. In a logistical context, firms can provide unique product packages, create customized unit loads, place prices on products, offer unique information services, provide vendor-managed inventory service, make special shipping arrangements, and so forth, to enhance customer success.

In reality, some of the value-added services that buyers and sellers agree to involve integrated service providers who are positioned to provide such services. Transportation carriers, warehouse firms, and other specialists may become intimately involved in the supply chain to make such value-adding activities a reality. At this point, a few specific examples of how they may work within a specific supply chain to provide value-added services are sufficient.

Warehouses, whether private or third-party, can be utilized to perform a number of customization activities. For example, a retail customer may desire a unique palletization alternative to support its cross-dock activities and meet the unique product requirements of its individual store units. Each store requires different quantities of specific product to maintain in-stock performance with minimum inventory commitment. In another situation, first-aid kits consisting of many different items are actually assembled in the warehouse as orders are received to meet the unique configuration of kit desired by specific customers. It is also common for warehouses to provide pick-price-repack services for manufacturers to accommodate the unique product configurations required by different customers.

Another form of value-added service involves the proper sorting and sequencing of products to meet specific customer requirements. For example, an auto assembly plant may require that components not only be received on time but also be sorted and sequenced in a particular manner to meet the needs of specific automobiles on the assembly line. The objective is to reduce assembly plant handling and inspection of incoming components. Meeting such exacting requirements for delivery is far beyond the basic service capability of many component suppliers. The use of third-party specialists is a necessity, especially when subcomponents from multiple suppliers must be integrated and then properly sequenced.

Value-added services can be performed directly by participants in a business relationship or may involve specialists. It has become more common in recent years to turn to specialists due to their flexibility and capability to concentrate on providing the required services. Nevertheless, regardless of how the specifics are organized and implemented, it is clear that logistics value-added services are a critical aspect of customer success programs.

Developing Customer Success: An Example

Customer success programs are typically focused on individual customers, as different customer organizations have unique requirements. Careful identification and selection of those customers who are most likely to respond to such efforts and who are willing to return loyalty to the supplier are essential to implementing success programs. In some instances, however, a firm may find it beneficial, or even necessary, to focus a success program on an entire segment of customers to ensure their long-term survival. Such a situation occurred in the wholesale drug distribution industry during the 1980s and 90s. Bergen Brunswig and other selected drug wholesalers revolutionized the independent, owner-managed segment of the retail drug industry. These retailers were faced with potential extinction due to the rise of chain and mass-merchant pharmacy operations but survived as a direct result of the wholesalers' success initiative.

Specifically, to enhance the business success of its retail drugstore customers Bergen Brunswig developed a classic four-stage model: cost-effectiveness, market access, market extension, and market creation. The long-term process is illustrated in Figure 3-4.

Overall, industry efficiency improvements were significant. Tailoring services to specific customers served to establish incentives for maintaining long-term alliances. The nature of Bergen Brunswig's initiative is reviewed below to illustrate how logistical competency can be used to achieve customer success and to gain competitive superiority.

Cost-Effectiveness
The first and most fundamental step was to gain cost-effectiveness. It was essential that the process and necessary related controls be in place to ensure that basic services

FIGURE 3-4

Development of business success based on logistical competency

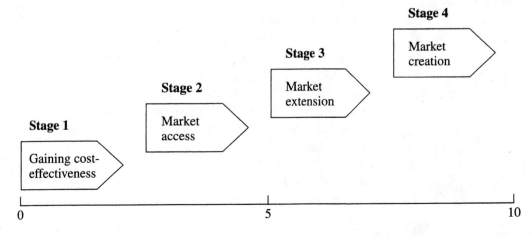

could be provided at a consistently high level of performance and in a cost-effective manner. From a managerial perspective, it is a prerequisite that a firm be able to efficiently perform the basic logistic services required by customers. Most firms that are serious about quality agree there is little room for basic operational error. Unless a firm is able to deliver basic service at reasonable cost, there is no reason for customers to commit additional business and there is limited possibility of moving forward toward a more exacting relationship.

Market Access

The market access stage consisted of higher-level commitments to customers who expressed a willingness to cooperate in efforts to achieve joint objectives. In other words, market access consists of buyers and sellers working together and sharing basic information to facilitate smooth joint operations. It is important to stress that no real level of customer selectivity was involved in market access. For example, Bergen Brunswig needed to establish a basic service commitment to all druggists who were willing to utilize it as a wholesale supplier. The only differential in the timing or level of service during the access stage was determined by the customer's purchase quantity. Once Bergen Brunswig offered retailers a specific service program, it became a principle of fundamental business fairness and legality that each druggist who purchased required volumes would receive equal basic services. For Bergen Brunswig, this commitment meant daily replenishment of exact inventory requirements within a consistent delivery schedule.

Market Extension

Market extension intensifies a business arrangement. Extension is based on moving toward zero defects and introducing value-added services in an effort to solidify and expand the business relationship. At this point the relationship became highly selective since the number of customers who were willing or able to participate was limited. In Bergen Brunswig's strategy, such value-added alliances consisted of a variety of programs to improve the competitiveness of selected customers who were willing to commit to Bergen Brunswig as almost a sole-source supplier. Typical of such value-added innovations were sophisticated bar coding, computer terminals for pharmacy checkout counters, point-of-sale encoding, shelf plan-o-gramming, immediate price change administration, profitability, and inventory turn reports. These innovations were designed to increase operating efficiency and extend overall competitiveness. Such value-added services were offered only to customers who committed to an extended business relationship.

Market Creation

The final stage, market creation, requires full commitment to a customer's success. While all previous stages contribute to competency, the final stage represents above-and-beyond initiatives to enhance success. In the case of Bergen Brunswig, one form of market creation consisted of researching and developing new and innovative ways to make relatively small druggists increasingly competitive with larger vertically integrated chains. For example, Bergen Brunswig pioneered and cooperatively tested such revenue-generating devices as selling cut flowers and carryout food. Creative arrangements also extended to the implementation of joint systems that electronically linked Bergen Brunswig to its retail customers for purposes of providing a full range of process control services.

The full impact of logistics is felt at every stage of the process. It is important to gain control and become cost-effective. High-level basic service is central to market access. During market extension, the commitment to perfect performance and value-added services solidifies the basic business arrangement. The relationship matures into a long-term situation wherein future growth is attained by helping the customer achieve the most successful business possible. The development of a business relationship built on such advanced principles takes time, as much as 10 years or more. The trust aspects of joint operations and free information exchange that are fundamental to such collaborations cannot be engineered and implemented in an untested, unseasoned business arrangement. The Bergen Brunswig model provides a classic illustration of the fusion of information technology and leadership collaboration required to achieve supply chain success.

Summary

The fundamental rationale for logistics is the need to accommodate customers, whether those customers are end users, intermediate, or even internal. The marketing concept provides the foundation for customer accommodation with its fundamental focus on customer needs rather than on products or services, the requirement to view and position products and services in a customer context, identification of market segments which differ in needs, and commitment that volume is secondary to profit.

Contemporary interpretation of the marketing concept suggests that it is more important to focus on the development of relationships with customers than to perfect individual transactions with customers. This interpretation focuses on the needs and requirements of individual customers as the core ingredient of one-to-one marketing. In a supply chain context, customer requirements related to spatial convenience, lot size, waiting time, and variety and assortment must be accommodated by logistical operations.

Organizations build their platform for accommodation on three levels of increasing commitment. The first of these is basic logistics customer service. To be competitive, a firm needs a basic service capability that balances availability, operational performance, and reliability for all customers. The level of commitment to each dimension of service requires careful consideration of competitive performance and cost/benefit analysis. The highest level of commitment is perfect order performance, which requires zero defects in logistics operations. Such high-level commitment is generally reserved for a firm's key customers.

Going beyond basic service to create customer satisfaction represents the second level of customer accommodation. Where basic service focuses on the organization's internal operational performance, customer satisfaction focuses on customers, their expectations, and their perceptions of supplier performance. Customer expectations extend beyond typical logistical operational considerations and include factors related to communication, credibility access, responsiveness, and customer-specific knowledge as well as reliability and responsiveness of operations. A firm can provide logistics service that is equal to or even better than competitors but still have dissatisfied customers. Failure to satisfy customers can arise from lack of knowledge about customer expectations, improper standards of performance, performance failure, poor communication, or incorrect customer perception of performance. As customer expectations escalate, logistics executives must continuously monitor customer satisfaction and improve logistics performance.

The highest level of customer accommodation is known as customer success. Where satisfaction programs seek to meet or exceed expectations, a success platform focuses on customer needs and requirements. Customer expectations are frequently different from needs and requirements. Achieving success requires intimate knowledge of a customer's needs, their operational requirements, and a commitment by the service provider to enhance a customer's ability to compete more successfully in the marketplace. Value-added services represent one way logistics can contribute to customer success. While customer success is normally associated with one-to-one marketing relationships, in isolated instances it may represent the most viable approach to ensuring the long-term survival of entire categories of customers. Bergen Brunswig and the retail pharmacy industry provide a classic example of how this approach worked.

Challenge Questions

1. Explain the differences between transactional and relationship marketing. How do these differences lead to increasing emphasis on logistical performance in supply chain management?
2. Why are the four primary service outputs of spatial convenience, lot size, waiting time, and product variety important to logistics management? Provide examples of competing firms that differ in the level of each service output provided to customers.
3. What is meant by availability in logistics customer service? Provide examples of the different ways to monitor a firm's performance in availability.
4. Compare and contrast speed, consistency, and flexibility as operational performance activities. In some situations, is one activity more critical than others?
5. Why is perfect order service so difficult to achieve?
6. Using the 10 categories of customer expectations in Table 3-1, develop your own examples of how customers might evaluate performance of a supplier.
7. Which of the gaps in Figure 3-1 do you think represents the major problem for most firms? How can a company attempt to eliminate the knowledge gap? The communications gap?
8. Compare and contrast the customer service, customer satisfaction, and customer success philosophies of supply chain management.
9. What is meant by value-added services? Why are these services considered essential in a customer success program?
10. How could a company use the four-stage process of cost-effectiveness, market access, market extension, and market creation to gain competitive superiority?

4   MARKET DISTRIBUTION STRATEGY

In the quest to accommodate customer requirements, no one activity is more important than any other and no one firm can be self-sufficient. This basic fact was discovered many years ago by no less than Henry Ford. Almost from the beginning, Ford envisioned an industrial empire, which was totally self-contained and relied on no other organization. He set out to develop the world's first totally vertically integrated firm.[1]

To support his auto manufacturing facilities, Ford invested in coalmines, iron-ore deposits, and steel mills. He bought land to grow soybeans used in the manufacture of paint and rubber plantations for tires. He owned railroads and ships for transporting materials and trucks for distribution of finished automobiles. He envisioned a network of automobile dealerships owned by Ford Motor Company and managed by his

---

[1]Henry Ford, *Today and Tomorrow* (Portland, OR: Productivity Press, 1926, 1988).

employees. The Ford Motor Company would be a highly integrated organization from raw material sourcing all the way to the final consumer.

Eventually, Ford found he needed help. Facing severe economic, regulatory, and labor barriers, he turned to a network of independent suppliers for needed materials, components, and services; for more effective marketing, a network of independently owned and operated dealerships. As time passed, Ford discovered that specialized firms could perform much of the essential work as well as or better than his own bureaucracy. The Ford strategy shifted from ownership-based control to one of orchestrating channel relationships.

This chapter is concerned with why and how firms develop and manage marketing channel distribution relationships. Chapter 5 deals with procurement, the activity that links a firm to its suppliers, and manufacturing, the activity that provides the form utility for customers. Throughout the two chapters, the focus is on the logistical integration of these activities to most effectively and efficiently accommodate customer requirements.

The study of marketing channels embraces a wide range of different ways that business operations are conducted. Supply chains are one of the popular marketing channel arrangements. The first section of this chapter deals with overall channel structure and the rationale for marketing channels in highly developed industrial economies. The second section deals with market distribution strategy, focusing on structure, channel design, and types of relationships among channel participants. Information technology, specifically electronic commerce, has had significant impact on market distribution strategy and is discussed in the third section of the chapter. The final section of the chapter focuses on the interrelationship of marketing strategy decisions related to pricing and logistics considerations.

Market Distribution in the Supply Chain

Imagine a society in which every individual is totally self-sufficient: each individual would produce and consume all of the products and services necessary for survival so there would be no need for any economic activity related to the exchange of goods and services between individuals. No such society can be found today. In reality, as individuals begin to specialize in the production of specific goods or services, a mechanism must arise for the exchange of those goods and services to satisfy the consumption needs of individuals. To do so efficiently and effectively, firms must overcome three discrepancies: discrepancy in *space,* discrepancy in *time,* and discrepancy in *quantity and assortment.*

Discrepancy in space refers to the fact that the location of production activities and the location of consumption are seldom the same. Consider, for example, the household furniture industry. Most household furniture in the United States is manufactured in a small geographic area in North Carolina and a great deal of office furniture is manufactured in western Michigan. Yet, where is furniture demanded? All over the United States! This difference between the location of production and the location of consumption is a fundamental problem that must be overcome to accomplish exchange. Overcoming this locational discrepancy provides customers the service output of spatial convenience discussed in Chapter 3.

Discrepancy in time refers to the difference in timing between production and consumption. Some products, agricultural commodities for example, are produced during short time periods but are demanded by customers continuously. On the other hand, many products are manufactured in anticipation of future customer demand. Since manufacturing often does not occur at the same time products are demanded, inventory and warehousing are required. The specific manner in which this discrepancy is overcome results in the service output related to waiting time discussed in Chapter 3. It should be noted here that much of the discussion in this text is devoted to the challenges firms face in more closely matching the rate of production with market consumption.

Discrepancy in quantity and assortment refers to the fact that manufacturing firms typically specialize in producing large quantities of a variety of items. Customers, on the other hand, typically demand small quantities of numerous items. This difference between the production and consumption sectors of the economy must somehow be reconciled to deliver the product variety and assortment to customers.

These basic problems of exchange are resolved by the overall market distribution process, through the mechanism typically referred to as the **channel of distribution.** A channel of distribution can be defined as a network of organizations and institutions that, in combination, perform all the functions required to link producers with end customers to accomplish the marketing task. An understanding of distribution channels is essential for logistics managers because it is within the channel that logistics strategy is actually executed to accommodate customer requirements. In this section, important elements of channel theory related to marketing functions, specialization, the sorting process, and channel separation are reviewed to highlight the interaction between marketing channel requirements and logistical accommodation.

Marketing Functions

Those who study marketing have long acknowledged that a number of specific acts or activities are essential to the successful completion of exchange. Although there are many ways to classify these functions, the traditional list includes selling, buying, transporting, storing, financing, standardization, market financing, risk bearing, and market information. In the typical channel arrangement, a function may alternately be performed by different channel members or it may be performed and duplicated numerous times.

Table 4-1 presents the traditional grouping of the eight universal functions into three subsets: exchange, logistics, and facilitation. The exchange functions represent

TABLE 4-1   Universal Marketing Functions Performed by Channel Arrangements

Group	Function
Exchange	Selling
	Buying
Logistics	Transportation
	Storage
Facilitation	Financing
	Standardization
	Risk
	Market information

the activities necessary for ownership transfer. Selling is necessary to cultivate product demand through development of products that satisfy market needs and through techniques of demand stimulation, such as advertising and personal selling. Buying involves the planning and acquisition of assortments so that proper quantities and qualities of products will be available to meet customer requirements. The logistics functions consist of getting the right products to the right place at the right time. In contemporary logistics the scope of concern is significantly broader than transportation and storage, encompassing all work related to inventory positioning, which may include aspects of satisfying form and possession requirements as well. The other four functions are collectively referred to as facilitation because their performance is necessary to complete the exchange and logistics activities.

Specialization

The need for functional performance leads directly to the economic concept of **specialization.** Specialization is a fundamental driver of economic efficiency. Manufacturers are specialists in the production of specific products. Wholesalers and retailers are specialists in the sense that they buy and sell specific assortments tailored to the requirements of the target markets they have chosen to serve. Warehousing and transportation firms are specialists in the performance of logistical functions. The logic of specialization is based on economies of scale and scope. When a firm specializes, it develops scale and scope to achieve operational efficiency. In fact, much of the economic justification for specialized channel participants lies in their ability to efficiently perform an activity.

The economic justification for using a specialist is challenged when a firm generates sufficient volume to consider performing the activity internally. Conversely, a firm may choose to spin off, or outsource, certain functions when it finds that it does not have sufficient economies of scale, or when it chooses to focus on other functions it deems more closely related to its core competency. The point is that essential functions may be shifted from one firm to another, absorbed, spun off, and the like.[2] Regardless of who performs the specific work, all functions must be performed to complete the distribution process.

Assortment

Product assortment is directly related to specialization and has received considerable attention in the business literature.[3] Market accommodation requires that distribution channels provide consumers and end users with their desired levels of product variety and assortment. In channel arrangements a number of independent businesses often cooperate to deliver the appropriate mix of products; at strategic positions in a distribution channel, products are concentrated, sorted, and dispersed to the next location in the overall supply chain. This process has four basic steps: concentration, allocation, customization, and dispersion.

---

[2]Rich literature exists concerning functional absorption and spin-off, based on the work of Bruce Mallen. For example, see Bruce Mallen, "Functional Spin-off: A Key to Anticipatory Change in Distribution Structures," *Journal of Marketing,* 37, no. 3 (July 1973), pp. 18–25.

[3]See Wroe Alderson, *Marketing Behavior and Executive Action* (Homewood, IL: Richard D. Irwin, Inc., 1957), chapter 7.

Concentration refers to the collection of large quantities of a product or of multiple products so they can be sold as a group. A manufacturer's consolidation warehouse, for example, brings the output of several different factories to a single location. Alternatively, an industrial distributor or wholesaler may purchase from several manufacturers and bring the items to a single location. One purpose of concentration is to reduce transportation cost. The cost reduction results from moving large quantities of product to the concentration location rather than each supplier individually shipping small quantities directly to customers.

Allocation refers to breaking down a homogeneous group of products into smaller and smaller lot sizes to more closely match customer requirements. Products received from suppliers in truckload quantities may in turn be sold in case quantities. Case quantities may be broken into individual product units. Allocation is also known as the process of breaking bulk.

Customization refers to regrouping the products into an assortment of items for resale to uniquely meet a specific customer's requirements. Manufacturers, through their consolidation facilities, allow wholesale and retail customers to purchase full truckloads of mixed products. Similarly, wholesalers build mixed assortments of products for retailers and retailers build assortments for consumers. For example, warehouse stores such as Costco may desire a unique product pack, such as two boxes of cereal wrapped together. Another retailer may require special promotional displays, which may even combine products from two different manufacturers. In contemporary supply chains, the ability to customize is vital.

Dispersion is the final step in assortment. It consists of shipping the customized assortments to customers when and where specified. A hypothetical example can illustrate the overall process of assortment and also provide insight into a critical economic principle of distribution: **the principle of minimum total transactions.** Figure 4-1(a) shows a simple structure with three manufacturers and six customers. The customers could be consumers or industrial users. For simplicity, assume the customers are retailers who are attempting to develop an assortment for resale to their consumer markets. In this figure, each retailer buys directly from each manufacturer, requiring a total of 18 separate transactions, each with its associated order placement, order processing, and order fulfillment cost, including the cost of transportation of relatively small quantities from the manufacturers to the individual retail locations.

Figure 4-1(b) introduces one wholesaler into the structure to accomplish the entire process of assortment. The wholesaler purchases the output of each manufacturer, which is delivered to one location. The wholesaler then breaks bulk and customizes quantities according to each retailer's specific requirements and transports these customized assortments to the individual retail locations. Using this intermediary, the total number of transactions is reduced to nine. Three transactions are required from manufacturer to wholesaler and six from wholesaler to retailer. The savings in order placement, processing, and fulfillment costs can be substantial. Furthermore, the cost of transportation is substantially reduced because there are only 9 transportation movements, each of large quantity, rather than 18 individual small quantity shipments. Of course, the intermediary must be compensated for the work performed. However, since both the manufacturers' and the retailers' costs are lower, the potential for a lower total cost system exists, even including the costs incurred by the intermediate wholesaler.

The assortment process provides considerable insight into the economics of market distribution. It also demonstrates how distribution channels provide different customers with their desired levels of product variety and lot-size requirements. It helps

FIGURE **4-1**

Principle of minimum transactions

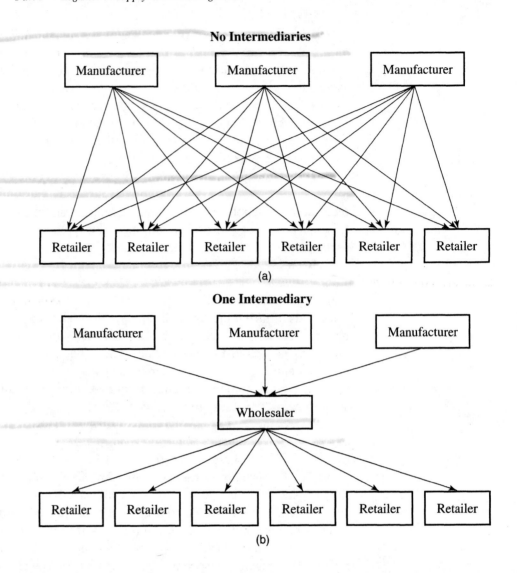

explain why a manufacturer such as Kellogg would have a small grocery store purchase cereal through a wholesaler to obtain a wide assortment of food products. On the other hand, Kellogg might deal directly with large supermarket chains that purchase cereal in large volume quantities.

Channel Separation

The preceding discussion of specialization of functions and assortment leads to one other important concept in market distribution: **channel separation.** Separation usually focuses on isolating the buying and selling functions related to ownership transfer from the functions related to physical distribution or logistics. Although both sets of activities are necessary and must be coordinated, there is no requirement that they be performed simultaneously or even by the same businesses. A product may change ownership without physically moving or may be shipped and warehoused several times without changing ownership. Thus, the ownership, or marketing, channel consists of a network of firms engaged in buying and selling. It consists of intermediaries such as agents, industrial distributors, full and/or limited function wholesalers, sales representatives, and retailers, all of which are involved in negotiating, contracting, and administering sales on a continuing basis.

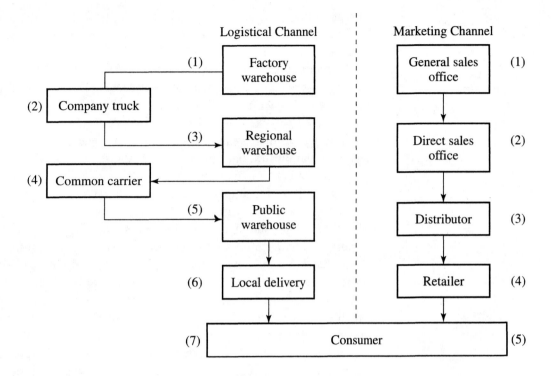

FIGURE 4-2

Logistical and marketing separation

The physical, or logistics, channel represents a network of organizations involved with achieving inventory movement and positioning. The work of logistics involves transportation, warehousing, storage, handling, order processing, and an increasing array of value-added services concerned with achieving time, space, lot-size, and assortment requirements.

It must be noted that it is certainly possible that any given firm may participate in both the marketing and the logistics channels for a product. Wholesalers, distributors, and retailers typically do physically handle, store, and transport products, as well as participate in the marketing flows. It is very useful conceptually, however, to recognize that there is no requirement that a firm participate in both channels.

Separation in Practice

Figure 4-2 illustrates potential separation of the overall distribution channel for color televisions. The only time the marketing and logistics channels formally merge is at the manufacturer's factory and the consumer's home. Three specialists are employed in the logistics channel: a common transportation carrier, a public warehouse, and a specialized local delivery firm. In addition, three levels of logistics operations are performed by the manufacturer. Television sets are initially stored in the company's factory warehouse, transported in private trucks, and then stored in a regional warehouse facility before specialized intermediaries begin to participate in the logistics channel.

In the marketing channel, the distributor has legal title to the television sets from the time they are shipped from the manufacturer's regional warehouse. Retailers are served from the public warehouse. During the logistics process, the distributor never physically warehouses, handles, or transports the television sets. When the retailer sells a set, delivery is made to the consumer's home from the distributor's stock being held in the public warehouse. The retailer maintains limited stock for point-of-sale display. Sales are negotiated between the retailer and consumer, including a commitment to deliver a specified television set model directly to the consumer's residence.

Direct-to-home customer shipment is completed from a strategically located public warehouse, which may be many miles from the point-of-sale transaction and product delivery destination.

Structural separation, as illustrated, reflects common practice in a wide variety of industries such as furniture, appliances, and television sets. These businesses offer products with a variety of options, models, and colors. As such, it would be difficult for a retailer to stock the full range of products. Instead, the retailer limits inventory commitment to display items, keeping color swatches and option books on hand for customer demonstration. The benefits of logistical specialization result in low-cost delivery and effective marketing.

An additional example of separation is a factory branch sales office that carries no inventory. The office exists for the sole purpose of stimulating ownership transactions. The physical product exchange between seller and buyer may logistically move in a variety of combinations of transport and storage, depending on value, size, bulk, weight, and perishability of the shipment. Generally, no economic justification exists for locating warehouses and inventories at the same site as the branch offices. The network of branch sales offices is best designed to facilitate maximum marketing impact. The logistical structure should be designed to accomplish the required delivery performance and economies.

A final example of separation comes from the rapidly growing home shopping industry. An order placed by phone, at a local catalog desk, or via the Internet is typically fulfilled from a factory or distribution warehouse directly to the buyer's home. All direct marketing systems exploit separation to realize separation benefits.

Interdependence of Marketing and Logistics

While the emphasis in this text is on logistical flows, separation of marketing and logistics should not be interpreted to mean that either can stand alone. Both are essential to create customer value. The major argument favoring operational separation is increased opportunity for specialization.

Structural separation does not necessarily require outsourcing work to specialized service firms. A single firm may be able to internally satisfy all marketing and logistical requirements. The desired degree of operational separation depends on available service providers, economies of scale, resources, and managerial capabilities. The benefits of separation are independent of combining internal organization units with outside specialists. From an ownership transfer viewpoint, the customer value-creation process is not complete until logistical promises are fully performed. Depending on the products involved, the logistical operations may start in anticipation of, be simultaneous with, or follow actual sale. Logistical performance with respect to time, location, and terms of delivery must comply with specifications established during sales negotiation.

Market Distribution Strategy Development

The marketing channel is one of the least understood areas of business strategy. The diversity and complexity of channel arrangements make it difficult to describe and generalize the challenges managers face when developing a supply chain strategy. Marketing channels do not have uniform dimensions and often defy simple description. Some are very direct, linking manufacturers or growers of a product directly to consumers. Others contain many intermediate institutions with ownership transfer oc-

FIGURE 4-3

Generic channels of distribution

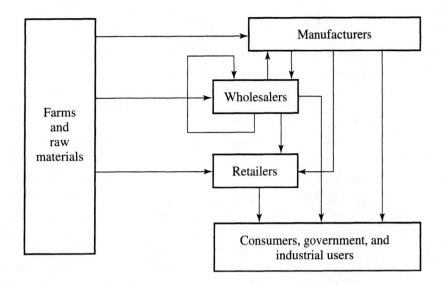

curring many times. Complicating the subject is the fact that almost all firms are engaged in multiple channel arrangements as they seek the most effective means to penetrate many different market segments and meet the requirements of those segments they choose to serve.

Distribution Structure

Figure 4-3 illustrates an overall generic channel structure required to complete the marketing process. While its simplicity is misleading, it serves to illustrate the major types of institutions that may be involved in the overall process. Manufacturers are primarily involved in creating products. As the creators, they were traditionally considered to be the originators of channel arrangements and became the focal point for channel discussions. Comprehensive channel study, however, must include more than the manufacturer's perspective. To do otherwise would incorrectly position wholesalers and retailers as passive institutions.

In many channel situations, retailers are powerful and dominant in determining how the overall distribution process will be organized and what the management practices will be. As the institution closest to final customers, retailers have a great deal at stake in channel performance. Wholesalers are less visible in the process, but their role in orchestrating and coordinating the activities of many manufacturers with those of retailers cannot be ignored. Understanding the roles of the many types of channel participants is critical in developing market distribution strategy.

Channel Participants

Primary channel participants are those businesses that assume risk during the value-added distribution process. Below, the basic nature of each business type is reviewed. The purpose is to illustrate the extent, size, and complexity of potential distribution arrangements in an economy encompassing over 375,000 manufacturers, 450,000 wholesalers, and 1.1 million retail establishments.[4]

---

[4]All statistics related to number of firms and sales are from *1997 Census of Business,* U.S. Department of Commerce.

Manufacturers.   The process of combining materials and components into products is typically called **manufacturing** or **production.** Manufacturing firms are highly visible channel participants because they provide form utility by creating the products that become the primary concern of the overall distribution process.

Manufacturers take on significant risk with the creation of products. For example, General Motors, Ford, and DaimlerChrysler invest hundreds of million of dollars in developing, testing, and launching new styles, new options, and improved automobiles. Reputable manufacturers assume full responsibility for the quality of their products and their ultimate acceptance by customers. The most visible manufacturers are the firms that produce consumer products such as automobiles, appliances, food, pharmaceuticals, clothing, etc. These products, produced for mass consumption, often have highly advertised and publicized brands with high levels of consumer identification. But in reality, these firms represent only a small percentage of all companies engaged in manufacturing. The majority of manufacturing firms produce components, subassemblies, or ingredients that are sold to other business firms. Such business-to-business (B2B) marketing is critical to the overall performance of final-product manufacturing and distribution. It must be noted that while the extent of manufacturer's risk in the overall distribution process is considerable, it is limited to the specific products produced. Each specific manufacturer's products typically represent a small proportion of those handled by the other primary channel participants: wholesalers and retailers.

Wholesalers.   Perhaps the least understood and least visible channel participant is the **wholesaler.** Wholesalers are businesses that are primarily engaged in buying merchandise from manufacturers and reselling to retailers, industrial users, or business users. They may also act as agents in buying merchandise for or selling merchandise to companies. In 1997, there were over 450,000 wholesaling establishments in the United States with total sales exceeding $4 trillion!

The primary business of wholesalers is their specialization in performing assortment in a manner that reduces costs and risk for other channel members. For many years in many industries it has been thought that mergers, acquisitions, and continued concentration in both the manufacturing and retailing sectors of the economy would eliminate the economic justification of wholesalers. Yet, in many industries, wholesaling continues to flourish. Such firms as Super Value, True Value, Sysco, McKesson, Grainger, as well as many others, maintain their viability through innovative specialization in performing the assortment process for a large number of manufacturers and retailers. They do so by reducing risk, duplication of effort, and the number of transactions required to satisfy customer requirements. As described in Industry Insight 4-1, Valu Merchandisers developed a program for its retail customers that combines several product categories into a one-stop solution for nutritional and whole health products.

Retailers.   In simplest terms, **retail** is the business of selling goods and services to consumers who buy for their own use and benefit. In 1997, there were over 1.1 million retail establishments with total sales of over $3.8 trillion. Ranging in size and scope from such firms as Wal★Mart, Kroger, Toys R Us, and The Limited to individually owned and operated stores, retailers are clearly the most visible channel participant to consumers. They perform functions that combine to offer their target customers the right products, at the right place, at the right time, in the right quantity, and at the right price. The specific strategies employed by individual retail firms in providing these *rights* to consumers vary dramatically and range from mass merchandising to discounting, to super specialty, to focused service, and many

INDUSTRY INSIGHT 4-1 ONE-STOP SUPPLEMENTS

Valu Merchandisers, a Kansas City, Missouri-based wholesaler and subsidiary of Associated Wholesale Grocers, has developed Natural Solutions to offer consumers a convenient and complete whole health shopping experience. Natural Solutions incorporates frozen foods, dairy, books and magazines, bulk products, beauty care, and vitamins and herbal supplements into a whole health section. In addition, the Health Notes Online computer provides online access to additional health tips and a nutritional database with extensive reference materials. The section requires approximately 140 linear feet for optimal success. Industry information indicates that sales of related natural products can increase significantly when sections are merchandised correctly.

The Natural Solutions concept is consumer-driven. Generally, consumers desire to decrease their shopping time while saving money and choosing from a broad product assortment. According to Bob Carlson, director of nutrition centers for Valu, "Our position is that if we can offer a host of different products with the same theme in the same area, we can get consumers more interested in the overall section. That is going to boost traffic and it is going to boost sales. It's all about one-stop shopping."

The section concept is based upon shopping synergies. "We are trying to set a tone for the section and the overall store," says Carlson. "We don't want consumers to do the bulk of their grocery buying in our stores and then run across the street or down the block to a natural foods store for natural products. This strategy, we think, can keep the consumer in our store for all their purchases."

Source: Anonymous, "One-Stop Supplements," *Supermarket Business,* June 1999, pp. 67–8.

---

others. Retailing, in fact, is a dynamic industry that constantly changes as firms seek ways to appeal to and serve consumers.

The component of retail strategy of most concern to logistic operations is merchandise assortment. The investment in merchandise and resulting inventory risk assumed by retailers are substantial. The types and varieties of merchandise the retailer carries are defined by the specific consumer needs and wants it attempts to satisfy. Additionally, retailers make merchandise decisions regarding the depth of assortment concerning different brands, colors, sizes, styles, etc., to be offered to consumers. Along with decisions regarding fashion and quality level, these factors combine to shape retail decisions regarding supply and which distribution channels each retailer will include in their supply chain strategy. Thus, as large as Wal★Mart may be, it is not a participant in the supply chain of every potential supplier. Wal★Mart, in fact all retailers, must carefully craft supply chain relationships to effectively and efficiently serve targeted consumers.

Direct versus Indirect Structures

Figure 4-4 presents a range of potential channel structures that might be utilized to accommodate a particular consumer segment's requirements. The alternatives range from the extreme on the left of direct from manufacturer to consumer with no intermediary involvement, to the extreme on the right, which includes wholesale agents, wholesale merchants, and retail outlets. Should the channel be *direct,* involving no or very few intermediaries, or should it be *indirect,* involving several different intermediate institutions? This notion of direct versus indirect structure represents a fundamental strategic decision.

FIGURE 4-4

Typical channel structures

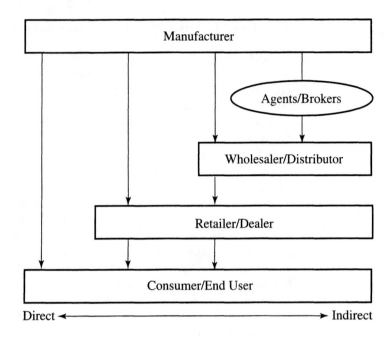

Earlier in this chapter the economies associated with intermediate stages of distribution were demonstrated. That discussion should not, however, be interpreted to mean that indirect distribution is always the appropriate solution. Furthermore, a question remains concerning the *degree of indirectness*. Which is the appropriate strategic choice? While no simple answer exists, the primary determinant lies in the consumer or end user's requirements. Recall from Chapter 3 that end-customer requirements were discussed in terms of lot sizes, variety and assortment, locational convenience, waiting time, and information. *As a general rule, as end-customer requirements for these outputs increase, the more likely it is that the required distribution structure will include intermediaries.* Several examples can be offered to demonstrate this point.

In Indonesia, and other developing countries, consumers with low discretionary income frequently purchase cigarettes one at a time from street vendors who purchase single packs from local wholesalers who purchase cartons from regional wholesalers. Because consumers desire to purchase in very small lot sizes, the distribution structure requires many intermediate levels. A direct manufacturer to consumer channel is infeasible. If consumers were willing to purchase in case lot quantities, however, a much more direct structure could be employed.

Perhaps a more comprehensive example can illustrate the nature of end-user requirements as the driver of channel structure. In the personal computer industry, Dell Computer pioneered the manufacturer direct-to-consumer distribution channel in the 1980s. Other PC manufacturers used, and most still use, a more indirect structure. The Dell channel is well suited for a particular type of consumer. A consumer who wants to buy one computer, who is willing to wait to receive the computer, does not desire to choose among several different brands, and has enough knowledge to intelligently specify all of the technical qualities desired can be well satisfied with the direct channel. Many other consumers, however, are not willing to wait days, or do not feel they personally have enough knowledge, or want to see an assortment of brands and models to compare features, quality, and prices. Their needs can only be satisfied through a structure that is less direct than that employed by Dell and which includes at least a retail intermediary.

As one thinks about the many different channel structures employed in the PC industry, it is worth also thinking about how each differs in the service requirements delivered to final consumers and end users. Gateway, for example, has a structure similar to Dell, with an important difference: the structure includes a retail level. In select markets, there are outlets called Gateway Country where potential customers can come to see, try out, and learn about Gateway computers. Customers can even buy a computer at Gateway Country. What they cannot do is take a computer home from a Gateway Country store. They still must wait for delivery. What is the advantage to Gateway of including this retail intermediary in its channel structure? The answer lies in the fact that it potentially satisfies a requirement of a number of customers—the requirement of information. Many consumers may feel that they do not have enough knowledge to make an intelligent choice of computers via the telephone or Internet. Gateway attempts to accommodate such information requirements through the Gateway Country retail store.[5]

Market Coverage

Related to the notion of channel structure is the decision concerning market coverage. Market coverage decisions involve choices concerning the relative intensity of outlets in any given geographic area so that the needs of existing and potential customers are adequately accommodated. Specifically, market coverage is most directly related to locational convenience for customers. Three basic market coverage alternatives exist: (1) intensive distribution, (2) selective distribution, and (3) exclusive distribution.

Intensive Distribution.   The placement of a product in as many outlets or locations as possible is known as **intensive distribution.** It is generally a logical choice for products that consumers purchase frequently and with minimal shopping effort, making locational convenience a key purchase requirement. Such products as soft drinks, candy, newspapers, gasoline, and aspirin represent just a few consumer products that are intensively distributed. For industrial end-users items such as maintenance, repair, and operating supplies (MRO), office supplies, and other industrial items may be intensively distributed.

On the surface it may seem that intensive distribution is the most logical alternative for all products and brands. After all, having a product available in many locations increases end-user convenience and, therefore, potential sales. Consider, however, what might happen to a manufacturer such as Sony if the decision were made to utilize intensive distribution. Sony might expand the number and types of outlets for televisions to include all mass merchandisers, discount stores, perhaps even drugstores and supermarkets, which frequently sell consumer electronics. As the number of outlets expands, Sony might increase market share in the short run, but several adverse consequences could also be expected. Some outlets might choose to sell Sony televisions at very low prices to attract consumers to their stores. This, in turn, might cause other outlets to reconsider their choice to participate in Sony's distribution channels. Some outlets could not provide the level of after-sales service necessary to support repair, and warranty, aggravating problems for those that do maintain such facilities. It is also likely Sony would take on more participation in marketing functions such as advertising, since many dealers who were once willing to promote Sony become reluctant to

---

[5]Robert Scally, "Gateway: The Crown Prince of Clicks-and-Mortar," *DSN Retailing Today,* May 8, 2000, pp. 75–6.

do so. While this discussion is, of course, speculative, it does demonstrate that intensive distribution is not the right choice for all products.

Selective Distribution.   The placement of a product or brand in a more limited number of outlets within a specific geographic area is called **selective distribution.** Of course, there can be many degrees of selectivity employed, ranging from almost intensive to almost exclusive. Again, the primary factor driving the choice is customer requirements for locational convenience and customers' willingness to spend time and effort to obtain the product. Sony televisions are, in fact, selectively distributed and made available through most electronics and appliance stores, and a limited number of other outlets, which will enhance its quality image and provide the level of support required for the brand.

Exclusive Distribution.   The exact opposite of intensive distribution, **exclusive distribution** involves placement of a brand in only one outlet in each geographic area. It is employed when consumers or end users are willing to expend considerable shopping effort and locational convenience is of little concern to them. It is also used when a firm wants to project an image of high quality, such as Rolex watches, or when very high levels of reseller support are required. Thus, construction and farm equipment, some brands of household furniture, designer fashion apparel, and similar products are exclusively distributed.

While certain types of products may seem to fit a particular market coverage alternative, generalizations can be misleading. It must be re-emphasized that companies choose which customers they will attempt to serve and that specific segments, or even individual customers, differ in their service requirements. Even in a product category such as candy, different choices have been made by competitive firms. Lifesaver mints, for example, are intensively distributed. Altoids, on the other hand, have more selective market coverage. Godiva is, for all practical purposes, available only through exclusive outlets. Finally, it should be noted that market coverage and channel structure are closely related. Intensive distribution generally necessitates indirect channels involving multiple intermediaries, whereas high selectivity and exclusivity may be supported through more direct channel structures.

Market Distribution Channel Design Process

The above discussion of structure and distribution coverage has emphasized the need to understand end-user requirements when developing market distribution strategy. As strategy is developed, the specific channel design must be defined. Two tools of significant assistance are channel mapping and a matrix approach to the design process. Each is explained below.

Channel Mapping

Figure 4-5 provides an example of channel mapping, the first of these tools. A **channel map** essentially is a flow diagram of the channels utilized by a specific firm. It is developed through careful research within an organization and discussions with numerous executives regarding how to go to market. As hard as it may be to believe, such research is an important step because, in most instances, very few people have a comprehensive understanding of the distribution channels utilized by their firm.

The purpose of mapping is to provide insight into current processes and establish a blueprint for change. Before channel design can be changed, or to decide whether

FIGURE **4-5**

Channel map—food processor

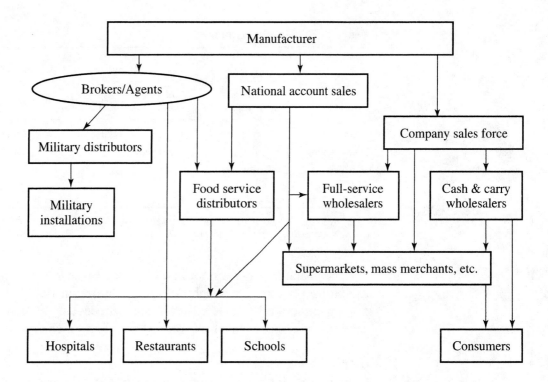

change is appropriate, a full understanding of the current process is needed. Even when designing from scratch for a new company or a new product, mapping the industry and key competitors is useful.

Developing a channel map should begin with clear delineation of the market segments being served. Figure 4-5 illustrates a simplified map of the distribution channels for a food manufacturer. Three distinct market segments are identified: (1) consumers, (2) institutional users, and (3) military installations. A more comprehensive map could be drawn to illustrate distinct subsegments within each of these categories but would result in more complexity than is needed to explain mapping. The mapping process then proceeds backward from the markets being served to identify the different types of channel participants capable of serving their market distribution requirements.

Channel mapping does not end with construction of a diagram. It should also include specification of the volume of activity related to each link in the map. For example, what percentage of the total volume goes to the military, institutions, and consumers? Each link should also be examined closely to see what are the specific functions and activities performed by the channel participants and what are the economic characteristics of the transactions. For example, what are prices, expenses, and margins associated with each link in the map?

One result of the mapping process is the ability to pinpoint areas of potential duplication of effort, waste, and/or shifting of functions. It provides a *roadmap* that can be used to ask questions such as what shortcuts are possible. For example, could the food processor depicted in Figure 4-5 rearrange functional performance in such a way that overlap between wholesale intermediary activities is eliminated or at least reduced? It also provides a framework for understanding functional performance in each channel echelon and for raising issues concerning the appropriate financial implications. For example, are the costs and margins involved between broker and full-function wholesaler justifiable, given the functional performance and volume activity? Or, might some rearrangement provide a more effective and efficient design?

TABLE 4-2   Matrix Approach

Sources	Demand Generation Tasks				
	Lead Generation	**Qualifying Sales**	**Presales**	**Closing**	**Postsales Service**
Direct Sales			Large Lot-Size	Large Lot-Size	Large Lot-Size
Telemarketing		All Customers			All Customers
Direct Mail	All Customers				
Distributors			Small Lot-Size	Small Lot-Size	Small Lot-Size

Source: Adapted from Rowland T. Moriarty and Ursala Moran, "Managing Hybrid Marketing Systems." *Harvard Business Review,* November/December 1990, p. 151.

The channel map does not in and of itself provide answers to such questions. It does, however, provide insight into possible design flaws and potential changes in strategy or tactics. Ultimately, such maps help develop an understanding of which aspects of the current channel are working well and which are not.

Matrix Approach

A second tool for use in channel design is a simple, yet effective, matrix approach.[6] Because most companies serve several segments of consumers and end users, different structures and combinations of channel participants may be needed to serve each of those segments as efficiently and effectively as possible. The matrix approach involves extending the concept of separation discussed earlier in this chapter and provides insight into the most appropriate participants and structures to accomplish objectives. In fact, the matrix approach is based on the concept of channel separation and marketing functions discussed earlier in this chapter.

Extending Channel Separation.   The earlier discussion of separation demonstrated that marketing and logistics channels may have different firms and no firm *necessarily* has to participate in both. The matrix design approach extends this concept by suggesting that each function can be further subdivided into specific individual activities. Each activity could potentially be performed by different channel participants. For explanatory purposes, consider the selling function and its related activities. Keep in mind that the same approach could be employed for other functions.

Table 4-2 shows a matrix for design of the selling channel for a hypothetical firm. Across the top, specific activities of the sales task are individually specified: generating sales prospects, qualifying those prospects, presale negotiation, closing the sale, and providing postsales service. The rows of the matrix consist of alternative means, some internal and some external, of performing each of the necessary activities. In the example matrix, four alternatives are under consideration: (1) a direct sales force, (2) telemarketing, (3) direct mail, and (4) independent distributors.

Relating Activities to Participants.   The art of the matrix design process comes in most efficiently and effectively assigning activities to participants for specific customer segments. A hypothetical example is used to illustrate this process.

---

[6]For the original discussion of the matrix design process, see Rowland T. Moriarity and Ursala Moran, "Managing Hybrid Marketing Systems," *Harvard Business Review,* November/December 1990, pp. 146–55.

Suppose the company has targeted two market segments to be served. These segments have been defined as customers who purchase in large lot-size quantities and those who purchase in small lot-size quantities. In this hypothetical example, it would not be cost-efficient to generate sales leads or quality prospects for customers who purchase in small lot-size quantities through use of a direct sales force. The lead generation task might be assigned to direct mail and prospect qualification to telemarketing. Note that all potential customers fall into these two segments for these two tasks. After customers have been qualified, large lot-size customers are assigned to the direct sales force for negotiation and closing the sale. Small lot-size customers are assigned to distributors for those tasks. Postsales service is accomplished for certain service activities by telemarketing. Other activities may require direct sales or distributor participation.

The final distribution channel design comes from consideration of which activities can most cost effectively meet customers' requirements for completion of which tasks. In our simple example, two critical points are clear. First, no one channel has to perform all of the activities required to complete a function. Note that telemarketing was used only for prospect qualification and for certain postsales service activities. Second, no activity has to be completely performed by any given channel member for any market segment. The direct sales force and the distributor channels perform only those activities related to their specific segments.

Channel Relationships

Throughout this chapter, it has been stressed that channel structures, based on specialization of function and activities, typically result in arrangements of independent firms. Each firm is dependent upon the others for success in the marketplace. As such, dependency provides a useful framework for understanding the types of behavioral relationships observed in distribution. Three channel classifications are identified ranging from least to most open expression of dependence: (1) single-transaction channels, (2) conventional channels, and (3) relational collaborative arrangements (RCAs). True supply chain arrangements are characterized as selected forms of RCAs.

Each form of channel involvement reflects a different degree of commitment by its participants. Figure 4-6 provides a graphic illustration of arrangements based on acknowledged dependence. This classification also provides a distinction between transaction and relational structures. In transactional arrangements little or no acknowledged dependency exists. Participants feel no responsibility to each other. The laws and obligations that govern buying and selling operate as the sole foundation for ownership transfer. In relational channels, participants recognize dependency and feel committed to one another. While all types of channels have logistical requirements, those classified as relational offer the greatest opportunity for developing supply chain arrangements.

Managing these relationships to reduce conflict, avoid duplication and waste, and develop cooperative solutions to common problems is the true essence of supply chain management. Relationship management is discussed in detail in Chapter 17.

Single-Transaction Channels
A great many business transactions are negotiated with the expectation that the exchange will be a one-time event. Examples of single-transaction channels are real estate sales, stock and bond ownership transfer, and the purchase of durable equipment such as processing plants and heavy machinery.

While single-transaction channel engagements are not important in terms of relationship management, they are significant to the businesses involved. Requirements to

FIGURE 4-6

Classification of channel relationships based on acknowledged dependency

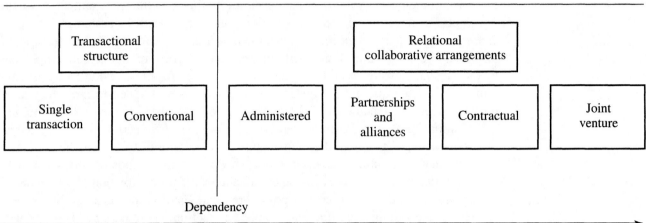

complete promised delivery are often technical and difficult to accomplish. The movement of oversized equipment, such as a printing press, typically requires special permits and is often restricted to specific times of the day or year. In some situations, special transportation and materials handling equipment are required to accommodate size and weight of the products involved. If a firm deals primarily with single transactions, logistics performance is critical and typically represents a significant cost of overall operations. Failure to develop repetitive patterns of business with repeat buyers makes each logistical assignment a unique event. Even if the logistical activity proceeds without a glitch and all parties are highly satisfied, the likelihood of a repetitive transaction is minimal.

Conventional Channels

Conventional channels are best viewed as loose arrangements or affiliations of firms that buy and sell products on an as-needed basis, without concern for future or repeat business. The prime determinant of the timing and extent of transactions is selling price.

Firms involved in a conventional channel develop operational capabilities to provide services necessary to fulfill their own basic business missions. They have little or no loyalty to each other and little motivation to cooperatively improve the efficiency of the supply chain.

Activity in a conventional channel is conducted on a transaction-to-transaction basis. The typical transaction is adversarial in that the negotiation is price-dominated, creating an us-against-them posture. In other words, the involved firms fail to work out a formalized long-term relationship; either party is free to exit the relationship whenever it wishes. Involvement occurs until a better deal comes along. In fact, it is not uncommon for firms to start and stop doing business with each other several times within a single year.

Two points are significant concerning conventional channels. First, they are an important part of the overall business structure because of their sheer transaction volume. Second, because firms do not develop synergisms with trading partners, opportunities to gain efficiency by virtue of cooperation are sacrificed in favor of maintaining autonomy.

Relational Collaborative Arrangements

The distinctive feature of RCAs is that participating firms acknowledge dependency and develop joint benefits through cooperation to achieve industry superiority. To participate in such systems, each channel member must be willing to perform specific duties. In this way, the various forms of RCAs represent relationship management characteristic of supply chains.

The overall relationship of an RCA is typically orchestrated by a firm that is acknowledged as the leader. The leader is most often the dominant firm in the channel in terms of market share, size, or technical skills. The firm that provides leadership typically has the greatest relative power in the arrangement.

While acknowledged dependency is the cohesive force in RCA arrangements, it also creates conflict. Managers may feel that their firm is not getting a fair share of benefits or that they are being placed in an unnecessarily risky position. When potential or real conflict develops, it is essential that it be resolved to maintain channel solidarity. For an RCA to have stability the leader must resolve conflict situations in terms of the long-term interests of the overall channel. Finally, since RCAs are expected to exist for a substantial time period, it is important that the leader provide a vision of the future, facilitate joint planning, and change management as necessary to maintain competitive superiority.

In a broad sense, all channel systems that involve two or more independent firms have a degree of relationship structure. When relationships are managed to achieve joint goals and participating firms feel obligated to each other, the relationship becomes a supply chain. Four forms of RCAs are common: (1) administered systems, (2) partnerships and alliances, (3) contractual systems, and (4) joint ventures. As one would expect, the acknowledgment of dependency increases as the arrangement moves from administered system to joint venture.

Administered Systems.   The least formal RCA is the **administered system.** The interesting feature of an administered arrangement is that typically no formal or stated dependency is acknowledged on the part of participants. Usually a dominant firm assumes leadership responsibility and seeks cooperation of trading partners and service suppliers. While bordering on a conventional channel arrangement, an administered system seems to be guided by a mutual understanding that all independent companies will be better off if they work together and follow the leader.

On the part of the leader, it is essential that decisions be made in a manner that takes each channel participant's welfare into consideration. All channel members must view the relationship as fair and equitable. Operational stability is dependent on the leader sharing rewards as opposed to purely adversarial give-and-take negotiation that typifies a conventional channel. With enlightened leadership, an administered system can be maintained over an extended period of time. The firm providing leadership can operate at any channel level; however, most examples of administered systems are led by dominant retailers.

Many firms perceive the benefits possible from working together in the channel but are not comfortable with the lack of formalization that is characteristic of the administered arrangement. In some situations, two or more relatively powerful firms such as Wal★Mart and Procter & Gamble may desire to work closer but feel the need to develop a more structured relationship. When such formalization takes place, the dependency of the relationship becomes widely acknowledged and the participating firms form partnerships and alliances.

Partnerships and Alliances.   As firms desire greater clarity and longer-term commitment than typically provided in an administered system, they may seek to formalize their relationships. The typical extension is to form a nonlegal partnership and over time extend the relationship toward an alliance. In these arrangements, the firms give up some of their operational autonomy in an effort to jointly pursue specific goals. The expectation is that the arrangement will prevail for a substantial period of time.

A great many business arrangements are referred to by the participating firms as **partnerships.** Along with administered systems, the partnership working relationship is at the lower end of the dependency scale. While firms acknowledge mutual dependence, their tolerance to be led is minimal. In other words, the acknowledgment of a degree of loyalty tends to solidify repetitive business transactions as long as everything else is satisfactory. The commitment to the arrangement typically falls short of a willingness to modify fundamental business methods and procedures. Nevertheless, a true partnership reflects a dependency commitment far greater than an administered arrangement. At the very least, such partnerships build on the expressed desire to work together that typically involves an attitude of working out differences and, most of all, a level of information sharing. The weak link of many fledgling partnerships is the inability to resolve truly disruptive differences of opinion. A typical example of such conflict often involves price increases. If a firm's response to a supplier's requested price increase is to open the business to bid, then the quality of the partnership arrangement is doubtful. A true partnership arrangement must approach such routine adjustments in a problem-solving format. If such interorganizational compatibility exists, the partnership is moving toward an alliance.

The essential feature of an **alliance** is a willingness of participants to modify basic business practices. If managers feel that the overall business arrangement can benefit from best practice modification and they are willing to change, then the relationship is a true alliance. The motivation behind alliances is more fundamental than simply locking in the business. While repetitive business is important, emphasis on best practice is aimed at reducing duplication and waste and facilitating joint efficiencies. *In essence, the alliance goal is to cooperatively build on the combined resources of participating firms to improve the performance, quality, and competitiveness of the channel.* Such cooperation requires a commitment to information sharing and problem solving. The expected result is a win–win for all participants. This type of RCA format represents the channel arrangement most often referred to as a supply chain.

While partnerships are relatively easy to find, true alliances are more difficult to identify. Several high-profile alliances in the drug, garment, building supply, mass merchandise, and food industries have recently gained national publicity. Developing alliances has appeal because they can magnify the economic and market leverage of individual firms without financial investment. What results is the *power of cooperation.* The human and financial resources of alliance members are pooled to improve the overall competitiveness of the channel arrangement. Industry Insight 4-2 describes a unique partnership arrangement between two competitors, Ford Motor Company and DaimlerChrysler, and Exel Logistics, which resulted in substantial efficiency in distributing auto parts to dealers.

Contractual Systems.   As the name implies, many firms desire to conduct business within the confines of a formal contract. The most common forms of contractual agreements in distribution relationships are franchises, dealerships, and agreements between service specialists and their customers. The commitment to a contract takes

INDUSTRY INSIGHT 4-2 DAIMLERCHRYSLER AND FORD MOTOR COMPANY—PARTNERS?

Though the idea runs counter to competitive rivalries in the auto industry, DaimlerChrysler and Ford Motor Company, along with Exel Logistics, have built a successful partnership to improve service and reduce the cost of parts distribution.

The pilot program was tested with 11 dealers in northern Michigan. Dealerships were spread across a wide geographic area, requiring a large number of delivery vehicles; however, the capacity of these vehicles was underutilized. Under the arrangement, Ford paid a fee to place its parts on the dedicated fleet operated by Exel for the distribution of DaimlerChrysler parts. The test was a success and both companies expect to establish shared-service agreements with other auto companies in the future. They are considering a second phase of the test that could include 50 to 100 dealerships.

The pilot program created a template for developing future shared-service agreements. Both companies found that a third-party provider was key to implementing the agreement. Exel had resources that the automakers lacked, including time, personnel, and technology. It was also critical to create detailed protocols.

After the test in Michigan, DaimlerChrysler and Ford ran a similar test in Mexico. The geography and dealership dispersion throughout Mexico was conducive to the shared-service concept. The routes were relatively long and the freight density was relatively low, creating available freight space. Auto dealers outside Mexico City bought less than 50 percent of the parts sold in the country, but distribution to them accounted for 90 percent of the miles. Additionally, each of the partners stood to realize some significant benefits. DaimlerChrysler would realize savings from current rates; Ford would increase service levels to its dealers; and Exel would gain added revenue from the route.

Jerry Campbell, manager of North American logistics and customs for Ford's customer service division, says that the shared services idea is one way of meeting the constant cost pressure. "Optimally, we should [share services] within our own company, then extend it to other customers and providers." In fact, Ford's customer service division already shares services with Volvo, which Ford Motor Company owns, and with Mazda, in which it has a major equity stake.

What makes a shared-services project successful? According to Tim Flucht, Exel's account manager for the Ford/DaimlerChrysler projects, "The basic paradigm you have to get past is competition. People have in their minds that certain parts of the supply chain are a competitive advantage. That may or may not be true. If it is true, you have to consider it very carefully. It is less of an issue when it is only a perceived advantage." The managers of Ford and DaimlerChrysler agreed that the consumer had already made the purchase choice. Flucht states, "Now it was a matter of sharing costs or continuing to pay the full amount."

Other important factors in the success of shared-services partnerships are a large degree of trust and openness in considering how to implement the program.

Source: Anonymous, "Auto Pilot," *Logistics*, July 2000, pp. 89, 90, and 92.

---

the relationship out of the pure voluntary framework that is characteristic of an alliance. In place of pure cooperation, the contractual arrangement establishes a set of legal obligations.

Many firms desire contracts because of the stability gained by formalizing commitment. In the case of a franchise or dealership, the formal agreement serves as guarantee concerning a firm's rights and obligations related to representing a service or product in a specific geographical area. The granting firm is ensured that conformance to specified ways of conducting business will occur and that a required minimum purchase will be made. Franchises and dealerships are most common in the marketing structure of automotive and fast food industries.

Many of the contractual arrangements are specifically directed to performance of the logistical activities necessary to complete distribution. For example, one of the most common forms of RCA contracting involves for-hire transportation. The most common contract between a shipper and carrier specifies the expected level of performance and establishes the fee or rate to be paid for the service. A typical example would be a carrier's agreement to regularly provide a predetermined amount of a specific type of equipment to a shipper. The shipper, in turn, may agree to load and position the equipment for efficient line-haul pickup by the carrier. The contract specifies the obligation of participating parties and the negotiated price.

The contract is a vital part of many logistical arrangements. Because many logistics relationships require extensive capital investment, participating company shareholders and financial providers desire contractual agreements to specify risk. Therefore, some degree of contracting is common throughout the range of voluntary relational arrangements.

Joint Ventures. Some distribution arrangements are simply too capital-intense for development by a single firm. Therefore, two or more firms may select to jointly invest in an arrangement. The strictest **joint venture** involves two or more firms joined economically to create a new business entity. While such start-ups from scratch are not common, opportunities exist for future development.

The more likely joint venture scenario occurs when a shipper decides to fully outsource all of its logistics requirements—including facilities, equipment, and day-to-day operations—to a third-party or contract service provider. A logical way to arrange this outsourcing is to establish a joint venture between the shipper and service firm. The establishment of a business relationship where all management groups participate serves to reduce the risk, especially when broad-based exclusive arrangements are required.

E-Commerce Impacts on Market Distribution

Perhaps no single subject has received as much attention in recent literature as the explosive growth of electronic commerce throughout the world. Almost daily, articles appear in the general, business trade, and academic press concerning the volume of business transacted currently, projections for the future, and the fundamental change being created by electronic commerce. Many articles focus on the so-called new economy and how the firms involved in the old economy are being challenged, or even made obsolete, by the dynamics of the new economy.[7] While electronic commerce has many different forms, including fax and traditional EDI (Electronic Data Exchange), much recent discussion focuses on the Internet and its implications for how businesses go to market.

The pace of change makes it very difficult to generalize precisely what will be the long-term impacts on market distribution. Below, attention is first focused on the development of a new retail format, the so-called e-tailers, which began to emerge in the late 1990s. Of course, many disappeared by early 2001. Discussion then is directed to

---

[7]For example, see Barry Janoff, "New Economy," *Progressive Grocer,* June 2000, pp. 18–28.

new channel alternatives and relationships among channel participants fostered by electronic commerce. Finally, an assessment is offered as to how these developments will impact the logistics activities required to support increased complexity of marketing channels. The focus in this chapter is on e-commerce in the consumer sector of the economy. The changing nature of B2B relationships as impacted by e-commerce is discussed in Chapter 5.

The Emergence of E-Tailing

It is unclear today just who was the first so-called e-tailer. Who first decided to take advantage of the fact that the widespread availability of personal computers and usage of the Internet presented a new business opportunity to present consumers with an alternative means of shopping? As early as 1992, Internet Service Providers (ISPs) such as America Online began to offer customers the ability to enter virtual shopping malls where they could browse through merchandise offered by a number of virtual stores, and select and order merchandise for delivery direct to the house. The earliest efforts, however, met with limited success as consumers initially resisted the concept of online ordering. While these virtual malls reported rather large numbers of consumers browsing the merchandise, actual sales transactions were limited.

In 1995, Jeff Bezos founded Amazon.com. While perhaps not the first e-tailer, the success of Amazon.com in generating both publicity and sales revenue makes it a prime example of how e-tailing emerged as a channel alternative. Amazon.com and other e-tailers offer an alternative shopping format, which has both advantages and disadvantages relative to traditional land-based bricks and mortar stores. One significant advantage is locational convenience, for what can be more convenient than shopping from your own personal computer?

A second advantage arises from the assortment that can be offered to consumers from this format. Unconstrained by physical limitations of store space, the e-tailer can offer for sale a complete assortment of product that cannot be matched by any bricks and mortar store. Even before it branched into numerous other product categories, Amazon.com offered consumers over one million choices of book titles. A third advantage offered is information. Potential buyers can access book reviews by both professional reviewers and those written by other consumers and can easily find books related to subjects of interest or books written by favorite authors.

The most important disadvantages for the consumer shopping via e-tailing are waiting time, the inability to physically browse, handle, or try the merchandise, and concerns related to security. Once purchased, the consumer must wait at least 1 day, with waiting times extending to weeks in many instances, depending upon actual inventory availability. Additionally, consumers frequently want to physically handle merchandise, whether it is skimming the pages of a book or trying on clothing to ensure proper fit. Finally, concerns about security include the potential for credit card fraud and the ability of companies to amass considerable personal information about individual backgrounds, tastes, and habits. Despite the limitations, it is clear that e-tailing has appeal to a significant number of consumers. Consumer purchasing from e-tailers was estimated at $20 billion in 1999 and is projected to be as much as $180 billion by the year 2004.[8]

---

[8]"Shopping Online Opens Strong in 2000," *USA Today,* March 1, 2000, p. B-1.

New Channel Alternatives

Considerable speculation has developed that the Internet will open a new world of relationships among manufacturers and service companies and their final consumers. The Internet potentially provides a mechanism for suppliers to gain inexpensive direct access to customers. Alternatively, it has been suggested that consumers desire to gain direct access to firms that manufacture products. Regardless, the speculation is that there is reduced need for complex market channel relationships involving agents, wholesalers, or retail stores. After all, if consumers are willing to shop via the Internet, why not deal directly with product/service manufacturers, bypass existing channel arrangements, and bring a new era characterized by emergence of direct channels as the primary mechanism for the new economy?[9]

In fact, many examples of just such direct channel development exist. In the air passenger industry, almost every airline has established a website providing detailed information concerning routes, flights, availability, prices, etc. Consumers can perform their own search, by time or price, and execute their own flight itineraries. Simultaneously, the airlines have reduced commissions paid to travel agents who traditionally perform these searches. Many product manufacturers also have established websites where consumers can access volumes of information concerning products, product use, and demonstrations, and receive promotional offers. In such instances, it is easy to imagine the consumer simply placing an order directly with the manufacturer.

Given the widespread availability and the low cost associated with the marketing transactions via the Internet, many have projected that the future will be an era of role redefinition and shifting of marketing functions back to the originators of products and services. In short, they predict an era of widespread channel *disintermediation* whereby traditional marketing channels will no longer be necessary to close the gaps between producers and consumers. The result, as hypothesized, will be lower prices to consumers and higher profits to suppliers.

The fact is that consumers have shown great willingness to interact directly with manufacturers via the Internet, increasing manufacturers' participation in marketing flows, which traditionally were more likely to be completed by or shared with channel intermediaries. Research shows that a large number of consumers do visit manufacturer websites; they visit frequently and at several stages of the buying process. Table 4-3 presents data from one study of online consumers showing that many consumers use manufacturer websites for such purposes as researching product and purchase information. The data shows, however, that only 27 percent of the consumers had used the manufacturer's website to make a purchase.

Of course, a large number of manufacturers do not provide consumers with the ability to make online purchases. Their slow adoption of the Internet as a mechanism to complete direct sales transactions stems from three sources. First, most manufacturers are not capable of efficiently completing the logistical fulfillment required by consumer-direct transactions. Second, there is tremendous reluctance by many manufacturers to bypass established distribution channels and disrupt relationships with existing channel intermediaries. In a highly publicized event in 1999, The Home Depot sent a letter to its suppliers informing them that The Home Depot would no longer do

---

[9]See, for example, Robert Benjamin and Rolf Wigand, "Electronic Markets and Virtual Value Chains on the Information Superhighway," *Sloan Management Review,* Winter 1995, pp. 52–62; Debra Spar and Jeffrey Bussgang, "Ruling the Net," *Harvard Business Review,* May/June 1996, pp. 125–33.

TABLE 4-3   Empowered Consumers Look at Manufacturers as Retailers*

"When in the purchase process are you likely to visit a manufacturer's website?"

When not buying their products	*Awareness*	45%
When researching a product	*Consideration*	75%
After deciding what to buy and where to buy it	*Preference*	16%
To make a purchase	*Purchase*	27%
After deciding what to buy, but not where to buy it		42%
After buying, to find out about repair and service options	*Post-sale*	25%
After buying, for help installing and configuring a product		31%
After buying, to register a warranty		40%

"What kind of information have you looked for on the manufacturer's
site within the last 6 months?"

Production information	79%	New product developments	37%
Product prices	79%	Warranty and guarantee information	35%
Where to buy specific products	49%	Installation and configuration info.	31%
Customer support	44%	General company information	31%
Accessory information about a product I already own	42%	How to connect with people with similar interests	4%

*Based on surveys from 8,842 online consumers. Data from Forrester's Technographics Online Retail & Media 2000 Field study (Forrester Research, Inc., Report: Channel Conflict Crumbles, March 2000, p. 2).

business with any manufacturer engaged in consumer-direct sales. Few manufacturers are willing to disrupt their relationships with established retail organizations. In the toy industry, Mattel discontinued efforts at online sales, and in the clothing industry, Levi-Strauss, which had been a pioneer in development of online capability, announced that it would stop selling jeans through its site.

Finally, it should be noted that while manufacturer direct-to-consumer sales via the Internet offer consumers many of the same advantages as e-tailing, it suffers a critical disadvantage. Manufacturers cannot offer the broad selection of products that can be offered by a retailer, whether a physical store or an Internet site. When consumers want a wide variety of product line and brand choices, direct transactions with manufacturers are not desirable. As a simple example, imagine trying to complete weekly grocery shopping via direct interaction with manufacturers.

Increased Channel Complexity

In contrast to disintermediation and channel simplification resulting from the Internet stands the potential for increased channel complexity. As existing businesses expand their activities in electronic commerce with consumers, and e-tailing gains in popularity with consumers, distribution relationships may proliferate and give rise to other forms of intermediaries. Many of these intermediaries were unheard of just a few years ago but currently play an important role in market distribution. Organizations with such names as affiliate sites, portals, and search engines have become an integral part of market distribution. Meanwhile, traditional wholesalers and retailers continue to operate, sometimes in conjunction with these new intermediaries. Consider, for ex-

INDUSTRY INSIGHT 4-3 CLICKS AS TRANSACTIONS

A simple, everyday example of Internet shopping will show how hypermediation works. Let's say that an occasional Web user—I'll call him Bob—becomes interested in the ubiquitous Harry Potter books. He thinks that he'd like to read them, but he wants to learn a little more about them. So he goes onto the Web and, since he's never bothered to change his browser's default home page, he ends up at the Netscape portal. In the search box he types the phrase "Harry Potter," and from a list of available search services he chooses, on a whim, GoTo.com. He's transported to the GoTo site, where his search results are posted. He chooses a promising-sounding site near the top called "Nancy's Magical Harry Potter Page."

Nancy's site, a personal home page with an unsophisticated but friendly design, is full of information that Bob finds useful. There are glowing reviews of the books by Nancy and a few of her friends, detailed plot summaries and character descriptions, and a discussion board where readers share their comments. There's also a link to a special Harry Potter page at eToys. Bob clicks on the link, and he finds that eToys is selling the first book in the series for just $8.97— 50 percent off its list price. He can't resist that kind of a bargain, so he takes out his Visa card and places an order. Three days later, the book is in his mailbox.

A fairly routine buying expedition on the Web, right? But consider the complex array of intermediaries that made money off Bob's modest purchase. There are the usual suspects, of course—the retailer eToys, the book distributor that eToys buys from, the bank that issued Bob's Visa card, the U.S. Postal Service. But there are less obvious players as well. First is Netscape. Netscape puts various search services on its home page and, in return, the services pay Netscape a penny or two every time a visitor clicks through to their sites. So when Bob was transferred to GoTo.com, Netscape received a little money. GoTo, for its part, auctions off its top search results to the highest bidders. Nancy, for instance, agreed to pay GoTo 1 cent for every searcher who clicks on her link. So when Bob chose Nancy's site, GoTo made a penny. GoTo didn't get to keep all of it, though. Because GoTo contracts with an outside provider, Inktomi, to conduct its searches, it had to pay Inktomi a fraction of that penny for processing Bob's search.

Then there's Nancy herself. Like thousands of other individuals who have personal Web pages, Nancy has signed up to be an affiliate of eToys. When she sends someone to eToys through a link on her page, the e-tailer pays her 7.5 percent of any resulting purchases. So Nancy made a cool 67 cents when Bob bought the book. What's more, eToys doesn't run its own affiliate program. It outsources the job to a company named Be Free. Be Free, in turn, takes a small cut on the purchases it administers. So it, too, got a little of Bob's money.

Add them up, and you'll find that no fewer than nine intermediaries had their fingers in Bob's $8.97 purchase. (And that doesn't even include the people who posted reviews on Nancy's site; they just haven't realized that they could be charging for their words.) In fact, every single time Bob clicked his mouse, a transaction took place: a little bit of value was created, and a little bit of money changed hands. Yes, the money usually amounted to only a penny or two, but it seems a safe bet that far more profit was made by the intermediaries that took those pennies than by eToys when it sold the book for half price. Bob's transaction is a microcosm of the emerging economic structure of e-commerce: the profits lie in intermediate transactions, not in the final sale of a good.

Source: Nicholas G. Carr, "Hypermediation: Commerce as Clickstream," *Harvard Business Review,* January/February 2000, pp. 46–7.

ample, that Barnes and Noble and Toys R Us have expanded their activities to include e-tailing. Rather than channel disintermediation, business-to-consumer e-commerce gives rise to what one author has called *hypermediation,* as channels of distribution adapt to the potential of the Internet.[10] Industry Insight 4-3 describes a consumer purchase of a book via the Internet and the many intermediaries involved in the purchase.

The most significant challenge posed by business-to-consumer electronic commerce is not the marketing and sales challenge; in fact, sales trends in 1999 and 2000 clearly demonstrate that some consumers are willing to shop and purchase electronically. Instead, the major challenge lies in the logistics process and efficient order fulfillment to satisfy consumer requirements. While e-commerce can significantly reduce marketing transaction costs related to generating and processing orders, it significantly impacts the economics related to physically picking, packing, and transporting those orders.

The business model on which a manufacturer's logistics process rests relies heavily on fulfillment of large orders shipped to a relatively small number of customer locations. Shipping truckloads to distribution centers is far different from shipping small parcels to consumer homes. E-distributors and e-retailers are not immune to the logistical challenges either. Preparing shipments of one or two items, documenting those shipments, tracing, and transporting within a very short time frame required to meet customer requirements and accomplishing these tasks in a manner which does not raise total costs to consumers is a primary concern of all Internet business-to-consumer organizations. In response to increasing customer requirements for fast delivery and increasing costs related to long-distance shipment of small parcels, Amazon.com embarked on a trail of building sophisticated distribution centers around the U.S. This strategy results in investment in facilities and equipment, not unlike that of traditional retail firms.

In fact, several alternative strategies for managing and accomplishing logistics exist for business-to-consumer e-commerce.[11] Some firms may accomplish fulfillment through a network of delivery centers in numerous markets where inventory is held in anticipation of customer orders. An alternative logistics strategy requires customer pickup at central locations, rather than home delivery. This approach has been called the *buy here/pick up there* strategy. In either case, such facilities could serve multiple sellers, providing some economies of scale. Another strategy may be to outsource the entire fulfillment process to partners who are specialists in physical fulfillment, especially third-party logistics firms that can consolidate operations for multiple sellers, provide flexibility in accommodating growth, and manage a more efficient flow of product from source to consumer destination. Sellers who have sufficient volume may choose to utilize dedicated fulfillment operations, as Amazon.com and Micro Warehouse have done.

Any strategic approach chosen will require careful examination of both cost and service level trade-offs. Each has implications for inventory investment, facility investment, transportation costs, and delivery to consumers. The analysis of these trade-offs is fundamental to logistical process design and is the subject of Chapter 16. Suffice it to say at this time that all organizations involved in business-to-consumer

[10]Nicholas G. Carr, "Hypermediation: Commerce as Clickstream," *Harvard Business Review,* January/February 2000, pp. 46–7.

[11]Fred R. Ricker and Ravi Kalakota, "Order Fulfillment: The Hidden Key to E-Commerce Success," *Supply Chain Management Review,* Fall 1999, pp. 60–6.

e-commerce are struggling to find the most appropriate logistics and fulfillment strategy for their firm.

Pricing and Logistics

Pricing is another aspect of marketing strategy that directly interacts with logistical operations. The terms and conditions of pricing determine which party has responsibility for performing logistics activities. A major trend in price strategy has been to *debundle* the price of products and materials so that services such as transportation, which were traditionally included in price, are now identified as separate items. Pricing practices have a direct impact on the timing and stability of logistical operations. In this section, several basic pricing structures are reviewed, followed by a discussion of pricing impact areas. No attempt is made to review the broad range of economic and psychological issues related to pricing decisions. The focus is on the relationship between pricing and logistical operations.

Pricing Fundamentals

Pricing decisions directly determine which party in the transaction is responsible for performance of logistics activities, passage of title, and liability. F.O.B. origin and delivered pricing are the two most common methods.

F.O.B. Pricing

The term *F.O.B.* technically means *Free On Board* or *Freight On Board*. A number of variations of F.O.B. pricing are used in practice. **F.O.B. origin** is the simplest way to quote price. Here the seller indicates the price at point of origin and agrees to tender a shipment for transportation loading, but assumes no further responsibility. The buyer selects the mode of transportation, chooses a carrier, pays transportation charges, and takes risk of in-transit loss and/or damage. In **F.O.B. destination** pricing, title does not pass to the buyer until delivery is completed. Under such circumstances, the seller arranges for transportation and the charges are added to the sales invoice.

The range of terms and corresponding responsibilities for pricing are illustrated in Figure 4-7. Review of the various sales terms makes it clear that the firm paying the freight bill does not necessarily assume responsibility for ownership of goods in transit, for the freight burden, or for filing of freight claims.

Delivered Pricing

The primary difference between F.O.B. and **delivered pricing** is that in delivered pricing the seller offers a price that includes transportation of the product to the buyer. In other words, the transportation cost is not specified as a separate item. There are several variations of delivered pricing.

Single-Zone Pricing.   Under a single-zone delivered pricing system, buyers pay a single price regardless of where they are located. Delivered prices typically reflect the seller's average transportation cost. In actual practice, some customers pay more than their fair share for transportation while others are subsidized. The United States Postal Service uses a single-zone pricing policy throughout the United States for first-class letters and parcel post. The same fee or postage rate is charged for a given size and weight regardless of distance traveled to the destination.

FIGURE 4-7

Terms of sale and corresponding responsibilities

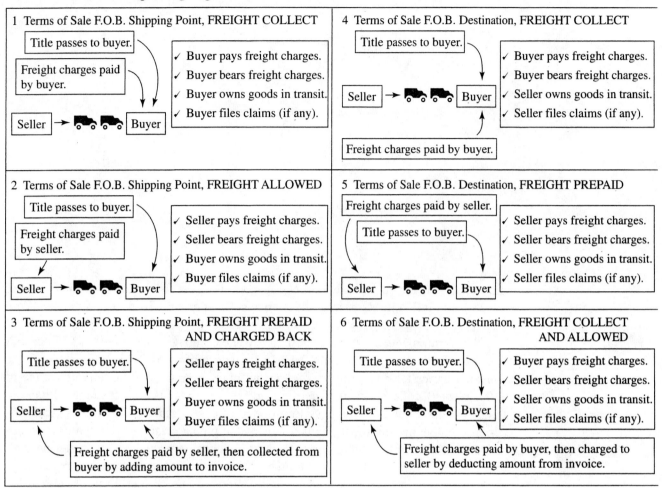

Reprinted with permission from The Purchasing Handbook, *National Association of Purchasing Management.*

Single-zone delivered pricing is typically used when transportation costs are a relatively small percentage of selling price. The main advantage to the seller is the high degree of control over logistics. For the buyer, despite being based on averages, such pricing systems have the advantage of simplicity.

Multiple-Zone Pricing.   The practice of multiple-zone pricing establishes different prices for specific geographic areas. The underlying idea is that logistics cost differentials can be more fairly assigned when two or more zones—typically based on distance—are used to quote delivered pricing. Parcel carriers such as United Parcel Service use multiple-zone pricing.

Base-Point Pricing.   The most complicated and controversial form of delivered pricing is the use of a base-point system in which the final delivered price is determined by the product's list price plus transportation cost from a designated base point, usually the manufacturing location. This designated point is used for computing the delivered price whether or not the shipment actually originates from the base location.

Figure 4-8 illustrates how a base-point pricing system typically generates different net returns to a seller. The customer has been quoted a delivered price of $100 per

FIGURE 4-8

Base-point pricing

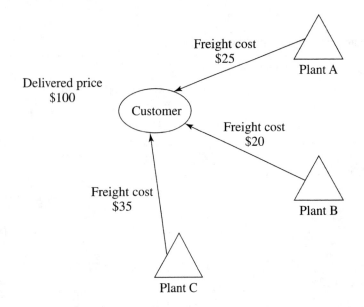

unit. Plant A is the base point. Actual transportation cost from plant A to the customer is $25 per unit. Plant A's base product price is $85 per unit. Transportation costs from plants B and C are $20 and $35 per unit, respectively.

When shipments are made from plant A, the company's net return is $75 per unit (the $100 delivered price minus the $25 transportation cost). The net return to the company varies if shipments are made from plant B or C. With a delivered price of $100, plant B collects $5 in *phantom freight* on shipments to a customer. Phantom freight occurs when a buyer pays transportation costs greater than those actually incurred to move the shipment. If plant C is the shipment origin, the company must absorb $10 of the transportation costs. **Freight absorption** occurs when a seller pays all or a portion of the actual transportation cost and does not recover the full expenditure from the buyer. In other words, the seller decides to absorb transportation cost to be competitive.

Base-point pricing simplifies price quotations but can have a negative impact on customers. For example, dissatisfaction may result if customers discover they are being charged more for transportation than actual freight costs. Such pricing practices may also result in a large amount of freight absorption for sellers.

Pricing Issues

Pricing practices are also integral to logistics operations in at least four other ways: potential discrimination, quantity discounts, pickup allowances, and promotional pricing.

Potential Discrimination

The legality of transportation pricing is an important consideration and must be carefully reviewed and administered to protect against potential discrimination. The Clayton Act of 1914 as amended by the Robinson-Patman Act of 1936 prohibits price discrimination among buyers when the practices "substantially lessen competition."

Zone pricing has the potential to be discriminatory because some buyers pay more than actual transportation cost while others pay less. Zone pricing systems are illegal when the net result is to charge different delivered prices for identical products to direct competitors. In recent years, determination of the legality of delivered zone pricing systems has centered around the issue of whether a "seller acts independently and not in collusion with competitors." The Federal Trade Commission is unlikely to take action unless there is clear-cut evidence of such conspiracy.

In the past, selected base-point pricing has been found illegal under both the Robinson-Patman Act and the Federal Trade Commission Act. The concern is whether it results in direct competitors having differential margins.

To avoid potential legal problems, the majority of firms use either F.O.B. or uniform delivered pricing policies. This strategy is generally preferable compared to defending average costing practices required in zone pricing or contending with the potential legal difficulties associated with base-point pricing. The following guidelines should be considered when establishing geographic pricing:

> Some of the geographic pricing strategies . . . may be illegal under certain circumstances. Three general principles can be used to guide policy in this respect. First, a firm should not discriminate between competing buyers in the same region (especially in zone pricing for buyers on either side of a zonal boundary) because such action may violate the Robinson-Patman Act of 1936. Second, the firm's strategy should not appear to be predatory, especially in freight absorption pricing, because such a strategy would violate Section 2 of the Sherman Act of 1890. Third, in choosing the basing point or zone pricing, the firm should not attempt to fix prices among competitors because such action would violate Section 1 of the Sherman Act.[12]

Quantity Discounts

Quantity discounts are generally offered by a firm as an inducement to increase order size or overall volume of business. To be nondiscriminatory, an identical discount structure must be available to all buyers. Under the Robinson-Patman Act, it is the responsibility of the seller to prove that the identical, noncumulative discounts are available to all qualified buyers. The quantity discount offered must be justifiable on the basis of direct cost saving.

The Robinson-Patman Act states that cost differences can be justified on the basis of savings in the manufacturing, delivery, or selling of goods. Quantity-related discounts based on reductions in manufacturing or selling cost are difficult to prove. Logistics-related savings are relatively easier to document since many are shipment-specific. Transportation and handling savings are often used to justify quantity discounts; thus, lower transportation rates for volume shipments are common.

In contrast to noncumulative discounts, cumulative discounts—based on consecutive purchases over some specified time period—are more difficult to justify. Cumulative discounts, by the very nature of their calculation base, favor large-volume purchasers while discriminating against smaller buyers. However, price discrimination can be proved only when potential or real injury to competition is determined.

Pickup Allowances

Pickup allowances are equivalent to purchasing merchandise on a F.O.B. origin basis. Buyers are given a reduction from the standard delivered price if they or their representatives pick up shipments at the seller's location and assume responsibility for transportation. A buyer may also use a for-hire carrier to perform merchandise pickup. In the food and grocery industry, which traditionally practiced delivered pricing, firms

---

[12]Gerard J. Tellis, "Beyond the Many Facets of Price: An Integration of Pricing Strategies," *Journal of Marketing* 50 (October 1986), pp. 146–60.

have realized significant savings by using private and for-hire carriers to pick up rather than purchasing merchandise on a delivered basis.

While some confusion exists concerning how to best establish a pickup allowance, a safe rule is that a seller should provide the same allowance to all directly competitive buyers. A uniform pickup allowance is often the price incentive offered to the customer closest to the shipping point. Other common policies offer pickup allowances equivalent to the applicable common carrier rate for the shipment.

The use of pickup allowances offers potential benefits for both the seller and the buyer. Shippers are required to deal with fewer small shipments, thereby reducing the need for extensive outbound consolidation. Buyers gain control over the merchandise earlier and are in a position to achieve greater utilization of captive transportation equipment and drivers.

Promotional Pricing

A final aspect of pricing that impacts logistical operations is the use of short-term promotions to provide incentives for purchases. Firms that pursue aggressive promotional strategies have a choice of designing their budgets to encourage consumers (via coupons) or wholesalers and retailers (via trade allowances) to purchase their products. For example, Procter & Gamble has an annual advertising and promotional budget that exceeds $2 billion. Marketing management must allocate these funds between media advertising focused on consumers and a combination of coupons and trade promotions. Budget dollars allocated to trade promotion push the purchase of P&G products and cause two results. First, the logistics systems of Procter & Gamble and its customers must handle increased product volume just before, during, and oftentimes immediately after a promotional period. Second, trade promotion spending lowers the effective price at which product is being sold. From a logistical perspective, the short-term increase in volume is of primary concern. Thus, while ultimate consumption may not demonstrate seasonal characteristics, logistical operations may have to deal with *seasonal surges* caused by promotional pushes.

The widespread practice of promotional pricing has traditionally been the way to provide an incentive for trade purchasing. Manufacturers establish list or sheet prices at an artificially high level with the expectation of reducing the effective price by trade promotion, consumer coupons, and new product slotting allowances. Administration of regular price changes usually involves advanced notification to customers, creating the opportunity for them to *forward buy*. This practice stimulates volume surges, which add excessive costs, and creates practices that do not add value. Forward buying involves purchasing merchandise beyond a customer's current needs. Sometimes these customers resell the extra product to other channel participants through the use of agents, a practice known as diverting. In effect, a firm is profiting by taking advantage of purchase incentives available to some channel participants and not others.

In an effort to stabilize promotional pricing, some firms have begun to develop coordinated programs. Manufacturers and retailers working together can negotiate *net prices* that are administered over a specific time horizon. The manufacturer and retailer jointly plan the promotion and advertising strategy for a product or merchandising category. A *dead net price* is determined that takes into account quantity purchase discounts, prompt payment discounts, and any other applicable price incentives. Finally, an agreement is reached concerning the duration of the negotiated price. These agreements also specify how performance will be measured during the operating period as a basis for future agreements.

The price negotiation framework described above has resulted in what is known as EveryDay Low Pricing (EDLP). Wal★Mart is generally credited with having created EDLP, the strategy around which it seeks to build customer loyalty. Other firms have developed EDLP purchase strategies with suppliers while following a promotional pricing format for consumer merchandising.

Few firms operate at the extremes of either EDLP or promotional pricing; however, most creative merchandisers develop a combination approach to stimulate consumer purchasing. While price or *loss leaders* are used to generate consumer traffic and encourage in-store impulse buying, few items are consistently sold as loss leaders, thereby reducing the risk of predatory pricing allegations.

In a more general sense, business in a free market society will and should engage in a wide variety of promotional and advertising activities. The challenge is to rationalize how such promotional efforts affect logistics. The timing and magnitude of promotional pricing need to be evaluated in terms of ability to consume and the capacity to efficiently handle volume surges. To a significant degree, *trade loading* practices result from end-of-period or end-of-year earnings pressures. This so-called Wall Street effect goes hand in hand with the use of promotional pricing to stimulate product flow so that sales can be booked during a specific time period. Such practices may offer short-term earnings relief but do little, if anything, to stimulate consumption. They are, however, guaranteed to increase logistics cost.

Menu Pricing

From a seller's perspective, a pricing program must be established to accurately and equitably charge customers for the products and services that they demand. Menu pricing is a technique used by many firms to accomplish this objective. An effective menu pricing system has three components: platform service price, value-added service specified costs, and efficiency incentives.

Platform Service Price
The first step in menu pricing is to establish the basic service platform to be offered to all customers and an appropriate price reflecting the costs related to providing that service level. The platform service price is expected to be paid by all customers, whether or not they require the service combination as specified. For example, the basic platform service price might be established for the following service level: "Full trailer of mixed products in unit load quantities on slip sheet from a distribution center for customer unload." The pricing quoted for this combination of delivery specifications, quantity, configuration, and unload requirements is the basis from which any additional charges or discounts are considered. Certain standard discounts may also be quoted as part of the basic service platform. For example, traditional quantity discounts and customer pickup allowances are typically considered to be a part of the basic platform price.

Value-Added Service Costs
The second aspect of menu pricing involves specifying charges for compliance to customer required additional activities. From the example above, an upcharge would be imposed for customized unit loading requested by a customer, such as layering products on the slip sheet in a specific order. A separate upcharge would be established for multiple stop-offs on the delivery, and a third upcharge would be

TABLE 4-4   Menu Pricing

Typical Value-Added Services Charges	Typical Efficiency Incentives
Using customer specified pallets	CHEP pallets
Multiple stop-offs	Expand receiving hours
Special packaging	Accept drop trailers
Sort/segregate loading	Timely unloading
Sequenced load	Flexibility on over/short/damage
Temperature control	Electronic ordering, invoicing, payment
Driver teams	Vendor-managed inventory
	Customer unload

established for delivery on pallets rather than slip sheets. This approach results in each customer paying for the specific combination of services it requires. Table 4-4 provides a listing of typical value-added services for which shippers frequently establish upcharges in their menu pricing programs. Of course, shippers may choose to offer some of these services as part of their basic service platform, in which case their basic price should include the appropriate charges.

Efficiency Incentives

The third step in a comprehensive menu pricing program is the establishment of efficiency incentives. Such incentives may be offered to encourage buyers to comply with specified requirements, which reduce logistics costs. The incentives provide a mechanism for sharing the benefits of such cost-reducing efforts. For example, a discount or allowance might be given to encourage ordering EDI, another incentive offered to receivers who guarantee truck unloading in 2 hours or less, and a third incentive for using CHEP pallets (CHEP pallets are specialized pallets which are bar-coded to allow constant monitoring and tracing of the pallet's specific location. CHEP pallets are leased on a per use basis rather than being purchased by a manufacturer.). Efficiency incentives frequently offered by shippers in a menu pricing program are listed in Table 4-4. Industry Insight 4-4 illustrates menu pricing as it is implemented at Campbell Soup Company.

Summary

No firm can be self-sufficient in meeting the requirements of its customers. Specialization in functions by organizations creates the need for a process to resolve the problems of efficient and effective exchange between those organizations. These problems relate to time, place, quantity, and assortment requirements. A market distribution mechanism must emerge to resolve these problems and create efficiency by minimizing the transactions required to meet customer demand. In fact, market distribution can be thought of conceptually as two separate structures: one to fulfill the buying and selling activities required and another to fulfill the logistical activities.

Developing market distribution strategy is a complex process. Alternative structural arrangements range from very direct between producer and consumer to very

INDUSTRY INSIGHT 4-4 CAMPBELL'S RECIPE FOR SAVINGS

Based in Camden, New Jersey, the Campbell Soup Company makes juices and sauces as well as the familiar red-and-white labeled cans of condensed soup. As a general rule, Campbell ships its product directly to U.S. retailers and grocery wholesalers from four plants located in Paris, Texas; Napoleon, Ohio; Sacramento, California; and Maxton, North Carolina. Campbell distributes its product via for-hire motor carriers to about 600 customers and more than 1,800 ship-to locations in this country. It shipped approximately 5.5 billion pounds of soups, sauces, and beverages in the United States last year.

Two years ago, the company began looking for ways to reduce its supply chain costs. Managers examined the operation, using the activity-based cost accounting method to establish the actual expense for specific logistics tasks. They identified factors such as pallet configuration, pallet type, shipment size, carrier unloading, and cash management practices that had a high impact on distribution costs. They concluded that customers that didn't order electronically and that ordered cases delivered via less than truckload transport were more costly to service than their counterparts that had automated their ordering procedures and ordered in truckload quantities.

In response, company executives decided to institute a strategic pricing program that would provide financial incentives for domestic customers to order product in full truckloads and in full pallets rather than in cases. The menu pricing program offers Campbell's customers a menu of pricing options—the choice of adopting certain practices and earning price reductions, maintaining their existing prices, or paying a higher price for additional services.

Customer orders get assigned to pricing brackets based on the cost Campbell incurs to service them. "If they order a certain percentage in full truckloads and full pallets, they qualify for different brackets," says Nicholas Bova, vice president for supply chain planning and logistics. "We also give them parameters around product unloading as well as electronic ordering and invoicing. In addition, customers are given allowances or price breaks for picking up the goods themselves and/or accepting direct plant delivery."

In the first 6 months of the program's operation, Campbell witnessed a significant change in its customers' buying practices. When the company launched the strategic pricing initiative, about 18 percent of Campbell's customers qualified for the best pricing bracket. Today, more than two-thirds of its customers meet the criteria for price discounts.

The program has enhanced the efficiency of Campbell's distribution operation. The company now consolidates more orders into full truckloads. Today, more than 90 percent of its domestic volume is ordered in full truckloads compared with 70 to 75 percent prior to the strategic pricing initiative. In addition, 85 to 90 percent of the volume moves on full pallets today compared with 70 percent in the past. Campbell exchanges electronic purchase orders and inventory information with about 90 percent of its customers as opposed to 60 to 65 percent when the program began.

Filling customer orders in the optimal way allows Campbell to improve its customer service, reduce distribution expenses, and share the savings with its trading partners. It now has fewer personnel and pays less overtime in its warehouse operation than in the past even though productivity has soared.

Campbell has been able to put into effect a 3-day processing time for standard orders from trading partners and a 2-day turnaround for customers in its continuous replenishment program. "If we move goods on full pallets, we have less handling," says Larry Venturelli, director of supply chain finance and customer logistics. "It shortens the amount of time it takes to fill an order. Because there's less handling, damage is reduced throughout the supply chain."

By motivating the customer to place more efficient orders, Campbell has realized major savings. Trading partners have also benefited through improved distribution and order handling practices, lowered transportation cost, upgraded warehouse and store service levels, and reduced administrative support.

Source: James Aaron Cooke, "Campbell's Recipe for Savings," *Logistics Management and Distribution Report,* March 2000, pp. 42–4.

indirect, involving various wholesale and retail intermediaries. End-user requirements form the basis for determining the appropriate structure. Their needs in terms of waiting time, lot-size purchase, locational convenience, and product assortment ultimately drive the decision concerning where and how producers must position their products. These decisions, in turn, influence the structure in terms of the number and types of intermediaries that should be included in the distribution process. A complicating factor is introduced by the fact that most companies attempt to serve multiple end-user segments. The best channel structure for one segment may not be best for all. Thus, most firms are engaged in multiple distribution channels.

Channel mapping is one tool used by organizations in designing distribution channels. A channel map outlines the alternative paths used to reach end customers, detailing the participants in each path as well as the functions performed and economic characteristics of each linkage in a path. A matrix approach, which details specific activities required to complete a function and alternative methods to complete each activity, can also be used to identify the most appropriate participants to meet specific customer requirements.

Different types of relationships are possible among channel participants. The basis for distinguishing among these relationships is the willingness of the members to acknowledge their mutual dependence. Ranging from single-transaction channels, which emerge for one-time exchange, to conventional channels, which operate with little recognition of dependency, to relational collaborative arrangements, such as partnerships and alliances, cooperation and information sharing among participants increase as the relationships become more formalized. Supply chains represent behavioral relationships that are advanced partnerships and alliances.

Perhaps no other development in recent years has as much potential impact on distribution channels as the Internet. Predictions for massive channel change such as the possibility that traditional retail stores will be replaced by e-tailers who have no store facilities, the disintermediation of channels as consumers interact directly with producers, and fundamental shifts of roles and responsibilities have dominated much of the discussion of the Internet's impact. It is too soon to actually determine what the long-term impact will be, but it is clear that logistical operations and fulfillment are a major concern for all businesses that interact with consumers directly via the Internet.

While price determination is not administered by logistics executives, pricing and logistics are highly interrelated. The continuum between F.O.B. and delivered pricing determines who controls logistics and how transportation expense is treated in price. Logistics also impacts such issues as price discrimination, discounts, allowances, and promotions. The development of menu pricing as a strategy allows a seller to most effectively charge for the actual services provided to a buyer.

Challenge Questions

1. Why is specialization so critical to distribution efficiency?
2. Describe how the process of assortment overcomes the problems created by specialization.
3. Given the principle of minimum transactions, explain why it is possible to have too many participants in a distribution channel.
4. What is the primary logic behind potential separation of marketing and logistics channel structure?

5. How does the risk related to inventory compare among manufacturers, wholesalers, and retailers?

6. Why wouldn't a manufacturer desire to always have intensive distribution coverage?

7. How could the matrix approach to design be applied to logistics activities?

8. Distinguish between the four types of relational collaborative arrangements. Provide an example of each.

9. What do you believe will be the impact of the Internet on market distribution by 2010?

10. What is a shipper's responsibility when terms of purchase are F.O.B. origin? F.O.B. destination? Why would a shipper prefer one over the other?

5   PROCUREMENT AND MANUFACTURING STRATEGIES

In Chapter 2, performance cycles were discussed as the foundation for integrated logistics in the supply chain. In fact, there are three performance cycles that must be linked through effective logistics. The *procurement cycle* links an organization with its suppliers; the *manufacturing support cycle* involves the logistics of production; and the *market distribution cycle* links the firm with its markets. As will be seen later in this chapter, manufacturing firms differ in their manufacturing strategies; thus, alternative approaches to procurement may be implemented to accommodate specific manufacturing requirements. Of course, all of this performance must meet customer requirements for quality products. This chapter begins, therefore, with a discussion of product quality from a customer's perspective and total quality management programs. Procurement and manufacturing are then each discussed with emphasis on alternative strategies employed. The chapter concludes with a discussion of logistical interfaces necessary to support an organization's chosen procurement and manufacturing strategies.

The Quality Imperative

An overriding concern of all organizations today is quality. In the competitive marketplace, no company dares to fall behind in providing quality to its customers, consumers, or end users. It has been argued that quality no longer provides an organization with an edge over its competitors but is a prerequisite for doing business in the global economy. Yet quality remains an elusive concept. In the end, quality rests in the eyes of customers and how they perceive an organization, its products, and its services. Many issues of quality were introduced in Chapter 3 with a perspective on the service expectations and requirements of customers. In this chapter, dealing with procurement of materials and manufacturing processes, critical issues of *product quality* are addressed. Much of the focus in supply chain management is ensuring product quality that meets customer requirements.

Dimensions of Product Quality

In the context of physical product form, quality is not as simple as it may first appear. In fact, the term *quality* means different things to different people. While everyone wants a quality product, not all may agree that a particular item or brand has the quality attributes desired. Eight different dimensions of product quality have been identified.[1]

Performance

Perhaps the most obvious aspect of quality from a customer's point of view is **performance,** or how well the product performs the task it was designed to perform. For example, personal computers may be judged with respect to their processing speed; audio components, in terms of sound clarity and lack of noise; or dishwashers, relative to how clean and spotless the dishes. Superior performance in a product is generally an objective attribute, which can easily be compared between items and brands. Of course, an item may actually have several performance dimensions, which complicates the comparison process. The personal computer is judged not only in terms of processing speed but also by such characteristics as internal memory, hard disk capacity, and numerous other aspects.

Reliability

Reliability refers to the likelihood that a product will perform during its expected life. It is also concerned with the number of breakdowns or repairs that a customer experiences after purchase. Consider, for example, Maytag's slogan "The Dependability People" and long-running advertising campaign featuring a company repairman as "the loneliest man in town." Maytag stressed that its products were more reliable than any other by showing that the Maytag repairman was never called to fix a broken appliance. Like performance, reliability is a characteristic of quality that can be objectively measured.

---

[1]David A. Garvin, "Competing on the Eight Dimensions of Quality," *Harvard Business Review,* November/December 1987, pp. 101–9.

Durability

While related to reliability, **durability** is a somewhat different attribute. It refers to the actual life expectancy of a product. An automobile with a life expectancy of 10 years may be judged by many consumers to be of higher quality than one with a life of 5 years. Of course, life span may be extended through repairs or preventative maintenance. Thus, durability and reliability are distinct but interrelated aspects of quality.

Conformance

Conformance refers to whether a firm's products actually meet the precise description or specifications as designed. It is frequently measured by looking at an organization's scrap, rework, or rate of defects. This quality measure is usually applied internally in an organization. For example, if 95 percent of a firm's products meet the specifications as designed, it has a 5 percent defect rate. The defective products may be scrapped or reworked to bring them into conformance. From a customer's viewpoint, conformance might be looked at as the number of "lemons." Suppose for example, that most of the automobiles sold by a manufacturer perform exactly as specified, have few breakdowns, and have a long life. However, if a small number of the autos are defective, the overall quality of the automobile may be judged as low.

Features

Customers frequently judge quality of specific products on the basis of **features**—the number of functions or tasks that they perform independent of aspects related to reliability or durability. For example, a television receiver with remote control, picture-in-picture, and on-screen programming is usually perceived to be of higher quality than is a basic model. But, in general, the more features a product contains, the greater is the likelihood that another quality attribute is lacking, particularly reliability.

Aesthetics

Aesthetics, the styling and specific materials used in a product, is an aspect used by many customers to judge quality. In clothing, cashmere sweaters are considered to be higher quality than polyester fabrics. In automobiles, the use of leather rather than cloth for seats, wood or metal rather than plastic, are aspects of style that imply quality. Included in aesthetics is the notion of *fit and finish* such as high-gloss paint on an automobile or seams that have no overlap. Product designs that are unique or innovative are also frequently regarded by customers to be of higher quality.

Serviceability

Serviceability, the ease of fixing or repairing a product that fails, is an important aspect of quality to some customers. Consider, for example, how some new appliances contain diagnostic capability, which alert users or service technicians that a failure is about to occur. Ideally, serviceability would allow the customer to fix the product with little or no cost or time lost. In the absence of such serviceability, customers generally consider those items or brands that can be repaired quickest with least cost to be better quality products.

Perceived Quality

As noted earlier, customers are the ultimate judges of product quality through their perception of how well the product meets their requirements. **Perceived quality** rests in customers' experiences before, during, and after the sale. Total product quality is a combination of the various dimensions, how they are blended by an organization, and how that blend is perceived. It is perfectly plausible that two different customers may perceive two different brands as being best quality, depending upon which blend of elements each considers to be most critical.

Total Quality Management

It is useful to remember that total quality encompasses much more than just the physical product. Of specific concern in this text are the elements related to service, satisfaction, and success discussed in Chapter 3. From the customer's perspective not only does the physical product have to incorporate the desired elements, but also the product must be available in a timely and suitable manner. Quality is, therefore, a responsibility of everyone in the organization.

Total Quality Management (TQM) is a philosophy and a system of management focused on meeting customer requirements in all aspects of their needs, from all departments or functions in the organization, whether the customer is internal or external, intermediate, end user, or consumer. While the specific tools and methodologies employed in TQM are beyond the scope of this text, the basic conceptual elements are: (1) top management commitment and support; (2) customer focus in product, service, and process design; (3) integration within and between organizations; and (4) commitment to continuous improvement.

Quality Standards

Establishing global standards for quality is extremely difficult due to different practices and procedures around the world. As a simple example, engineering tolerances in one country might be measured in millimeters, while in another, they are measured in tenths of an inch. Nevertheless, a set of standards has emerged from the **International Organization for Standardization (ISO)** and has gained worldwide acceptance.

In 1987, a series of quality standards was issued under the name ISO 9000. Incorporating several subsets (ISO 9001, 9002, etc.), these quality guidelines provide basic definitions for quality assurance and quality management. ISO 9001, for example, deals with the quality system in place for product design, development, production, installation, and service. Several organizations around the world are authorized to perform audits of companies and their practices and procedures for TQM. A company that meets the ISO guidelines can receive certification. In 1998, another set of guidelines, ISO 14000, was released. ISO 14000 deals with guidelines and procedures for managing a firm's environmental impact. Certification in both ISO 9000 and ISO 14000 would indicate that a company has in place both a world-class quality management and environmental management system.

Interestingly, the ISO certification process is accomplished by an audit of a firm's policies, systems, and procedures for quality and environmental management. It does not include actual testing of products or audits of customer satisfaction. Despite this limitation, ISO certification is an important indicator of a firm's commitment to TQM. It is also important because many companies and even the European Union are demanding that supply chain partners be ISO certified.

Another important quality standard, particularly for U.S. companies, is the **Malcolm Baldrige National Quality Award.** Established in 1987, the award is intended to recognize those companies that excel not only in quality management processes but also in quality achievement. Figure 5-1 lists the criteria for the award and the point values assigned to each. Notice that customer focus is critical not only in the third

FIGURE 5-1

Malcolm Baldrige criteria and values

1 Leadership (120 pts.)
The **Leadership** Category examines how your organization's senior leaders address values and performance expectations, as well as a focus on customers and other stakeholders, empowerment, innovation, learning, and organizational directions. Also examined is how your organization addresses its responsibilities to the public and supports its key communities.

2 Strategic Planning (85 pts.)
The **Strategic Planning** Category examines your organization's strategy development process, including how your organization develops strategic objectives, action plans, and related human resource plans. Also examined are how plans are deployed and how performance is tracked.

3 Customer and Market Focus (85 pts.)
The **Customer and Market Focus** Category examines how your organization determines requirements, expectations, and preferences of customers and markets. Also examined is how your organization builds relationships with customers and determines their satisfaction.

4 Information and Analysis (90 pts.)
The **Information and Analysis** Category examines your organization's performance measurement system and how your organization analyzes performance data and information.

5 Human Resources (85 pts.)
The **Human Resource Focus** Category examines how your organization enables employees to develop and utilize their full potential, aligned with the organization's objectives. Also examined are your organization's efforts to build and maintain a work environment and an employee support climate conducive to performance excellence, full participation, and personal and organizational growth.

6 Process Management (85 pts.)
The **Process Management** Category examines the key aspects of your organization's process management, including customer-focused design, product and service delivery, support, and supplier and partnering processes involving all work units.

7 Business Results (450 pts.)
The **Business Results** Category examines your organization's performance and improvement in key business areas—customer satisfaction, product and service performance, financial and marketplace performance, human resource results, supplier and partner results, and operational performance. Also examined are performance levels relative to competitors.

Source: Obtained from the National Institute for Quality website at **www.NIST.gov.**

category but also in several other of the criteria. Other countries have also initiated their own quality award programs. While there is only one winner in each of three categories for the Baldrige award each year, many executives believe that the process of applying and being judged for the awards focuses an organization's attention on TQM. Some companies, such as Motorola, even insist that their suppliers at least apply for such awards as a mechanism to ensure that those companies are providing top-quality materials and services.

Procurement

Every organization, whether it is a manufacturer, wholesaler, or retailer, buys materials, services, and supplies from outside suppliers to support its operations. Historically, the process of acquiring these needed inputs has been considered somewhat of a nuisance, at least as compared to other activities within the firm. Purchasing was regarded as a clerical or low-level managerial activity charged with responsibility to execute and process orders initiated elsewhere in the organization. The role of purchasing was to obtain the desired resource at the lowest possible purchase price from a supplier. This traditional view of purchasing has changed substantially in the past two decades. The modern focus on supply chain management with its emphasis on relationships between buyers and sellers has elevated purchasing to a higher, strategic-level activity. This strategic role is differentiated from the traditional through the term **procurement,** although in practice many people use the terms purchasing and procurement interchageably.

The increasing importance of procurement can be traced to several factors. The most basic of these factors has been the recognition of the substantial dollar volume of purchases in the typical organization and the potential dollar savings from a strategic approach to managing the activity. The simple fact is that purchased goods and services are one of the largest elements of cost for many firms. In the average manufacturing firm in North America, purchased goods and services account for approximately 55 cents of every sales dollar.[2] By way of contrast, the average expense of direct labor in the manufacturing process accounts for only about 10 cents of every sales dollar. While the percentage spent on purchased inputs does vary considerably across manufacturing industries, it is clear that the potential savings from strategic management of procurement are considerable.

Related to the cost of purchased inputs is the emphasis on outsourcing, which has dominated many industries over the last two decades. The result is that the amount spent on procurement has increased significantly in many organizations. Firms today purchase not only raw materials and basic supplies but also complex fabricated components with very high value-added content. They spin off functions to suppliers to focus resources on their core competencies. This means that more attention must be focused on how the organization interfaces and effectively manages its supply base. For example, General Motors uses its first-tier supplier network and third-party logistics providers to complete subassemblies and deliver finished components on a just-in-time basis for incorporation into automobiles on the assembly line. Many of these activities were once performed by General Motors itself. Developing and coordinating these relationships are critical aspects of effective procurement strategy. The logistical requirements related to effective procurement strategy are identified below.

Procurement Perspectives

The evolving focus on procurement as a key capability in organizations has stimulated a new perspective regarding its role in supply chain management. The emphasis has shifted from adversarial, transaction-focused negotiation with suppliers to ensuring that the firm is positioned to implement its manufacturing and marketing strategies with support from its supply base. In particular, considerable focus is placed on ensuring supply, inventory minimization, quality improvement, supplier development, and lowest total cost of ownership.

Continuous Supply
Stockouts of raw materials or component parts can shut down a production plant and result in extreme cost to an organization. Downtime due to production stoppage increases operating costs and results in an inability to provide finished goods for delivery to customers. Imagine the chaos that would result if an automobile assembly line had all parts available but tires. The almost completed automobiles would have to wait until a supply of tires was received and, in fact, production would have to be halted until tires were available. Thus, one of the core objectives of procurement is to ensure that a continuous supply of materials, parts, and components is available for use.

---

[2]Shawn Tulley, "Purchasing: New Muscle," *Fortune,* February 20, 1995, p. 75.

Minimize Inventory Investment

In the past, downtime due to material shortages was minimized by maintaining large inventories of inputs to protect against potential disruption in supply; but maintaining inventory is expensive and utilizes capital that might be used elsewhere in the organization. One goal of modern procurement is to maintain supply continuity with the minimum inventory investment possible. This requires balancing the costs of carrying excessive materials against the possibility of a production stoppage.[3] The ideal, of course, is to have needed materials arrive just at the moment they are scheduled to be used in the production process, in other words, *just-in-time.*

Quality Improvement

Procurement can play a critical role in the quality of an organization's products. The quality of finished goods and services is obviously dependent upon the quality of the materials and parts used in producing those items. If poor-quality components and materials are used, then the final product will not meet customer quality standards.

Simply ensuring that each individual item purchased is of the appropriate quality level may not be sufficient. If a standard part is sourced from many different suppliers, and each supplier meets specified quality requirements, it is still possible that the final product may encounter quality problems. Industry Insight 5-1 describes the quality failures encountered by Tenant, a manufacturer of floor-cleaning machines. Ultimately, Tenant discovered that the key to improving quality of its products lay in a different approach to procurement.

Quality improvement through procurement also has substantial implications for cost in an organization. If defective materials are the cause of poor-quality finished products, the costs of scrap and rework in the production process go up. If the problems are not detected until customers receive the product, costs associated with warranties, guarantees, repair, and replacement increase substantially. Ultimately, procurement must maintain a quality perspective in dealing with suppliers to ensure that customer requirements are met in a cost-effective manner.

Supplier Development

In the final analysis, successful procurement depends on locating or developing suppliers, analyzing their capabilities, and selecting and working with those suppliers to achieve continuous improvement.[4] Developing good supply relationships with firms that are committed to the buying organization's success is critical in supplier development. The next step is to develop close relationships with those suppliers, working with them through sharing of information and resources, to achieve better results. For example, a manufacturer might share a production schedule with suppliers, which allows them to better meet the buyer's requirements for delivery. A retailer might share promotional plans to ensure that a supplier will be able to meet its needs for increased quantities at a specific time. This perspective on effective procurement stands in stark contrast to the traditional mode of purchasing which inherently created adversarial relationships with the supply base.

Lowest Total Cost of Ownership

Ultimately, the difference in perspective between traditional purchasing practice and contemporary procurement strategy can be summarized as a focus on **Total Cost of**

---

[3]James Carbone, "Suppliers as Strategic Business Partners," *Purchasing,* November 21, 1996, p. 23.

[4]Daniel Krause, "Suppliers Development: Current Practices and Outcomes," *Journal of Supply Chain Management,* Spring 1997, pp. 12–20.

INDUSTRY INSIGHT 5-1 SWEPT AWAY BY TENNANT

Tennant was experiencing severe oil leak problems in its floor sweepers and scrubbers. Quality checks found oil leaks in 1 out of every 75 hydraulic joints, or 2 per machine. To a floor-cleaning company a sweeper that leaked oil was the equivalent of a mortal sin. Fortunately, most leaks were caught before the machines were shipped from the plant, but rework was required. In 1979, Tennant was spending about 33,000 hours on manufacturing rework, at a cost of $2 million or 2 percent of revenues.

Investigating the cause of these quality problems revealed that purchasing was ordering hydraulic hoses and fittings from no less than 16 suppliers. Tennant switched between different suppliers based on price and availability. Consequently, parts didn't always fit together properly.

Douglas Hoelscher, Tennant's VP of operations, established a special multidisciplinary sourcing group for fluid connectors with the express purpose of selecting one hydraulic hose supplier. Eventually, Parker Hannifin was chosen and has been Tennant's only supplier of hydraulic hoses and fittings. As a result, Tennant was counting leaks per 100 joints in 1980; by 1985, it was down to 1 leak per 1,000 joints; and, by 1992, Tennant had quit counting altogether.

Tennant learned an important lesson from this experience. Quality could be greatly influenced by sourcing policies and relationships with suppliers. Consequently, Tennant gave Parker the opportunity to plumb an entire machine, which was previously done in-house. Tennant had always been reluctant to let outsiders see products still in the developmental stage. Now, the company routinely seeks suppliers' advice. "We saw the need to surround ourselves with suppliers that could provide engineering and design support, and that weren't just parts makers," says Don Carlton, Tennant's purchasing director.

Tennant has narrowed its supplier base to improve relations with its suppliers and improve quality. From 1,100 suppliers in 1980, active suppliers now number 250, with approximately 50 receiving the majority of Tennant's business.

Source: Ernie Raia, "Swept Away by Tennant," *Purchasing,* September 22, 1994, pp. 42–9.

Ownership (TCO) instead of a focus on purchase price. Procurement professionals recognize that although the purchase price of a material or item remains very important, it is only one part of the total cost equation in their organization.[5] Service costs and life cycle costs must also be considered.

Purchase Price and Discounts.   Whether established through competitive bidding, buyer–seller negotiation, or simply from a seller's published price schedule, the purchase price of an item is obviously a concern in procurement. No one wants to pay a higher price than necessary. Related to the price quote is normally a schedule of one or more possible discounts that the buyer may receive. For example, quantity discounts may be offered as an inducement to encourage buyers to purchase larger quantities or cash discounts may be offered for prompt payment of invoices.

Consideration of suppliers' discount structures immediately takes the buyer beyond simple quoted purchase price. Other costs associated with purchasing must be considered. For quantity discounts to be factored in, the buyer must also consider the costs associated with holding inventory. Larger purchase quantities increase inventory of materials or supplies. Size of purchase also impacts administrative costs associated

---

[5]Zeger Degraeve and Filip Roodhooft, "Effectively Selecting Suppliers Using Total Cost of Ownership," *Journal of Supply Chain Management,* Winter 1999, pp. 5–10. See also Lisa M. Ellram, "Total Cost of Ownership," *International Journal of Physical Distribution and Logistics,* August 1995, pp. 4–23.

with purchasing. Lot-size techniques such as **Economic Order Quantity (EOQ),** discussed fully in Chapter 10, can help resolve this rather simple cost trade-off.

Supplier terms of sale and cash discount structures are also an aspect of purchase price. A supplier offering more favorable trade credit terms is, in effect, impacting the purchase price from the buyer's perspective. For example, a discount for prompt payment of an invoice offered by one supplier must be compared with other suppliers' offers, which may have different percentages or time periods involved.

What normally is not considered in traditional purchasing practice is the impact of such pricing and discount structures on logistics operations and costs. For example, while traditional EOQ does include consideration of inventory carrying costs, it generally does not include such factors as the impact of order quantity on transportation costs or the costs associated with receiving and handling different size orders. Many of these logistical considerations had been ignored or given cursory consideration as buyers attempted to achieve the lowest purchase price of the goods and services acquired for the organization but there is now increasing recognition of the importance of these logistics costs.

Service Pricing and Debundling.   Sellers typically offer a number of standard services that must be considered in procurement. Additionally, a wide variety of value-added services must be evaluated as organizations attempt to find the lowest TCO. Many of these services involve logistical operations and the logistical interface between buyers and sellers.

The simplest of these services is delivery. How delivery will be accomplished, when, and to where are all aspects for cost consideration. As discussed in the previous chapter, in many industries it is standard practice to quote a price that includes delivery to the customer's plant, warehouse, or store location. Alternatively, the seller may offer the buyer a pickup allowance if the buyer picks up the merchandise at the seller's location and assumes responsibility for transportation. The buyer may be able to reduce total costs, not only through taking advantage of the allowance but also by more fully utilizing its own transportation equipment. The buyer may even find it beneficial to use a common carrier for these pickups, if the economics of the pickup allowance justify it.

There may also be different prices depending upon the destination preferred by the buyer. For example, delivery of a single large load to a retailer's distribution center might represent one level of service, whereas delivery of smaller quantities to individual store locations represents another. Each alternative service involves different costs for the seller and the buyer.

In Chapter 3, numerous other potential services were discussed, ranging from special packaging to preparation of promotional displays. Performance of subassembly operations in a supplier's plant or a third-party distribution center represents a further extension of potential value-added service. The point is that each potential service has a cost to the supplier and a price to the buyer. A key aspect of determining the TCO for purchased requirements is to consider the trade-offs involved in terms of value-added versus cost and price of each service. To do so, the purchase price of an item must be *debundled* from the price of services under consideration; that is, each of the services should be priced separately so that appropriate analysis can be made. In Chapter 4, this practice was referred to as *menu pricing*. Where traditional purchasing might overlook value-added services in seeking lowest possible purchase price, effective procurement executives consider whether such services should be performed internally, by suppliers, or at all. Debundling allows the buyer to make the most appropriate procurement choice.

FIGURE 5-2

Major categories for the components of total cost of ownership

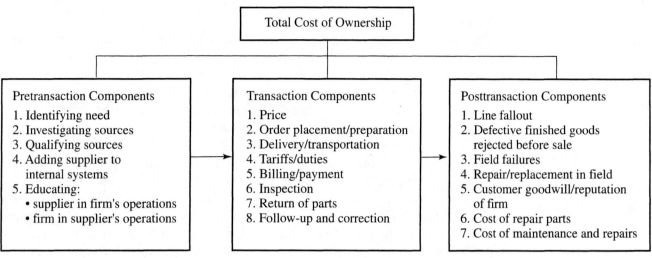

Source: Michel Leenders and Harold Fearon, *Purchasing and Supply Management,* 11 ed. (Chicago, IL: Irwin, 1997), p. 334. Reprinted with permission.

Life Cycle Costs. The final aspect of lowest TCO includes numerous elements known as **life cycle costs.** The total cost of materials, items, or other inputs extends beyond the purchase price and elements of value-added service to include the lifetime costs of such items. Some of these costs are incurred before actual receipt of the items, others are incurred while the item is being used, and some occur long after the buyer has actually used the item.

One aspect of life cycle costs involves the administrative expense associated with the procurement activity itself. Expenses related to screening potential suppliers, negotiation, order preparation, and transmission are just a few of the administrative costs of procurement. Receiving, inspecting, and payment are also important. The costs related to defective finished goods, scrap, and rework, which are associated with poor supplier quality, must also be considered, as well as related warranty administration and repair of items that consumers have purchased. Even the costs associated with recycling or recovery of materials after the useful life of a finished product may have an impact on TCO.

Figure 5-2 presents a model of the various elements that comprise TCO. When each of these elements is considered in procurement, it is clear that numerous opportunities for improvement exist in most companies. Many of these opportunities arise from closer working relationships with suppliers than is possible when adversarial price negotiation dominates the buyer–seller relationship. When working cooperatively with suppliers several strategies may be employed to reduce both the buyers' and the sellers' costs, making the total supply chain much more efficient and allowing it to more effectively meet the requirements of downstream partners. Such strategies are discussed next.

Procurement Strategies

Effective procurement strategy to support supply chain management concepts requires a much closer working relationship between buyers and sellers than was traditionally practiced. Specially, three strategies have emerged: **volume consolidation, supplier operational integration,** and **value management.** Each of these strategies requires an increasing degree of interaction between supply chain partners; thus, they may not be considered as distinct and separate but rather as evolutionary stages of development.

Volume Consolidation

The first step in developing an effective procurement strategy is volume consolidation through reduction in the number of suppliers. Beginning in the 1980s many firms faced the reality that they dealt with a large number of suppliers for almost every material or input used throughout the organization. In fact, purchasing literature prior to that time emphasized that multiple sources of supply were the best procurement strategy. Numerous advantages were seen to this approach. First, potential suppliers were continually bidding for the buyer's business, ensuring that prices would be quoted as low as possible. Second, maintaining multiple sources reduced the buyer's dependence on any one supplier. This in turn served to reduce the buyer's risk should a specific supplier encounter problems such as a strike, a fire, internal quality problems, or other disruptions in ability to supply. For example, when UPS drivers went on strike in 1998, numerous shippers were unable to deliver their products to customers because of their extreme reliance on UPS for delivery service. Although other suppliers of package delivery service exist, none had the available capacity to cope with large volumes of shipments that had been handled by UPS. While other reasons for multiple supplier relationships exist, these reasons constitute the primary rationale.

By consolidating volumes with a reduced number of suppliers, procurement is able to leverage its share of a supplier's business. At the very least, it raises the buyer's negotiating strength in relationship to the supplier. More importantly, volume consolidation with a reduced number of suppliers provides a number of advantages for those suppliers. As working relationships with a smaller number of suppliers are developed, those suppliers can, in turn, pass these advantages to the buying organization. The most obvious source of advantage is that by concentrating a larger volume of purchases with a supplier, the supplier can gain greater economies of scale in its own internal processes, partially by being able to spread its fixed costs over a larger volume of output. In the example of Tennant cited in Industry Insight 5-1, reduction in hydraulic hose suppliers from 16 to 1 meant that the preferred supplier's increased sales to this one customer allowed economies in marketing, delivery, and production. Additionally, if a supplier can be assured of a larger volume of purchase, it may be more willing to make investments in capacity or in processes to improve customer service. When a buyer is constantly switching suppliers, no one firm has an incentive to make such investments.[6]

Clearly, when a single source of supply is used risk increases. For this reason, supply base reduction programs are almost always accompanied by rigorous supplier screening, selection, and certification programs. In many instances, procurement executives work closely with others in their organization to develop such preferred or certified suppliers. It should be noted that volume consolidation does not necessarily mean that a single source of supply is utilized for every, or any, purchased input. It does mean that a substantially smaller number of suppliers are used than was traditionally the case in most organizations. Even when a single source is chosen, it is wise to have a contingency plan in place.

The savings potential from volume consolidation is not trivial. One consulting firm has estimated that savings in purchase price and other elements of cost can range

---

[6]Matthew G. Anderson, "Strategic Sourcing," *International Journal of Logistics,* January 1998, p. 1–13.

from 5 to 15 percent of purchases.[7] If the typical manufacturing firm spends 55 percent of its revenue on purchased items and can save 10 percent through volume consolidation, the potential exists to deliver a $5.5 million improvement on revenue of $100 million to bottom-line, pretax income!

Supplier Operational Integration

The next level of development in procurement strategy emerges as buyers and sellers begin to integrate their processes and activities in an attempt to achieve substantial operational performance improvement in the supply chain. The integration begins to take the form of alliances or partnerships with selected participants in the supply base to reduce the total costs and improve the operating flows between the buyer and the seller.

Such integration can take many specific forms. As one example, the buyer may allow the seller to have access to its sales and ordering information system, giving the seller early warning of which products are being sold and what future purchases to expect. Such information allows the seller to be better positioned to effectively supply requirements for materials at a reduced cost. Cost reduction occurs because the seller faces more certain demand from the buyer and can reduce the need for cost-inefficient practices, such as expediting.

Further operational integration can occur by buyer and seller working together to identify the processes involved in maintaining supply, searching for ways to redesign those processes. Establishing EDI linkages to reduce order time and eliminate errors is a simple form of such integration. More sophisticated efforts may involve eliminating redundant activities that both parties perform. For example, in some sophisticated relationships, activities such as buyer counting and inspection of incoming deliveries have been eliminated as greater reliance is placed on the supplier's capabilities. Many firms have achieved operational integration focused on logistical arrangements, such as continuous replenishment programs and vendor-managed inventory. Such integration has considerable potential for reducing TCO.

Some of the efforts in operational integration strive to reduce total cost through two-way learning. For example, Honda of America works closely with its suppliers to improve those suppliers' capability in quality management. Using its own personnel, Honda visits supplier facilities and helps identify ways that those suppliers can increase the quality of their output. Such improvements ultimately benefit Honda by reducing the suppliers' costs of rework and by providing Honda with higher levels of quality materials.

The primary objective of operational integration is to cut waste, reduce cost, and develop a relationship that allows both buyer and seller to achieve mutual improvements. The above examples are merely illustrative of some of the ways that integration can aid in this objective. Combined creativity across organizations can provide synergy that one firm, operating in isolation, would be unable to achieve. It has been estimated that operational integration with a supplier can provide incremental savings of 5 to 25 percent above the benefits achieved through volume consolidation.[8]

Value Management

Achieving operational integration with suppliers leads quite naturally to the next level of development in procurement strategy, value management. Value management is an

---

[7]Matthew Anderson, Les Artman, and Paul B. Katz, "Procurement Pathways," *Logistics,* Spring/Summer 1997, p. 10.

[8]Matthew Anderson, Les Artman, and Paul B. Katz, op. cit.

FIGURE 5-3

Flexibility and cost of design changes

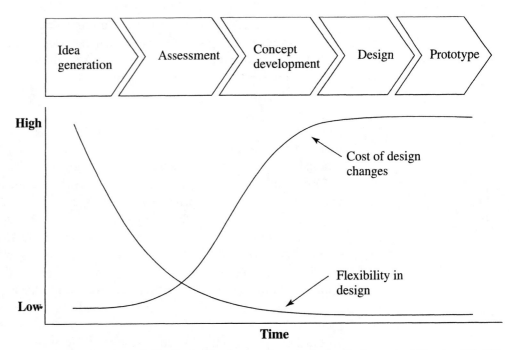

Source: Robert M. Monczka, et al., *New Product Development: Strategies for Supplier Integration* (Milwaukee, WI: ASQ Quality Press, 2000), p. 6.

even more intense aspect of supplier integration, going beyond a focus on buyer–seller operations to a more comprehensive relationship. Value engineering, reduced complexity, and early supplier involvement in product design represent some of the ways procurement can work with suppliers to reduce further the TCO.

Value engineering is a concept that involves closely examining material and component requirements at the early stage of product design to ensure that the lowest total cost inputs are incorporated into that design. Figure 5-3 shows how early supplier involvement can be critical in achieving cost reductions. As a firm's new product development process proceeds from idea generation through its various stages to final commercialization, the company's flexibility in making design changes decreases. Design changes can easily be accommodated in the early stages, but by the time prototypes have been developed, a design change is extremely difficult. The expense associated with a design change has the opposite pattern, becoming extremely high after a prototype is developed. The earlier a supplier is involved in the process, then, the more likely an organization is to capitalize on the supplier's knowledge and capabilities.

An example from an automobile manufacturer demonstrates the potential arising from early supplier involvement. In designing the front bumper for a new model, the design engineer was completing design of the bracket assembly for the bumper. During the process, an engineer from the assembly supplier, which had already been chosen even though production was still several years into the future, asked if the bracket location could be moved by about 1/2 inch. The design engineer, after some consideration, replied that it could be done with no impact on the final product. The design engineer was interested to know why the supplier's engineer requested the change. The answer was that by moving the bracket, the supplier would be able to use existing tools and dies to manufacture the piece. Under the original design, major capital investment would have been required for new tooling. The result was approximately a 25 to 30 percent reduction in cost due to the modification.

Clearly, value management extends beyond the procurement activity in an organization and requires close cooperation between numerous participants, both internal and external. Teams representing procurement, engineering, manufacturing, marketing and sales, and logistics as well as key supplier personnel attempt to find solutions to lower total cost, improve performance, or better meet customer requirements by investigating the cost and functionality of purchased inputs. Research by Mercer Management Consulting reveals that the potential payoffs from this approach vary widely in organizations but can be greater than the payoffs already achieved in volume consolidation and supplier operational integration.[9]

Purchase Requirement Segmentation

The Pareto effect applies in procurement just as it applies in almost every facet of business activity. In the procurement context, it can be stated simply: a small percentage of the materials, items, and services that are acquired account for a large percentage of the dollars spent. The point is that all procured inputs are not equal; however, many organizations use the same approach and procedures for procuring small items as they do for acquiring their most strategic inputs. One result is that they spend as much in acquiring a large $10,000 order of raw materials as they do for a $100 order of copying paper. Since all purchased inputs are not equal, many firms have begun to pay attention to segmented purchase requirements and prioritizing resources and expertise against those requirements.

It would be a mistake, though, to simply use dollar expenditure as the basis for segmenting requirements. Some inputs are strategic materials; others are not. Some inputs have potential for high impact on the business success; others do not. Some purchases are very complex and high risk; others are not. For example, failure to have seat assemblies delivered to an auto assembly line on time could be catastrophic, while failure to have cleaning supplies might be merely a nuisance. Obtaining a new computer order-processing system has major ramifications for the entire organization; purchasing a laptop for a new sales representative is a relatively simple task. The key is for the organization to apply the appropriate approach to procurement as needed. Volume consolidation and supply base reduction most likely can be justified for almost every material and service. The benefits described earlier from this approach can be gained for office supplies as well as raw materials. Because operational integration focuses heavily on improving the flow of products and information between organizations, it is particularly appropriate for inputs which have a high degree of logistical cost and potential value-added from logistics operations. A value-management approach should be reserved for the firm's most critical resource suppliers.[10]

E-Commerce and Procurement

The explosion in technology and information systems is having a major impact on the procurement activity of many major organizations. Much of the actual day-to-day work in procurement has traditionally been accomplished manually with significant amounts of paperwork, resulting in slow processes subject to considerable human

---

[9]Matthew Anderson, Les Antman, and Paul B. Katz, op. cit.

[10]An interesting approach to segmentation of supplier relationships is described in Rasmus Friis Olsen and Lisa M. Ellram, "A Portfolio Approach to Supplier Relationships," *Industrial Marketing Management,* March 26, 1997, pp. 101–13.

error. Applying technology to procurement has considerable potential to speed the process, reduce errors, and lower cost related to acquisition.

Basic Electronic Procurement

Probably the most prevalent use of electronic commerce in procurement is **Electronic Data Interchange (EDI).** EDI, as the term implies, is simply the electronic transmission of data between a firm and its supplier. This allows two or more companies to obtain and provide much more timely and accurate information. There are many types of data being transmitted directly, including purchase requisitions, purchase orders, purchase order acknowledgment, order status, and tracking and tracing information. The explosion in EDI usage during the late 1990s was a direct recognition of its benefits, including standardization of data, more accurate information, more timely information, shortening of lead times with associated reductions in inventories, and reduced TCOs.

At its most basic level, EDI is a major component of integration between buyers and sellers. At least in theory, buyers can communicate quickly, accurately, and interactively with suppliers about requirements, schedules, orders, invoices, and so forth. It provides a tool for transparency between organizations, which is needed to integrate processes in the supply chain.

Another basic application of electronic commerce in procurement has been the development of electronic catalogs.[11] In fact, making information available about products and who can supply them is a natural application for computer technology. Electronic catalogs allow buyers to gain rapid access to product information, specifications, and pricing. When tied to EDI systems, electronic catalogs allow buyers to quickly identify and place orders for needed items. Many companies have developed their own online electronic catalogs and efforts have also been devoted to developing catalogs containing products from many suppliers, which will allow buyers to compare features, specifications, and prices very rapidly. These tools potentially can bring significant savings in procurement, especially for standard items for which the primary criterion is purchase price.

The Internet and B2B Procurement

The real excitement in procurement related to e-commerce is the development of the Internet as a B2B tool. Even more so than in the business-to-consumer realm, the Internet and the World Wide Web are expected to have a major impact on how businesses interact with one another. As early as 1996, several major organizations, including General Motors and Wal★Mart, announced that suppliers who were not capable of conducting business via the Internet would be eliminated from consideration. Estimates of the future for B2B e-commerce vary even more wildly than business-to-consumer, but at least one respected authority predicts B2B Internet transactions could reach over $1 trillion by 2005.[12]

One advantage of the Internet relative to traditional EDI is that it overcomes some of the technical issues of compatibility of computer systems, which is required in EDI. The Internet itself provides capability for buyers and sellers to exchange files and information easily. General Electric created a "Trading Process Network" that turned a once completely manual process for procuring custom-designed parts into an elec-

---

[11]Doris Kilbane, "E-Catalogs Becoming Standard," *Automatic I.D. News,* August 1999, pp. 19–20.
[12]Reported in *USA Today,* May 10, 2000, p. B-1.

tronic system. The system sends requests for quotation along with drawings and specifications to vendors worldwide. GE reports that the system has reduced acquisition costs significantly and, perhaps more importantly, reduced cycle times by as much as 50 percent.[13]

Another example of how the Internet can transform B2B exchange is seen in the development of e-Chemicals. The company is known as an *infomediary* because it acts as intermediary, providing information between companies. Traditionally, purchasing small quantities of chemicals was extremely difficult both for the buyer and the seller. Chemical processors do not like to deal with numerous small orders, finding it very expensive from sales, marketing, and logistics standpoints. Small quantity purchasers likewise find that dealing with large chemical processors is difficult and costly. While there are industrial distributors in the industry, they are plagued by several problems, including maintaining inventories of a wide variety of chemicals from numerous manufacturers. E-Chemicals offers a solution to these problems via the Internet. It has developed relationships with major processors, which allows it to take orders of small quantities from numerous buyers. As illustrated in Figure 5-4, e-Chemicals takes these small orders, processes them, consolidates them into larger orders for the suppliers, makes arrangements with a third-party logistics provider for pickup and delivery, and conducts the invoicing and collection through an arrangement with a financial institution. Chemical suppliers benefit by no longer dealing with numerous small orders. Buyers benefit by receiving one shipment of items from several suppliers, receiving one invoice, making one payment, and having greater assurance of supply than is typically available from traditional distributors. Although e-Chemicals charges for its services, the cost reductions more than offset this expense. Developments similar to that of e-Chemicals have arisen in numerous industries, including steel, hardware, and farm equipment and supplies. Industry Insight 5-2 describes Farmbid.com, a website at which farmers can buy supplies.

Buying exchanges are another Internet-related development. While some companies have formed their own trading networks for dealing with their suppliers, buying exchanges represent cooperative efforts among companies, frequently competitors, to deal with their common base of suppliers. In the auto industry, General Motors, Ford, and DaimlerChrysler, each of which had initially formed separate trading networks, announced that they are forming a joint online buying exchange.[14] The auto companies will allow their suppliers to view requirements for parts and supplies, look at technical specifications, and even see production schedules. Since the auto manufacturers in many instances deal with common suppliers, these suppliers will be able to better plan their own production and delivery requirements by having access to information concerning all of their customers in one location. It is even considered possible that the buyers may pool some of their requirements for standard parts to achieve greater economies through volume consolidation.

The potential volume of procurement activity through buying exchanges is enormous. Exchanges have been developed in the aircraft parts industry, chemicals, steel building products, food distribution, and even retailing. For example, Sears and Carrefour, two of the world's largest retailers, formed GlobalNetxchange to combine their

[13]Richard Wough and Scott Eliff, "Using the Internet to Achieve Purchasing Improvements at General Electric," *Hospital Material Management Quarterly,* November 1998, pp. 81–83.

[14]Robert Simson, Farn Werner, and Gregory White, "Big Three Carmakers Plan Net Exchange," *The Wall Street Journal,* February 28, 2000, p. A-3.

FIGURE 5-4

E-Chemicals

The e-Chemicals Solution . . .
The Role of an Infomediary

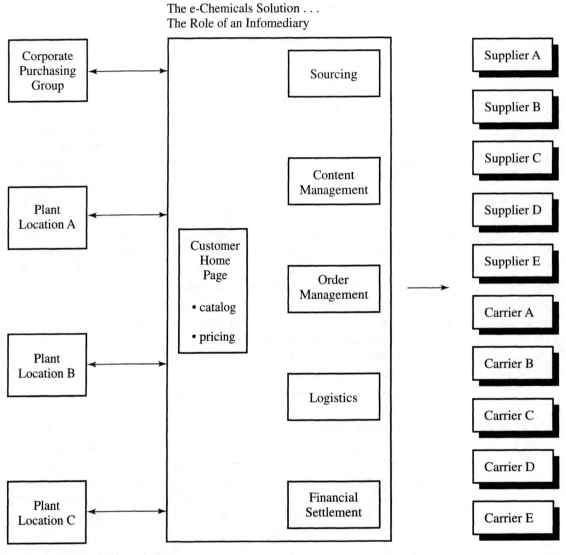

Source: e-Chemicals, Inc. Reprinted with permission.

joint $80 billion in purchases into one online network for dealing with suppliers.[15] Suppliers will be able to view the retailers' sales and inventory levels and better plan their production requirements. The entire procurement process, from request for quotes to purchase orders to invoicing and payment, can be conducted electronically via the website.

While numerous benefits are envisioned for trading exchanges and buying exchanges, there is a potential downside. Many suppliers fear that the exchanges will become a mechanism that ultimately will return procurement to focus strictly on purchase price. If buyers post their requirements and needs on the Web primarily for the purpose of soliciting bids from alternative suppliers, or use the technology to have suppliers enter into an auctioning process, it is feared that many of the advances in

[15]Calmetta Coleman, "Sears, Carrefour Plan Web Supply Exchange," *The Wall Street Journal,* February 29, 2000, p. A-4.

INDUSTRY INSIGHT 5-2 FARMING VIA THE INTERNET

Ted Farnsworth became frustrated as he searched the Internet for farming equipment for his brother-in-law's New York dairy farm. As a result, he has started his own farming website, Farmbid.com. Approximately 90,000 customers have registered to buy and sell seed, chemicals, machinery, and other agricultural products.

Farmbid is one of more than a dozen farming websites that have sprouted in recent months. Some auction cattle, pigs, sheep, and horses; while others sell everything from seed to animal vaccinations to farm insurance. These B2B sites are trying to cash in on the distance and isolation that many rural farmers face. By providing one-stop shopping, the sites hope to get a slice of the lucrative agricultural industry, estimated to be a $1 trillion market by 2004. Online agricultural transactions are expected to account for 12 percent, or $120 billion, in sales over the next 4 years.

The sites are welcome news for farmers, who are facing some of the lowest prices in history for their crops and goods. Farm sites allow customers to comparison shop among different manufacturers and have companies compete for their business. The digital marketplaces can lower prices as companies look to unload excess grain, seed, or equipment at relatively low prices. Farmers have traditionally bought products from catalogs, local dealers, and traveling salesmen. While the current system works, many farmers are restricted in what brand or type of product they can buy and don't always get the best prices.

The sites make money through advertising, transaction fees, or by taking a percentage of each sale executed over the site. Few sites are profitable, and most don't expect to be for at least a year.

Although there's a strong market for B2B farming sites, analysts say there's only room for two or three competitors. The industry is beginning to consolidate. Companies like DuPont and Cargill have strong relationships with farmers and other firms. To succeed, B2B sites need a critical mass of customers. But with only 1.9 million U.S. farms, the pool of available customers is limited.

Gary Carlson, CEO of Rooster.com, a soon-to-be-launched electronic mall, states that his site will be inclusive toward all agricultural companies. It will allow dealers to set up virtual storefronts where they can sell seed, chemicals, and other goods. However, according to Carlson, it will work "very closely" with agriculture dealers that already have established relationships with Cargill, Cenex, and DuPont and help them set up virtual shops.

Farmbid's Farnsworth expects a tough battle. But Farmbid "has advantages, such as having a lot of farmers signed up," he says. "We're building a Web site around the farmer and giving them everything they need," such as auctions, weather, classified, and even farm chat rooms.

The greatest hurdle for all the B2B players is the limited Internet access in rural areas. Few farms are served by high-speed Internet services, such as cable modems or digital subscriber lines (DSL). Most farmers can access dial-up Internet service providers, but often face long-distance charges. This curtails farmers' use of the Net and could limit the revenue of many sites, according to analysts.

Source: Deborah Solomon, "Farm B2Bs Find Fertile Soil on Net," *USA Today,* April 20, 2000, p. 1B.

---

supplier integration and value management will suffer. The future will show whether the result will be positive or negative.

In a supply chain management context, the link between a company and its external suppliers is critical. It provides for the integration of materials and resources from outside the organization into internal operations. Procurement is charged with the responsibility of ensuring that this transition is accomplished as efficiently and as effectively as possible. Much of the concern in procurement is focused on the logistical interface between the organization and its supply base. Ultimately, the purpose of procurement is to integrate material flow in accordance with manufacturing requirements. In the next section, alternative manufacturing strategies are discussed with a focus on their logistical requirements.

Manufacturing

A substantial number of firms in the supply chain are involved in manufacturing products. Whereas almost all business firms are engaged in procurement and market distribution operations, manufacturers add value by converting raw materials into consumer or industrial products. They create value by producing and marketing product/service bundles to either end customers or intermediate members of the supply chain. For example, retailers purchase a wide range of product from varied manufacturers to create an appealing assortment for consumers. This section reviews supply chain structure and strategy from a manufacturing perspective. Similar to the previous section that discussed procurement, the objective is to identify logistics requirements and challenges necessary to integrate and support manufacturing into supply chain operations.

Manufacturing Perspectives[16]

The range of products a firm manufactures evolves from its technological capability and marketing strategy. Firms perfect manufacturing competencies based upon market opportunity and willingness to take innovative risk. At the outset, a manufacturing firm creates or invents a new product assortment as its entry point as a value-added participant in a supply chain. Initial market success serves to define and clarify a firm's competency as perceived by customers and suppliers. A firm initiating manufacturing operations to produce automotive parts will be viewed by trading partners as being distinctly different from one that produces garments. While the products produced are clearly different, the real differentiator between firms is found in competencies related to knowledge, technology, process, and strategy. Once established, a manufacturing firm's image and focus are continuously modified in the eyes of supply chain partners as it conducts business, researches and develops new products, and performs agreed-to value-added services. Thus, the combination of capabilities and competencies that are exhibited by a manufacturing firm are dynamic. In terms of supply chain participation, the combination of products, services, capabilities, and competencies represents a firm's value proposition and provides dimension to its supply chain opportunities. A firm's manufacturing competency is based on **brand power, volume, variety, constraints,** and **leadtime requirements.**

Brand Power
Many manufacturers spend a great deal of promotional money to create brand awareness and acceptance among prospective buyers; as a result, they are typically identified by their product brands. The measure of a customer's purchase preference based on a manufacturer's reputation, product quality, and supply chain capabilities is known as brand power.

Buyers along the supply chain range from end customers to industrial purchasing agents. Under market conditions wherein a brand has high customer awareness, ac-

[16]This section draws upon Steven A. Melnyk and David R. Denzler, *Operations Management: A Value Driven Approach* (Chicago, IL: Richard D. Irwin, 1996).

INDUSTRY INSIGHT 5-3 THIRD-PARTY INNOVATION

Tradeteam is a joint venture of Exel Logistics, along with its parent company NFC Plc., and Bass Brewers to provide a national distribution network service to the U.K. beverage industry.

Tradeteam was developed in response to changing pressures and shifting market conditions in the industry. The beer market in the United Kingdom had been in long-term decline, with pub consumption shrinking at approximately 1 percent per year. Overall, the industry had been suffering from excess capacity and lower margins. On top of this, the government had required brewers to divest themselves of their interest in pubs, a directive with major marketplace implications. Between 1992 and 1999, for example, pub ownership by regional and national brewers declined from 74 percent to 33 percent. The end result was typical of low-growth industries: Brewers were consolidating and repositioning and were in need of a fresh approach to marketing and distribution.

As the United Kingdom's largest provider of brewery distribution services, Exel Logistics had a significant interest in protecting a business that was under pressure from individual brewers and emerging pub ownership groups. Exel's idea was to take over one major brewer's existing distribution infrastructure to achieve the critical mass associated with that company's market share. Leveraging that infrastructure, it would then offer cost-effective logistics services to other beverage suppliers. This concept led to the formation of the Tradeteam joint venture between Exel Logistics and Bass, which already was the industry's low-cost producer.

Tradeteam is now the U.K.'s leading independent logistics provider to the beverage industry. It has annual revenues of $200 million and delivers approximately 280 million gallons of beer and other beverages to more than 27,000 retail customers on behalf of a number of beverage suppliers. Uniquely situated as a multiuser distributor between the consumer and the supplier, Tradeteam has revolutionized the beverage industry supply chain.

Results to date have been encouraging. Tradeteam has enabled the brewers and beverage suppliers to reduce their operating costs, increase revenues through market expansion, and provide superior service levels to their customers. Market share for this innovative joint venture has reached the 40 to 50 percent range. In fact, this represents the largest outsourcing initiative yet undertaken in the United Kingdom.

Source: Anonymous, "One Example of Third-Party Innovation," *Supply Chain Management Review*, Fall 1999, p. 87.

---

ceptance, and preference, manufacturers can be expected to have a great deal of influence. As a general rule, *the stronger a firm's product brand image among buyers, the more leverage the manufacturing organization will have in determining supply chain structure and strategy.* For instance, Deere & Company dominates how farm machinery, as well as lawn and garden products, is sold, distributed, and maintained.

Independent of customer acceptance is the reality that a firm that brands and markets a particular line of products may not, in fact, be engaged in either the actual manufacturing/assembly or in the performance of supportive logistics services. It is common practice for an organization to outsource some or even all manufacturing and logistics operations required to market a specific product. The nature of the manufacturing process, cost, and next destination in the supply chain go a long way to determine the attractiveness of outsourcing. Logistical requirements in terms of inbound materials and finished product distribution are created by the geographical relationship between location of manufacturing operations and those of suppliers and customers. However, the power to determine the range of value-added services, physical product movement requirements, timing, and characteristics of flow along the supply chain is directly related to brand power. As illustrated in Industry Insight 5-3 a third-party supplier can help a firm develop effective brand power.

Volume

Manufacturing processes can be classified in terms of the relationship of cost per unit to volume of output. The traditional perspective is to treat volume in terms of the well-established principle of **economy of scale.** The scale principle defines a relationship wherein the average cost of producing a product declines as its manufacturing volume increases; that is, a product quantity should be increased as long as a per unit increase in volume decreases the average cost per unit manufactured. Economy of scale results from efficiencies generated by specialization of process, workforce, fixed asset utilization, procurement economies, and limited need for process changeover.

Economy of scale is extremely important in manufacturing situations involving high fixed cost machinery to convert raw material into finished products. Typical examples are found in the paper, steel, and refining industries. In fact, some petroleum processing firms have decoupled their refineries from their supply chain marketing structure and positioned them as independent external suppliers. The refineries are then able to sell in the open market to all potential buyers and fully exploit economy-of-scale advantage.

In volume-sensitive industries, high capital investment coupled with high cost of changeover tends to encourage extremely long production runs. In terms of logistical support, two considerations related to volume influence supply chain design. First, supply chain operations must accommodate the number of times a specific product is manufactured during a specific planning period. Such *manufacturing frequency* has a direct impact on both inbound and outbound logistical requirements. Second, the quantity or lot size typically produced during a specific manufacturing run determines the product volume that must be handled and warehoused in a supply chain structure.

Variety

In contrast to manufacturing situations dominated by scale, other production technologies feature flexibility. These manufacturing processes are characterized by relatively frequent product runs and high repetition of small lot sizes. As contrasted to economy of scale, manufacturing processes that feature variety rapidly switch production from one product to another while retaining efficiency are referred to as having **economy of scope.** Scope means that a manufacturing process can use varied combinations of materials, equipment, and labor to produce a variety of different products.

Variety refers to the *range* of product variations that are capable of being manufactured in a given manufacturing process. Such variation may result from the nature of how products are routed throughout a manufacturing plant and/or the use of general as contrasted to specialized equipment. The achievement of economy of scope is also directly related to the speed and cost of changeover from one product to another. In terms of logistical support, high variety translates to relatively small manufacturing lot sizes, flexible material requirements, and a broad range of product outputs. High manufacturing variety directly impacts the type of transportation and warehousing services required to accommodate flexible manufacturing.

Constraints

All manufacturing processes reflect a balance between economy of scale and economy of scope. Volume and variety drive logistical support requirements. Constraints interact with volume and variety to create manufacturing plans. The three primary constraints that influence manufacturing operations are *capacity, equipment,* and *setup/*

changeover. Each of these constraints forces compromise concerning ideal manufacturing operations. Such compromise planned in the context of forecasted sales and planned promotions reconciles into a production plan.

Capacity, as the name implies, is a measure of how much product can be produced per unit of time. Of particular interest is a firm's *demonstrated* capacity of quality production. Whereas a factory, process, or machine may have a *rated* capacity, the relevant measure is a firm's demonstrated ability to reach and maintain a specific level of quality output in a predictable time period. A measure of manufacturing competency is the speed to which a particular process reaches demonstrated capacity given an unexpected change in requirements.[17] Such scalability reflects a combination of manufacturing, procurement, and logistical agility.

Equipment constraints are related to flexibility concerning the use and sequencing of specific machines to perform multiple manufacturing tasks. Clearly the variety a factory can produce is constrained by the range of available equipment and the required sequence of work. However, some manufacturing requirements are more easily accommodated across a family of machines and by using variable work sequences than are others. In many situations, a specific machine or work task tends to constrain or act as a bottleneck to the overall manufacturing process. Likewise, logistical capability to accommodate different patterns of equipment utilization may serve to enhance or constrain flexibility of the manufacturing process. Manufacturing executives devote substantial time and resources to eliminating bottlenecks that serve to constrain operations. The structure for focusing managerial attention is captured in *theory of constraint* methodology.[18]

Setup/changeover constraints are directly related to the earlier discussion concerning variety. Substantial progress has been made in manufacturing management to speed up both process changeover time and the time required to reach demonstrated capacity. Whereas several hours and even days were once required for changeover, today the tasks are being performed in hours. For example, modular-manufacturing units, such as paint sprayers, are being set up and calibrated offline and then being inserted ready to flow into assembly lines. Of course all efforts to increase setup/changeover speed are directly dependent upon logistical support.

Leadtime

Manufacturing **leadtime** is a measure of the elapsed time between release of a work order to the shop floor and the completion of all work necessary to achieve ready-to-ship product status. Any given manufacturing process consumes operational and interoperational time.[19]

Operational time is the combination of setup/changeover and running or actual production time. In any manufacturing situation the greater the amount of total leadtime accounted for by actual production, the inherently more efficient is the conversion process. Efficient operational time must be traded off against the issues discussed earlier concerning volume and variety.

---

[17]Thomas G. Gunn, *21st Century Manufacturing* (Essex Junction, VT: OM NEO, 1992), Chapter 8.

[18]For origins of this logic, see Eliyahu M. Goldratt and J. Cox, *The Goal* (Croton on Hudson, NY: North River Press, 1984); and Eliyahu M. Goldratt and Robert E. Fox, *The Race* (Croton on Hudson, NY: North River Press, 1986).

[19]Steven A. Melnyk and R. T. Christensen, *Back to Basics: Your Guide to Manufacturing Excellence* (Boca Raton, FL: St. Lucie Press, 2000), pp. 15–17.

Manufacturing processes also encounter unexpected losses of time. During periods that a process, line, or machine is idle due to queuing, waiting, breakdown, or failure in logistical support, manufacturing efficiency is negatively impacted. All forms of unexpected delay represent serious bottleneck issues. For example, Melnyk and Christensen estimate that between 75 and 95 percent of all nonproductive delays result from unplanned queuing in manufacturing processes.[20] Needless to say, most manufacturing executives have little or no tolerance for unexpected production delays that result from late or damaged arrival of critical materials or components. Logistical delay on the part of a supplier who provides parts or materials can result in manufacturing failure to meet planned output. A firm's strategic impact is directly impacted by leadtime performance. As a general rule, firms that compress manufacturing leadtimes and control or eliminate unexpected performance variance exhibit greater flexibility to accommodate customer requirements while enjoying low-cost manufacturing.

Logistical operations committed to supporting manufacturing can impact operating efficiency in a variety of ways. The potential benefits of brand power are based on a firm's track record regarding timely performance of customer order-to-delivery commitment. Lot-size efficiencies related to manufacturing frequency and repetition are dependent on reliable logistical support. The decision to produce large manufacturing lot sizes directly creates need for logistical support. Economy of scale drives procurement best practice and average inventory investment across the supply chain. The decision to focus on variety in manufacturing impacts the logistics requirements by adding the complexity of frequent changeover. Logistical performance is also a key variable in managing constraints. Such constraints can be caused or resolved based on the quality and flexibility of logistical support. Finally, logistics is critical to achieving high levels of leadtime performance. In particular, logistical failure can increase manufacturing leadtime by introducing unexpected delays.

The above logistical interfaces, as well as all other factors that impact manufacturing performance predictability, serve to create operational gaps that are resolved by inventory. Inventory stocks occur, in part, when the timing of customer expectation exceeds a firm's, or its suppliers', ability to deliver the correct assortment of products to the right place at the right time. The management of these raw material and finished inventory stocks is a prime responsibility of logistics.

Manufacturing Strategy

The unique nature of each manufacturing process and the market served limit the practical range of alternative strategies. Manufacturing strategic range is constrained by both marketing and technological forces. Prevailing marketing practices serve to ground manufacturing strategy in terms of customer acceptability. Technology drives strategy to a manufacturing model that is competitive. For example, a manufacturer having a process dominated by economy of scale may desire to improve process flexibility. However, significant investment will typically be required to increase frequency and repetition.

Over time, the changing nature of the market and available technology serve to alter a firm's existing strategic posture. Consider, for example, the steel industry, which was long dominated by processes highly dependent on economy of scale. Recent years have witnessed market acceptance of a wide range of new steel-based materials combined with value-added services. The birth of the Steel Service Center has in-

---

[20]Steven A. Melnyk and R. T. Christensen, op. cit., p. 17.

troduced postponement as a way to increase customer accommodation. The nature of basic steel production has also undergone dramatic change. New process methods are being perfected that reduce long-time dependence on high-scale manufacturing processes. The combined impact of these changes in market and process has shifted the strategic posture of steel producers.

Matching Manufacturing Strategy to Market Requirements

In Chapter 3, typical marketing strategies were classified as being mass, segmental and focused, or one-on-one.[21] These strategies are differentiated, in part, in terms of the required degree of product and service accommodation. Mass marketing requires limited product/service differentiation. In contrast, one-on-one marketing strategy builds on unique or customized product/service offerings for each and every customer. The strategic marketing posture of a firm in terms of flexibility and agility to accommodate specific customer requirements is directly related to manufacturing capability. To a significant degree, a firm's manufacturing capability drives the feasible range of effective marketing strategy. For a manufacturing firm to effectively compete, it must be able to integrate manufacturing capability into a meaningful marketing value proposition.

Strategic Alternatives

The most common manufacturing strategies are **make-to-plan (MTP), make-to-order (MTO),** and **assemble-to-order (ATO).** It is also common to refer to MTP as **make-to-stock (MTS).**[22]

As a general rule, MTP strategies are characteristic of industries exploiting economy of scale that results from long production runs. Significant finished goods inventory is typically manufactured in anticipation of future customer requirements. The logistical requirement to support MTP is warehousing capacity to store finished product and to facilitate product assortment for specific customers. When flexible manufacturing is introduced to speed up switchover, the inventory lots produced are typically smaller in quantity. However, warehouses are still required for temporary storage and to facilitate product assortment.

In contrast, MTO manufacturing strategies seek to manufacture to customer specification. While MTO may not be as limited as the traditional job shop, exact quantities and configurations are produced in relatively small quantities. Logistical capacity may be required for temporary storage and to achieve outbound transportation consolidation, but most product produced in a MTO environment is shipped direct to customers.

In ATO situations, base products and components are manufactured in anticipation of future customer orders; however, the products are not fully assembled or customized until a customer's order is received. Such final assembly reflects implementation of the principle of manufacturing or form postponement.[23] The need for logistical capacity is critical in ATO operations. In fact, an increasing amount of ATO product finalization is being performed in distribution warehouses. The attractiveness of an ATO manufacturing strategy is that it has the potential to combine some facets of economy of scale typical of MTP with a degree of MTO flexibility. Full implementation of an ATO strategy requires that warehouse operations be integrated in the process to perform customizing and assembly operations. Industry Insight 5-4 illustrates the importance of logistically supporting an original equipment manufacturer.

---

[21]Chapter 3, p. 69.

[22]This general classification draws upon Robert H. Hayes and Gary P. Pisano, "Beyond World Class: The New Manufacturing Strategy," *Harvard Business Review,* January/February, 1994, pp. 77–86.

[23]See Chapter 1, p. 18.

INDUSTRY INSIGHT 5-4 CRITICAL PARTS DELIVERED WITHIN HOURS

Speed is increasingly a key supply chain differentiator, especially in the supply of critical parts, where customers expect delivery within hours, not days.

Two primary forces are driving development of this service niche. First, original equipment manufacturers have warranty contracts with their end users, which frequently include protections against downtime losses. Second, many parts supply operations are fragmented as companies generally have multiple service territories and different service providers for each. Faced with pressures to reduce inventory levels and associated investments, OEMs and other companies need greater visibility, not only to parts availability, but also to pipeline contents—a difficult challenge when responsibilities are spread across numerous networks.

"OEMs are always looking to improve their service to their end users, and having a service parts network with a high parts availability and rapid response time to their field engineers enables them to improve system uptime," says Scott Collins, VP of service parts logistics for Sonic Air, a division of United Parcel Service. Throughout the last decade Sonic Air, in conjunction with UPS, has focused on designing a service network to specifically meet the needs of these OEMs. "We give the OEMs a single point of contact, we use our own network, and we have systems connectivity across that entire network," states Collins.

Sonic owns a central parts distribution center with more than 1 million square feet of space within 3 miles of the UPS air hub in Louisville, an arrangement that enables Sonic to provide late-night processing of orders with delivery guaranteed by 10:30 A.M. the next day, or even earlier if customers use premium services. From that distribution center, Sonic replenishes its network of more than 400 field support bank locations worldwide. With the exception of a few dedicated sites, the field support banks are multiclient facilities.

Orders can come in to Sonic from customers by EDI, Internet, fax, or via one of several call centers Sonic operates, as late as 1 A.M. for next-day availability. Orders are routed to the appropriate dispatcher, who then alerts the respective branch operations that the particular part has to be pulled and dispatched for delivery. Parts can be sent overnight directly to certified engineers (CEs) in the field. Another option is a hold-for-pickup service at any of the 1,430 UPS service counters designated as sites where CEs can snag the parts as early as 7:30 A.M.

The Sonic strategy is to locate field support banks close to the end-user population of their customers to minimize the time from order entry to delivery. "Our network runs 24×7, and right now we can serve 68 percent of the U.S. business population within an hour, 88 percent in two hours, and 99 percent in four hours," says Collins.

Sonic also uses its Louisville distribution center to provide repair and refurbishment services, maintaining a staff of more than 300 technicians to provide rapid turnaround of equipment such as laptop computers, hard drives, monitors, and telecommunications devices, including the programming of cell phones.

Getronics (formerly Wang Getronics) is currently in the ramp-up phase of a new service program. Sonic technicians now perform 1,100 repairs a month for Getronics on a wide array of computer parts, peripherals, and point-of-sale equipment and Sonic expects to see that number rise from 6,000 to 8,000 as the program comes fully online.

Sonic also provides Getronics with end-of-runway central warehousing, which improves Getronics' efficiency and reduces some of the fixed and variable costs associated with the parts operation. "The Sonic/UPS relationship has allowed Getronics to enhance our overall logistics services to our customers by consolidating our freight services—ground, air, and next-flight-out, warehousing, and repair—in one central facility," says Richard Fogarty, VP of service delivery for Getronics. "This allows us to take advantage of freight savings and enables us to reduce our investments in parts by cutting the cycle time for returning defective parts to a serviceable condition. Getronics can also offer a higher level of logistics consulting services to our customers by using the Sonic nationwide network of parts distribution centers, which provide four-hour parts delivery in major business areas for our client base."

Sonic is reconfiguring its information systems. "By the first quarter of next year, we are going to have a fully integrated service parts system that ties together order entry, dispatch, order management, repair, inventory management, billing, and financials," says Collins. An inventory management system interconnecting the network will help identify which parts to store at particular locations, based on the frequency of failures experienced by the end-user population. "Hopefully, this visibility across the entire network will enable customers to do a better job planning and thus be able to reduce the total cost of the inventory in the pipeline," he adds.

Sonic provides much of this information on the Web. Using a browser, customers can pull tracking information on parts shipments and confirm deliveries, giving them visibility of a part from order entry through to delivery. "On the reverse side, where we have recovery operations for monitors and hard drives and laptops, the customer can track the reverse flow of those units through the pipeline and check the status of a particular repair as it moves through the shop floor in Louisville," says Collins.

Source: Kurt C. Hoffman, "With Critical Parts, Delivery is Counted in Hours, Not Days," *Global Logistics & Supply Chain Strategies,* June 2000, pp. 58–60, 62.

Total Cost of Manufacturing

The marketing and manufacturing strategies of a firm drive logistical service requirements. For example, MTO manufacturing strategies typically require less finished goods inventory than MTP and ATO strategies. However, MTO strategies typically require component inventory support and may result in high-cost market distribution. In light of such cost trade-offs, the design of a logistics support system should be based on the **Total Cost of Manufacturing (TCM).**

Total cost of manufacturing consists of production/procurement, inventory/ warehousing, and transportation. All of the above costs are impacted by manufacturing strategy. As such, TCM represents the foundation for formulating a market distribution strategy. Figure 5-5 represents a generalized model of the TCM *per unit* ranging across strategic alternatives from MTO to ATO to MTP. Naturally, exact cost relationships will depend upon specifics related to each business situation. The design objective is to identify the manufacturing strategy that best fits the marketing opportunity confronted.

FIGURE 5-5

Total cost of manufacturing

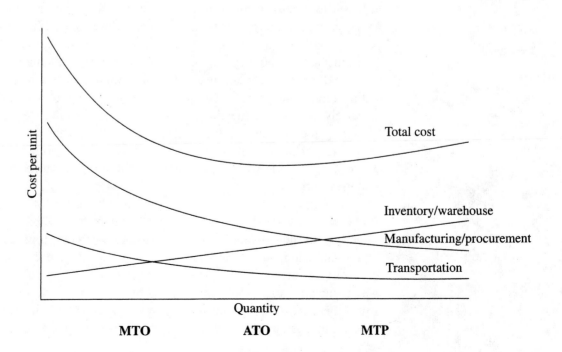

285

In Figure 5-5, the cost of manufacturing and procurement declines as quantity increases, reflecting economy of scale associated with MTP. Inventory and warehousing costs increase, reflecting the impact of larger manufacturing lot sizes. Transportation cost per unit decreases as a result of shipment consolidation. In contrast, MTO strategies reflect high per unit manufacturing and procurement costs which are, in part, offset by lower inventory and warehousing costs. In the MTO strategy, transportation cost per unit is higher, reflecting small shipment and/or premium transportation. The value of Figure 5-5 is to generalize relationships and visualize important trade-offs. The TCM results from functional integration of manufacturing, procurement, and logistics. From a perspective of integrated management it is important for manufacturing firms to design a supply chain strategy that achieves lowest total cost of manufacturing across the entire process.

Logistical Interfaces

The efficient and effective coordination of manufacturing strategy with the procurement of materials and components ultimately relies on logistics. Resource inputs must be procured and made available when needed for manufacturing operations. Whether the manufacturing strategy is MTO, ATO, or MTP, logistics links the supplier base with manufacturing processes. Clearly, the more seamless the interface, the better the opportunity is for achieving lowest cost of ownership and, ultimately, lowest total cost of manufacturing. Such operations only emerge when there is high-level supplier integration in both operations and in design. Just-in-Time, Materials Requirements Planning, and Design for Logistics represent three approaches to achieving desired coordination.

Just-in-Time

Just-in-Time (JIT) techniques have received considerable attention and discussion in recent years in every functional area related to supply chain management. Sometimes referred to as just-in-time production, often called just-in-time purchasing, and frequently referred to as just-in-time delivery, the goal of JIT is to time-phase activities so that purchased materials and components arrive at the manufacturing or assembly point just at the time they are required for the transformation process. Ideally, raw material and work-in-process inventories are minimized as a result of reducing or eliminating reserve stocks. The key to JIT operations is that demand for components and materials depends on the finalized production schedule. Requirements can be determined by focusing on the finished product being manufactured. Once the production schedule is established, just-in-time arrival of components and materials can be planned to coincide with those requirements, resulting in reduced handling and minimal inventories.

The implications of JIT are numerous. Obviously, it is necessary to deal with suppliers who have high and consistent levels of quality, as their components will go directly into the finished product. Absolutely reliable logistical performance is required and eliminates, or at least reduces, the need for buffer stocks of materials. JIT generally requires more frequent deliveries of smaller quantities of purchased inputs, which may require modification of inbound transportation. Clearly, to make JIT work, there must be very close cooperation and communication between a manufacturer's purchasing organization and suppliers. In JIT operations, companies attempt to gain the benefits of backward vertical integration but avoid the formal tie of ownership. They achieve many of the same ends through coordination and process integration with suppliers.

Originally, JIT was applied to manufacturing processes characterized as MTP, since the effective functioning of the system is dependent upon a finalized production schedule. However, as manufacturing strategies have evolved with more emphasis on flexibility, reduced lot-size production quantities, and quick changeovers, JIT concepts have evolved to accommodate ATO and MTO manufacturing as well. In many situations, lead suppliers are used by manufacturers to sort, segregate, and sequence materials as they flow into assembly operations. The goal is to reduce handling and facilitate continuous JIT.

Some organizations, seeing the benefits of JIT systems and recognizing the benefits of supplier integration, have gone so far as to bring their suppliers' personnel into their production plants. The supplier personnel are empowered to use the customer's purchase orders, have full access to production schedules, and have responsibility for scheduling arrival of materials. Originally introduced by the Bose Corporation, the term **JIT II** has been applied to these efforts to reduce leadtimes and cost.

Requirements Planning

In complex manufacturing organizations a process known as **Materials Requirements Planning (MRP)** is frequently used to aid in the interface between purchaser and supplier. MRP systems attempt to gain benefits similar to those of JIT, minimize inventory, maintain high utilization of manufacturing capacity, and coordinate delivery with procurement and manufacturing activities. Implementation of MRP systems requires a high level of technological sophistication. Software applications such as advanced planning and scheduling systems have been developed to deal with the complexity of information required, such as leadtimes, quantities on-hand and on-order, and machine capacities for literally thousands of materials across multiple manufacturing locations.

Design for Logistics

The logistics interface with procurement and manufacturing, as well as with engineering and marketing, can be greatly enhanced by incorporating a concept known as **Design For Logistics** into the early phases of product development. Recall that the objectives of JIT and MRP are to minimize inventories and handling, with materials and components being ready for assembly or transformation as they are needed. How a product is designed and design of the components and materials themselves can have a significant impact on this process. In particular, product packaging and transportation requirements need to be incorporated into the design process. For example, if inbound components are packaged in containers with a standard quantity of 50 but only 30 components are needed to meet production requirements, then waste will occur. Additionally, product and component design must have consideration of transportation and internal materials handling methods to ensure that cost-efficient, damage-free logistics performance can be achieved. Similar design considerations must be made for the finished product itself.

Table 5-1 summarizes the critical relationships between market distribution, manufacturing/procurement, and logistical requirements. The framework is useful in positioning how logistical requirements flow from the marketing and manufacturing strategy.

Table 5-1   Strategic Integration Framework

Market Drivers	Manufacturing Capabilities	Procurement	Logistics
Focused:	**Make-to-Order:**	B2B	**Direct Fulfillment:**
One-on-one strategies	Maximum variety	Discrete quantities	Time postponement
Unique product/service offerings	Unique configuration	Supplier VMI	Small shipment
Response-based	Flexible manufacturing		
	High variety		**Form and Time Postponement:**
Segemental:	**Assemble-to-Order:**	B2B	
Limited size	Wide variety	JIT	Warehouse ATO
Customer groups	Quick changeover		Combination direct and warehouse fulfillment
Differentiated products	Product customization		
Mixed response and anticipatory	High variety and volume		Consolidated shipment
Mass Marketing:	**Make-to-Plan:**	B2B	**Warehouse Fulfillment:**
Anticipatory	Long product runs	Commodity	Full stocking strategy
Little product differentiation	Focus low cost	Auction	Assortment mixing
	High volume/low variety	E-procurement	Volume shipment

Summary

Managing logistics in the supply chain requires an interface between logistics, procurement, and manufacturing strategies.

A primary concern of procurement and manufacturing is product quality, a prerequisite for any firm that desires to be a global competitor. In fact, product quality has several different dimensions. It can mean reliability, durability, product performance, and conformance to engineered specifications. From a customer's perspective it may also include aspects of product features, aesthetics, or serviceability. World-class companies have implemented Total Quality Management programs in all their activities in their efforts to achieve quality from their customers' perspective.

Procurement in an organization is charged with responsibility for obtaining the inputs required to support manufacturing and operation. The focus is multidimensional, attempting to maintain continuous supply, minimize leadtimes from suppliers and inventory of materials and components, and develop suppliers capable of helping the organization achieve these goals. Ultimately, modern procurement professionals focus on the Total Cost of Ownership of acquired resources, not just the purchase price of those inputs. This requires that they consider carefully the trade-offs among purchase price, supplier services and logistical capability, quality of materials, and how the materials affect costs over the life cycle of the product into which they are incorporated.

Procurement strategies today involve consolidation of the volumes purchased into a smaller, more reliable, number of suppliers. They include efforts to integrate supplier and buyer operations to achieve better and lower-cost logistics performance. Supplier integration in new product design represents another strategy to reduce total ownership costs.

In Chapters 4 and 5, strategic considerations related to market distribution, procurement, and manufacturing have been discussed in terms of their combined impact on logistical requirements. A number of important trade-offs were identified. We have seen that isolated optimization of any specific functional area without considering cross-functional impact will not likely result in maximum performance. Operational integration is the focus of Chapter 6.

Challenge Questions

1. Using television receivers as an example, how could three different brands be perceived by different consumers as being the best quality brand in the market?

2. Why does the contemporary view of procurement as a strategic activity differ from the more traditional view of "purchasing"?

3. How can strategic procurement contribute to the quality of products produced by a manufacturing organization?

4. Explain the rationale underlying volume consolidation. What are the risks associated with using a single supplier for an item?

5. How does lowest TCO differ from lowest purchase price?

6. What is the underlying rationale that explains why firms should segment their purchase requirements?

7. Explain how constraints in manufacturing are interrelated with a company's decisions regarding volume and variety.

8. Why would a company's costs of manufacturing and procurement tend to increase as the firm changes from an MTP to an MTO strategy? Why would inventory costs tend to decrease?

9. How does a firm's marketing strategy impact its decisions regarding the appropriate manufacturing strategy?

10. Explain how logistics performance is crucial to JIT.

6 OPERATIONAL INTEGRATION

The dominant theme of supply chain collaboration is the advancement of operational integration. The benefits attainable from collaboration are directly related to capturing efficiencies between functions within an enterprise as well as across enterprises that constitute a domestic or international supply chain. This chapter focuses on the challenges of integrative management by examining why integration creates value and by detailing the challenges of collaboration at the firm, domestic, and global levels of supply chain operations.

Why Integration Creates Value

The basic benefits and challenges of integrated management were introduced in Chapter 1. To further explain the importance of integrated management, it is useful to understand that customers have at least three perspectives of value.

The traditional perspective of value is **economic value.** Economic value builds on economy of scale in operations as the source of efficiency. Economy of scale seeks to fully utilize fixed overhead to achieve the lowest, total landed cost. The focus of economic value is efficiency of product/service creation. Economic value is all about doing things as well as possible. The customer take-away of economic value is *high quality at a low price.*

A second value perspective is **market value.** Market value is about presenting an attractive assortment of products at the right time and place to realize effectiveness. Market value focuses on achieving economy of scope in product/service presentation. The creation of multimerchant shopping malls, large-scale mass-merchandising retail stores and multivendor e-commerce fulfillment operations are all initiatives to achieve market value. The customer's take-away in terms of market value is *convenient product/ service assortment and choice.*

Realization of both economic and market value is important to customers. However, increasingly firms are recognizing that business success also depends upon a third perspective of value referred to as **relevancy.** Relevancy involves customization of value-adding services, over and above product and positioning that make a real difference to customers. Relevancy value means the right products and services, as reflected by market value, at the right price, as reflected by economic value, modified, sequenced, synchronized, and otherwise positioned in a manner that creates valuable segmental diversity. In a consumer context, for example, relevancy means transforming ingredients into ready-to-eat meals. In general merchandise retailing, relevancy means transforming products into fashionable apparel. In manufacturing and assembly, relevancy is achieved by integrating specific components into products to increase functionality desired by a specific customer. The customer's take-away in terms of relevancy is a unique *product/service bundle.*

The simultaneous achievement of economic value, market value, and relevancy value requires total integration of the overall business process and is known as the integrative management value proposition, as illustrated in Table 6-1.

Industry Insight 6-1 illustrates how the value proposition of traditional supermarkets is being challenged by alternative retail formats that offer greater value to customers.

TABLE 6-1 Integrative Mangement Value Proposition

Economic Value	Market Value	Relevancy Value
• Lowest total cost	• Attractive assortment	• Customization
• Economy-of-scale efficiency	• Economy-of-scope effectiveness	• Segmental diversity
• Product/service creation	• Product/service presentation	• Product/service positioning
Procurement/Manufacturing Strategy	**Market/Distribution Strategy**	**Supply Chain Strategy**

Industry Insight 6-1 Threats to Traditional Retail Food Supply Chains

Conventional supermarkets seek to simultaneously satisfy value drivers across many consumers. This initial supermarket strategy of trying to be all things to all shoppers may be its eventual downfall. Several retail formats now provide alternatives that focus on specific consumer value drivers, creating greater value.

A major and growing competitive threat to traditional supermarkets is meals prepared away from home. This segment represented 54 percent of the dollars spent for food in the U.S. for 2000 and is projected to enjoy the most future growth in food consumer expenditure. Heat-and-eat foods are available at a wide range of outlets, including supermarkets, or are available for home delivery. Restaurants are selling as many meals for carryout as they are for on-site consumption. This segment focuses on providing time and form value, giving customers what they want, when and where they want it.

The rapidly growing mass merchants pose the second threat to traditional supermarkets. Merely 5 years ago, Wal★Mart was not considered a player in food distribution. Today it is the second largest retailer of grocery products in the United States, outsized only by the merger of Albertson's and American Stores. Of course, Wal★Mart's entry into retail food stores is not unique. Many other mass merchandisers are following a similar strategy of focusing on a limited assortment of grocery products sold at the same stores with numerous nonfood products.

The convenience store format presents a third threat to the prominence of traditional supermarkets by creating value of time and place. Today, a growing variety of meal solutions are sold at convenience stores. These stores also provide a quick way to obtain select items, thereby avoiding a prolonged trip to the supermarket.

A final alternative to traditional food supply chains is home delivery. As early as the 1930s, A&P used bicycle delivery boys to deliver groceries direct to customer homes all over Manhattan. Grocery home delivery sales are not currently a serious volume threat to the conventional supermarket; nevertheless, all of the essential technology is in place to make home delivery a viable alternative format. Industry observers predict home delivery variations to range from 10 to 20 percent of total ingredient purchases in the first decade of the new millennium. The economics of this alternative are becoming more competitive. A total cost comparison of supermarkets and home delivery must quantify the "convenience cost" associated with shopping time and the reclamation cost of clearing unsalable product from the marketplace. The industry's $2 billion annual expenditure for reclamation is virtually nonexistent in the home delivery format. As long as the product is delivered within its expiration date, it will be consumed. Home delivery creates value through time and place.

Other competitive arrangements—such as vending machines—are also chipping away at the traditional supermarket's share of the consumer food dollar. All alternative formats build on the fact that the traditional supermarkets' custom of creating value through price and assortment does not offer sufficient *relevancy*. The success of these alternatives pressures supermarkets to reinvent themselves and streamline the supply chain. Selected companies are using efficient replenishment to counter alternative formats.

Source: Donald J. Bowersox et al., "Threats to Traditional Retail Food Supply Chains," *Supply Chain Management* (Washington, DC: Food Market Institute, 1999), pp. 59–60.

Systems Concept and Analysis

The **systems concept** is an analytical framework that seeks *total* integration of components essential to achieving stated objectives. The components of a logistics system are typically called functions. The logistical functions, as discussed in Chapter 2, were identified as order processing, inventory, transportation, warehousing, materials handling and packaging, and facility network design. **Systems analysis,** applied to logistics, seeks to quantify trade-offs between these five functions. The goal of systems analysis methodology is to create a whole or integrated effort, which is greater than the sum of the individual parts or functions. Such integration creates a *synergistic* interrelationship between functions in pursuit of higher overall achievement. In systems terminology, functional excellence is defined in terms of contributions a function makes to the overall process as contrasted to isolated performance in a specific area. Until the last few decades of the 20th century, process integration was generally neglected by managers who were trained to pursue functional excellence. Rapid advancement in information technology has increased the ability to identify and understand enhancement trade-offs to better facilitate logistics and supply chain initiatives.

When analyzed from a process perspective, the goal is balanced performance between functional areas within an enterprise and across the supply chain. For example, manufacturing economics are typically minimized by long production runs and low procurement costs. In contrast, integrated process management raises questions concerning the total cost and customer impact of such practices. A traditional financial orientation typically seeks to minimize inventories. While inventory should always be maintained as low as practical, arbitrary reductions below a level required to facilitate integrated operations typically increase total cost. Marketing's basic desire is to have finished goods inventory available in local markets. Inventory stocked in close geographical proximity to customers is believed to facilitate sales. Such anticipatory deployment of inventory is risky and may be in direct conflict with the least total cost process. In fact, e-commerce connectivity and fulfillment strategies are driving entirely different inventory stocking and fulfillment strategies.

In systems analysis, attention is focused on the interaction between components. Each component contributes a specific functionality essential to achieving system objectives. To illustrate, consider a high-fidelity stereo system. Many components are integrated for the single purpose of sound reproduction. The speakers, transistors, amplifier, and other components only have purpose if they contribute to quality sound. However, failure of any component will cause the output of the stereo system to fail.

Some principles can be stated concerning general systems theory. First, the performance of the total system or process is of singular importance. Components are only important if they enhance total system performance. For example, if the stereo system can achieve superior sound with two speakers, then it is unnecessary to include additional speakers. Second, individual components need not have best or optimum design. Emphasis is on the integrated relationship between components that constitute the system. Transistors, as an example, are hidden from view inside the stereo system. As such, they do not need to be aesthetically pleasing. To spend money and time designing an appealing transistor is not necessary in terms of system integration. Third, a functional relationship, called *trade-off,* exists between components that serve to stimulate or hinder total system performance. Suppose a trade-off allows a lower-quality amplifier to be used if an extra transistor is added to the system. The cost of the extra transistor must be justified in terms of savings in amplifier cost. Finally, components linked together as an integrated system may produce end results greater than possible through individual performance. In fact, the desired result may be unattainable without such integrated performance. A stereo system will technically operate without speakers, but audible sound is impossible.

The principles of systems analysis are basic and logically consistent. An integrated process with cross-functional integration can be expected to achieve greater results than one deficient in coordinated performance. In logistical systems, synergistic performance is targeted customer service at the lowest possible total cost. Although logical and indisputable in concept, effective application of systems integration is operationally difficult. In the final analysis, it matters little how much a firm spends to perform any specific function, such as transportation, as long as overall performance goals are realized at the lowest total cost expenditure.

Logistical Integration Objectives

To achieve logistical integration, six operational objectives must be simultaneously achieved: (1) responsiveness, (2) variance reduction, (3) inventory reduction, (4) shipment consolidation, (5) quality, and (6) life cycle support. The relative importance of each is directly related to a firm's logistical strategy.

Responsiveness

Responsiveness is concerned with a firm's ability to satisfy customer requirements in a timely manner. As noted repeatedly, information technology is facilitating response-based strategies that permit operational commitment to be postponed to the last possible time, followed by accelerated delivery. The implementation of response-based strategies serves to reduce inventories committed or deployed in anticipation of customer requirements. Responsiveness, as developed in Chapter 1, serves to shift operational emphasis from forecasting future requirements to accommodating customers on a rapid order-to-shipment basis. In a response-based system, inventory is not deployed until a customer commits. To support such commitment, a firm must have inventory availability and timely delivery once a customer order is received.

Variance Reduction

All operating areas of a logistical system are susceptible to variance. Variance results from failure to perform any expected facet of logistical operations. For example, delay in customer order processing, an unexpected disruption in manufacturing, goods arriving damaged at a customer's location, and/or failure to deliver at the right location on time all create unplanned variance in the order-to-delivery cycle. A common solution to safeguard against the detrimental variance is to use inventory safety stocks to buffer operations. It is also common to use premium transportation to overcome unexpected variance that delays planned delivery. Such practices, given their associated high cost, can be minimized by using information technology to maintain positive logistics control. To the extent that variance is minimized, logistical productivity will improve. Thus, **variance reduction,** the elimination of system disruptions, is one basic objective of integrated logistics management.

Inventory Reduction

To achieve the objective of **inventory reduction,** an integrated logistics system must control asset commitment and turn velocity. Asset commitment is the financial value of deployed inventory. Turn velocity reflects the rate at which inventory is replenished over time. High turn rates, coupled with desired inventory availability, mean assets devoted to inventory are being efficiently and effectively utilized; that is, overall assets committed to support an integrated operation are reduced.

It is important to keep in mind that inventory can and does facilitate desirable benefits. Inventories are critical to achieving economies of scale in manufacturing and procurement. The objective is to reduce and manage inventory to the lowest possible level while simultaneously achieving performance objectives.

Shipment Consolidation

One of the most significant logistical costs is transportation. Approximately 60 cents of each logistics dollar is expended for transportation. Transportation cost is directly related to the type of product, size of shipment, and movement distance. Many logistical systems that feature direct fulfillment depend on high-speed, small shipment transportation, which is costly. A system objective is to achieve **shipment consolidation** in an effort to reduce transportation cost. As a general rule, the larger a shipment and the longer the distance it is transported, the lower is the cost per unit. Consolidation requires innovative programs to combine small shipments for timely consolidated movement. Such programs require multifirm coordination because they transcend the supply chain. Successful e-commerce fulfillment direct-to-consumers requires innovative ways to achieve effective consolidation. Industry Insight 6-2 discusses logistics challenges of e-commerce to illustrate the importance of effective consolidation.

Quality

A fundamental operational objective is continuous **quality** improvement. Total Quality Management (TQM) is a major initiative throughout most facets of industry. If a product becomes defective or if service promises are not kept, little if any value can be added by the logistics process. Logistical costs, once expended, cannot be reversed or recovered. In fact, when product quality fails after customer delivery and replacement is necessary, logistical costs rapidly accumulate. In addition to the initial distribution cost, products must be returned and replaced. Such unplanned movements typically cost more than original distribution. For this reason, commitment to zero-defect order-to-delivery performance is a major goal of leading-edge logistics.

Logistics itself is performed under challenging conditions. The difficulty of achieving zero-defect logistics is magnified by the fact that logistical operations typically are performed across a vast geographical area during all times of day and night without direct supervision.

Life Cycle Support

The final integration design objective is **life cycle support.** Few items are sold without some guarantee that the product will perform as advertised. In some situations, the initial value-added inventory flow to customers must be reversed. Product return is common as a result of increasingly rigid quality standards, product expiration dating, and responsibility for hazardous consequences. Reverse logistics also results from the increasing number of laws encouraging recycling of beverage containers and packaging materials. The significant point concerning reverse logistics is the need to maintain maximum control when a potential health liability exists, such as a contaminated product. The operational requirements for reverse logistics range from lowest total cost, such as returning bottles for recycling, to maximum control in situations involving defective products. Firms that design efficient reverse logistics often are able to reclaim value by reducing the quantity of products that might otherwise be scrapped or sold at

Industry Insight 6-2 Delivering the E-Commerce Purchase

E-commerce companies that will survive growth will be those that achieve the best logistical support systems and the most dependable delivery. These goals are easily described, but not so easily accomplished.

Many e-commerce people fail to understand that the actual process of getting the product from factory to home remains the same, whether the customer has ordered through a retail store, an 800 number, a direct-mail catalog, or an e-commerce website.

The customer receiving the package doesn't know or care whether it originated at a warehouse, factory, or retail store but does care whether it arrives on time, is in good condition, and is the product ordered. The customer doesn't care whether it arrives via FedEx, UPS, USPS, or pony express as long as quality is maintained.

Home delivery is highly labor-intensive and most communities in the United States face a significant labor shortage. As a result, it is increasingly difficult to find a delivery service that shares the company's dedication to customer satisfaction. For some products, such as major appliances and furniture, proper delivery service includes final assembly; hooking up to water, gas, or electric lines; final quality check; and removal of the shipping carton. Finding a carrier with the skills and experience to do these jobs is not a simple task.

One potential solution is to subcontract the logistics function to a growing number of service providers who have targeted Internet vendors as a major new marketing opportunity. The best third-party providers understand the problems of home delivery; they have performed similar functions for other firms with similar operations. They have the trained staff, equipment, and software to handle the fulfillment process.

Consider these criteria when evaluating potential third-party providers:

1. Order acceptance and processing: Does the potential vendor have a state-of-the-art order acceptance system with satisfied users?
2. Assembly/packaging/value-added activities: Does the vendor have experience with home delivery and setup?
3. Credit card verification: If some deliveries are COD, can the vendor handle both credit cards and cash?
4. Returns handling: Is there a system in place to handle returns?

Sometimes a perfect delivery may be unacceptable to a customer. When the product is in the home, it may not have the color, feel, or look that was expected. Consequently, the customer wants to return it. This reverse logistics process is the least recognized and yet possibly the greatest challenge that faces the e-commerce industry.

Catalog sales companies have always experienced a higher return rate than other retailers, and it is probable that e-commerce will follow a similar pattern. Key planning questions include:

- What is the anticipated volume of returned goods?
- Are returned goods labeled or bar coded? If so, where is the coding?
- What are the returned goods procedures and the conditions of return goods authorization?

Reverse logistics is more complicated than normal outbound distribution; however, there are third-party specialists with substantial experience in the processing of customer returns. For example, one third-party reverse logistics company handles all of the customer returns for a major retail chain. When a customer returns an item to the store, the store sends it to a reclamation center in Indiana. At the center, each returned item goes through a grading process to determine whether the item can be locally repaired, repackaged, and returned to the vendor, or whether it must be destroyed. In some cases, substandard product is segregated and sold at a discount in an overseas market.

With the explosive growth of Internet vendors, there is a substantial opportunity for logistics specialists to provide support that these fast growth entrepreneurs desperately need.

Source: Alex Metz, "Where the Rubber Meets the Road . . . Delivering Your E-Commerce Purchase," *Hunt's Profiles in Logistics Management,* March/April 2000.

a discount. Sound integrative strategy cannot be formulated without careful review of reverse logistical requirements.

For some products, such as copying equipment, primary profit lies in the sale of supplies and aftermarket service to maintain the product. The importance of life cycle support is significantly different in situations wherein the majority of profits are achieved in the aftermarket. For firms marketing consumer durables or industrial equipment, the commitment to life cycle support constitutes a versatile and demanding marketing opportunity as well as one of the largest costs of logistical operations. Life cycle support requires *cradle-to-cradle* logistics. Cradle-to-cradle logistical support goes beyond reverse logistics and recycling to include the possibility of aftermarket service, product recall, and product disposal.

Enterprise Integration

The basic level of integration is the internal operations of individual firms. To inexperienced managers, the integration of functions under the managerial control of one enterprise might appear easy to achieve. In actual practice, some of the most challenging integration issues involve cross-functional trade-offs within a specific company. As noted earlier in the discussion of systems analysis, functional management is deeply embedded as best practice within most firms.

Internal Integration Barriers

Managers do not attempt to integrate operations in a vacuum. It is important to recognize barriers that serve to inhibit process integration. Barriers to internal integration find their origins in traditional functional practices related to organization, measurement and reward systems, inventory leverage, information technology, and knowledge hoarding.

Organization

The organization structure of a business can serve to stifle cross-functional processes. Most business organizations seek to align authority and responsibility based on functional work. In essence, both structure and financial budget closely follow work responsibility. The traditional practice has been to group all persons involved in performing specific work into functional departments such as inventory control, warehousing operations, or transportation. Each of these organizations has an operational responsibility, which is reflected in its functional goals.

To illustrate, transportation and inventory have traditionally been managed by separate organizational units. Created in isolation, goals for managing transportation and inventory can be contradictory. Transportation decisions aimed at reducing freight cost require shipment consolidation, but transportation consolidation typically causes inventory to increase.

Popular terms to describe such function myopia are a *sandbox* or *silo* mentality. The traditional managerial belief was that functional excellence would automatically equate to superior performance. In integrated process management, it matters little how much is spent to perform a specific function as long as process performance goals are achieved at the lowest total cost expenditure. Successful integration of processes, such as logistics, requires that managers look beyond their organizational structure and achieve cross-functional coordination. This may or may not require organizational change. Regardless, successful process integration requires significant traditional management behavioral modification.

Measurement and Reward Systems

Traditional measurement and reward systems serve to make cross-functional coordination difficult. Measurement systems typically mirror organization structure. Most reward systems are based on functional achievement. To facilitate internal process integration, new measures, increasingly called *balanced scorecards,* must be developed. Managers must be encouraged to view specific functions as contributing to a process rather than a stand-alone performance. A function may, at times, have to absorb increased costs for the sake of achieving lower total process cost. Unless a measurement and reward system is in place that does not penalize managers who absorb cost, integration will remain more theory than practice.

Inventory Leverage

It is a proven fact that inventory can be leveraged to facilitate functional performance. The traditional position is to maintain sufficient inventory to protect against demand and operational uncertainty. Stockpiling both materials and finished inventory leverages maximum manufacturing economy of scale. Such economy of scale can result in low per unit cost of manufacturing. Forward commitment of inventory to local markets can leverage sales. While such practices create functional benefits, they may be achieved at a cost, which is not typically allocated to that function. The integrative challenge is the cost/benefit balance of such leveraging and risks associated with potential inventory obsolescence.

Infocratic Structure

Information technology is a key enabler of process integration. A significant problem results from the fact that structure and availability of information have traditionally been based on functional organization requirements. As a result, information is typically formatted in terms of functional accountability. This early practice in formatting information has resulted in what is referred to as *infocratic structure.* The content and flow of available information follow long-standing functional organization. When managers attempt to reorganize to enable the cross-functional processes, the infocratic structure serves as an invisible force to maintain traditional functional practice. The impact of infocratic structure is one of the driving reasons why Enterprise Resource Systems (ERP) have great general management appeal. The infocratic structure also helps explain why ERP implementations are so difficult.[1]

Knowledge Hoarding

In most business situations, knowledge is power, so unwillingness to share and a general lack of understanding concerning how to best share knowledge are not uncommon. But by reinforcing functional specialization and by encouraging a workforce composed of experts, organizations inherently doom process integration. Consider, for example, the case when an experienced employee retires or for some other reason departs a firm. Replacement personnel must be given sufficient time to learn, but if information is concealed, all the time in the world may not help bring the new employee up to speed.

A more serious situation occurs when managers fail or are unable to develop procedures and systems for transferring cross-functional knowledge. Much process work

---

[1]See Chapter 8 for a detailed discussion of Enterprise Resource Systems.

FIGURE 6-1

The great divide: The challenge of managing across functional boundaries

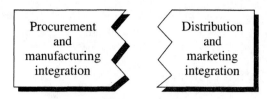

is shared between jobs and is not restricted to a specific functional area, so transfer of knowledge and experience is vital.

The Great Divide

Clearly many obstacles make functional integration difficult. To some extent, the five barriers discussed above have contributed to a common situation in business referred to as the great divide. The great divide reflects an organizational condition wherein achieved integration is partial but not complete on an end-to-end process basis, as illustrated in Figure 6-1. The most common situation is when a firm achieves only partial integration of distribution/marketing on the outbound side of the enterprise and procurement/manufacturing on the inbound side. The paradox is that firms seem to be capable of achieving highly integrated operations with suppliers from whom they purchase materials and components. Firms also join operations in market distribution to service end consumers. Such initiatives reflect cross-functional integration that, in fact, extends beyond a single business enterprise. Despite these accomplishments, managers report considerable difficulty in linking these two types of external collaboration into an enterprisewide integrative process. In short, managers seem to achieve more successful integration with external business partners than they do with managers and departments within their own firm.[2]

The phenomenon of the great divide is interesting and challenging. The fact that such operational discontinuity is common among firms in many different industries supports generalization. First, integration appears to be easier with groups external to a firm, such as suppliers and distribution agents, at least in part because the balance of power is typically clear and integrative objectives such as sales and costs can be quantified. Second, senior managers in most organizations do not have a sufficiently clear vision of internal process requirements and related measures to drive across-the-enterprise integration. Finally, the barriers outlined earlier serve to render end-to-end integration a difficult, if not impossible, end state in most traditional organizations.

Several authors writing on the challenges of implementing integrative processes have concluded that the typical traditional organization cannot accommodate sufficient change to transform from a functional to process orientation.[3] This group advocates that successful implementation of integrative process management requires a major structural and philosophical shift in traditional command and control practice. Some go so far as to advocate the need to fully disintegrate traditional organization structure.

Most observers of current logistics practice feel significant inroads into improved process performance are being realized as a result of modifying and repositioning functional capabilities. The key is to align, focus, and measure functional performance in terms of process contribution. At stake in closing the great divide is commitment to

---

[2]Donald J. Bowersox, David J. Closs, and Theodore P. Stank, *21st Century Logistics: Making Supply Chain Integration a Reality* (Oak Brook, IL: Council of Logistics Management, 1999).

[3]Christopher Meyer and David Power, "Enterprise Disintegration: The Storm Before the Calm," *Commentary* (Lexington, MA: Barker and Sloane, 1999).

a single strategy, facilitated by well-defined processes, relevant measurement, common forecasting and planning, and a supportive reward system.

How Much Integration Is Enough?

The critical question concerning a firm's ability to participate in supply chain collaboration is, How much internal integration within a participating firm is necessary or desirable to achieve across-the-supply-chain collaborative success? This is a difficult question to answer. Any assessment must acknowledge two facts.

First, few, if any, existing supply chain arrangements are, in fact, end-to-end integrations. The more common examples reflect integration of cross-organizational processes involving either procurement and manufacturing or marketing and distribution. In other words, the separation of these cross-organizational processes serves to disrupt a firm's continuous supply chain operations. However, even limited integration appears to create value for the participating organizations. Therefore, one could conclude that limited collaboration offers sufficient benefits to justify supply chain initiatives.

Second, the number one reason given by executives to explain the limited scope of and high failure rate of such supply chain collaborations is the inability of participating partners to perform as promised. For example, collaborations fail because a firm's manufacturing cannot or does not produce the products marketing promised to customers. Likewise, collaborations fail because marketing does not provide manufacturers with timely and detailed promotional plans of market distribution partners. Of course collaborations also fail because logistics is not able to perform to the expectations of manufacturing and/or marketing. This second assessment point serves to support the insight that comprehensive across-the-supply-chain collaborations will not occur until participating firms achieve high levels of credible internal integration. In short, long-term supply chains' success will require that participating firms resolve their internal great divides.

Domestic Supply Chain Integration

Extending an enterprise across the supply chain requires a vision concerning how the firms involved in the collaboration will structure and manage their combined or joint affairs. The following discussion develops interorganizational behavior guidelines.

Supply Chain Competitiveness

A supply chain perspective shifts the relevant business model from a loosely linked group of independent businesses to a multienterprise coordinated effort focused on channel efficiency improvement and increased competitiveness. While not all supply chain collaborative arrangements involve logistics, most do. In such arrangements, attention shifts from firm-based logistical management to the coordination of supply chain performance. Two beliefs facilitate this drive for efficiency and competitiveness.

First, the fundamental belief is that cooperative behavior will reduce risk and greatly improve efficiency of the overall logistical process. To achieve a high degree of cooperation it is necessary for supply chain participants to share strategic information. Such information sharing must not be limited to transaction data. Equally or more important is a willingness to share information concerning future plans so participating firms can jointly develop the best way to satisfy customer requirements. Collaborative information is essential to positioning and coordinating participating firms to jointly do the right things faster and more efficiently.

The second belief is the opportunity to eliminate waste and duplicate effort. As a result of collaboration, substantial inventory deployed in a traditional channel can be eliminated. Supply chain collaboration can also eliminate or reduce risk associated with inventory speculation. Significant inventory can be eliminated. One grocery industry study concluded the average dry grocery product requires 104 days to reach the supermarket checkout counter from the time it is packaged by a food processor.[4] The average inventory in the health care industry ranges between 12 and 18 months' supply.[5] The notion of supply chain rationalization is *not that inventory is bad* and should be totally eliminated; rather, inventory deployment should be driven by economic and service necessities and not tradition and anticipatory practices.

In the mass-merchandise industries, retailers like Wal★Mart, K-Mart, J.C. Penney, Target, and Walgreens are facilitating supply chain arrangements aimed at improved competitiveness. Using a combination of internal resources and collaboration with suppliers, these firms have positioned their logistical competency as a core business strategy. Their record in terms of retail growth and profitability speaks for itself.

Several manufacturers are facilitating supply chain collaborations in such diverse industries as chemicals, textiles, building supplies, and household tools. Firms such as DuPont, Levi-Strauss and Company, Owens-Corning Fiberglass, and Black & Decker are implementing revolutionary new strategies to improve the value processes of their specific supply chains.

At the wholesale level, drug suppliers such as McKesson and Bergen Brunswig have moved from near extinction to dominant suppliers in their industry. Food wholesalers and cooperatives such as Sysco, Spartan Stores, Fleming, and SuperValu are revolutionizing traditional logistics practices in their industries. Similar developments can be observed in the paper and supplies industry by firms such as Unisource and ResourceNet International. Likewise, Ace in the hardware business and W.W. Grainger in industrial supplies have revolutionized conventional logistics practice in their respective industries.

This diverse list of firms that have increased supply chain competitiveness exhibit several similarities. First, their collaborative practices are technology driven. Second, their business solutions achieve competitive superiority. Finally, most initiatives combine the experience and talents of key supply chain participants blended with a combination of third-party service providers. At the heart of several of the firms highlighted is a solid commitment to creating and maintaining a unique supply chain culture. Such cultures are forged on a fundamental understanding of risk, power, and leadership.

Risk, Power, and Leadership

Dependency is a primary driver of supply chain solidarity. To the degree that participating enterprises acknowledge mutual dependency, the potential exists to develop collaborative relationships. Dependency drives a willingness to plan functional integration, share key information, and participate in joint operations. The concepts of

---

[4]"Efficient Consumer Response: Enhancing Value in the Grocery Industry," Kurt Salmon Associates, Inc., New York, NY, January 1993.

[5]"Efficient Healthcare Consumer Response," CSC Consulting, Inc., Cleveland, Ohio, November 1996.

risk, power, and *leadership* are essential to understanding acknowledged dependency and how it makes supply chain integration work.

Risk

Enterprises that participate in supply chain arrangements must acknowledge they have responsibility for performing specific roles. They must also believe that their business will be better off in the long run as a result of collaboration. Each enterprise must be positioned to specialize in an operational area or function based on its unique core competency. The driving force behind supply chain integration is to leverage these core competencies.

As a general rule, a supply chain member whose competency is highly specialized will assume comparatively less risk with respect to overall performance. Conversely, firms that have a great deal at stake will be positioned as the prime facilitators and will confront the most risk in the supply chain arrangement. Firms with unique specialization, more often than not, will participate in multiple supply chains. For example, a wholesaler incurs risk as a result of stocking products for a specific manufacturer. The traditional practice among wholesalers is to hedge such risk by offering customers an assortment of many different manufacturers' products, thereby reducing reliance on any supplier.

In contrast, a manufacturer with a limited product line may be totally captive to a few supply chain arrangements. In essence, the manufacturer may be betting the business that the collaboration will be successful. For manufacturers, commitment to supply chain arrangements can be risky business. The disproportionate risk among channel members is of primary importance because it structures dependency relationships and determines how the collaboration will be managed. Some participants have a deeper dependence on supply chain success than others. Therefore, participants with the most risk can be expected to assume active roles and shoulder greater responsibility for facilitating collaboration.

Power

In a practical sense, the prerogative and even the obligation to spearhead collaboration rests with the supply chain participant who enjoys the greatest relative power. In many situations, that participant will also be the firm having the greatest risk. Over the last decade significant power shifts have occurred in business. One of the most significant is the increased power of retailers, which resulted from four somewhat independent developments.

First, the general trend of retail consolidation translated into fewer but more dominant retailers with more extensive market coverage. Second, the proliferation of point-of-sale data, frequent shopper programs, and credit card use provide retailers with easy access to vital market information. As a result, consumer trends can be rapidly identified and accommodated. Many mass merchants even maintain in-store computers and continuous satellite transmission to keep merchandise buyers fully involved in developing market trends. A third factor favoring retailers is the increasing difficulty and high cost manufacturers confront in developing new brands. The fact is that many private label products owned by retailers have greater category penetration than so-called national brands. For example, the Gap and The Limited almost exclusively distribute private branded merchandise. Finally, as noted earlier, the process of logistical replenishment has shifted to a more response-based posture. The exact timing and sophisticated orchestration of a high-velocity market-paced logistics system are ideally driven from the point of consumer purchase. When consumers purchase products, the final or ultimate value of the supply chain is a reality.

While the above noted forces are a modern reality, not all forces are shifting power forward in the supply chain. One major countervailing force has been the rapid development of Internet-based purchase sites that allow direct consumer involvement with manufacturers. In the not so distant past, marketing channels were structured to accommodate product line. Today's scrambled merchandising environments result in products increasingly being cross-channel distributed to accommodate specific markets that are volatile and rapidly changing. New retail formats, both Web-based and traditional brick and mortar, are blurring channel arrangements. The result is that manufacturers confront new supply chain arrangements for distributing their products.

As a substitute for full reliance on traditional brand power, selected manufacturers have reengineered their operations to become the dominant supplier for selected consumer product or categories. The movement toward category dominance allows manufacturers to offer greater value to their prospective supply chain partners. In addition to superior brands at competitive prices, dominant category position can involve several key operational capabilities that increase a firm's attractiveness as a supply chain participant.

The drive to establish dominant category positioning involves the following capabilities: (1) willingness to develop collaborative arrangements; (2) manufacturing and logistical flexibility to accommodate a wide range of supply chain requirements; (3) rationalization and supplier integration to assure accommodation of frequent schedule changes; (4) segmental or custom marketing and merchandise programs; (5) availability of information connectivity to accommodate cross-organizational operations; and (6) short, responsive, flexible, and reliable order cycles to facilitate rapid replenishment of customer requirements. Of course it goes without saying that the ideal supplier will perform at or below average industry logistics cost.

Because both manufacturers and distributors have repositioned traditional operations, the potential exists to leverage collaboration. *As a general rule, powerful firms tend to link together in the development of supply chain arrangements.* For the arrangement to be successful the dominant parties to the cooperative arrangement need to agree to a leadership model.

Leadership

Just as individual organizations need leaders, so do supply chains. At the present stage of supply chain maturity no definitive generalization can be made concerning how firms gain leadership responsibility. In many situations, specific firms are thrust into a leadership position purely as a result of their size, economic power, customer patronage, or comprehensive product portfolio. In other arrangements, for less obvious reasons, there is a clear presence of leadership on the part of one enterprise, which is acknowledged in the form of mutual dependency and respect on the part of other participating supply chain members. In other situations leadership appears to gravitate to the firm that initiates the relationship.

The essence of channel leadership is to orchestrate the core competencies of participating firms into integrated performance. Constructive leadership is necessary to stimulate and reward collaborative behavior. Maintaining an overall supply chain perspective is particularly important. The leadership role involves creating function spin-off and absorption agreements between businesses participating in the arrangement. The role also requires problem-solving negotiation and mediation of risk and reward sharing. Such fusion between participating firms can be facilitated by the supply chain integrative framework.

FIGURE 6-2

Supply chain flows

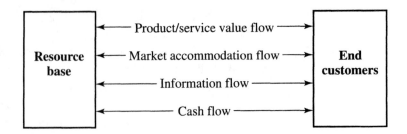

Supply Chain Integrative Framework[6]

A supply chain integrative framework is required to identify the range and continuity to achieve comprehensive collaboration. Such a framework requires that capabilities and competencies essential to integrating supply chain logistics are identified and implemented. The creation of value related to supply chain integration is best achieved by simultaneous orchestration of the four critical flows shown in Figure 6-2: product/service, market accommodation, information, and cash.

The product/service value flow represents the value-added movement of products and services from the raw material source to the end customers. Product value increases as it flows along the supply chain as a result of physical modification, packaging, market proximity, customization, service support, and related activities that enhance end-consumer desirability of the product.

While the product/service flow generally moves from the resource base to end customers, as noted earlier, supply chain arrangements must also accommodate critical reverse flows such as product recalls, reclamation, and recycling. The market accommodation flow provides a structure to achieve postsales service administration. Market accommodation also involves information exchange concerning sales patterns and product usage essential for supply chain planning. Examples are product customization requirements, point-of-sale (POS) data, end-customer consumption, and warehouse releases. This information provides supply chain members with channel visibility concerning the timing and location of product consumption. Planning and operations can be better synchronized when all participants share a common understanding of demand and consumption patterns.

The information flow is bidirectional exchange of transactional data, inventory status, and strategic plans between supply chain participants. Typical examples of this aspect of collaboration are forecasts, promotional plans, purchase orders, order acknowledgments, shipping and inventory information, invoices, payments, and replenishment requirements. Information exchange initiates, controls, and records the product/service value flow. Historically paper-based, an increasing amount of the information flow is now being exchanged via EDI and Web-based connectivity.

Cash typically flows in the reverse direction of value-added activities. However, in arrangements involving promotion and rebate, cash flows to facilitate product and service movement. Cash flow velocity and asset utilization are critical to superior supply chain performance.

Naturally, these four flows must occur between channel participants even when the supply chain is not integrated. However, situations characterized by low coordination and integration between supply chain participants typically result in delay, redun-

---

[6]Donald J. Bowersox, David J. Closs, and Theodore P. Stank, op. cit.

FIGURE 6-3

Supply chain framework

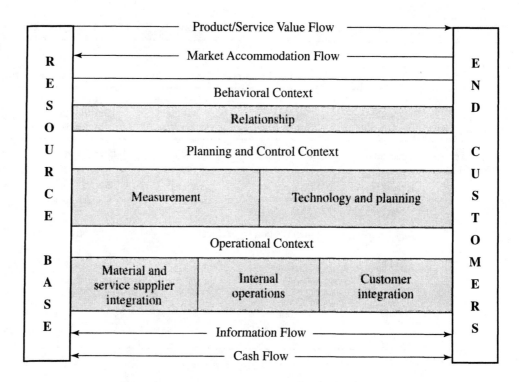

dancy, and inefficiency. To facilitate effective and efficient supply chain flows, competencies and their supporting capabilities must be integrated.

Framework Constructs

The supply chain integrative framework illustrated in Figure 6-3 encompasses a broad range of capabilities and competencies. The framework serves to facilitate operations into a supply chain context by integrating basic work, functions, capabilities, and competencies.

A job or *basic work,* such as order picking or truck driving, is the most visible part of the logistical operations. Jobs are often industry- or firm-specific in content; however, they are usually grouped into organizational units to facilitate control. For example, all the jobs related to warehousing are often grouped. Another common grouping is to organize all jobs related to transport into a transportation department. These functional groupings are significant because they are highly visible elements of an organization. Departments have traditionally been the focal point for financial budgeting, performance measurement, and operational control. Functional work arrangements constitute the drivers of logistical best practice. It is the functions or drivers that combine to create value. The critical shift in operational thinking is to view functional excellence in terms of process performance that enhances *overall* supply chain integration.

To achieve integration, functional value should be focused in terms of universal capabilities. A **capability** is the knowledge and achievement level essential to developing integrated performance. Capabilities relate to *why work is being performed* as contrasted to a functional perspective concerning *how it is performed*. The capability reflects the value contribution of the work. Inherent in a capability is the application of integrative principles that allow multiple functions to be synchronized into value-creating competencies. Whereas jobs and functions may be highly relevant to specific industries and work situations, capabilities are universal. Capabilities span the supply

TABLE 6-2   Supply Chain Context, Competencies, and Supportive Capabilities

Competencies	Operational Context			Planning and Control Context		Behavioral Context
	Customer Integration	**Internal Integration**	**Material/Service Supplier Integration**	**Technology and Planning Integration**	**Measurement Integration**	**Relationship Integration**
Supportive Capabilities	Segmental focus	Cross-functional unification	Strategic alignment	Information management	Functional assessment	Role specificity
	Relevancy	Standardization	Operational fusion	Internal communication	Activity-based and total cost methodology	Guidelines
	Responsiveness	Simplification	Financial linkage	Connectivity	Comprehensive metrics	Information sharing
	Flexibility	Compliance	Supplier management	Collaborative forecasting and planning	Financial impact	Gain/risk sharing
		Structural adaptation				

chain and are equally applicable to suppliers, manufacturers, wholesalers/distributors, and across the full range of retail formats. Capabilities also transcend industries, nations, and even cultural boundaries. Furthermore, they are observable and most importantly measurable within firms of all sizes. Research has firmly established that capabilities reflecting best logistics practice are to some degree observable in all firms that participate in a supply chain.

Examples of capabilities include the ability to (1) identify and accommodate the needs of specific customers; (2) work with supply chain partners to achieve integrated operations; (3) effectively share operating and planning information between supply chain partners; (4) measure and understand overall supply chain performance; and (5) share benefits and risks.

The fusing of capabilities results in universal **competencies.** Table 6-2 details the capabilities related to each of the six integrative competencies grouped in terms of their supply chain context. The operational context includes traditional processes related to procurement, production, and market distribution. The planning and control context incorporates information technology and planning systems, as well as measurement competency. The behavioral context relates to how a firm manages internal and external relationships among supply chain entities.

The Operational Context

Operations involve the processes that facilitate order fulfillment and replenishment across the supply chain. To achieve leading performance in an operational context, firms must be customer-focused, must achieve interorganizational coordination, and must excel in functional and process performance.

Customer integration builds on the philosophies and activities that develop intimacy and is the competency that builds lasting competitive advantage. Firms have always paid attention to the needs of customers but only recently have begun to identify and consider their differences in terms of capable operational segmentation. Any firm seeking supply chain integration must also demonstrate strong commitment to the supportive capabilities of relevancy, responsiveness, and flexibility.

Internal integration focuses on the joint activities and processes within a firm that coordinate functions related to procurement, manufacture, and market distribution. Many firms have attempted to integrate internal functionality but, as discussed earlier, anecdotal and quantitative evidence strongly indicates there are significant gaps. Managers often report more success in coordinating with customers than with their own manufacturing, logistical, and marketing operations. The capabilities that support internal integration are cross-functional unification, standardization, simplification, compliance, and structural adaptation.

Supplier integration focuses on capabilities that create operational linkages with material and service providing supply chain partners. While the customer is the overriding focal point or supply chain driver, overall success also will depend on strategic alignment, operational fusion, financial linkage, and supplier management. Competency in supplier integration results from performing the capabilities seamlessly in internal work processes. Firms that desire to excel must blend their operating processes with those of supply partners to meet increasingly broad and demanding customer expectations.

It is not insignificant that the thirteen capabilities that support customer, internal, and supplier integration can be identified, quantified, and organizationally learned.

The Planning and Control Context

Operational excellence must be supported by integrated planning and measurement capabilities. This involves joining technology across the supply chain to monitor, control, and facilitate overall supply chain performance.

Planning and control integration concerns the design, application, and coordination of information to enhance purchasing, manufacturing, customer order fulfillment, and resource planning. This competency includes database access to enable sharing of appropriate information among supply chain participants. It also concerns transaction systems to initiate and process replenishment and customer orders. In addition to information management, it is essential that capabilities related to internal communication, connectivity, and collaboration be developed.

Measurement integration is the ability to monitor and benchmark functional and process performance, both within the firm and across the supply chain. Because each firm is unique, the collaborative effort must define, operationalize, and monitor standard or common measures. Competency in measurement requires the capabilities of functional assessment and activity-based methodologies. Comprehensive metrics and financials impact assessment.

The Behavioral Context

Effective relationship management is the final competency essential in supply chain engagements. Successful implementation of supply chain strategy rests on the quality of the basic business relationship between partners. In general, managers are far more experienced in competition than they are in cooperation.

Whereas guidelines exist for the development of meaningful and distinctive supply chain relationships, no two situations are identical. No shortcuts or substitutes exist for the detailed commitment necessary to build and develop successful long-term relationships. In dealing with customers, suppliers, and service providers, firms must specify roles, define guidelines, share information, share risk and gains, resolve conflict, and, when necessary, be able to dissolve an unproductive arrangement. The managerial skill sets required for successful supply chain integration require development of an interorganizational culture. This is particularly true since the dynamic environment in which firms compete requires regular review of assumptions, processes, and measures to

Industry Insight 6-3 The Eight I's to Creating Successful We's

The characteristics of effective intercompany relationships challenge many decades of Western economic and managerial assumptions. For example, most Westerners assume that modern industrial companies are run most effectively by professional managers operating within limited, contractual Western obligations. And most Westerners assume that any person with the requisite knowledge, skills, and talents can be a manager in the modern corporation. Although smaller companies, family businesses, and companies that are operating in developing countries have retained "premodern" characteristics, the "rational" model has been considered the ideal to which all organizations would eventually conform.

Intercompany relationships are different. They seem to work best when they are more family-like and less rational. Obligations are more diffuse, the scope for collaboration is more open, understanding grows between specific individuals, communication is frequent and intensive, and the interpersonal context is rich. The best intercompany relationships are frequently messy and emotional, involving feelings like chemistry or trust. And they should not be entered into lightly. Only relationships with full commitment on all sides endure long enough to create value for the partners.

Indeed, the best organizational relationships, like the best marriages, are true partnerships that tend to meet certain criteria:

Individual Excellence. Both partners are strong and have something of value to contribute to the relationship. Their motives for entering into the relationship are positive (to pursue future opportunities), not negative (to mask weaknesses or escape a difficult situation).

Importance. The relationship fits major strategic objectives of the partners, so they want to make it work. Partners have long-term goals in which the relationship plays a key role.

Interdependence. The partners need each other. They have complementary assets and skills. Neither can accomplish its goals apart from the other.

Investment. The partners invest in each other (for example, through equity swaps, cross-ownership, or mutual board service) to demonstrate their respective stakes in the relationship and each other. They show tangible signs of long-term commitment by devoting financial and other resources to the relationship.

Information. Communication is reasonably open. Partners share information required to make the relationship work, including their objectives and goals, technical data, and knowledge of conflicts, trouble spots, or changing situations.

Integration. The partners develop linkages and shared ways of operating so they can work together smoothly. They build broad connections between many people at many organizational levels. Partners become both teachers and learners.

Institutionalization. The relationship is given a formal status, with clear responsibilities and decision processes. It extends beyond the particular people who formed it, and it cannot be broken on a whim.

Integrity. The partners behave toward each other in honorable ways that justify and enhance mutual trust. They do not abuse the information they gain, nor do they undermine each other.

Source: Rosabeth Moss Kanter, "Collaborative Advantage: The Art of Alliances," *Harvard Business Review,* July/August 1994, p. 100.

---

assure those relationships remain relevant. Industry Insight 6-3 summarizes research that identified the *Eight I's* that are essential to achieving a supply chain *We.* Tables 6-3 and 6–4 summarize success factors and common obstacles directly related to supply chain integration.

Finally, ample evidence suggests that managers must plan for the ultimate dismantling or renovation of supply chains. While some arrangements may encounter a natural death as a result of losing momentum, others may persevere to the point that they no longer embody leading edge practice. Thus, like most managerial concerns, supply chain integration is a dynamic situation that must be continuously re-evaluated.

TABLE 6-3   Factors Increasing Likelihood of Supply Chain Relationship Success

Retailers	Manufacturers
• High level of cooperation	• Information sharing
• Similarity of goals/objectives	• Recognition of mutual benefits
• Clear communications	• Controlled implementation
• Senior management support	• Joint task force
• Control of inventory	• Commitment/resource dedication
	• Benefits realization

Source: Reprinted by permission of Accenture Consulting.

TABLE 6-4   Common Obstacles Confronted When Creating Supply Chain Relationships

Retailers	Manufacturers
• Low-volume stockkeeping units (SKUs)	• Lack of communication
• Resistance of manufacturers to change	• Trust level
• Information systems	• Noncompatible systems
• Noncompatible data formats	• Understanding of technical issues
	• Resistance of customers to change
	• Readiness of retailers

Source: Reprinted by permission of Accenture Consulting.

Integration and Logistical Competency

Three points are significant concerning supply chain logistical competency. First, when an overall integrated process becomes one of the most admired and differentiating proficiencies between supply chains, it has the potential to become the strategic cornerstone. Logistical core competency is common in today's competitive environment.

Second, from an academic viewpoint, the abstraction of logistics from function to capability to competency in a supply chain context forms the constructs of a viable theory. The identification of capabilities offers the first level of generalization. The fusing of capabilities into universal competencies serves to blend the specific discipline of logistics into the sum of the business. The positioning of logistics as a core competency expands the value generation of supply chain integration.

Third, logistics is the operationally based process across the supply chain that must be truly integrative for the supply chain to provide overall customer value.

Global Supply Chain Integration

Whereas an effective logistics system is important for domestic supply chain integration, it is absolutely *essential* for successful global manufacturing and marketing. Domestic logistics focuses on performing value-added services to support supply chain integration in a somewhat controllable environment. Global logistics must accommodate operations in a variety of different national, political, and economic settings while also dealing with increased uncertainties associated with the distance, demand, diversity, and documentation of international commerce.

The operating challenges of global logistics systems vary significantly within different operating regions of the world. The North American logistics challenge is one of open geography with extensive land-based transportation and limited need for cross-border documentation. The European logistician, in contrast, is confronted by relatively compact geography involving numerous political, cultural, regulatory, and language situations. The Pacific Rim logistical challenge is island-based, requiring extensive water or air shipment to transcend vast distances. These different perspectives require firms that have global operations to develop and maintain a wide variety of capabilities and expertise. Industry Insight 6-4 illustrates the complexity of introducing change in a global context.

In the past, an enterprise could survive by operating with a unique North American, European, or Pacific Rim business strategy. While regionalization remains viable for some firms, those which desire to grow and prosper are facing the challenges of globalization. Strategic business initiatives must change as a firm and its supply chain become progressively more globalized.

Logistics in a Global Economy

Global operations increase logistics cost and complexity. Estimated 1997 logistics cost for industrialized nations exceeded $5 trillion, or 13.4 percent of estimated global Gross Domestic Product (GDP). Table 6-5 lists GDP and estimated logistics cost by country. In terms of complexity global operations, in contrast to domestic, are characterized by increased uncertainty and decreased ability to control. Uncertainty results from greater distances, longer lead times, and decreased market knowledge. Decreased ability to control results from the extensive use of international service firms coupled with potential government intervention in such areas as customs requirements and trade restrictions.

These unique challenges complicate development of an efficient and effective global supply chain strategy. Fortunately, there are forces that both drive and facilitate globalization and necessitate borderless logistics operations.

Stages of International Development

The continuum of global trade perspectives ranges from *export/import* to *local presence* to the concept of a *stateless enterprise*. The following discussion compares conceptual and managerial implications of strategic development.

Export/Import: A National Perspective

The initial stage of international trade is characterized by exporting and importing. A participating organization typically is focused on internal operations and views international transactions in terms of what they will do for domestic business. Typically, when firms are committed to an export/import strategy they use service providers to conduct and manage operations in other countries.

A national export/import business orientation influences logistical decisions in three ways. First, sourcing and resource choices are influenced by artificial constraints. These constraints are typically in the form of use restrictions, local content laws, or price surcharges. A **use restriction** is a limitation, usually government imposed, that restricts the level of import sales or purchase. For example, the enterprise

Industry Insight 6-4 Virtual Europe

Because of the complexity, it took a team of KPMG consultants 2.5 years to successfully develop and implement centralized Customs clearance in the European Union (EU). They used a virtual warehousing strategy supported by the European Commission and individual national Customs authorities.

Initially, the pilot targeted Belgium and Finland. Now other countries are giving the idea serious attention. The hope is it's a first step toward a reformed, centralized, and simplified Customs accounting and revenue collection process within the EU. Multinational companies operating in Europe can expect to see improved compliance and greater efficiency from the audit-based Customs reporting systems. The ultimate goal—a single European authorization—is within reach.

In practice, this virtual warehouse exists only on paper (or the Web), but it earns the same duty determent benefits as a Customs warehouse. Just as important, it lets all goods imported into the EU clear Customs at a single point. That means all Customs activities can be conducted with a single Customs authority even though goods may be received in several countries. If the company meets the requirements for constant stock control, goods can be stored in a number of locations.

Information systems replace physical Customs control over stock inventories. It's all done with computers, but those computer data must measure up to EU Customs standards. Most importantly, they must accurately tally the taxes due each EU member country from participating companies.

It's been legal to pick your Customs authority since 1985, but figuring out how to do it was the challenge. In fact, figuring out how to slice the money collected was the main reason the initial pilot project took so long. "We worked with Belgium, Finland, Germany, and UK to reach agreement for the pilot projects," says Terry Shaw, partner with KPMG in charge of trades and customer practice in Europe. Shaw also was the partner responsible for the KPMG virtual warehouse team. "We went live in May 1998—it has taken all that time to work it out."

Cooperation of participating countries is fundamental and there are still some issues, says Shaw. In the short term, he insists companies will need an intermediary. It is absolutely essential that participants have a good stock tracking system and a clear understanding of current Customs procedures. Centralized stock control is critical to acceptance of centralized reporting to a single Customs authority.

Shaw claims the virtual warehouse uses a versatile reporting system so it can customize different aspects of Customs reporting for various scenarios. A company might export, then reimport product which could be entitled to re-enter duty-free. For example, a wheel manufacturer in Europe exports wheels to a U.S. automotive manufacturer, then reimports the car to several countries in Europe. They might qualify for relief from the full Customs duty for the wheel.

To make this intricate system work, data have to be forwarded in the right format to be used by the Customs authority. Goods arrive physically in two or three countries. When they're ready for free circulation, the main controller is notified. This triggers a notice to Customs and the goods are freed to move.

The virtual warehouse concept does not eliminate the need for visual inspection, however. Customs will always have the right to inspect all goods to control smuggling, regardless of where goods are stored or cleared.

If successful, the virtual warehouse will grant new freedom to U.S. companies who now may be restricted as to which ports they can use to funnel goods through and distribute from.

Source: Anonymous (within article written by Helen Richardson), "Virtual Europe," *Transportation & Distribution*, March 2000, p. 42.

TABLE 6-5   Sizing 1997 Global Logistics Expenditures ($U.S. in Billions)

Region	Country	GDP	Logistics ($)	Logistics (%GDP)
North America	Canada	658	$ 80	12.1%
	Mexico	695	106	15.3
	United States	8,083	849	10.5
	Total	9,436	1,035	11.0
Europe	Belgium/Lux.	240	27	11.4
	Denmark	123	16	12.9
	France	1,320	158	12.0
	Germany	1,740	228	13.1
	Greece	137	17	12.6
	Ireland	60	8	14.0
	Italy	1,240	149	12.0
	Netherlands	344	41	11.9
	Portugal	150	19	12.9
	Spain	642	94	14.7
	United Kingdom	1,242	125	10.1
	Total	7,238	884	12.2
Pacific Rim	PRC	4,250	718	16.9
	India	1,534	236	15.4
	Hong Kong	175	24	13.7
	Japan	3,080	351	11.4
	Korea	631	78	12.3
	Singapore	85	12	13.9
	Taiwan	308	40	13.1
	Total	10,063	1,459	14.5
South America	Brazil	1,040	156	15.0
	Venezuela	185	24	12.8
	Argentina	348	45	13.0
	Total	1,573	225	14.3
Remaining Other Countries		9,690	1,492	15.4
TOTAL		38,000	$5,095	13.4%

Sources: Donald J. Bowersox, David J. Closs, Theodore P. Stank, *21st Century Logistics: Making Supply Chain Integration a Reality* (Oak Brook, IL: The Council of Logistics Management, 1999); and Donald J. Bowersox and Roger J. Calantone, "Executive Insights: Global Logistics," *Journal of International Marketing* 6, no. 4 (1998), pp. 83–93.

may require that internal divisions be used for material sources even though prices or quality are not competitive. **Local content laws** specify the proportion of a product that must be sourced within the local economy. **Price surcharges** involve higher charges for foreign-sourced product imposed by governments to maintain the viability of local suppliers. In combination, use restrictions and price surcharges limit management's ability to select what otherwise would be the preferred supplier.

Second, logistics to support export/import operations increases planning complexity. A fundamental logistics objective is smooth product flow in a manner that facilitates efficient capacity utilization. Barriers resulting from government intervention make it difficult to achieve this objective.

Third, an export/import perspective attempts to extend domestic logistics systems and operating practices to global origins and destinations. While a national perspective simplifies matters at a policy level, it increases operational complexity since exceptions are numerous. Local managers must accommodate exceptions while remaining within corporate policy and procedure guidelines. As a result, local logistics management must accommodate cultural, language, employment, and political environments without full support and understanding of corporate headquarters.

International Operations: Local Presence
The second stage of international development is characterized by establishment of operations within a foreign country. Internal operations include combinations of marketing, sales, production, and logistics. Establishment of local facilities and operations serves to increase market awareness and sensitivity. This is often referred to as gaining **local presence.** At the outset of a local presence strategy, foreign operations typically use parent company management and personnel, and practice home country values, procedures, and operations. However, over time, business units operating within a foreign market area will adopt local business practices.

This adoption typically means hiring host country management, marketing, and sales organizations and may include the use of local business systems. As local presence operations expand, the host country philosophy will increasingly emerge; however, the company headquarters' strategic vision remains dominant. Individual country operations are still measured against home country expectations and standards.

Globalization: The Stateless Enterprise
The stateless enterprise contrasts sharply to operations guided by either an export/import or international perspective. The stateless concept was originally popularized in a *Business Week* article describing enterprises that effectively make decisions with little or no regard to national boundaries.[7]

Stateless enterprises maintain regional operations and develop a headquarters structure to coordinate area operations. Thus, the enterprise is stateless in the sense that no specific home or parent country dominates policy. Senior management likely represents a combination of nationalities. Denationalized operations function on the basis of local marketing and sales organizations and are typically supported by world-class manufacturing and logistics operations. Product sourcing and marketing decisions can be made across a wide range of geographical alternatives. Systems and procedures are designed to meet individual country requirements and are aggregated as necessary to share knowledge and for financial reporting.

Consider an enterprise that has its historical foundations in Germany, Japan, or the United States, but with a high percentage of its sales, ownership, and assets maintained and managed in China, for example. China is estimated to be the world's third largest economy, but it very much remains a third-world country in many respects—including logistics and supply chain infrastructure. China has poor communications, no intermodal systems, no boxcar or container location tracing, no cargo airlines, and virtually nonexistent roads outside major cities. For these reasons, a stateless enterprise operating in China would rely on local management that fully understands underdeveloped business systems, the rapid rate of change, and exploding trade volume.

---

[7]"The Stateless Corporation," *Business Week,* May 14, 1990, p. 98.

Examples of firms that fit the specification of stateless enterprises are ABB (Switzerland), Dow Chemical (United States), ICI (Britain), Hoechst (Germany), Nestlé (Switzerland), and Philips (Netherlands).

While most enterprises engaged in international business are operating in stages one and two, a truly international firm must focus on the challenges of globalizing operations. Such globalization requires a significant level of management trust that transcends countries and cultures. Such trust can only grow as managers increasingly live and work across cultures. Table 6-6 provides a comparison of characteristics of firms that operate at different stages of global supply chain integration.

Managing the Global Supply Chain

To meet the challenges discussed above, management must evaluate the complexity of global supply chains and focus on five major differences between domestic and international operations: (1) performance cycle structure, (2) transportation, (3) operational considerations, (4) systems integration, and (5) alliances.

Performance Cycle Structure

The performance cycle length is the major difference between domestic and global operations. Instead of 3- to 5-day transit times and 4- to 10-day total performance cycles, global operational cycles are measured in weeks or months. For example, it is common for automotive parts from Pacific Rim suppliers to take 60 days from replenishment order release until physical order receipt at a U.S. manufacturing facility.

The reasons for a longer performance cycle are communication delays, financing requirements, special packaging requirements, ocean freight scheduling, slow transit times, and customs clearance. Communication may be delayed by time zone and language differences. Financing causes delays since international transactions often require letters of credit. Special packaging may be required to protect products from in-transit damage since containers typically are exposed to high humidity, temperature, and weather conditions. Once a product is containerized, it must be scheduled for movement between ports having appropriate handling capabilities. This scheduling process can require up to 30 days if the origin and destination ports are not located on high-volume traffic lanes or the ships moving to the desired port lack the necessary equipment. Transit time, once the ship is en route, ranges from 10 to 21 days. Port delays are common as ships wait for others to clear harbor facilities. Customs clearance may further extend total time. Although it is increasingly common to utilize electronic messaging to preclear product shipments through customs prior to arrival at international ports, the elapsed performance cycle time is still lengthy.

The combination and complexity of the above factors causes international logistics performance cycles to be longer, less consistent, and less flexible than is typical in domestic operations. The reduced consistency, in particular, increases planning difficulty. The longer performance cycle also results in higher asset commitment because significant inventory is in transit at any point in time.

Transportation

The U.S. initiative to deregulate transportation during the early 1980s has extended globally. Three significant global changes have occurred: (1) intermodal ownership and operation, (2) privatization, and (3) cabotage and bilateral agreements.

Historically, there have been regulatory restrictions concerning international transportation ownership and operating rights. Transport carriers were limited to

TABLE 6-6 Characteristics of Global Development

Typical Characteristics

Three Stages of Development	Product Focus	Marketing Strategy	Supply Chain Strategy	Management	Information and Decision Support	Human Resource Development
Export/import	Domestic production and distribution	Specific customers	Agents and third-party logistics service providers	Transportation driven with integrated financials	Home country focused with limited EDI	Management with "home country" focus and limited international experience
International operations; local presence	Local market customization supported by postponement or local production	Focused specific market areas which may cross national boundaries	Subsidiaries and local distributors with specific business charters and visible local presence	Decentralized management of local operators and strategic alliances with local profit responsibility	Independent database and decision support	Limited top management with international experience and strong "home country" decision focus
Globalization; the stateless enterprise	Global brands	All economic regions	Worldwide flow of key resources to leverage global sourcing and marketing advantages	Centralized planning with locally flexible distribution supported with common systems	Integrated database and decision support	International training and experience required for all upper-level management with some requirements for mid-level management

315

operating within a single transportation mode with few, if any, joint pricing and operating agreements. Traditionally, steamship lines could not own or manage integrated land-based operations such as motor or rail carriers. Without joint ownership, operations, and pricing agreements, international shipping was complicated. International shipments typically required multiple carriers to perform freight movement. Specifically, government rather than market forces determined the extent of services foreign-owned carriers could perform. Although some ownership and operating restrictions remain, marketing and alliance arrangements among countries have substantially improved transportation flexibility. The removal of multimodal ownership restrictions in the United States and in most other industrialized nations served to facilitate integrated movement.

A second transportation impact on global operations has been increased carrier privatization. Historically, many international carriers were owned and operated by government in an effort to promote trade and provide national security. Government-owned carriers often subsidize operations for their home county businesses while placing surcharges on foreign enterprises. Artificially high pricing and poor service often made it costly and unreliable to ship via such government carriers. Inefficiencies also resulted from strong unionization and work rules. The combination of high cost and operating inefficiencies caused many government carriers to operate at a loss. A great many such carriers have been privatized.

Changes in cabotage and bilateral service agreements are the third transportation factor influencing international trade. Cabotage laws require passengers or goods moving between two domestic ports to utilize only domestic carriers. For example, water shipment from Los Angeles to New York was required to use a U.S. carrier. The same cabotage laws restricted Canadian drivers from transporting a backhaul load to Detroit once a shipment originating in Canada was unloaded in Texas. Cabotage laws were designed to protect domestic transportation industries even though they also served to reduce overall transportation equipment utilization and related efficiencies. The European Community has relaxed cabotage restrictions to increase trade efficiency. Such reduced cabotage restrictions will save U.S. corporations 10 to 15 percent in intra-European shipping costs.

Operational Considerations

There are a number of unique operational considerations in a global environment. First, international operations typically require multiple languages for both product and documentation. A technical product such as a computer or a calculator must have local features such as keyboard characters and language on both the product itself and related manuals. From a logistics perspective, language differences dramatically increase complexity since a product is limited to a specific country once it is language-customized. For example, even though Western Europe is much smaller than the United States in a geographic sense, it requires relatively more inventory to support marketing efforts since separate inventories may be required to accommodate various languages. Although product proliferation due to language requirement has been reduced through multipurpose packaging and postponement strategies, such practices are not always acceptable. In addition to product language implications, international operations may require multilingual documentation for each country through which the shipment passes. Although English is the general language of commerce, some countries require that transportation and customs documentation be provided in the local language. This increases the time and effort for international operations since complex documents must be translated prior to shipment. These communication and

---

TABLE 6-7   Common Forms of International Logistics Documentation

---

- *Export irrevocable commercial letter of credit.* A contract between an importer and a bank that transfers liability or paying the exporter from the importer to the (supposedly more creditworthy) importer's bank.
- *Bank draft (or bill of exchange).* A means of payment for an import/export transaction. Two types exist: transaction payable on sight with proper documents (*sight draft*), and transaction payable at some fixed time after acceptance of proper documents (*time draft*). Either type of draft accompanied by instructions and other documents (*but no letter of credit*) are a documentary draft.
- *Bill of lading.* Issued by the shipping company or its agent as evidence of a contract for shipping the merchandise and as a claim to ownership of the goods.
- *Combined transport document.* May replace the bill of lading if goods are shipped by air (*airway bill*) or by more than one mode of transportation.
- *Commercial invoice.* A document written by the exporter to precisely describe the goods and the terms of sale (similar to a shipping invoice used in domestic shipments).
- *Insurance certificate.* Explains what type of coverage is utilized (fire, theft, water), the name of the insurer, and the exporter whose property is being insured.
- *Certificate of origin.* Denotes the country in which the goods were produced to assess tariffs and other government-imposed restrictions on trade.

---

documentation difficulties can be somewhat overcome through standardized electronic transactions.

The second operational difference in global commerce is unique national accommodations such as performance features, power supply characteristics, and safety requirements. While they may not be substantial, the small differences between country requirements may significantly increase required SKUs and subsequent inventory levels.

The third operating difference is the sheer amount of documentation required for international operations. While domestic operations can generally be completed using only an invoice and bill of lading, international operations require substantial documentation regarding order contents, transportation, financing, and government control. Table 6-7 lists and describes common forms of international documentation.

The fourth operating difference is the high incidence of countertrade and duty drawback found in some international situations. While most established firms prefer cash transactions, countertrade is important. Countertrade, in essence, is when a seller agrees to take or purchase products from the buyer as part of a sales agreement. While such agreements have financial consequences, they also have major implications for logistics and marketing in terms of disposal of goods received as payment.

For example, Pepsi supplies syrup to the Soviet government, which bottles and markets the soft drink with practically no control from Pepsi. In return, Pepsi is paid for the syrup by receiving exclusive rights to distribute Russian Stolichnaya vodka in the United States. This exclusive right requires marketing and logistics support.

Systems Integration

Few firms currently enjoy global systems integration. Since firms typically globalize by acquisition and merger, the integration of systems typically lags. Operational integration requires the ability to route orders and manage inventory requirements electronically throughout the world. Development of supportive technology integration represents substantial capital investment. The overall process was significantly facilitated by the global initiative to achieve Y2K compliance. However, there remain few enterprises that have integrated global systems.

Alliances

A final difference in international operations is the extended role of third-party alliances. While alliances with carriers and specialized service suppliers are important in domestic operations, they are essential in international commerce. Without alliances, it would be necessary for an enterprise operating internationally to maintain contacts with retailers, wholesalers, manufacturers, suppliers, and service providers throughout the world. International alliances offer market access and expertise and reduce the inherent risk in global operations. The number of alternatives and the complexity of the globalization require increased use of alliances.

Globalization is an evolving frontier that is increasingly demanding supply chain integration. As international business develops, the demand for logistical competency increases due to longer supply chains, less certainty, and more documentation. While the forces of change push toward borderless operations, supply chain management still confronts market, financial, and channel barriers. The barriers are exemplified by distance, demand, diversity, and documentation. The challenge is to position an enterprise to take advantage of the benefits of global marketing and manufacturing by developing world-spanning logistical competency.

Summary

Operational integration is a managerial challenge at the level of individual enterprises, across domestic supply chains, and for the conduct of international business. Operational integration creates value as a result of coordinated cross-functional efficiency. The application of systems analysis and assessment of total cost provides a methodology to integrate functions into a productive process. Integrated processes offer distinct cost and service benefits.

At the individual firm level operational integration is difficult. Barriers exist and serve as obstacles to internal operational integration. This resistance to integration can be traced to long-standing functional management practices and related information systems and reward practices. Conventional measurement practices and metrics serve to reinforce functionalism. The resistance to process integration is sufficiently strong and can be universally observed. The commonly observed phenomenon referred to as the great divide reflects the common difficulty in achieving enterprise end-to-end integration.

The paradox is that many firms successfully integrate with customers and/or suppliers. Thus, firms often integrate more outside their specific enterprise than they do internally. This means that many attempts at extending the enterprise across the supply chain are, at best, partial solutions. However, many such limited supply chain engagements appear to be valuable arrangements for their participants. It remains unclear just how much internal integration is necessary for a firm to be a viable supply chain participant. Of course, the risk is that failure to achieve internal operational integration may cause a firm to be unable to meet supply chain commitments.

The reason that partial supply chain integration achieves value is directly related to the significant potential to reduce waste, duplication, and operational redundancy. In particular, collaboration offers ways to reduce inventory investments and related risk for participating firms. Successful supply chain integration requires cross-organizational programs to facilitate operations, technology and planning, and relationship management collaboration. While few, if any, across-the-supply-chain collaborations exist today, the potential benefits of such holistic integration are staggering.

As a supply chain strategy moves into the international arena, new complexities are encountered. These complexities result from longer distances, difference in demand, cultural diversity, and complex documentation. Firms will increasingly confront the need to expand operations into the global arena. Strategies to achieve a share of the rapidly expanding world market range from export/import to local presence to true globalization. Regardless of the strategic focus, success will, to a large extent, be dependent upon a firm's logistical capabilities.

Challenge Questions

1. Compare and contrast economic, market, and relevancy value.
2. Illustrate the differences in product/service creation, presentation, and positioning.
3. Explain the following statement: "The methodology is systems analysis and the theoretical framework is the systems concept."
4. Why is variance reduction important to logistical integration? Illustrate in terms of logistical operations.
5. What is the meaning of the phrase *cradle-to-cradle* logistics? Discuss the operational differences of original versus reverse logistics.
6. How do reward systems serve as barriers to enterprise integration?
7. In your words, describe and illustrate the *great divide*. Do you believe the great divide phenomenon is as widely experienced as the text indicates? Support your position with an illustration.
8. What creates power in the context of supply chain collaboration? Why do many observers feel power is shifting forward or closer to end consumers in many supply chain arrangements?
9. Demonstrate your understanding of the relationship between logistical capabilities and competencies by tracing the evolution of logistical work to universal competencies. Does this logic have any practical application in understanding logistical sophistication? If so, what is the practical benefit?
10. Compare and contrast export/import operations to local presence. What are the logistics ramifications of each stage of international development?

7　INFORMATION NETWORKS

Supply chain information systems initiate activities and track information regarding processes, facilitate information sharing both within the firm and between supply chain partners, and assist in management decision making. This chapter describes these comprehensive information systems as a combination of communication networks, transaction systems, and decision support systems. All component systems must be integrated to provide comprehensive functionality for analyzing, initiating, and monitoring supply chain operations.

Information System Functionality

From its inception, logistics focused on product storage and flow through the distribution channel. Information flow and accuracy was often overlooked because it was not viewed as being critical by customers. In addition, information transfer rates were limited by the speed of paper. There are four reasons why timely and accurate information has become more critical for effective logistics systems design and operations. First,

192

customers perceive information about order status, product availability, delivery schedule, shipment tracking, and invoices as necessary elements of total customer service. Customers demand access to real time information. Second, with the goal of reducing total supply chain assets, managers realize that information can be used to reduce inventory and human resource requirements. In particular, requirements planning using the most current information can reduce inventory by minimizing demand uncertainty. Third, information increases flexibility with regard to how, when, and where resources may be utilized to gain strategic advantage. Fourth, enhanced information transfer and exchange capability utilizing the Internet is changing relationships between buyers and sellers and redefining channel relationships.

Supply chain information systems (SCIS) are the thread that links logistics activities into an integrated process. The integration builds on four levels of functionality: (1) *transaction systems,* (2) *management control,* (3) *decision analysis,* and (4) *strategic planning.* Figure 7-1 illustrates logistics activities and decisions at each level of information functionality. As the pyramid shape suggests, management control, decision analysis, and strategic planning enhancements require a strong transaction system foundation.

A **transaction system** is characterized by formalized rules, procedures, and standardized communications; a large volume of transactions; and an operational, day-to-day focus. The combination of structured processes and large transaction volume places a major emphasis on information system efficiency. At the most basic levels, transaction systems initiate and record individual logistics activities and functions.

FIGURE 7-1

Information functionality

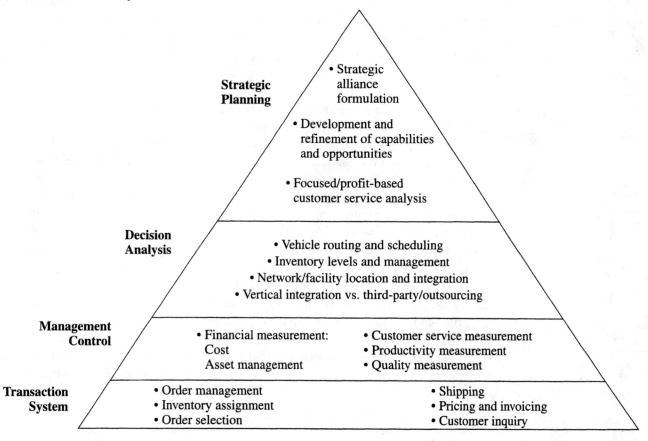

Transaction activities include order entry, inventory assignment, order selection, shipping, pricing, invoicing, and customer inquiry. For example, customer order entry represents a transaction that enters a customer request for product into the information system. The order entry transaction initiates a second transaction as inventory is assigned to the order. A third transaction is then generated to direct warehouse operations to select or pick the order from the warehouse storage location. A fourth transaction initiates transport of the order to the customer. The final transaction develops the invoice and records an account receivable. Throughout the process, the firm and customer expect the availability of real time information regarding order status. Thus, the customer order performance cycle is completed through a series of information system transactions.[1]

The second SCIS level, **management control,** focuses on *performance measurement and reporting.* Performance measurement is necessary to provide management feedback regarding supply chain performance and resource utilization. Common performance measures include cost, customer service, productivity, quality, and asset management measures. As an example, specific performance measures include transportation and warehousing cost per pound, inventory turnover, case fill rate, cases per labor hour, and customer perception.

While it is necessary that SCIS report historical system performance, it is also necessary for the system to identify operational exceptions. Management exception information is useful to highlight potential customer order or operational problems. For example, proactive SCIS should be capable of identifying future inventory shortages based on forecasted requirements and planned inventory. Management exception reporting should also be capable of identifying potential transportation, delivery warehouse, or labor requirements that exceed capacity limitations.

While some control measures, such as cost, are well defined, other measures, such as customer service and quality, are less specific. For example, customer service can be measured internally, from the enterprise's perspective, or externally, from the customer's perspective. While internal measures are relatively easy to track, external measures are more difficult to obtain since they require monitoring performance regarding specific customers.

The third SCIS level, **decision analysis,** focuses on software tools to assist managers in identifying, evaluating, and comparing supply chain and logistics strategic and tactical alternatives for improved effectiveness. Typical analyses include supply chain design, inventory management, resource allocation, routing, and segmental profitability. Decision analysis SCIS must also include database maintenance, modeling, analysis, and reporting over a wide range of potential logistics situations. Similar to management control, decision analysis includes some tactical analysis considerations such as vehicle routing and warehouse planning. Decision analysis applications are also being used to manage customer relationships by determining the trade-offs associated with having satisfied and successful customers, as discussed in Chapter 3. Because decision analysis is used to guide future operations and needs to be unstructured and flexible to allow consideration of a wide range of alternatives, users require more expertise and training to benefit from its capability.

Strategic planning, the final SCIS level, organizes and synthesizes transaction data into a wide range of business planning and decision-making models that assist in evaluating the probabilities and payoffs of various strategies. Essentially, strategic

---

[1]For a review of performance cycle structure and dynamics, see pp. 55–64.

FIGURE 7-2

SCIS usage, decision characteristics, and justification

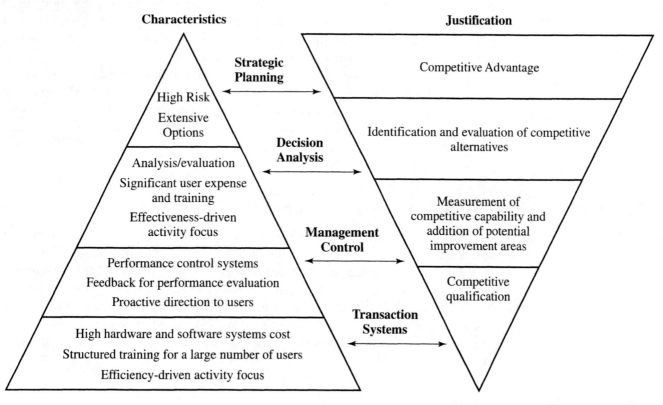

planning focuses on information support to develop and refine supply chain and logistics strategy. These decisions are often extensions of decision analysis but are typically more abstract, are even less structured, and have a longer-term focus. Examples of strategic planning decisions include the desirability of strategic alliances, development and refinement of manufacturing capabilities, and market opportunities related to customer responsiveness.

The relative shape of Figure 7-2 illustrates relative SCIS development costs and benefits. The left side of the figure illustrates development and maintenance characteristics while the right side reflects benefits. Development and maintenance costs include hardware, software, communications, training, and personnel expenses.

In general, a solid base requires significant SCIS investments for transaction systems. Transaction system costs are high due to the large number of system users, heavy data communications requirements, high transaction volume, and significant software complexity. Transaction systems costs are also relatively well defined and exhibit more certainty and limited payoff with respect to benefits or returns. A comprehensive transaction system does not provide a substantial competitive advantage in today's environment; it is a competitive requirement. Virtually all firms that are still in business have made substantial investments to achieve transaction system efficiency. Therefore, while the investment is substantial, the relative return is often quite small. Higher level systems such as management control, decision analysis, and strategic planning typically require fewer hardware and software resources but often involve greater uncertainty and risk with regard to potential system benefits.

Management control and decision analysis systems, on the other hand, focus on providing insight into problem processes and alternatives. For example, benchmarking management control systems can identify processes where a firm lags competitors while external customer service audits may identify opportunities for selective, customer-focused programs. Finally, strategic planning systems with the ability to assess supply chain design, customer/product profitability, segment contribution, or alliance benefits can have a major impact on enterprise profitability and competitiveness even though they are not particularly hardware or software intensive.

In the past, most systems development focused on improving transaction system efficiency. While these investments offered returns in terms of speed and lower operating costs, anticipated cost reductions have often been elusive. SCIS development and implementation now focus on enhanced supply chain system integration and more effective decision making.

Comprehensive Information System Integration

A comprehensive information system initiates, monitors, assists in decision making, and reports on activities required to complete logistics operations and planning. There are many components that must be combined to form an integrated information system, and there are many ways to organize and illustrate the combined components.

The major system components include: (1) Enterprise Resource Planning (ERP) or legacy systems, (2) communication systems, (3) execution systems, and (4) planning systems. Figure 7-3 offers one illustration of these components and their typical interfaces.

ERP or Legacy Systems

The **ERP** or **legacy systems** highlighted in Figure 7-4 are the backbone of most firms' supply chain information systems. This backbone maintains current and historical data and processes transactions to initiate and track performance. Legacy systems refer to the mainframe applications that were developed prior to 1990 to automate transactions such as order entry, order processing, warehouse operations, inventory management, transportation, and related financial transactions. For example, systems related to customer orders were often labeled Order Management Systems (OMS) since they managed the order fulfillment process. In addition to order information, legacy systems typically maintain information regarding customers, products, inventory status, and facility operations. In many cases, these legacy systems represent independently developed software modules that lack integration and consistency; consequently, problems with data reliability and integrity abound. These problems are further complicated by the fact that multidivisional firms often use different legacy systems for each division or country.

During the 1990s, many firms began to replace legacy systems with ERP systems designed as integrated transaction modules with a common and consistent database. ERP systems facilitated integrated operations and reporting to initiate, monitor, and track critical activities such as order fulfillment and replenishment processing. In addition to data integrity and consistency, ERP systems gained rapid popularity as a way to minimize potential problems with the Year 2000 millennium bug. ERP systems also incorporate an integrated corporatewide database, sometime referred to as a data warehouse, along with appropriate transactions to facilitate logistics and supply chain operations. Typical transactions can accommodate order entry and fulfillment, procurement, and production transactions. Beyond these operational applications, ERP

FIGURE 7-3

Integrated supply chain system modules

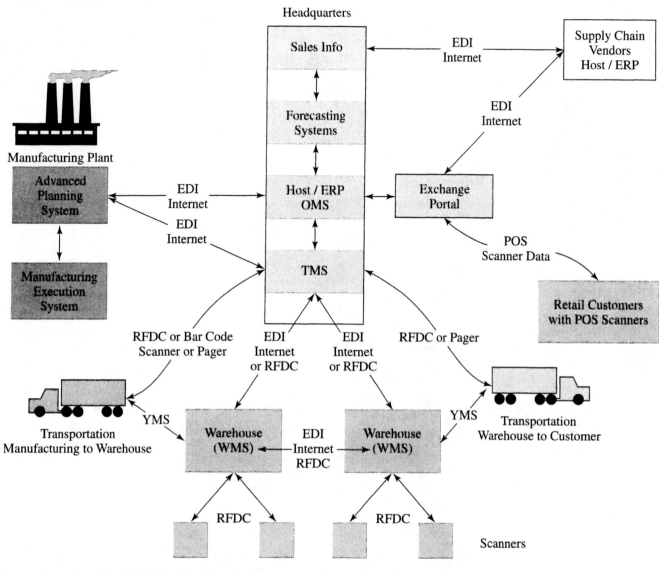

Source: Adapted from Cahner's Publishing, "The Information Flow Across an Integrated Supply Chain," *Logistics Online* (**www.manufacturing.net/scl/yearbook/**). Used with permission.

systems typically include financial, accounting, and human resource capability. Table 7-1 lists the traditional and emerging capabilities characteristic of ERP systems, and Industry Insight 7-1 describes how one company (Cisco) has used ERP systems to facilitate tremendous growth, support acquisitions, and develop superior customer service.

To capitalize on the benefits of integration, headquarters systems are beginning to include two other system components, forecasting and Customer Relationship Management (CRM), as illustrated in Figure 7-3. The CRM or sales management system is one of the newer applications designed to facilitate information sharing between the sales force and operational management. CRM provides sales representatives and customers with current information gained through the ERP system regarding sales history, shipment history, order status, promotional summary, and shipment information. The history and current status information, combined with information regarding

FIGURE 7-4

Enterprise resource planning

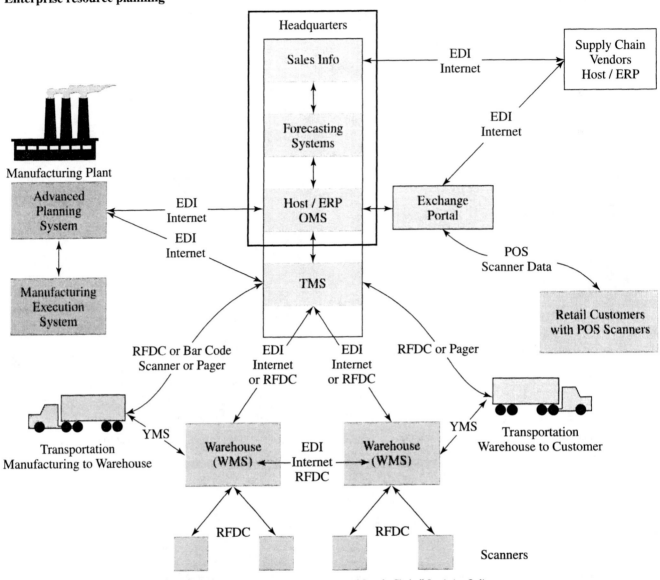

Source: Adapted from Cahner's Publishing, "The Information Flow Across an Integrated Supply Chain," *Logistics Online* (**www.manufacturing.net/scl/yearbook/**). Used with permission.

product development, pricing, and promotion, allows CRM to forecast customer orders that will maximize customer success as discussed in Chapter 3. Such timely and accurate information exchange between a firm and its customers increases the likelihood that product sales and promotion plans will be supported with available product.

Communication Systems

The communication module facilitates information flow between functional areas within the firm and between supply chain partners. Figure 7-5 highlights the major communication components required for supply chain operations. Logistics information consists of real time data on company operations—inbound material flows, production status, product inventories, customer shipments, and incoming orders.

TABLE 7-1   Capabilities of ERP Systems

What do you get with ERP?

As monolithic as ERP may sound, it isn't. In fact, the software is composed of many different modules (as many as 60) that connect to the company's financial system. That collected data is then used to project the performance of key corporate financials. This enterprise-centric model of ERP is now being expanded to include new modules that allow ERP to be part of the planning process by the company and its suppliers and customers.

Traditional Capabilities:
- Bill of materials
- Accounts payable and accounts receivable
- General ledger
- Inventory control
- Order entry
- Purchasing
- Project requirements planning
- Routings
- Capacity requirements planning

Emerging Capabilities:
- Enterprise application integration
- Visibility
- Collaborative planning, forecasting, and replenishment
- Customer relationship management
- Web-enabled applications
- Hosting

Source: Gary Forger, "ERP Goes Mid-Market," *Modern Materials Handling,* January 2000, p. 71. Reprinted with permission.

From an external perspective, firms need to make order, shipment, and billing information available to suppliers, financial institutions, transportation carriers, and customers. Internal operating units must be able to share and exchange information on production schedule and status. Typical supply chain communication technologies include bar coding, scanning, Electronic Data Interchange (EDI), satellite communication, radio frequency, and the Internet. Standards and formats to exchange data are discussed later in this chapter.

Execution Systems

Enterprise execution systems work in conjunction with the firm's ERP to provide specific functionality to support logistics operations. While some ERP systems include reasonable logistics functionality, many lack the capabilities to facilitate contemporary warehouse and transportation operations. Figure 7-6 highlights selected execution system modules. Most execution systems are "bolted-on" or integrated into the ERP system to facilitate data exchange. In addition to facilitating standard warehouse management functionality such as receiving, storage, shipping, and warehouse automation, Warehouse Management Systems (WMS) typically include management reporting, support for value-added services, and decision support capability. The Transportation Management System (TMS) typically includes routing, load building, consolidation, and management of reverse logistics activities as well as scheduling and documentation. Yard Management Systems (YMS) track inventory in vehicles stored in facility yards. Chapter 8 provides a more detailed discussion of logistics execution systems.

Planning Systems

The final information system components are the planning systems highlighted in Figure 7-7. While the ERP system processes transactions to execute specific logistics

INDUSTRY INSIGHT 7-1 ACHIEVING INTEGRATION THROUGH DECENTRALIZATION

Since its founding in 1984, Cisco has always seemed to be able to look a bit further over the horizon than its competitors. It concentrated on networking when the rest of the world was point-to-point. It specialized in the enhanced functionality of routing when most people thought switches were all they'd ever need. And it moved rapidly to put a large portion of its sales operations online before most people thought this was practical.

As a result, Cisco now manages 75 percent of its revenues through its website: $25 million per day, $8 billion per year. This is believed by many industry observers to be the largest electronic commerce site in the world.

Despite Cisco's indisputable record of success, the journey hasn't always been an easy one. Growth was one reason. By 1994, Cisco had rapidly outgrown its application systems. "We were experiencing growth rates of more than 70 percent per year," says Andy Starr, IS Manager. Revenues had reached nearly $1 billion, but Cisco was still operating on applications meant to support a company half that size. To remedy the situation, Cisco embarked on an aggressive ERP implementation using an Oracle database and applications. In 1995, after only 9 months, the company went live with a big bang implementation—a complete switch of all worldwide transactions systems. Five thousand orders in backlog were converted in just one weekend. Peter Solvik, Cisco's CIO, says, "The applications provided the architecture on which we could very, very rapidly grow, adapt, and scale the company."

Acquisitions were another reason. In 5 years Cisco has acquired 27 companies. When acquiring a company, systems integration is critical to support the 60- to 90-day closing period applied by Cisco. The goal is to take orders for that company's products on Cisco's information system the day the deal is closed. The acquired firm's legacy systems are then replaced quickly, creating a common worldwide ordering environment. "We wouldn't have acquired these companies if we didn't have the ability to integrate them fluidly. They wouldn't provide value to our customers or our shareholders," says Solvik.

Cisco's ERP framework has grown from a single server into three U.S.-based servers and one in the Netherlands. This network of servers coordinates Cisco's manufacturing and order fulfillment processes, providing immediate response to requests and better availability of products to its customers.

For example, an order loaded into the Amsterdam server is scheduled for delivery using the U.S. Available-to-Promise (ATP) server. The ATP server schedules according to the supply said to be available by the U.S. manufacturing server. The customer order is then built and shipped from one of five manufacturing sites and invoiced from the Amsterdam server. All of these servers combined provide Cisco with four benefits: increased reliability, reduced risk of server failure, enhanced flexibility and scalability of the ERP system, and a reduction in lead times from 4 weeks to 1.

Solvik states that Cisco's entire Internet commerce initiative is based on a simple truth: "customers prefer self-service." To achieve a higher degree of self-service, Cisco was the first company to integrate its website with an Oracle Applications ERP infrastructure. The Cisco Connection Online (CCO) Internet site offers customers and suppliers global communications with 49 pages of country- or region-specific support services and product and contact information translated into 14 different languages. It operates with dedicated server links located in Australia, China, France, Hong Kong, Japan, the Netherlands, and South Korea that support 200 offices in 54 countries around the world.

Within the CCO is the "Internet Product Center" where customers can configure and place orders; look up pricing, lead times, and order status; and access invoicing information. This has reduced order entry cycle time from 1 week to less than 3 days. It has also reduced order acknowledgment cycle time from 12 hours to 2 hours, with the goal of achieving real time acknowledgment in the next 6 months. Cisco has the unique ability to process billing in multiple currencies and manage tax and regulatory issues in every country where it conducts business, yet consolidate financial performance based upon U.S. currency. "The CCO allows the salesperson to focus on the strategic aspect of the relationship," says Solvik, "and improves responsiveness to the customer through automation of mundane tasks."

Thanks to the capabilities of its Oracle ERP infrastructure, Cisco has been able to add out-sourced manufacturing to its operations over the last 4 years. "Over 50 percent of the units shipped are untouched by a Cisco factory or a Cisco employee," Solvik says. "We run our worldwide out-source factory across almost 50 suppliers entirely on Oracle Manufacturing Applications."

Cisco has also extended its communications throughout the supply chain to about 100 suppliers. "Now our component suppliers can bid against each other on a new product over the Internet," says Solvik. Changes in Bills of Materials are broadcast to suppliers through the CCO site. "We've reduced the engineering change order cycle time from 25 to 10 days within the last four years. This improves quality significantly and reduces inventory write-offs," says Solvik.

Most important, Solvik can appreciate the benefits of a good relationship in dollars and cents. "By adding together the benefits of electronic commerce, electronic self-service, manufacturing initiatives, and a few [benefits] offered by the Internet, the annual contribution to the company amounts to over $550 million from these top areas alone."

Source: **http://www.oracle.com/customers/sia/cisco.html.**

FIGURE 7-5

Communication modules

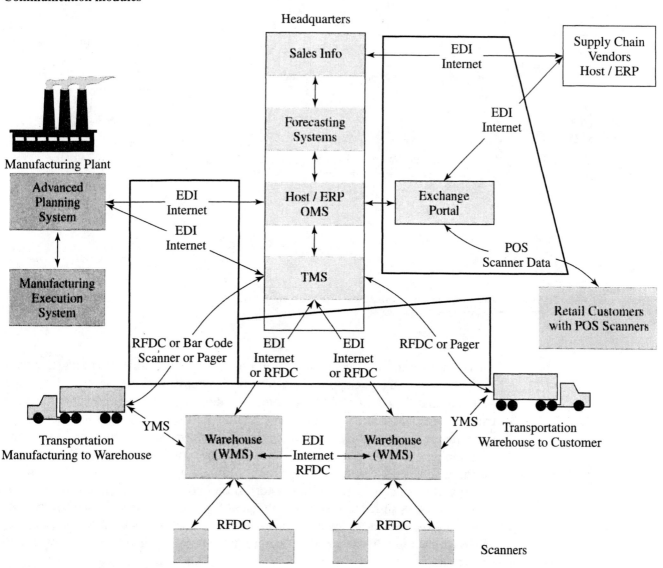

Source: Adapted from Cahner's Publishing, "The Information Flow Across an Integrated Supply Chain," *Logistics Online* (**www.manufacturing.net/scl/yearbook/**). Used with permission.

FIGURE 7-6

Execution modules

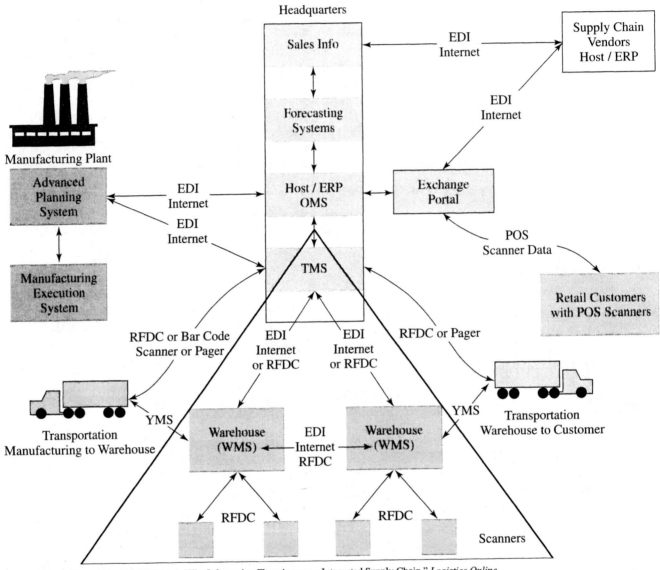

Source: Adapted from Cahner's Publishing, "The Information Flow Across an Integrated Supply Chain," *Logistics Online* (**www.manufacturing.net/scl/yearbook/**). Used with permission.

activities, transaction systems in general don't evaluate alternative strategies or assist with decision making. Supply chain planning systems, now being termed Advanced Planning and Scheduling (APS) systems, are designed to assist in evaluating supply chain alternatives and advise in supply chain decision making. Sophisticated supply chain planning systems are becoming increasingly common to allow for consideration of complex alternatives under tight decision time constraints. Typical supply chain planning applications include production scheduling, inventory resource planning, and transportation planning. Using the historical and current data maintained in the data warehouse, APS software systematically identifies and evaluates alternative courses of action and recommends a near optimal solution within the constraints imposed. Typical constraints involve production, facility, transportation, inventory, or raw material limitations.

FIGURE 7-7

Advanced planning and scheduling components

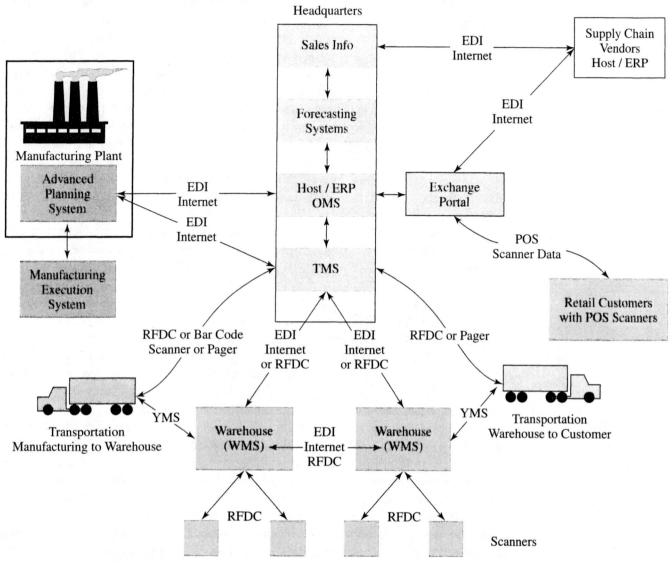

Source: Adapted from Cahner's Publishing, "The Information Flow Across an Integrated Supply Chain," *Logistics Online* (**www.manufacturing.net/scl/yearbook/**). Used with permission.

Planning systems can generally be grouped into two categories, strategic and tactical. Strategic planning systems are designed to assist in analyses where there is a large number of alternatives and data outside the range of current history is required. Examples of strategic planning applications include supply chain network design and structural analyses such as which combination of supplier, production, and distribution facilities should be used and how product should flow between existing or potential facilities.

Tactical planning focuses on operational issues as constrained by short-term resource constraints such as production, facility, or vehicle capacity. The information support for tactical planning is typically available from a firm's data warehouse. Tactical planning processes evaluate customer requirements and identify an operational combination of production, inventory, facilities, and equipment utilization that can be applied within capacity constraints. The result is an action plan to guide short-term operations.

Accessing Supply Chain Applications

The maintenance of comprehensive information system technology can be extremely expensive. The hardware is extensive, and the software is complex. The hardware typically includes a network of servers and personal computers to provide the computing power and storage capacity to track a large number of customers, products, inventory, and order transactions. The software must allow for a wide range of options for users that are frequently located throughout the world. In addition, both the hardware and the software must incorporate substantial security and redundancy to prevent loss of critical capabilities and information if either the software or the hardware fails. Hardware and software also require substantial human expertise for both implementation and ongoing maintenance. Although smaller firms may not require the same level of system scale, redundancy, and globalization, the required operational functionality is essentially the same. There are three ways firms obtain access to necessary hardware, software, and support.

The first is through *direct ownership*. The firm purchases the hardware and software for implementation within its facilities. While the initial cost can be substantial, the direct ownership route offers high security and low variable cost. Firms can reduce capital investment by leasing equipment or software from vendors or a third-party financing company. However, there are also risks associated with the direct ownership plan. The firm must employ or contract individuals who can provide the expertise to implement, modify, and maintain both the hardware and the software. Management and financial support of information technology resources may use capital and talent that are needed to develop core competency of a firm. In addition, direct ownership of information technology resources must carefully evaluate redundancy requirements. SCIS require that global operations be supported 24 hours a day, 7 days a week.

A second strategy is to *outsource* information management to a third party with the competency and expertise to implement, maintain, and manage such technologies. Firms such as International Business Machines (IBM), Electronic Data Systems (EDS), and Accenture provide comprehensive information technology outsourcing and consulting. The hardware and software can be dedicated or shared with other clients of the service provider. In either case, both the hardware and the data are reasonably secure. The benefits of outsourcing are that operational responsibility is assigned to a specialist that has extensive resources to focus on both hardware and software implementation and operations. In addition, such management firms typically offer backup services by sharing substantial resources across a number of clients. The major disadvantage of using a third-party service provider is increased variable cost. To provide the service, a profit margin must be added to the cost of equipment and software. However, the cost differential may be more than justified since the service provider should be in a position to achieve economies of scale by sharing resources and personnel across multiple clients.

The third strategy is the use of an *Application Service Provider* (ASP). An ASP is a relatively new type of service provider that has emerged via the Internet. ASPs are third-party service firms that own and maintain computer hardware and software which they rent to clients on a usage or transaction basis. With an ASP, the hardware and software are typically limited to a personal computer, a Web browser, and an Internet connection. The ASP owns websites that offer a variety of software and client computer files. In what is coming to be called *Apps on tap*, the ASP maintains and upgrades the computer software and database and makes it available to the firm. The

TABLE 7-2   Application Service Provider Benefits and Risks

Benefits	Risks
Cost savings: Not necessary to purchase or upgrade software	Security: Proprietary information possibly vulnerable due to ASP failures
Time savings: Firm can focus on core business	Infrastructure: ASP requires high-speed Internet connection
Staffing: ASP provides technical staff to support implementation and maintenance	History: No clear business model yet.
Flexibility: Client can remotely access software with a Web browser	

Source: ASPNews.com. Cherry Tree & Co. Reprinted with permission.

ASP is responsible for the security, redundancy, and integrity of the website. Table 7-2 lists major ASP benefits and risks.

In most cases, firms will employ a combination of the three strategies to accommodate information technology requirements. The basic order entry and management software may be acquired and operated by a firm using internal computers to minimize cost and provide security. More complex software such as planning systems may be rented from ASPs. In any case, the combination of the ownership and access methods provides firms with the capability to create a comprehensive information system without extensive in-house expertise and significant initial funding.

Communication Systems

Information technology is also critical for information sharing to facilitate logistics and supply chain planning and operations. Historically, coordination of logistics has been difficult since logistics activities are often performed at locations distant from information technology hardware. As a result, information was not available at the location of essential work in terms of both time and content. The past decade has witnessed remarkable advances in logistical communication systems capability. EDI, the Internet, Extensible Markup Language (XML), and satellite technology exist to facilitate communication between firms and facilities. Radio frequency allows short-range communication within facilities such as warehouses. Image, bar coding, and scanner technologies allow communication between supply chain information systems and their physical environment.

Electronic Data Interchange

While the phone, fax, and direct computer connection have enabled information exchange in the past, EDI and the Internet are quickly becoming the standards for effective, accurate, and low-cost information exchange. EDI is defined as intercompany computer-to-computer exchange of business documents in standard formats to facilitate high-volume transactions. It involves both the capability and practice of communicating information between two organizations electronically instead of via the traditional forms of mail, courier, or even fax.

Direct EDI benefits include increased internal productivity, improved channel relationships, increased external productivity, increased ability to compete internationally, and decreased operating cost. EDI improves productivity through faster information transmission and reduced redundancy. Accuracy is improved by reducing repetitive data entry and interpretation. EDI impacts logistics operating cost through (1) reduced labor and material cost associated with printing, mailing, and handling paper-based transactions; (2) reduced telephone, fax, and Telex; and (3) reduced clerical cost. The graphics industry has found that EDI can eliminate up to 90 percent of paper-based systems, can reduce receipt processing time by 50 percent, and can save $8.00 per invoice document.[2] In another example, Texas Instruments reports EDI has reduced shipping errors by 95 percent, field inquiries by 60 percent, data entry resource requirements by 70 percent, and global procurement cycle time by 57 percent.[3]

While EDI has made significant inroads into logistics communication, its penetration is beginning to plateau at about 50 percent of the transactions. Large manufacturers, distributors, and retailers have adopted EDI as a means to exchange information with major trading partners, but the substantial setup costs and expertise required have limited its application by medium and small firms. Annual surveys of logistics firms by The Ohio State University indicate the majority of EDI activity is with vendors and key accounts.[4]

Communication and information standards are essential for EDI. Communication standards define technical characteristics so that the computer hardware can correctly perform the interchange. Communication standards deal with character sets, transmission priority, and speed. Information standards dictate the structure and content of the message. Standards organizations have developed and refined two general standards as well as numerous industry-specific standards in an effort to standardize both communication and information interchange.

Communication Standards

The most generally accepted communication standards are ANS X.12 (American National Standards Committee X.12) and UN/EDIFACT (United Nations/Electronic Data Interchange for Administration, Commerce, and Transport). X.12 is promoted as the U. S. standard, while EDIFACT is promoted by the United Nations as more of a global standard.[5] Each organization has defined a structure for exchanging common data between supply chain partners. Experts indicate that the most likely migration path is to EDIFACT standards.[6] Table 7-3 illustrates the difference between paper and electronic communications. The left side of the table illustrates the line item detail necessary to communicate a four-line order. The specific data include the quantity, unit-of-measure, item number, description, and unit price. The table's right side illustrates the information in coded form with field separators. Note that this approach is limited as fields must be transferred in a commonly accepted and understood sequence because the X.12 format does not include a variable definition. Lack of consistency in variable definition and interpretation has further reduced the adoption rate for EDI and

---

[2] Anonymous, "EDI Benefits Are Seen in the Dealer Channel," *Graphic Arts Monthly,* March 1999, p. 20.

[3] Clay Youngblood, "EDI Trial and Error," *Transportation and Distribution,* April 1993, p. 46.

[4] The Ohio State University, "Careers Patterns Survey," 1998; available under "careers" at the Council of Logistics Management website, **www.clm1.org.**

[5] Gregory B. Harter, "What Can We Expect," *Transportation and Distribution* 34, no. 4 (April 1993), p. 42.

[6] Ibid.

TABLE 7-3   Comparison of Communication Transaction Formats

Quantity	Unit	No.	Paper Format Description	Price	ANS X.12 Format
3	Cse	6900	Cellulose sponges	12.75	IT1•3•CA•127500•VC•6900 N/L
12	Ea	P450	Plastic pails	.475	IT1•12•EA•4750•VC•P450 N/L
4	Ea	1640Y	Yellow dish drainer	.94	IT1•4•EA•9400•VC•1640Y N/L
1	Dz	1507	6″ plastic flower pots	3.40	IT1•1•DZ•34000•VC•1507 N/L

Source: Mercer Management, Inc. Reprinted with permission.

TABLE 7-4   Primary Logistics Industry EDI Standards

UCS (Uniform Communication Standards): grocery

VICS (Voluntary Interindustry Communication Standards Committee): mass merchandisers

WINS (Warehouse Information Network Standards): warehouse operators

TDCC (Transportation Data Coordinating Committee): transportation operators

AIAG (Automotive Industry Action Group): automotive industry

motivated the advancement of XML, a flexible computer language discussed later in this chapter.

The National Institute of Standards and Technology (NIST) and automotive experts are further driving information integration by experimenting with approaches to exchanging data for the entire business cycle. The program, known as STEP (Standard for the Exchange of Product Model Data), was designed for exchanging design and engineering data between supply chain partners. STEP should allow users to integrate business and technical systems data involving all elements of the business cycle including design, analysis, manufacturing, sales, and service.[7]

EDI Transaction Sets

Communication standards are implemented via transaction sets. A transaction set provides a single common standard to facilitate information interchange between partners in any industry and country. Table 7-4 lists the common logistics-related industry transaction standards. For each industry, the transaction set defines the types of document that can be transmitted. Documents cover common logistics activities such as ordering, warehouse operations, and transportation. Table 7-5 lists the transaction set usage matrix. The transaction set consists of a transaction code (or ID) and is followed by the required data. The transaction code indicates whether the electronic communication is a warehouse shipping order (code 940) or a warehouse stock transfer receipt (code 944), for example. In addition to the transaction code, a warehouse transaction contains warehouse number, item number, and quantity.

While applications are migrating toward common standards, there is still conflict regarding the ultimate goal. A single common standard facilitates information

---

[7]Amy Zukerman, "Standards, Technology, and the Supply Chain," *Transportation and Distribution,* May 2000, p. 44.

TABLE 7-5 Transaction Set Usage Matrix

TS ID	Transaction Set Name	UCS	VICS EDI
102	Associated Data		✓
180	Return Merchandise Authorization and Notification	✓	✓
204	Motor Carrier Load Tender	✓	
210	Motor Carrier Freight Details and Invoice	✓	
214	Transportation Carrier Shipment Status Message	✓	
753	Request for Routing Instructions		✓
754	Routing Instructions		✓
810	Invoice	✓	✓
812	Credit/Debit Adjustment	✓	✓
816	Organizational Relationships	✓	✓
818	Commission Sales Report	✓	
820	Payment Order/Remittance Advice	✓	✓
824	Application Advice	✓	✓
830	Planning Schedule with Release Capability	✓	✓
831	Application Control Totals	✓	✓
832	Price/Sales Catalog		✓
846	Inventory Inquiry/Advice	✓	✓
850	Purchase Order	✓	✓
852	Product Activity Data	✓	✓
853	Routing and Carrier Instructions		✓
855	Purchase Order Acknowledgment	✓	✓
856	Ship Notice/Manifest	✓	✓
857	Shipment and Billing Notice	✓	
860	Purchase Order Change Request—Buyer Initiated		✓
861	Receiving Advice/Acceptance Certificate		✓
864	Text Message	✓	✓
867	Product Transfer and Resale Report	✓	
869	Order Status Inquiry		✓
870	Order Status Report		✓
875	Grocery Products Purchase Order	✓	
876	Grocery Products Purchase Order Change	✓	
877	Manufacturer Coupon Family Code Structure	✓	
878	Product Authorization/De-Authorization	✓	
879	Price Information	✓	
880	Grocery Products Invoice	✓	
881	Manufacturer Coupon Redemption Detail	✓	
882	Direct Store Delivery Summary Information	✓	✓
883	Market Development Fund Allocation	✓	
884	Market Development Fund Settlement	✓	
885	Store Characteristics	✓	
886	Customer Call Reporting	✓	
887	Coupon Notification	✓	
888	Item Maintenance	✓	
889	Promotion Announcement	✓	✓
891	Deduction Research Report	✓	
893	Item Information Request	✓	✓

TABLE 7-5   Continued

TS ID	Transaction Set Name	UCS	VICS EDI
894	Delivery/Return Base Record	✓	
895	Delivery/Return Acknowledgment and/or Adjustment	✓	
896	Product Dimension Maintenance	✓	
940	Warehouse Shipping Order	✓	✓
944	Warehouse Stock Transfer Receipt Advice	✓	
945	Warehouse Shipping Advice	✓	
947	Warehouse Inventory Adjustment Advice	✓	✓
997	Functional Acknowledgment	✓	✓

Source: Deborah Faraqher, Uniform Code Council, Inc., 1995.

FIGURE 7-8

Value-added networks (VANs). The VAN collects transaction messages and information from a manufacturer and then translates those messages and information into appropriate industry-specific communication standards.

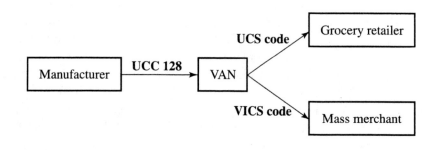

interchange between partners in any industry and country, but many firms believe that strategic advantage can be achieved only with proprietary EDI capabilities. Proprietary capabilities allow a firm to offer customized transactions that efficiently meet information requirements.

Additionally, a standard transaction set would have to accommodate the needs of all types of users and, as a result, would be more complex. For example, the grocery industry requires a 12-digit universal product code (UPC), while the electrical supply industry requires a 20-digit item code. Standardized logistics EDI transactions would have to accommodate both.

Many firms resolve this dilemma through the use of value-added networks (VANs). A VAN, illustrated in Figure 7-8, is a common interface between sending and receiving systems. The VAN adds *value* by managing transactions, translating communication standards, and reducing the number of communication linkages. Transaction management includes broadcast of messages to subsets of suppliers, carriers, or customers and receipt of messages from customers using different communication standards.

The Uniform Code Council (UCC), in partnership with EAN International, is the organization responsible for international numbering standards and is committed to developing common global standards for products and transaction sets. Information regarding the status of their current initiatives can be found on their website at **www. uc-council.org.** Another source documenting the evolving commercial standards is the Voluntary Interindustry Commerce Standards (VICS) at **www.vics.org.**

Internet

The widespread availability of the Internet and standardized interfaces offered through Internet browsers such as Netscape and Internet Explorer have substantially expanded the opportunities and capability to exchange information between firms of all sizes. The Internet is quickly becoming the supply chain information transmission tool of choice for forecasted requirements, orders, inventory status, product updates, and shipment information. In conjunction with a PC and an Internet browser, the Internet offers a standard approach for order entry, order status inquiry, and shipment tracking. The Ohio State University survey predicts the Internet will carry 20 percent of customer orders by the year 2010.[8] Industry Insight 7-2 describes how OshKosh B'Gosh uses document templates along with the Internet to provide inventory and transportation visibility.

The increasing availability of the Internet has also enabled the development of the exchange portal, a communication medium that has significant supply chain implications. An exchange portal is an *infomediary* that facilitates horizontal and vertical information exchange between supply chain partners. Figure 7-9 illustrates an exchange portal of a firm designed to facilitate communication between the firm's customers and suppliers. The firm can provide information regarding raw material requirements, product availability, or price changes and allow the marketplace to react by placing bids or orders based on the most timely information. It is projected that 60 percent of Fortune 500 firms will have exchange portals by 2003 to facilitate communication with key customers and suppliers.[9] While a single firm site might provide good Internet advertising, it does increase complexity, as all the partners have to contend with multiple, unique interfaces resulting in high transaction cost.

A second type of exchange portal is industry-based. It facilitates communication between all supply chain partners within an industry and can substantially reduce transaction costs. Figure 7-10 illustrates the exchange portal that the automobile industry has developed to facilitate communication between the original equipment manufacturers and their multiple tiers of suppliers. This portal offers a common framework for exchanging information including design information, proposal requests, commodity availability, bids, and schedules. While the information can be made available to all interested parties, it is also possible to restrict information availability. There is increasing fear that industry portal collaborations might increase the potential of monopolistic practices and trade restraints. The Federal Trade Commission (FTC) can be expected to play an increasing role in the evolution of the exchange portals, particularly for B2B activities.[10]

A third type of exchange portal is cross-industry-based and is designed to facilitate communication between firms that have common interests in commodities and services. Figure 7-11 illustrates a cross-industry exchange portal for manufacturers, suppliers, service providers, and customers. When one of the member firms has a need for raw material, product, or service, it can access the exchange portal to determine availability and potential price. Similarly, when one of the member firms has excess product or service capacity, such availability can be posted on the portal to solicit interest or a possible bid by one of the exchange members. Industry Insight 7-3 provides a detailed description of the Tradematrix.com exchange portal.

---

[8]The Ohio State University, "Careers Patterns Survey," 1998; available under "careers" at the Council of Logistics Management website, **www.clm.org.**

[9]Sanjiv Sidhu, "Harvesting Value in the Eye of the Hurricane," presented at the Planet 2000 Conference, San Diego, CA: October 9, 2000.

[10]Kim S. Nash, "Really Check," *Computerworld*, June 5, 2000, pp. 58–9.

INDUSTRY INSIGHT 7-2   USING THE INTERNET SAVES TIME AND MONEY

From its base in White House, TN, OshKosh B'Gosh's logistics management activities extend to the nation's borders and beyond. To manage the inevitable paperwork that accompanies international shipping, logistics managers have implemented a number of steps to streamline operations. "We've taken all of our documents and made templates," says Dennis Defnet, OshKosh's corporate transportation manager. This allows the company to send import documentation to its Customs brokers via the Internet, eliminating the use of faxes. Not only does that improve speed and reduce the amount of paper, it has been a hit with Customs officials, who appreciate the clarity of the documents. "It's done tremendous things for accuracy, speed, and pre-clearing shipments," Defnet says. In addition, he reports, the cost per document using the Internet versus EDI is significantly lower.

By linking its systems with suppliers' and carriers' systems, OshKosh also has the information it needs to manage inbound shipments. Gaining visibility of inbound shipments is crucial, explains Joe Burgert, the company's director of distribution. OshKosh has a large number of contractors shipping from Asia. The distribution center may receive 20 or more ocean containers per day. Knowing what product is in each container allows distribution center managers to locate seasonal product quickly and determine the best unloading sequence.

For those international shipments, OshKosh relies on shipment arrival information provided by its Customs brokers. "We have visibility as to the contractor, the seasonality, and the number of units and cartons," Burgert says. "We have all the information sent to the receiving department at White House." The data, provided electronically, are loaded into spreadsheet files, which OshKosh managers can use for planning.

Defnet adds that knowing the time of arrival allows the company to manage warehouse space and time for unloading air and ocean shipments. "We know exactly where our shipments are, when they clear Customs, when the trucking company is notified, and so on," he says.

Source: "Big Results From Small Packages," *Inbound Logistics*, November 1999.

FIGURE 7-9

Single-firm exchange portal

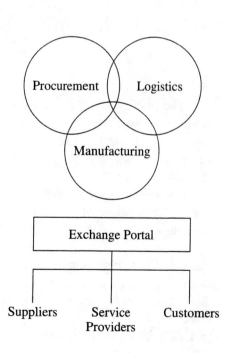

FIGURE 7-10

Automobile industry exchange portal

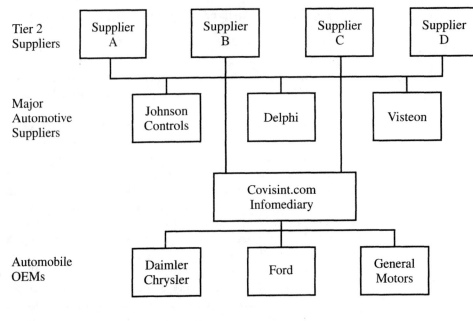

| Tier 2 Suppliers | Supplier A | Supplier B | Supplier C | Supplier D |

Major Automotive Suppliers: Johnson Controls, Delphi, Visteon

Covisint.com Infomediary

Automobile OEMs: Daimler Chrysler, Ford, General Motors

FIGURE 7-11

Cross-industry exchange portal

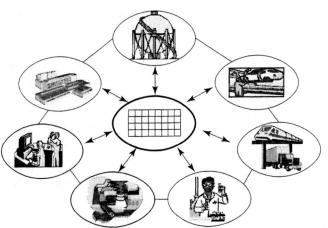

The Internet and the exchange portal have advanced supply chain communication from one-to-one or limited capability to a one-to-many environment capable of being extended to a many-to-many capability. The result is that extended Internet communication is a reality that offers substantial challenge in terms of exploiting widely available information.

One of the major challenges to the wide adoption of exchange portals is the definition and acceptance of online catalogs. Much like the paper version, an online catalog contains a listing of the products and services offered along with their descriptions and specifications. A catalog that is consistent across participating firms is critical to facilitate effective comparison of products and services across firms. For example, a firm desiring to purchase a simple T-shirt from a portal would like all the T-shirt suppliers on that portal to have a similarly formatted entry describing the shirt, its coloring, its contents, as well as other minute details so that the customer can make an effective comparison. While customers prefer consistent catalogs, suppliers prefer to use a catalog as a differentiator and are thus reluctant to deviate from their proprietary format. To facilitate information sharing and exchange, the Voluntary Interindustry Commerce Standards (VICS) and Collaborative Planning, Forecasting, and Replenishment (CPFR) are actively promoting common and consistent catalog definitions and standards.

INDUSTRY INSIGHT 7-3 AN INFOMEDIARY FOR SUPPLY CHAINS

TradeMatrix.com is an e-business platform that enhances design, operations, and evaluation of B2B marketplaces to better meet consumer demands. This electronic marketplace allows firms to focus efforts on key customers, determine segmental profitability, and accelerate time-to-market.

The TradeMatrix concept is to allow firms to build, launch, and service Internet marketplaces that facilitate very focused customer relationships. The Internet becomes the central trading system for major manufacturers and service providers. For example, participating firms can now instantly check the inventory—and the production capacity—of all their major suppliers at the same time to determine how quickly orders can be delivered. Such information sharing can substantially reduce supply chain uncertainty and results in less inventory and shorter, more consistent performance cycles. The visibility can also assist in new product development by allowing suppliers, manufacturers, and even customers to design, refine, and source components prior to initiating production.

A cross-industry trade portal supported by the collaboration of a number of supply chain product and service providers, TradeMatrix includes the application functionality to support procurement, marketing, fulfillment, planning, product development, and customer care. While many of the participating firms offer e-business services, through TradeMatrix they are also providing the hardware and software infrastructure to allow other firms to initiate e-business activities. TradeMatrix provides the complete suite of software, tools, and services to facilitate design and launch of an electronic marketplace and improve trading with supply chain partners.

The establishment of an online marketplace like TradeMatrix requires a combination of shared technology services and e-marketplace management. Shared technology services provide a set of guidelines and standards to facilitate applications design, deployment, runtime operations, and monitoring. The e-marketplace management provides the managerial and technical expertise for system hosting, catalog management, personalization, billing, profile management, relationship management, and services management.

Sun Microsystems and IBM applied the TradeMatrix concept to their own supply chains. Sun operates in a fabless (no internal component manufacturing) environment with contract manufacturers who produce its electronic components. With this model, Sun must oversee and coordinate the business processes of several component suppliers, their contract manufacturers, and third-party logistics providers. The system has allowed Sun to address some of its most critical business challenges, including large fluctuations in forecasted product mix, long product lead times through the supply chain, long collaborative planning lead times with suppliers, and balancing inventory turns with customer satisfaction.

IBM Personal Systems Group focused its efforts on reducing channel inventory while enhancing service levels. IBM enhanced communications with distribution channel partners by using POS data provided using EDI along with other data to create a recommended forecast. The channel partners collaboratively edit the forecast and provide it back to IBM planners. The resulting forecasts then form the input to an integrated planning process for supply/demand matching and allocation. The collaboration reports increased customer service levels to near 100 percent availability, reduced channel inventory by 80 percent, and reduced order scheduling time from 10 to 3 days.

Source: **www.TradeMatrix.com** and **www.i2.com/marketspaces/case_studies/index.htm.**

Extensible Markup Language

Extensible Markup Language (XML) is a flexible computer language that facilitates information transfer between a wide range of applications and is readily interpretable by humans. It was published in 1998 by the World Wide Web Consortium to facilitate information transfer between systems, databases, and Web browsers. Since EDI is very structured, the setup cost and required expertise are relatively high, limiting applications to situations involving high transaction volumes. XML is emerging as the information transfer medium between firms and service providers that do not have transaction volumes to justify EDI. XML is facilitating communication by breaking down many information technology barriers that have constrained EDI adoption.

A basic XML message consists of three components: the actual information being transmitted, data tags, and a DTD (Document Type Definition) or schema. The data tag is a key feature as it defines the data being transmitted. For example, in a shipment XML, the tag for address would be "address" and might appear <address>123 Main St.</address>. The tags tell computers what the data between the brackets are and where the data should go in a database or Web page. The use of common terms and the lack of sequencing requirements make XML transactions much easier to use than EDI. The XML DTD or schema tells the computer what document format to refer to when decoding a message. A DTD is essentially a template that maps out a standard form, its tags, and their relation to a database. For example, there would be separate schema for customer orders, advanced shipping notifications, or transportation documentation.

In situations characterized by low volume, XML is superior to EDI for three reasons. First, it is not expensive to install. It is easy to design an application and requires much less time to implement. Second, XML is easy to maintain because it can be easily converted to HTML (HyperText Markup Language), the language of Web browsers. This makes it much easier to modify and share data between applications. Finally, XML is more flexible, allowing for broad applications and quick definition and extension of standards.[11] One of the major challenges for the growth of XML is the definition of industry standards. Launched in 1998, Rosettanet, a consortium of over 60 companies, has begun developing common definitions for business practices and products as well as standards for using XML to transmit information through the supply chain.[12] Such a common vocabulary is necessary to enable supply chain participants to communicate with each other and have the confidence that the information exchange is secure.

Satellite Technology

Satellite technology allows communication across a wide geographic area such as a region or even the world. The technology is similar to microwave dishes used for home television in areas outside the reach of cable. Figure 7-12 illustrates two-way communication between corporate headquarters and both vehicles and remote locations such as stores.

Satellite communication provides a fast and high-volume channel for information movement around the globe. Schneider National, a nationwide truckload carrier, uses communication dishes mounted on its trucks to enable two-way communication between drivers and their dispatchers. Such real time interaction provides up-to-date information regarding location and delivery information and allows dispatchers to redirect trucks based on need or congestion. Retail chains also use satellite communication to quickly transmit sales information back to headquarters. Wal★Mart uses daily sales figures to drive store replenishment and to provide input to marketing regarding local sales patterns.

---

[11]For more detail, see Gordon Forsyth, "XML: Breaking Down IT Barriers in Logistics," *American Shipper,* June 2000, pp. 20–6.
[12]James Aaron Cooke, "New Wave," *Logistics,* January 2000, pp. 67–70.

FIGURE 7-12

Logistics satellite communication applications

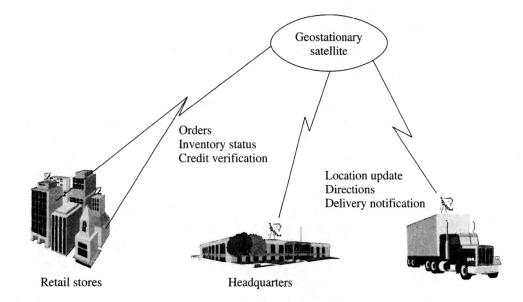

Radio Frequency Exchange

Radio Frequency Data Communication (RFDC) technology is used within relatively small areas, such as distribution centers, to facilitate two-way information exchange. A major application is real time communication with mobile operators such as forklift drivers and order selectors. RFDC allows drivers to have instructions and priorities updated on a real time basis rather than using a hard copy of instructions printed hours earlier. Real time instructions to guide work flow offer increased flexibility and responsiveness and have the potential to improve service using fewer resources. Logistics RFDC applications also include two-way communication of warehouse selection cycle count verification and label printing.

Advanced RFDC capabilities in the form of two-way voice communication are finding their way into logistics warehouse applications. Instead of requiring warehouse operations personnel to interface with a mobile or handheld computer, voice RFDC prompts operators through tasks with audible commands and waits for verbal responses or requests. United Parcel Service uses speech-based RFDC to read zip codes from incoming packages and print routing tickets to guide packages through their newer sortation facilities. The voice recognition systems are based on keywords and voice patterns of each operator. The primary benefit of voice-based RFDC is easier operator interface; since keyboard data entry is not required, two hands are available for order picking.[13]

Radio Frequency Identification (RFID) is a second form of radio frequency technology. RFID can be used to identify a container or its contents as it moves through facilities or on transportation equipment. RFID places a coded electronic chip in the container or box. As the container or box moves through the supply chain, it can be scanned for an identifying code or even for the list of contents. Retailers are beginning to use RFID to allow entire cartloads of merchandise to be scanned simultaneously. The U.S. Department of Defense uses RFID to list the contents of pallets so that they can be tracked as they are loaded on transportation equipment or move through facilities.

---

[13]Patti Satterfied, "Voice-Directed Systems Boost Warehouse Picking," *Parcel Shipping & Distribution,* September 1999, pp. 22–4.

Image Processing

Image processing applications rely upon facsimile (fax) and optical-scanning technology to transmit and store freight bill information, as well as other supporting documents such as proof of delivery receipts or bills of lading. The rationale for this new service is that timely shipment information is almost as important to the customer as delivering the goods on time. As freight is delivered to customers, support documentation is sent to image processing locations, electronically scanned, and logged into the system.

Electronic images of the documents are then transmitted to a main data center where they are stored on optical laser disks. By the next day, customers can access the documents through computer linkages or a phone call to their service representative. Customer requests for a hard copy of a document can be filled within minutes by a facsimile transmission. Customer benefits include more accurate billing, faster response from carrier personnel, and easy access to documentation. The carrier also benefits because the system eliminates the need to file paper documents, reduces the chance of loss, and provides improved credibility with customers.

Satellite technology, RF, and image processing require substantial capital investment prior to obtaining any returns. Experience has shown, however, the primary benefit of these communication technologies is not lower cost but improved customer service. Improved service is provided in the form of more timely definition of tasks, quicker shipment tracing, and faster transfer of sales and inventory information. There will be increased demand for these communication technology applications as customers observe the competitive benefits of real time information transfer.

Bar Coding and Scanning

Auto Identification (ID) systems such as bar coding and electronic scanning were developed to facilitate logistics information collection and exchange. Typical applications include tracking receipts at warehouses and retail sales. These ID systems require significant capital investment for users, but necessarily replace former paper-based information collection and exchange processes that were error-prone and time-consuming. In fact, increased domestic and international competition is driving shippers, carriers, warehouses, wholesalers, and retailers to develop and utilize Auto ID capability to compete in today's marketplace.

Auto ID allows supply chain members to quickly track and communicate movement details with a low probability of error, so it is fast becoming a fundamental service requirement for freight tracking by carriers. Both consumers and B2B customers expect to be able to track the progress of their shipment using the Web-based system offered by carriers such as United Parcel Service and FedEx.

Bar coding is the placement of computer readable codes on items, cartons, containers, pallets, and even rail cars. Most consumers are aware of the Universal Product Code (UPC) that is present on virtually all consumer products. UPC bar codes, used first in 1972, assign a unique 12-digit number to each manufacturer and product. Standardized bar codes reduce errors when receiving, handling, or shipping product. For example, a bar code distinguishes package size and flavor. European Article Numbering (EAN) is the European and United Nations standard for bar coding of items. It is likely that the UPC and EAN systems will become more harmonized due to pressures of global trade.

While UPC/EAN symbology is suitable in the consumer goods industry, some supply chain members desire more comprehensive information. Shippers and carriers, for example, are concerned with contents of pallets or containers. Therefore, a need exists for bar codes to identify cartons, pallets, or containers of products, rather than an individual retail item. Although it is possible to have a paper document listing pallet contents, the document may be lost or damaged in transit. A computer readable code that contains information regarding shipper, receiver, carton contents, and any special instructions and can be attached to an in-transit shipment is necessary; however, incorporating this amount of information into a bar code overwhelms the capability of a 12-digit UPC/EAN code. The basic problem is that marketers do not want bar codes to take up valuable space on packages because it reduces product information and advertising design space. On the other hand, including more information within existing space would make the codes too small and increase scanning errors.

To resolve these problems, bar code research and development have proceeded in a number of directions. There are now other symbologies that are particularly relevant for logistics. These include Code 39, Code 128, Interleaved 2 of 5, and PDF 417.

Code 39 was developed because some industries needed to encode alphabetic as well as numeric data into a bar code. Code 39 is typically the nonfood standard bar code and is used for identification, inventory, and tracking purposes in various industries, such as manufacturing. Code 39 produces relatively long bar codes and may not be suitable if label length is a consideration.

Code 128 evolved when the need for a wider selection of characters arose than Code 39 could provide and is used in the shipping industry when label size is an issue. Code 128 is gaining wide acceptance as the international standard container code, as it uniquely identifies each container in a shipment and improves routing and traceability. Code 128 allows manufacturers and distributors to provide container identification from production to point of sale. UCC 128 is used in conjunction with an EDI Advance Ship Notice (ASN) that precisely identifies carton contents.

It is projected that over 90 percent of all shipments in the medical, retail, apparel, and wholesale drug industry will use Code 128 symbology to track expiration dating, lot numbers, and production dates.[14]

Interleaved 2 of 5 is another symbology commonly used in the shipping industry. It is a very compact symbology that is widely used on corrugated boxes for shipment to retailers. The Interleaved 2 of 5 is a one-dimensional code that records a 10-digit numeric value.

PDF 417 is a two-dimensional, high-density, nonlinear symbology that has substantial data capacity. The PDF is really a Portable Data File as opposed to being simply a reference number. PDF 417 utilizes a stacked matrix design that can store 1800 characters per inch.

Table 7-6 presents an overview of common bar codes along with their relative strengths and weaknesses. Bar code development and applications are increasing at a very rapid rate. Table 7-7 summarizes the benefits and opportunities available through Auto ID technologies. While the benefits are obvious, it is not clear which symbologies will be adopted as industry standards. Standardization and flexibility are desirable to accommodate the needs of a wide range of industries, but they also increase cost, making it more difficult for small- and medium-size shippers, carriers, and receivers to

---

[14]For a discussion of bar coding and scanning trends, see Rick Gurin, "Scanning Technologies Adapt to Changing Times," *Automatic I.D. News,* December 1999, p. 28.

TABLE 7-6   Comparison of Common Bar Codes

Background	Strengths	Weaknesses
Datamatrix (Datacode)		
• Developed for small-item marking	• Readable with relatively low contrast • Density for small numbers of characters	• Limited error correction capability • Proprietary code • Not laser readable • Only readable with expensive area scanner
Codablock 39/128		
• Developed in Europe	• Straightforward decoding based on one-dimensional symbology • Public domain	• No error correction • Low density • Does not support full ASCII
Code 1		
• Most recent matrix code	• Best error correction capability of matrix codes • Public domain	• Limited industry exposure • Not laser readable • Only readable with expensive area scanner
Code 49		
• Developed for small-item marking	• Readable with current laser scanners • Public domain	• No error correction • Low capacity
Code 16K		
• Developed for small-item marking	• Readable with current laser scanners	• No error correction • Low capacity
PDF 417		
• Developed to represent large amounts of data in small physical areas • Reduces reliance on EDI (knowledge travels with the labor)	• Dramatically increased capacity • Error correction capability • Reads information vertically and horizontally • Public domain	• Requires technological development to reduce scanning cost • Testing required for highly advanced applications

Notes: *Capacity* refers to the number of characters that can be coded within a specific area.
Public domain means that the code can be used freely without paying royalties.
Error correction means that coding errors can be identified and corrected.

implement standardized technologies. Finally, while continued convergence to common standards is likely, surveys indicate that select industries and major shippers will continue to use proprietary codes to maximize their competitive position.

Another key component of Auto ID technology is the **scanning process,** which represents the eyes of a bar code system. A scanner optically collects bar code data and converts it to usable information. There are two types of scanners: handheld and fixed position. Each type can utilize contact or noncontact technology. Handheld scanners are either laser guns (noncontact) or wands (contact). Fixed position scanners are either automatic scanners (noncontact) or card readers (contact). Contact technologies require the reading device to actually touch the bar code. A contact technology reduces scanning errors but decreases flexibility. Laser gun technology is the most popu-

TABLE 7-7   Benefits of Automatic Identification Technologies

Shippers	Warehousing
Improve order preparation and processing	Improved order preparation, processing, and shipment
Eliminate shipping errors	Provide accurate inventory control
Reduce labor time	Customer access to real time information
Improve record keeping	Access considerations of information security
Reduce physical inventory time	Reduced labor costs

Carriers	Wholesalers/Retailers
Freight bill information integrity	Unit inventory precision
Customer access to real time information	Price accuracy at point-of-sale
Improved record keeping of customer shipment activity	Improved register checkout productivity
Shipment traceability	Reduced physical inventory time
Simplified container processing	Increased system flexibility
Monitor incompatible products in vehicles	
Reduced information transfer time	

lar scanner technology currently in use, outpacing wands as the most widely installed technology.[15]

Scanner technology has two major applications in logistics. The first is Point-of-Sale (POS) in retail stores. In addition to ringing up receipts for consumers, retail POS applications provide accurate inventory control at the store level. POS allows precise tracking of each Stock Keeping Unit (SKU) sold and can be used to facilitate inventory replenishment. In addition to providing accurate resupply and marketing research data, POS can provide more timely strategic benefits to all channel members.

The second logistics scanner application is for materials handling and tracking. Through the use of scanner guns, materials handlers can track product movement, storage location, shipments, and receipts. While this information can be tracked manually, it is very time-consuming and subject to error. Wider usage of scanners in logistical applications will increase productivity and reduce errors. The demand for faster and less error-prone scanning technology drives rapid changes in the marketplace for applications and technology.[16]

Summary

Supply chain information systems link logistics activities in an integrated process based on four levels of functionality. The transaction system provides the foundation by electronically taking the order, initiating order selection and shipment, and completing appropriate financial transactions. Management control systems record functional and firm operating performance and provide appropriate management reporting.

---

[15]For more detailed information regarding bar coding processes, hardware, and cases, see the Symbol Technology website at **www.symbol.com.**

[16]Rick Gurin, op. cit., pp. 28–9.

Decision analysis systems assist management in the identification and evaluation of logistics alternatives. Strategic planning systems provide top management with insight regarding the impact of strategic changes such as mergers, acquisitions, and competitive actions. While the transaction system provides the foundation, management control, decision analysis, and strategic planning systems are becoming critical for high-performance supply chain management.

ERP or legacy systems are the backbone of most SCIS because of their integrated database capabilities and modular transactions. The communication systems facilitate information exchange internally within the firm's functions as well as externally across global sites and with other supply chain partners. The execution systems are becoming more critical for controlling warehouse and transportation operations. Supply chain planning systems will likely become the critical competitive differentiator for the future as firms strive to improve their asset productivity through reduced inventory and physical assets.

There are three alternative approaches for obtaining supply chain hardware, software, and support. While direct ownership remains common, outsourcing and the use of ASPs are becoming increasingly popular. Outsourcing turns over the entire information technology responsibility to an outside service provider, while an ASP uses the Internet to access key software applications, particularly for communications and planning.

Remarkable advances have been made to facilitate logistical communication both within a given firm and among its supply chain partners. EDI, satellite, and more recently XML continue to enable quicker and more consistent communication between supply chain partners. Other technologies, such as bar coding, scanning, and radio frequency, are substantially enhancing the communication effectiveness between logistics information systems and the physical environment in which they must operate.

The increasing accessibility and capabilities of these information and communication systems substantially increase the availability and accuracy of supply chain information. Communication technology advances have dramatically reduced the uncertainty between large firms, but substantial opportunities remain for improved communications between smaller firms which make up the majority of supply chain participants. While further communication system improvement will continue to reduce uncertainty, it is likely that major opportunities for future performance enhancers will be through supply chain analysis and strategic planning systems.

Challenge Questions

1. Compare and contrast the role of ERP systems and planning systems in enhancing firm performance and competitiveness.
2. Compare and contrast the role of ERP systems and logistics execution systems.
3. Compare and contrast the role of supply chain ERP systems and advanced planning and scheduling systems in enhancing firm and supply chain competitiveness.
4. How can smaller firms remain competitive in the exchange of logistics information?
5. Discuss and compare the role that EDI and the Internet will play in facilitating communication between supply chain partners.

6. Compare and contrast the role of EDI and the Internet for logistics and supply chain information exchange.

7. Describe and contrast the role of RFDC and RFID for logistics and supply chain applications.

8. Discuss the relative benefits of software purchase, use of third-party providers, and use of application service providers.

9. Compare and contrast the benefits and risks of firm level, industry level, and cross-industry trade portals.

10. Discuss the relative differences between contact and noncontact scanning.